LESSONS FROM THE EDGE

LESSONS
FROM
THE
EDGE

A Memoir

MARIE YOVANOVITCH

MARINER BOOKS
Boston   New York

LESSONS FROM THE EDGE. Copyright © 2022 by Marie Yovanovitch. Printed in the United States of America. All rights reserved. No part of this book may be used or reproduced in any manner whatsoever without written permission except in the case of brief quotations embodied in critical articles and reviews. For information, address HarperCollins Publishers, 195 Broadway, New York, NY 10007.

HarperCollins books may be purchased for educational, business, or sales promotional use. For information, please email the Special Markets Department at SPsales@harpercollins.com.

FIRST EDITION

Designed by Emily Snyder

Library of Congress Cataloging-in-Publication Data has been applied for.
ISBN 978-0-358-45754-1

The opinions and characterizations in this book are those of the author and do not necessarily reflect those of the U.S. government.

22 23 24 25 26 LSC 10 9 8 7 6 5 4 3 2 1

To my parents, Nadia and Michel

And now these three remain:
Faith, hope, and love;
but the greatest of these is love.

— 1 CORINTHIANS 13:13

Contents

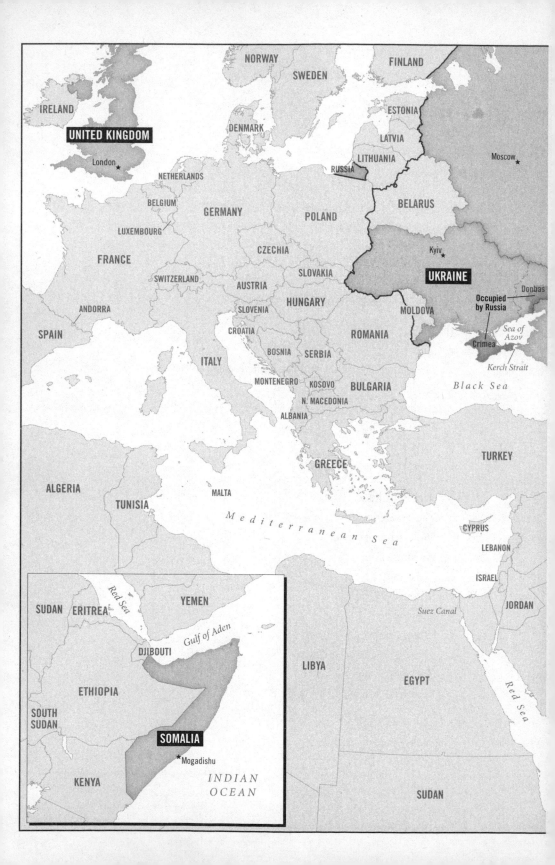

RUSSIA

KAZAKHSTAN

* Bishkek
KYRGYZSTAN

CHINA

Caspian Sea

UZBEKISTAN

TAJIKISTAN

GEORGIA

AZERBAIJAN
* Yerevan
Nagorno-Karabakh

ARMENIA

TURKMENISTAN

AFGHANISTAN

SYRIA

IRAQ

IRAN

PAKISTAN

INDIA

KUWAIT

Persian Gulf

BAHRAIN

QATAR

SAUDI
ARABIA

U.A.E.

OMAN

Arabian Sea

YEMEN

N

——— 1991 border of the Soviet Union
All other borders shown are 2019 political borders.

Author's Note

THIS BOOK IS MY STORY, as I remember it. It is based on my memories, my experiences, and my thoughts. In the case of my family's history, it's based on the recollections my parents passed on to my brother and me. Throughout I have tried to take different points of view into account, but no doubt others will have divergent memories and interpretations of some of the same events. I must also note that many of the events described occurred relatively recently, and new information continues to come to light.

By necessity, this book relates only a partial story, with much left out, especially when it comes to my time in the Foreign Service. Diplomacy is a team effort, and while I have tried to make that clear, I know I have not given enough credit to the many individuals who contributed to the successes described in this book.

Writing also can sometimes be a team effort, as I have discovered. And while I have benefited from the help and advice of many in the course of writing this book, any errors are entirely my own.

In order to protect the privacy of a few individuals, in rare cases I have used pseudonyms. But in all cases the people I describe here are very real.

Dialogue that appears between quotation marks is exactly what was said. When memory or sources do not allow for precise quotes, I have paraphrased what was said to the best of my recollection and put the words in italics.

The Russian and Ukrainian languages are closely related, but they are not the same. In the U.S., we often use the Russian version of transliterated words, even when writing about Ukraine. In this book, when writing about Russian people and places, I have transliterated the names from the Russian language; when writing about Ukrainian people and places, I have transliterated the names from the Ukrainian language. For example, the capital city of Ukraine is transliterated "Kiev" from the Russian language but "Kyiv" from the Ukrainian language, so this latter spelling is the one that I have used. Similarly, "Chernobyl" is the Russian transliteration of the Ukrainian power plant. "Chornobyl" is the Ukrainian transliteration, and I have used the Ukrainian version. In rare instances I have not adhered to this rule for proper names because the individual has a preference for a different spelling.

Finally, I consider myself fortunate to have lived all over the world and experienced the diversity of many countries and many peoples. I hope that I have succeeded in describing the richness and the beauty of the cultures that I have encountered in a way that allows readers to appreciate and enjoy them as much as I have.

Prologue

"Pledge to Serve"

I KNEW IT WAS OVER. The coordinated campaign of lies and innuendo had done its job. I wasn't going to be the U.S. ambassador to Ukraine for much longer.

It was Saturday, March 23, 2019, and I was at my official residence, a historic building in downtown Kyiv. That morning offered my first moment of relative calm after a typically busy seventy-hour workweek. I finally had the time to fully focus on the storm brewing back home.

Before me on the kitchen table was a packet of materials that had grown to considerable size since my press staff had begun sending it to me early Thursday morning. The first articles in the packet dated to Wednesday, when the Washington-based political website *The Hill* had posted several stories alleging American malfeasance in Ukraine, including by me. One quoted a corrupt Ukrainian prosecutor who claimed — falsely — that I had tried to shield certain favored Ukrainians from prosecution by his office. A companion article detailed an equally untrue but even more damaging assertion in Donald Trump's Washington: that I had "repeatedly" spoken with "disdain" about the president's administration.

Other pages in the packet revealed that the *Hill* stories had gone viral back home. Most concerning, President Trump himself had tweeted about a piece appearing in *The Hill* after one of his favorite news sources, Fox News host Sean Hannity, had devoted part of his primetime show that first night to the manufactured scandal.

The rest of the news packet included follow-on news articles, interviews, blog postings, and tweets from right-wing commentators, many of whom had Trump's ear. They were filled with vitriol, slamming me for fictitious acts of corruption and disloyalty to the president. One alarming tweet directed at me featured a photo of a noose with the words "It's for you."

Over the course of my thirty-three-year career in the Foreign Service, much of it spent in the countries of the former Soviet Union, I had seen this type of disinformation operation before. Oligarchs, unscrupulous officials, and government agencies, or some combination of the three, had frequently launched disinformation campaigns to destroy commercial competitors and domestic political opponents. They disseminated their fictions so effectively that baseless rumors quickly became generally accepted facts — or viewed as factual enough.

Sometimes American diplomats were targeted, as a way to discredit our diplomacy. But such efforts universally failed with the only audience that counted in America. In my experience, the State Department had always responded robustly, making clear that the information was false and that the embassy and the targeted diplomat enjoyed the full support of the U.S. government.

Not this time. This was something as new as it was threatening. Corrupt actors in Ukraine were colluding with corrupt actors in the U.S., and they were successfully influencing *our* government and *our* people. It was a shock made all the more devastating by the fact that rather than stopping it, people close to the president of the United States were aiding and abetting the effort. And when Trump waded into the fray by sharing the results of this disinformation campaign with his tens of millions of Twitter followers, he showed how effective the operation had been.

I knew that Trump's tweet almost certainly meant that the plan to remove me would be successful, but I wasn't going down without a fight. I wasn't just concerned with defending my honor, as important as that was to me. I was also thinking about the integrity of the U.S. government, our national security interests, and the continuing success of our bipartisan agenda in Ukraine. The people who were working against me wanted me gone because of the embassy's efforts to help reformers fight corruption in Ukraine — efforts that stood in the way of their unprincipled plans, which included Trump's tarring his expected 2020 rival, former vice president Joe Biden, with manufactured dirt. If these bad actors won, not only would U.S. interests be undermined, but the victory would also reveal the extent to which personal interests were running U.S. public policy. Even worse, it would encourage shady characters in the U.S. and around the globe to believe that they too could manipulate our policy or get rid of American officials who stood in their way. And it would hand them a road map for how to do it.

I had no choice; I *had* to fight this. And I firmly believed that the State Department should fight it too. In a flurry of email and WhatsApp messages to my colleagues back in D.C., I urged the department to issue a statement of support. Word came that David Hale, the department's number-three official, was recommending that I "deny on the record saying anything disrespectful." Using the abbreviations for Foreign Service officer and president of the United States, he also suggested that I publicly "reaffirm [my] loyalty as Ambassador and FSO to POTUS and the Constitution."

It was a devastating response. Rather than jumping to defend me, the department wanted to review the situation and was telling me to put out my own statement. I couldn't believe that I was in this position. And my incredulity was laced with a sense of betrayal. Just two weeks earlier, Hale had asked me to extend my tour as U.S. ambassador to Ukraine; now it felt like I was being hung out to dry. I had served in five previous administrations, both Republican and Democrat. I had never seen anything like this.

Even worse was the nature of the statement that I was being asked to record. Americans pledge allegiance to the flag and to the republic for which it stands; Foreign Service officers, like all government officials, swear an oath to support and defend the Constitution. Pledging fealty to an individual, in contrast, felt downright un-American. We had disposed of that idea in 1776.

I knew in my bones that it was wrong — and futile. If the department wasn't going to defend me, and do so very quickly, then defending myself would achieve nothing. But I told myself that I had to try. If foreign and private interests were able to remove me, the message it would send — to allies, adversaries, and Americans — would be extremely damaging. Even more damaging than the political theater I was being instructed to perform.

I sat down at the big wooden desk in my home office, took a sip of my favorite lemon-ginger tea, and tried to center myself. Then I pecked out a short statement and printed it out to review.

As I looked over the piece of paper in my hands, my misgivings grew. What I had written was a message meant for an audience of one. I felt sure that after I had debased myself and our country, Trump would fire me anyway.

There wasn't time to call around for advice, so I asked myself what people whom I admired would do. I thought in particular about my late father. A gentle man born into the chaos of the early Soviet Union, he had fled the Communists and then escaped the Nazis before finding his home in America. He was the most principled person I have ever known. I could almost feel Papa's strong and loving presence in the room that day as I sat alone with my words in the gathering gloom. He was reminding me that no job was worth my soul.

Papa's memory was the only instruction that I needed. I had spent a lifetime trying to put integrity first. This was not the time to stop.

I set aside the printout and wrote a second statement. This one focused on Ukraine's upcoming presidential election. I urged Ukrainians to vote and underscored the importance of free and fair elections and the peaceful transfer of power in a democracy. I added that "diplomats like me make a pledge to serve whomever the American people, our fellow citizens, choose . . . I promote and carry out the policies of President Trump and his administration. This is one of the marks of a true democracy." Even if it wasn't the Trump loyalty pledge that Hale had suggested, I hoped that by embedding the words "pledge to serve," I'd be giving my colleagues something to take back to State Department leadership. I knew it was unlikely to change their minds, but it was the best I could do without losing my integrity.

Our embassy tweeted out my recording of the second statement the following morning, but, not surprisingly, it did nothing to stem the tide against me. Within a matter of weeks I was called back to D.C. to hear the deputy secretary of state tell me that my ambassadorship was over. What I didn't know then — what I couldn't ever have imagined — was how much more was to come.

WHEN I RETURNED to the United States, I wanted to put the Ukraine events behind me and move on. I confided in only a few friends. It was just too difficult to explain what had happened to me. I barely understood it myself. When I told people that I had somehow gotten caught up in Trump's reelection maneuvering, it sounded crazy, even to me. Ambassadors serve at the pleasure of the president and can be recalled for any reason — or for no reason. If Trump wanted me out of Ukraine, all he had to do was order me home, and nobody would give it a second thought. There was no need to drag me through the mud. For those paying attention, it was clear that something else was going on.

As political events unspooled and led to the first impeachment trial of President Trump, my name and face were splashed across the front pages of the newspapers, in the lead stories of broadcast and cable news, and in every dark corner of the Internet. I didn't recognize the person depicted in the media, a heroine for some, a villain for others.

Nor did I anticipate that hundreds of strangers from all over the U.S. would write me letters of support. After such a tumultuous year, I appreciated their words more than they could ever know, but I was taken aback by how little many of my correspondents had previously known about the State Department, and at how surprised they were to learn about the service and the sacrifice of our nation's diplomats. Many suggested that I write a book. Their encouragement stayed with me when I retired in early 2020.

I am a private person: an introvert by nature and a behind-the-scenes type by profession. Before 2019, I would never have believed that anyone other than my family would find my life story of interest. But the reaction to my testimony changed that, and so I started writing, thinking that perhaps others might have something to gain from the story of my Foreign Service journey.

Some of my friends likely will think that what I have written in this book is too personal, too raw. I share my lifelong insecurities, the painful experience of my recall from Ukraine, and the ordeal that ensued. Some friends will feel that dispelling the notion that I am the one-dimensional heroine depicted in the wake of my testimonies will lead readers to think less of me. I decided to take that risk nevertheless.

Too many people have praised me for testifying — for speaking truth to power — and suggested that they never could have done the same. Especially women. They seem to believe that I must have been born a defiant truth-teller, ready to cross swords with the powerful, harboring no doubts. Someone inherently different from them. A "badass," as some have described me.

It was far more complicated than that. And, I hope, actually more compelling. Mine is not a story of someone who is somehow stronger or more courageous than other people. It is of someone who is, frankly, ordinary, but who dug deep and met a challenge just as most Americans would do in similar circumstances.

As I began to write this book, I looked back on my life and saw a straight line to the person I am today from the little girl whose immigrant parents raised her on the old-fashioned values of faith, hope, and love. I saw the power that persistence and resilience played throughout my career. I saw the hurdles that I and so many women of my generation overcame. And I saw how believing in myself empowered me to realize my dreams, especially the dream of representing America. As a Foreign Service officer, I got to live that dream — although I also saw it sorely tested.

I entered the Foreign Service as the final years of the Cold War were giving way to the American-led, unipolar world of the 1990s. I advanced to a leadership role just as 9/11 and the War on Terror reshuffled our global priorities and transformed our foreign policy. I eventually became an ambassador three times, each time to a country that once formed a part of the Soviet Union. I ended my career in a world that in some senses resembled the one in which I started — one with great power competition threatening to divide the world, as Russia and China, each in its own way, try to upend the post–Cold War order that the U.S. and its democratic allies have worked so hard to establish. The difference between the world of the early 1990s and today, though, is that the U.S. is no longer the uncontested preeminent power in the world. As a result, we need to work harder and smarter if we want a world in which the American people are safe, prosperous, and free.

The best way to do this is by working together with allies, and our best allies are other democracies. We share the same values and often the same interests, and when we work together, we are more likely to get better results for our citizens than if we work alone.

When the Soviet Union dissolved, many of the countries that emerged expressed an interest in transitioning to democracy and a market economy and asked for U.S. assistance to achieve it. We were eager to respond: we knew any investment we made in helping these countries become rule-of-law nations would benefit not just them but us. The people would be better off, and the stable, thriving, and democratic countries that would result would become better partners for the U.S., make the world safer, and create markets and investment opportunities for Americans and their products.

But there was resistance to change as well. Promoting reform often required me to navigate the edge between the aspirations of the peoples of the former Soviet Union and the frequent resistance of their elites. I tried to help my government counterparts understand that the hard work of building a democracy was worth the effort; it would make their country stronger, more resilient, and ultimately more successful. And if they followed through with it, they would foster the kind of economies with which other countries would want to partner and conduct commerce.

But as I was pushing my counterparts for reform, I also understood that politics and policy aren't always so neat and tidy. The United States didn't get to choose who led other countries, and sometimes simply inching a corrupt leader or a backsliding government toward better governance was the best we could hope for. At other times decision-makers in Washington concluded that we couldn't risk sacrificing our short-term interests by insisting on strict adherence to America's ideals. In the perfect world, our interests and our values would always align, but the rough-and-tumble of the real world sometimes requires us to balance the two.

As ambassador, I didn't always agree with the decisions our leaders made, but it was my job to implement them. And until recently I had always believed that the decision-makers in Washington were making the choices they thought served our national interests, even if they sometimes made different choices than I would have, and even if subsequent events proved their decisions were incorrect.

The truth is that it's impossible to always get it right. Diplomacy is an art, not a science. At its core, diplomacy is about building trust and creating relationships, so that when necessary we can call on a leader and a country to do what the U.S. needs them to do. And the U.S. can only do that successfully and over the long term if we work hard at maintaining our relations with other countries, and our partners believe that we have the integrity to hold up our part of the bargain and our adversaries believe that we have the resolve to carry out our threats.

Drive-by diplomacy is rarely successful. In the words of George Shultz, Reagan's secretary of state, diplomats must "tend the garden," working constantly to maintain good relations with countries around the globe. It is mostly unremarkable work, except for that moment when the crisis comes and we are successful in getting a country to accept refugees, allow us to use a military base, or contribute to bailout funds for a third country.

In foreign relations, as in so many other human affairs, there is no guidebook, no easy answers. We have to deal with imperfect knowledge and flawed — sometimes criminal — leaders as well as our own domestic limitations. We operate in realms of immense complexity, and yet we Americans are often uncomfortable with nuance. We want to divide the world into white hats and black hats, an understandable impulse that nevertheless can oversimplify analysis and impair decision-making.

At least in principle, our values and our interests are nowhere more aligned than when it comes to fighting corruption. When leaders view their positions in government as sinecures serving their personal interests rather than those of their constituents, it not only contravenes our values, it also goes against our interests, especially our long-term interests. Corrupt leaders are inherently untrustworthy as partners, and the loathing they engender at home almost inevitably leads to instability within — and sometimes beyond — their borders. But in practice there are times when we have to balance our interests against our values, because the U.S. has important priorities that often require dealing with unprincipled leaders who are stealing their country's heritage.

Often my job was to try to find that right balance between our values and our interests in the countries where I served. Because the culture of corruption that communism bequeathed to the new post-Soviet countries was so inimical to the interests of these countries, as well as to our own, I spent much of my time in the Foreign Service trying to help reformers inside and outside government battle against the poor governance and corruption that were bleeding their countries. That was in the interests of these countries and the long-term interests of the United States, and I was proud that there was strong bipartisan support in the U.S. for our policies.

But when I returned to the U.S. in the late spring of 2019, I found a situation uncomfortably reminiscent of what I had seen abroad. The U.S. had become a profoundly divided country, marked by democratic backsliding and increasingly on edge. Our long-accepted norms were under attack and the resilience of our institutions in doubt. I had never anticipated such a turn of events in America. It seemed we had forgotten that our democracy is a privilege, one that we need to protect, to defend, and work to strengthen every day.

This is a lesson that countless citizens of other nations are learning today. Having lived all over the world, I wondered whether we in the U.S. could find wisdom and strength in the examples of other countries that have navigated similar challenges. In retelling the story of my own education as a Foreign Service officer, I have tried to find out.

Part I

Travelers

1921–1986

1

Origins

M AMA ALWAYS SAID that our people are travelers. I suppose that means my career in the Foreign Service was encoded in my genes long before I came into the world.

For me, travel means anticipation and excitement. It's an opportunity to see new places, engage with different cultures, and challenge my preconceived notions about how the world works. Traveling provides moments to learn and to grow. On occasion it gives me a chance to spend time with family members scattered across the globe.

But for my parents and their parents before them, travel wasn't a professional privilege or a leisure pastime. It was an act of survival: a series of stress-filled journeys to escape the tyranny and oppression that defined so much of the early twentieth century in the unfree world. And it was, in its final form for Mama and Papa, a leap of faith, an act of hope, a gift of love to their children — one that brought us to this country and enabled me to turn what had been a necessary activity for my parents into not just an avocation but a vocation.

MY PARENTS, Nadia and Michel, met in Montreal, Canada, in 1957, both seeking refuge and opportunity in the New World. Each had roots in Russia. Papa had been born there, in Chita, to a Russian mother and a Serbian father. My paternal grandparents, George and Maria, met while George labored as a POW in Siberia, the unfortunate end point of his service in the Austro-Hungarian army in World War I. Just a couple of years into Papa's life, the Soviets allowed foreigners to leave Russia because of widespread famine. George took his family back to Belgrade, in what was then Yugoslavia. Tragically, Papa was orphaned within a few years of the move, when first his father and then his mother died. Papa either didn't know the cause or blocked out those sad times. All he told us was that their difficult circumstances no doubt contributed to their ill health and untimely deaths.

In a stroke of good fortune, the Russian expatriate community in Yugoslavia took Papa in. He lived as a charity case, eventually ending up at the Russian Imperial Cadet Corps, a military boarding school established to replace the one the Bolsheviks had closed down in St. Petersburg. Papa's cadet school classmates became his family, one with a common dream of one day helping to liberate Russia from the Communists and restore the czar to the throne.

Papa rarely spoke about his childhood. But one story stuck with me, because it illuminated so much about his character and the values that he wanted to instill in his children. Papa recalled a night when the cadet school's director stormed into the boys' sleeping quarters, angry that one of them had committed some infraction of the school's strict code. He lined up the pajama-clad boys in the cold, dark hallway and demanded to know who was at fault. If the boys gave up the perpetrator or themselves took responsibility for the act even if they didn't do it, they could go back to bed. As the night wore on and it got colder, boy after boy apologized for a deed he had not committed. Except my father. He wasn't a tattletale, but neither was he going to be bullied into apologizing for a wrong that wasn't his. He spent the rest of the night standing with his back against the wall, all alone.

Years later, my father was still proud of the strength of character that had enabled him to stand up to the powerful director. He raised my brother and me to believe that if we were presented with such a challenge, we needed to do the same.

MAMA SHARED MORE about her childhood than Papa did. When I heard her stories as a child in the comfort of our 1960s Connecticut home, I frequently felt that I was listening to a work of fiction; her childhood and the world she grew up in were that inconceivable to me. But the older I got, the more I came to understand how painfully real her experiences had been.

Mama was born in Wiesbaden, Germany, to a Russian father who had fought and then fled the Bolsheviks and an Indonesian-born, half Dutch, half German mother. My grandparents met in church: the gold-domed St. Elizabeth's Russian Orthodox Church on the outskirts of Wiesbaden, where my Opa Mikhail served as choirmaster and my Oma Louise sang in his choir.

Their marriage produced seven children, with my mother, Nadezhda (Nadia for short), arriving second, in 1928. But their union also eventually brought something less welcome: shared statelessness. As Mama explained it, Opa Mikhail lost his Russian citizenship when he refused to go back to almost certain charges of treason in what had become the Soviet Union, and Oma Louise's marriage to a foreigner cost my grandmother her German citizenship.

At first the family's lack of citizenship and their Russian surname — Theokritoff — didn't seem to matter too much, at least not to the children. Their lives centered on the church, each other, and the hard work it took to survive without much money. They shared with three other families a house on the church grounds with no running water, no electricity, and no gas. Opa's chickens out back often served as dinner, and shopping for food or coal required a long walk or sled ride down the steep hill to town — and a challenging slog back up with a full load. All the children were expected to pitch in, but as the second oldest, Mama bore a disproportionate responsibility for helping with the housework and raising her younger siblings.

Despite the challenges, Mama recalled those early days as happy ones, because the family had what mattered most: love and companionship. But like so much else in Weimar Germany, it was not to last.

As the Nazis assumed and then consolidated power, the realities of fascism began to come home for the Theokritoffs. The government confiscated the church in 1934, and Opa lost his job. The family was allowed to stay on in the house, but my grandfather, a highly regarded composer and choirmaster, was forced to take whatever menial jobs he could get to feed his family.

My mother and her siblings soon learned what it meant to be viewed as inferior in a society that devalued anyone not a member of the so-called Aryan race. Other kids bullied and teased the Theokritoff children, and when Mama started school, she found that she had to struggle against her teachers' low expectations for their "Russian" student. But Mama loved learning and yearned for an education. Against the odds, she managed to keep an optimistic attitude and stay in school for most of her childhood, living up to the Russian meaning of her name: "hope." Even then Mama knew that education was the ticket to a better future.

When World War II started, the Nazis sent Opa to work in a factory 125 miles away. The family had to leave the church house and move into an apartment in the center of Wiesbaden, seeing Opa only when he came home on weekends.

Even as a child Mama knew that something was wrong with the world in which she was growing up, though she was too young to understand it all. She recalled receiving treasured books from a Jewish friend whose family suddenly left Germany in the prewar years. The next day Oma was called in by the school principal and reprimanded for receiving so-called Jewish books. Mama couldn't understand why the principal was angry about the gift of books.

Decades later she still remembered one particular incident with both anger and anguish. Early in the war, nighttime air raids dropped bombs that blew out the windows of the family's apartment building. Mama fled, shoeless, but didn't make it far after broken glass bloodied her bare feet. A Jewish neighbor came to the rescue and carried her to the bomb shelter door, knowing that he himself would not be allowed to enter. The shelter warden rebuked the man for even touching Mama before shutting the door and leaving Mama's neighbor to fend for himself as the air raid continued. When she told the story so many years later, Mama's sense of gratitude for her neighbor's selflessness remained — as did her distress that nothing could rectify the wrong done to this honorable man.

Reared in a world controlled by the Nazi propaganda machine, Mama found it difficult to understand what was going on. Her stateless parents wouldn't discuss the bomb shelter incident or any others. Already in a precarious position, they didn't want to risk having their children innocently repeat any criticism of the Nazis.

Still, they repeatedly took another risk — a big one. In the evenings Oma and Opa, if he was there, would post a child at the door as they secretly listened to British radio to get reports on the fighting. In Nazi Germany, listening to the BBC could have gotten the whole family detained or even imprisoned, so my grandparents did not share the news with their children. I always wondered what it felt like for Mama and her siblings: caught in the Nazi era, sensing the threat, seeing the cruel actions, hearing the lies, but having no broader context or true understanding of events enveloping them.

As the war years wore on, life got tougher for Mama and everyone else.

Most of the family eventually moved to join Opa nearer his factory town, but Mama stayed with an elderly couple in Wiesbaden so that she could continue her high school education. Her time there ended when an Allied bomb hit their house. Everyone survived, but the couple did not want to take responsibility for Mama anymore and sent her back to her parents.

In wartime that was not a simple — or safe — proposition, especially for a fifteen-year-old girl. Wiesbaden was still in flames when Mama set out to reunite with her family. She literally ran through a street on fire as she headed for the train station. The police kept buckets of water at street corners, and Mama plunged a blanket in the water, covered herself, and ran down the street, darting around small fires and falling debris. She made it to the closest train station, but Allied bombs had arrived first, so she walked to the next station. She eventually made her way onto a train, but low-flying Allied bombers soon approached. The train stopped so that passengers could seek safety by hurling themselves into a ditch. Sobbing with fear, Mama tried to calm down by telling herself that she was too young to die. She survived that terrifying night and eventually found another train to take her to her family. Her education, however, did not survive. Mama never returned to high school.

Near the end of the war the Nazis came for Mama's family. With ranks so depleted that even men well into their fifties were being called up, the German army was considering drafting Opa. But first the secret police had to determine his race; apparently they believed they could verify whether Opa was genetically desirable by examining each family member. Fearful that a visit to Gestapo headquarters could end with the family separated or worse, Oma had a family photo taken. She put the resulting photograph in each child's pocket to help the children find each other if the family was split up. The picture shows a grim-faced Oma, a resigned Opa, and seven happy children apparently unaware of the gravity of their situation.

Mama never learned what the Gestapo decided about the Theokritoff genes, but the whole family was allowed to go home after the examination and was not contacted again. Fortunately, the war came to a close soon thereafter, without Opa having to take up arms. While the fighting ground on elsewhere, March 28, 1945, marked the end of the war for the family, by then living back in Wiesbaden. Mama recalled standing on the side of the road as an endless column of brightly painted American tanks roared by. Just like in the movies, the soldiers threw candy to the kids — and just like in the movies, Mama and her siblings eagerly caught the sweets. The entire family had survived the war. It was nothing short of a miracle.

LIKE MAMA, PAPA spent the war years struggling to survive. After graduating from the cadet school, he attended the Yugoslav Military Academy, just months before the Nazis invaded. The Yugoslav army collapsed almost immediately, and Papa found himself deported to a POW camp in Germany, Stalag XII-F.

The prisoners received only subsistence rations, and Papa was hungry. But he was also resourceful. Like his future father-in-law, Papa was an avid churchgoer and gifted singer. He formed a choir of fellow prisoners to sing Russian and Serbian patriotic and liturgical music. When the Nazi guards heard the music, they commanded the choir to perform for them, but my father refused until he received extra food in exchange for their song.

Here's how I imagined it as a kid: David against Goliath, with my father and his faith winning. Undoubtedly that's the lesson he wanted to convey. As an adult, I wonder whether the Nazis really would have brooked such insubordination from a prisoner. Was this more a matter of my father being forced to sing and receiving scraps from the Nazi table as a "reward"? By the time I asked myself this question, my father was gone, so I'll never know the answer — and perhaps by the time I knew him, my father didn't either.

In any case, soon Papa and his friends started making plans to escape, with the help of two local boys they had befriended while working at a construction site in the nearby town. The local boys smuggled them some civilian clothes, and when the scheduled day arrived, Papa and two friends put them on underneath their prison uniforms and waited patiently until nightfall. Having figured out the sequence of the floodlights raking the dark field outside the camp, they timed their breakout to avoid detection and, as Papa put it, "ran like the wind." Somehow all three evaded capture.

The trio eventually made their way to Paris, where the Russian expatriate community again came to Papa's aid. He spent the remainder of the war working as a hired hand for the daughter of the famous Russian composer Sergey Rachmaninoff. It was not always easy. At one point the Gestapo arrested him, beat him, and interrogated him. Good fortune again intervened, although the nature of the intervention later became a matter of good-natured dispute. As Papa's friends told it, they secured his release by bribing one of the guards. But Papa told a different story. He proudly insisted that his singing won his release. Papa said that one Nazi guard, a drunk, told him that anyone with a voice like Papa's couldn't be all bad and let him out of the jail. Either way, Papa was free.

In August 1944, American troops liberated Paris. Papa was there, jubilantly waving an American flag with his Russian émigré friends. I wish I had a photo of that, but I can see it in my mind's eye. And right next to it I can see Mama, months later, catching the candy American soldiers were throwing as they advanced through Germany.

MAMA WAS GLAD the war was over, but back in Wiesbaden, the Theokritoffs still struggled to put food on the table. Mama and her sisters stepped up and found menial work at the large military base the U.S. had opened in the city. Ironically, having once been harassed by German schoolchildren because she was Russian, Mama was now viewed with some suspicion by her new employers because she was German. But the family needed to eat, and the girl who had run through a burning street to rejoin her family was not going to let them down now.

Through a brother who had fled Russia for London decades earlier, Opa arranged to emigrate to England and made plans to take the rest of the family over as soon as possible. Once he was sufficiently settled, he was able to send for three of the older children, but Mama stayed in Germany to help Oma until Opa had saved enough for everyone to reunite. As the family's main support in Wiesbaden, Mama worked constantly and had no friends. The three years she spent waiting to go to England were among her saddest.

Finally, on New Year's Eve 1949, she set out for her new life. Reuniting with her father and siblings in London was a joy, but with the double burden of a German accent and a Russian name, she found that the British capital presented its own challenges. Still, Mama's drive and abilities ensured that she soon prospered in a series of jobs. Even more importantly, with Opa back working as a choirmaster, Mama rediscovered the church. She joined his choir and developed a faith that would form the strongest part of her for the rest of her days.

As much as she loved her family, Mama began to chafe at the familial responsibilities that seemed destined to continue indefinitely if she remained in London. She wanted to build her own life. So, in a bold move for a single woman in the 1950s, Mama convinced her employer, Lloyd's of London, to give her a job in Montreal. In March 1957 she left London for a new start in Canada.

It's hard to imagine today, but when Mama sailed to Canada, an ocean away from her entire family, she thought she would never see any of them again. She was twenty-eight, all alone, and on her way to the New World.

WITH NO STRONG TIES to France, Papa too had decided to try for a better life away from war-torn Europe. Canada was taking in people displaced by the war, so Papa gave it a try. By the time Mama immigrated, he was working by day as a draftsman on the Montreal metro project and studying for a master's degree at the University of Montreal by night. He spent his free time in church, singing in the choir and developing an interest in choir-directing. And when Mama arrived and joined his church, he also took an interest in her.

Less than a year after they first met, on February 2, 1958, Mama married Papa. She looks radiant in the photos. Papa, as ever, looks serious, but there is definitely a smile at the corners of his lips.

I arrived nine months later, almost to the day, and was baptized Marie Louise in honor of my two grandmothers. Mama worked until I was born and then quit, as was expected at the time. She and Papa settled into a happy life as he finished his degree and started applying for teaching jobs in Canada and the U.S. Most importantly, they were looking forward to the birth of their second child. Tragically, the baby, Michael Nicholas, died hours after his birth. Almost instantly their place of refuge became a source of heartbreak.

When a boarding school in Connecticut offered Papa a job, Mama and Papa saw it as an opportunity for a fresh start. So on a hot Friday in August 1962, we piled into our ancient black Austin. It was packed so tightly it would have made the Beverly Hillbillies proud. As we said goodbye to Canada, my parents — travelers of necessity their entire lives — looked forward to what they hoped would be their final destination, the United States.

SET IN THE FOOTHILLS of the rolling Berkshire mountains and on the banks of the Housatonic River, Kent, Connecticut, is surely one of the most beautiful places on earth. Older than the republic but populated by fewer than 1700 people when we arrived, Kent was a typical rural New England town — the kind of place where a steepled white clapboard church graces the main street (called Main Street, of course) and the whole town turns out for the Memorial Day parade.

On the east side of town and across the bridge stood the Kent School, Papa's workplace for the next three decades. The boarding school had a coed student body of roughly five hundred. Kent's motto, "Simplicity of Life, Directness of Purpose, Self-Reliance," resonated with my parents, who lived by those same values. But that was just about the only familiar thing they found in Kent. Kent had no Russian Orthodox Church, no cultural scene to speak of, nobody who had experienced the war as they had — in short, seemingly no one like them.

We moved into a postage-stamp-sized house next door to a family of eight kids. I spoke no English, but my eight tutors corrected that quickly. Within a week I came home and announced that I was going to speak only English — no more Russian with Papa or German with Mama. My startled parents decided not to fight it; instead of the French they had spoken as their common language in Montreal, they had already decided to speak only English to each other so that Mama could help Papa master the language. Just like that we became an English-speaking household. I lost my Russian and German — a lifelong regret, even though I would eventually, although not without difficulty, learn Russian again.

For my parents the Russian Orthodox Church was integral to their spiritual and cultural identity. Not attending church was not an option, even though Russian Orthodox churches were few and far between in rural Connecticut. Every Sunday we drove an hour on a windy, hilly country road to the closest one. I was never able to embrace my parents' enthusiasm for going to church, perhaps because the long and bumpy ride almost always left me carsick and the long and elaborate service didn't resonate with me. But I did absorb the church's teachings through my parents' word and example — especially the imperative to treat all God's children the way I wanted to be treated.

My parents were more successful at imbuing in me a lifelong love for Russian culture and tradition. Every year that we lived in Kent, they would throw lavish Easter feasts that I still heard about on visits twenty-five years after they had retired and moved away. As Easter approached, Mama would convert the kitchen into command central, and the delightful smells of celebration would drive us all crazy. She baked kulich, a yeasty Easter cake shaped like a cupola, and prepared a special sweet Easter cheese called paskha. Papa decorated the table with enormous bouquets of spring flowers gathered from the garden he cultivated in our backyard. The whole family dyed dozens of hard-boiled eggs deep red, blue, purple, green, and yellow, so that all the guests could battle it out in egg fights — a tradition in which competitors use their own egg to try to crack their opponents' eggs. Papa, a master strategist, managed to emerge victorious every time. We had an enormous ham, several different salads, and plenty of vodka. People came early in the afternoon and stayed late into the night — typical Russian-style hospitality.

Throughout my childhood I just wanted to fit in. I loved my parents, and like most kids was thoroughly embarrassed by them at the same time. In a place where it seemed to me everyone could recall their *Mayflower* ancestors, we were fresh off the boat. My parents spoke with thick accents, marking them as foreign. Worse, they were German and Russian immigrants, after World War II and in the middle of the Cold War. They made me wear funny clothes that my mother sewed to save money. We didn't eat the same food or worship in the same way. My parents didn't even know about holidays like Halloween and Thanksgiving.

Maybe all the kids I grew up with felt the same way — that they had weird parents with funny ways and that everyone else was cool and self-confident. Maybe everyone I saw as well-adjusted was also just struggling to fit in and do the best they could. But there's no doubt that, as often happens, my parents passed on their own sense of displacement to me. Their insecurity, their sense of not belonging, was a legacy as formative as the gifts of love, hope, and faith. As much as I battled against my differences, I also allowed them to define me.

That feeling of otherness led me to develop early on what turned into a lifelong habit of observing before acting — of making sure that I fully understood a situation before I made a move. I like to think that as I aged, I kept the mental and emotional process to myself, but it was out there on both sleeves when I was a kid. Mama loved to recall — to my great embarrassment — how when I was seven, my best friend's mom observed that I was a complicated soul: *With most kids you tell them to jump into the water, and they jump. Masha, though, starts thinking about all the possibilities*

— could there be a shark in there, a large rock, or perhaps a lovely underwater garden? (Masha was my nickname.)

Our family's never-ending money concerns also had a lifelong impact on me. As we settled into our life in Kent, my parents were beyond happy that Papa had found a good job in the United States. But with four mouths to feed — my brother, André, arrived in 1967 — the constant worry over money inhabited our home like a fifth member of the household. We didn't face the kind of poverty that my parents had experienced in Europe, when they sometimes went hungry. But Papa's salary never quite seemed enough to make ends meet. We bought things secondhand or made them ourselves, and we always worried as the end of the month approached. To this day, just like my parents, I repurpose everything. Old rubber bands and used aluminum foil and grocery bags all have a permanent home with me until I figure out a way to launch them into their second life. And despite having had a steady paycheck all my adult life, I've always harbored a worry that financial ruin could be just around the corner.

None of this is to say that my childhood was unhappy; on the contrary, my anxieties were tempered by the feeling of security that comes from being loved unconditionally. And I had a large community of friends my age too: the children of Kent School faculty who lived close by. The mountains, the river, and the fields were our playgrounds. We created little houses in the rock caves for our games of imagination. We swung on the vines that choked many of the trees. In the summer we swam and rode the river's small rapids in inner tubes. In the winter we sledded and skated.

I loved the outdoors, but my very favorite thing was reading. I lived the books I read, and my dolls, my stuffed animals, and André all played important supporting roles. My favorite books were fantasy stories like the Narnia series. I loved the fictional world where good and evil battled it out and good always prevailed — if not without sacrifice. I also loved biographies of famous women, courageously making the world a better place through their work and their example: Clara Barton, Betsy Ross, Amelia Earhart, Florence Nightingale, Eleanor Roosevelt. They inspired me to want to do the same.

TEACHING AT a boarding school is a family affair, one that pretty much defined our home life throughout my childhood. It consumed the vast majority of Papa's waking hours: not just preparing for and teaching different levels of French and Russian every day, but also coaching sports teams, eating meals with students in the dining hall, and — most time-consuming, yet most rewarding — advising students and often their parents.

Mama got pulled into the job as well. A nurturer by nature, Mama enjoyed opening our doors to homesick students who benefited from her tasty cooking, served up with lots of love. She had a vast repertoire of recipes that she would stretch for every student in crisis, each worried parent, or the ever-growing collection of family friends who would drop by for a chat and end up staying for a meal. Still the same lover of learning who as a teenager had risked her life to stay in school, Mama blazed a trail for me and my friends by getting a high school degree, then a bachelor's, and eventually two master's degrees. She started working at Kent School, first as a librarian and then as a German teacher. She still made time, though, to serve up equal measures of food and love to the students.

Papa didn't offer a warm shoulder to cry on. He was stern, sometimes remote, but if you wanted someone in your corner, he was your man. Still as disciplined as he had been in the cadet corps, he had a reputation as a strict but fair teacher and a stickler for the rules, whether he was teaching Russian grammar or enforcing the many rules that governed student life. Many parents valued my father's tough-love approach, including some whom I wouldn't have expected. Papa took pride in telling us how the ruthless Nicaraguan dictator Anastasio Somoza told his son to quit complaining about Papa: *Mr. Yovanovitch will make a man out of you,* Somoza admonished. While it may have been a different matter back home in Nicaragua, Somoza appreciated that his son was learning that at Kent the same rules applied to everyone, no matter who your daddy was.

For my part, I spent my grade school years looking up to the girls at Kent School and yearning for the day that I could join them. Kent girls seemed confident, smart, athletic, and so cool — traits I thought I would acquire magically upon enrollment. When the time came, I moved onto the girls' campus. It was just four miles from home but a galaxy away as an experience. I cried for the first month, sure I wouldn't measure up. Papa said what he always said: "Just do your best, that's all we can expect." His nonjudgmental words helped me adjust to the higher expectations that were my new normal at Kent.

The school's motto was in many ways an extension of the lessons my parents had taught André and me at home. The bedrock values of faith, self-reliance, and the importance of giving back to the community infused just about everything the school did. Three times each week the bells of St. Joseph's Chapel called us to mandatory worship services. Every student had to pitch in to keep the dorms and campus clean. Although the faculty had the last word, seniors were in charge of the dorms, in charge of the dining hall, and in charge of meting out discipline if students fell short. I disliked the rules and routine, but they had the intended impact; to this day I am a disciplined rules-follower who believes in giving back.

The academics at Kent tested me — and engaged me — in a way grade school had not. I especially loved English and history. My formative years coincided with a period of turmoil and change in the United States — the Vietnam War, the civil rights movement, the Watergate scandal — and the discussions about these topics, their historical roots, and my generation's ability to make positive change in our world were invigorating.

During my junior year I heard about the Foreign Service for the first time. Two friends told me about their father, a U.S. diplomat in Moscow. They described a life of traveling the globe, meeting important people, and shaping foreign policy. It sounded exciting, and much more interesting than anything rural Connecticut could offer.

But at that point in my life probably anything that promised to take me away from Kent would have sounded enticing. The truth was that Kent and the Kent School were starting to feel increasingly small to me. Although I excelled academically, I never felt like I could make much of a mark at the school. Status derived from athletic achievement, and I was neither interested in nor very good at sports. Worse, my Kent School years were filled with a low-level tension that made me keep my head down — for my parents' sake, if not my own.

Several years before I started high school, the administration had opted not to renew a teacher's contract after catching his kid smoking. I didn't know the details or whether there was more to the story, but I was still that complicated overthinking soul my friend's mom had described. I told myself that I had to be on my best behavior — not an easy thing for any teenager, and not something that I always succeeded at doing. But I was worried that if I didn't try my hardest, I would upend the secure life my parents had worked so hard to achieve.

It turned out that I wasn't completely crazy. In my senior year I channeled my inner Woodward and Bernstein for the school paper, writing an article about a small break-in at one of the dorms and commenting on the lax security and the need to address it. The headmaster found out about the story prior to publication and called me into his office. He never told me not to publish the piece, but he did observe that if the school put more money into security, they'd have to cut the teaching staff. I understood he was talking about my father, and I made the decision not to run the article. It was crushing. And it served as one of many life lessons about how hard it can be to do the right thing — and how hard it can sometimes be even to know what the right thing is.

By the time my senior year was coming to an end, I couldn't wait to leave Kent and the Kent School. Kent had given me a phenomenal education and I valued my group of friends, but I was in a hurry to start a new and independent life. After a childhood filled with stories of my parents' adventures in faraway places, I was ready to quit my small town and the pressure of constantly living up to the expectations of others. I wanted to start living for myself.

My protective father wanted me to go to Smith; he liked the idea of an all-girls college for me. I think he would have sent me to a convent if he could have. But I decided to go to Princeton, where I knew I'd get a good education and thought I'd have a good time. Both proved to be true.

OUR PRINCETON ORIENTATION that September of 1976 started with a welcome from Bill Bradley, the legendary basketball player who was soon to embark on a second career in the U.S. Senate. I had recently read John McPhee's classic on Bradley, *A Sense of Where You Are,* which attributed Bradley's basketball success not just to talent but to his hard work and discipline. I had to pinch myself, because there I was listening to Bradley, in person, telling the freshman class that we had the same opportunities to make an important contribution in our chosen fields. He reminded us of the university's motto, "Princeton in the Nation's Service," as almost every speaker did over the next four years.

The university's administration imbued every orientation event with Princeton history and tradition and ensured we knew we were following in the footsteps of presidents, Supreme Court justices, and other leaders. It was intimidating but awe-inspiring to think that I was part of that continuum. Like Kent, Princeton imposed expectations of excellence.

Just as Kent had been a quantum leap from grade school, Princeton challenged me in a way Kent never had. It seemed that all my classmates had
graduated first in their high school class or captained their school's basketball team. Princeton raised the bar for all of us, and as usual, I was worried
that I wouldn't measure up.

But I was all in, even though I was again an outlier — along with about
one third of my incoming class. Princeton had not admitted women to its
undergraduate ranks until 1969, and remarkably, the Princeton community
was still debating the wisdom of the decision to go coed when I arrived.
We'd come a long way, but there was still a long way to go.

Just *how* far I began to realize soon after I signed up for a European history class with Professor Jerome Blum. He had literally written the (text)
book on European history, and I was thrilled when I was assigned to the
weekly discussion group he led rather than one run by a graduate student.
I was the only woman in the discussion group, and at the first meeting Professor Blum declared that he had not been in favor of admitting women to
Princeton — a comment I interpreted to mean I was not welcome in his
class. I didn't know what to do. The thought of challenging a famous professor never even crossed my mind, nor did the idea of dropping the class. So
I did what I frequently did when facing adversity: I kept my head down, my
mouth shut, and my mind working hard, hoping that this would be enough
to get me through.

Six weeks later, after giving me an A on my midterm exam, Professor
Blum called me into his office. He wanted to know why I didn't speak in
class. Finding my voice, I reminded him of what he had said at the first discussion group and explained that I had thought he didn't want me in the
class. I don't recall an apology, but to his credit, in the second half of the se-
mester, he made a point of including me in the discussion. I never learned
what precisely Blum had intended to convey by his remark in that first
meeting, but his later behavior made clear he was open to having women
prove themselves. Perhaps most importantly, I learned that if I didn't speak
up for myself, it was unlikely that anyone else would.

Despite or maybe even because of that European history course, I decided to major in history. I also decided to get a certificate in Russian studies, so that I could learn more about where our family had come from. I still
couldn't speak my father's native language, but I found that I now had an
interest in trying.

Despite my success in Professor Blum's class, my academic performance was shockingly modest for most of my college years, although it wasn't all my fault. Princeton had awarded me a generous scholarship package, but the campus job it came with wasn't enough to cover my expenses. By junior year I had found a different job, waitressing in town. Tips paid for my food and rent, but working an almost full-time job meant I didn't have a lot of time for other things.

All of a sudden it was senior year, and I realized I wasn't quite sure what I wanted to do next. It seemed that everyone else had a plan. I was so scattered that I even missed my thesis deadline and ended up graduating after the rest of my class. (In later years, when my professors heard about my professional successes, they were delighted but a bit bemused.)

I *did* know what I *didn't* want to do: go to graduate school or work for one of the multinational corporations recruiting on campus. So I punted, and enrolled in a three-month Russian-language program in Moscow. It seemed like a good bridge between my student life and the responsibilities of adulthood. Besides, after learning about the Soviet Union for the past four years, I wanted to study the country up close — and possibly even to meet some of the relatives Mama's father had left behind when he fled Russia. Alex Haley had recently published his blockbuster novel *Roots,* and the resulting genealogy craze inspired me to want to see where my family came from. It was the right time and the right place to fulfill my genetic destiny and become a traveler.

2

Into the Foreign Service

I N THE LATE SUMMER of 1980, Russia's experiment in Communist rule was nearing its end, although we didn't know it at the time. The Soviet Union was still a nuclear-armed superpower and the center of gravity for much of the world. Eastern Europe remained firmly behind the Iron Curtain, with failing economies and unfree people — and with sclerotic authoritarians gripping power as firmly as ever. The Soviet Union and the United States battled around the globe for influence, allies, and resources, nowhere more directly than in Afghanistan, where U.S.-supplied insurgents fought Soviet forces seeking to prop up the country's Communist government. Superpower competition often felt abstract and distant to most Americans, but President Jimmy Carter's decision to boycott the 1980 summer Olympics in Moscow to protest the Soviet invasion of Afghanistan put it front of mind that summer. When I arrived in Moscow shortly after the conclusion of the games, the Cold War was positively frigid.

I had studied my ancestral homeland while at Princeton, and my parents had tried to pass cultural traditions on to me. But I knew as I embarked on my trip that I had little real sense of life inside the Russian Soviet Federated Socialist Republic, one of twelve republics making up the Union of Soviet Socialist Republics — the Soviet Union, or the USSR for short. Russia for me was just as Churchill had described it decades earlier: "a riddle wrapped in a mystery inside an enigma." Very few Soviets were allowed to travel outside their so-called workers' paradise, and the KGB — the intelligence and internal security agency — closely monitored all Western visitors to the USSR, making most Russians fearful of meeting with foreigners. Yet there was much that could be learned about the country if you knew where

to look and who to talk to, as I was about to discover in my post-gradua-
tion travels.

I TOOK a late-summer flight to Amsterdam to meet the fifteen or so other
Americans in my study program. To save money, we planned to take the
train from Amsterdam to Moscow, 1500 miles away. We departed in the
evening, and, exhausted by jet lag, I fell asleep almost immediately, but my
slumber didn't last.

As clichéd as it sounds, sometime after midnight I woke up to the sound
of dogs aggressively barking. We had arrived at Germany's infamous Checkpoint Charlie, the crossing point between East and West Berlin. Searchlights
flooded the station, lighting up the otherwise dark train. East German border guards entered our car, and we could hear them brusquely knocking on
the door of each sleeping compartment. When they got to ours, one guard
pointed his flashlight directly at our eyes and demanded our passports. As
he closely examined them, his partner tightly held the leash of his German
shepherd. I hoped he was in full control of the animal. There was no small
talk. The first guard returned our passports, swept the compartment with
his flashlight one last time, and banged the door shut. It was just like in the
movies.

This border crossing gave me new insight into my parents, whose experience of growing up under totalitarian rule was never distant. One of my
earliest memories was of our move from Montreal to Kent. I was only three
years old, but the stress my parents felt as we waited to cross the American border was so palpable, I remember it still. I saw that anxiety reemerge
whenever we drove back to Canada to visit friends and on our rare trips to
London to see Mama's family. Any interaction with authorities examining
their "papers" triggered painful memories from my parents' youth.

I hadn't understood their reaction until I experienced Checkpoint Charlie. I had done nothing wrong, and yet at that moment I too felt anxious —
taken aback by the coldness of the border guards and the deliberate display of power. We soon got underway again, but despite the gentle rocking
of the train, the adrenaline racing through my body made it hard for me to
fall back to sleep that night.

We pulled into the Polish capital of Warsaw later that day for a city tour
and overnight stay. I was on the lookout for signs of revolution: the news in
the U.S. had been full of stories about the shipyard workers in the northern

coastal city of Gdansk striking for greater rights, an almost unheard-of oc-
currence in an eastern bloc country. Although it wasn't then clear whether
the workers would succeed, I was excited to be in Poland, close to what I
hoped was a groundswell movement for change. But when we arrived in
Warsaw, I saw no sign of the struggle; everything on the streets seemed as
normal as could be.

It wasn't until years later that I realized that epic and consequential
events could be afoot in one part of a country or even a city and yet seem
completely invisible elsewhere. The Gdansk strikes led to the emergence of
the Solidarity movement, and its leader, Lech Wałęsa, was later elected Poland's first post-Communist president. But at the time I wondered whether
the U.S. press had overstated the significance of the strikes.

We rolled into Moscow late the following afternoon, checked into our
dormitories, and immediately went to Red Square. By the time we got there,
night had already fallen. I could feel the cobblestones digging into my soft-
soled sneakers as we marveled at the many-colored onion-shaped domes of
St. Basil's Cathedral, the towering red-brick Kremlin walls, and the squat
sarcophagus where Lenin's embalmed remains rested. I wish I could say
that I imagined my Opa Mikhail walking around Red Square sixty-odd
years earlier, blissfully ignorant that he soon would flee his homeland. But
in fact I was just reveling in the adventure, too excited to be the least bit in-
trospective. It was a fairy-tale start to the three-month program.

We studied Russian language at the Pushkin Institute during the day and
spent evenings chasing cognac with bread and cheese at a little café around
the corner from the school. It felt very sophisticated and very far from my
undergraduate days. On weekends we took road trips. Chaperones from In-
tourist, the government travel agency, made sure we didn't stray, doubling
as both tour guides and minders. They booked us into bleak hotels with
amenities so limited that they frequently lacked even hot water. In Leningrad, as a special bonus, I contracted giardia from the unclean water, but
somehow I saw even that discomfort as part of the adventure.

It was fascinating to visit the places I had read about, but whatever ide-
alistic visions I might have had about what it was like for those who lived
in the land of my forebears quickly dissipated in the face of the harsh everyday realities for the average Soviet. Although there never seemed to be a
shortage of inexpensive cognac, vodka, and cigarettes, the food supply was
limited and unpredictable. Coming from the land of plenty, I took a while

to adjust, but by the time I departed, I had become like every other Muscovite at least in one way: I never left home without my collapsible string bag or *avoska*. *Avoska* means "maybe" — as in *maybe* some rarity like oranges or imported shoes would be for sale, and *maybe* I would get lucky by spotting the line of people waiting to buy it, and *maybe* I'd manage to purchase one of the coveted items before they ran out. And like everyone else, I would first join the line and *then* ask what the line was for. I was enjoying my time in Moscow because it was different and exciting, but the need for an *avoska* was one of many reasons I couldn't imagine actually living there.

I wanted to get to know the country, and for me that meant getting to know Soviets other than those the government presented to us. At the time Soviets rarely had foreign friends, and especially not American friends; it was simply too dangerous for them. The few Soviets willing to befriend us were what I called "internal exiles," people who wanted to leave the Soviet Union at a time when that was forbidden. Maybe they couldn't leave physically, but mentally and emotionally they had long since departed. They toed the party line in public but questioned it in private. Contact with foreigners was a way to glean information and taste a bit of freedom. They had to be careful, and I am sure they wondered whether we were CIA, just as I wondered whether they were reporting on us to the KGB — or simply befriending us for access to American jeans and other black-market goods.

One particular incident put their heartbreaking plight into stark relief for me. An older Russian woman whom I greatly admired invited me to meet a friend she described as an "important" man. I expected an evening of intellectual and enlightening conversation. That's not what I got. The "important" friend turned out to be a man who looked ancient to my twenty-one-year-old self, although he probably wasn't older than fifty. He almost immediately expressed an interest in me and then spent the evening plying me with vodka, which quickly interacted with my giardia medication, causing me to break out in big red spots all over. The spottier I got, the more insistent the man became. Pretty quickly his intent became clear: he wanted to leave the Soviet Union and saw me as his ticket. Love must be blind, because I received my first marriage proposal that night. Romantic it wasn't. I politely made my excuses and escaped from that apartment as quickly as I could.

Unfortunately, my suitor couldn't escape the USSR so easily. I never saw him again, but I have thought a lot about this man over the years. He was successful by any measure. He had a prestigious job and a great apartment in central Moscow, but the price was lip service to the Communist system. At some point the cognitive dissonance must have become too great for him. This was a much sharper way of learning than studying a history book, but even so, I knew that I would never be able to really understand what it was like to grow up in the USSR — the self-censorship of every thought that didn't conform, the life planned out for you from cradle to grave, the constant compromises.

Although I had come to the Soviet Union aware of its failings, I still had wondered whether the Communist system had any lessons for us. Our country wasn't perfect, after all, and like so many of my generation, I couldn't help but look at the U.S. — the domestic upheavals of the 1960s, the inequities that plagued American society, the Vietnam War, and the Watergate scandal — and think that we had much room for improvement. Against that backdrop, the Communist slogan promising "from each according to his ability" and "to each according to his needs" sounded superficially appealing.

But what I found in the Soviet Union made me wonder what I had been thinking. I saw a completely broken system, one that not only featured a deprived population fearful of its own government but a government that hadn't even delivered on communism's basic promise of equality. Seeing how the Soviet system failed its people — materially, intellectually, spiritually — I was reminded again of that old saw about democracy being the worst form of government except for all the others. I realized how fortunate I was that my grandparents on both sides had decided to leave, starting a chain of events that eventually brought me to the United States.

Not all the members of our extended family had been lucky enough to get out, however. My British relatives had given me the contact information for Opa's youngest sister, my octogenarian great-aunt Vera, and I found her widowed and living alone in a room in a communal apartment in Moscow. As soon as she greeted me at the front door, Aunt Vera hustled me down a long, narrow corridor with peeling paint and into her small space. She turned up the radio and told me to speak quietly so we wouldn't be overheard. She didn't want the other families knowing that an American, especially an American relative, was her guest.

Her room was threadbare, and the floorboards were curling up. Laundry was hanging in a corner. At that point my Russian was only serviceable, and it was hard to bridge the divides of language, age, and experience. Vera had lived through the revolution, the famines, Stalin's purges, World War II, and more. I wanted to hear about her life and how our family had fared in the decades after Opa departed from Russia, but she wouldn't discuss any of it with me. Vera may have been small and hunched, as though she physically carried the burdens of all the tragedies she had lived through, but she was a survivor. She wasn't going to let a kid from the U.S. get her into trouble with the authorities by discussing anything that could be considered sensitive — which was everything I wanted to know about.

Even with that limited interaction, my great-aunt proved herself braver than the rest of the family. Or maybe, at her age, she just had less to lose. I sensed as much when I asked Aunt Vera if I could meet her daughter, Ksenya, and granddaughter, Aleksandra, who was about my age. What could be more natural than for my second cousin Aleksandra and me to be friends? But Aunt Vera told me it wasn't possible. No reason given, but I assumed that the family had decided it was too risky.

I had seen the lingering effects of totalitarianism on my parents, but seeing its effects in real time was something else entirely. As a young American, I found it beyond me to imagine a state so powerful that it could leave a family afraid to meet a relative. But that, I learned, was the evil genius of the totalitarian state. The USSR didn't need to explicitly forbid such a gathering or even exert any power to achieve this specific end. People were conditioned from birth to know that a snooping neighbor could expose any behavior at any time, and that even purely innocent actions could be spun in the wrong way, sometimes with dire consequences. From my Russian family's perspective, meeting the American relative just wasn't worth the risk.

PARADOXICALLY, BECAUSE MOSCOW was so challenging and unpredictable, I often felt more alert and alive than I did at home, where life seemed too comfortable and programmed. Three months flew by, and when the language program concluded, I didn't want to leave. So I got a job as a nanny with a Canadian diplomatic family, one of the few ways I could legally remain in the Soviet Union. But I could put off my real life for only so long.

In the spring of 1982 I moved to Manhattan to get a real job, as I had always imagined I would. But with the economy in recession, no one was eager to take on a recent college grad with no qualifications, despite my energetic networking and interviewing. I was taken aback when one interviewer, after noting the low entry-level salary, assured me that my parents would support me until I got married. Not *my* parents, I thought to myself. To cover the bills, I got temporary secretarial work and once again fell back on waitressing.

I finally received a job offer through a family friend: secretarial work at an advertising firm, with a salary of $14,000 a year. Even then, that wasn't enough to live on, although on the bright side, the offer included a promise of rapid promotion. With no other options, I accepted the job, hung up the phone — and cried. This was not where I had expected a Princeton degree to lead.

As it turned out, I did get promoted to account executive six months later. For the next three-plus years I worked with clients on their marketing and advertising strategy and ensured that the creative team stayed focused and on budget. To my surprise, I was good at it, and I moved up quickly. But once the initial challenge and excitement of succeeding in the workforce was behind me, I realized that selling products wasn't inherently interesting to me.

My epiphany had come around a year into my advertising job. In October 1983 the U.S. invaded the Caribbean island nation of Grenada, ostensibly to protect American medical students from the violent fallout of infighting among the island's Communist rulers. I was shocked when I read about it on the subway going to work. It looked like we were using our medical students as a pretense to justify replacing a regime we didn't like. But what gave us the right to interfere with this nation's government? If our concern was really the safety of the medical students, why hadn't we been able to find a nonmilitary way to get them out? What would we have said if the Soviets had done the same thing?

I was eager to discuss the news, but when I got to work, the *New York Times* in hand, my coworkers weren't interested. They wanted to talk about which colors to use in the ad layout we were working on. At that moment I realized that I needed to find a job better aligned with my interests. I wanted to work on something that I was passionate about — and which was bigger than me or a corporate account.

As I mulled over the possibilities, my mind turned back to that high school conversation about the Foreign Service. I loved foreign affairs, politics, and history, and I wanted to live abroad again. Plus I wanted to find a way to give back to the country that had given the Yovanovitch family a home.

I didn't know much about what the Foreign Service did, other than that it was part of the State Department and that it offered diplomats the opportunity to represent the U.S. while living and working overseas. It seemed like it was a meaningful career, one in which I could serve our country, be involved in promoting our security, supporting our prosperity, and protecting American citizens. I didn't really understand what all that meant in practice, but it sounded like exciting work — and important. Maybe I could help our government resolve future challenges like the one we faced in Grenada through diplomacy rather than pushing our interests through the military, I grandly thought to myself.

The eligibility requirements for the Foreign Service were minimal. You had to be an American citizen, have a high school degree, and be at least twenty-one years of age. Check, check, and check.

The first step was to sign up and take the written test, given once a year. So that's what I did. Then I failed the grammar portion by one point. I hung on to my advertising job and studied Strunk and White's grammar bible. Persistence paid off, and I passed the following year. Shortly thereafter I made it through the oral exam on the first try, and then I waited some more.

It took over a year for diplomatic security agents to complete the necessary background check, probably because I had so many foreign relatives, including in the Soviet Union. One of the agents who interviewed me told me that my family ties would preclude me from ever serving in the USSR. That was disappointing news, but I was ready to serve almost anywhere, as long as I was covering the political events of the day.

In December 1985 I finally received an offer to join the Foreign Service. I was thrilled — at least until I learned that I was unlikely to get the kind of job I had envisioned when I applied. When I had decided to pursue the Foreign Service, I had simplistically assumed that all Foreign Service officers (FSOs for short) followed political events and negotiated with foreign diplomats to protect U.S. interests. But as it turned out, FSOs had responsibility for a lot of other work as well, and new FSOs didn't necessarily have a choice in the type of assignment they received.

When I joined, FSOs were assigned to one of four different "cones" — clearly delineated areas of specialization — and expected to spend their ca-

reers working in those cones. Consular officers provided important services to American citizens abroad, from helping families adopt a child to
evacuating people after a natural disaster or a political crisis; they also determined whether foreigners were eligible for visas to travel to the United
States. Economic officers reported on and negotiated economic and trade
issues and promoted U.S. commercial interests; they helped America pros-
per by working to open markets for American products. Management officers kept the whole embassy operation going by managing budgets, people,
and the physical plant.

Any of those cones would have provided challenging work, but I wanted
to join the fourth cone and be a political officer. I wanted to follow political developments, maintain relationships with foreign countries, and negotiate solutions to international crises. So did a lot of other aspiring diplomats, apparently; candidates with the best scores got first choice on the
available openings, and by the time my turn came, only one career track
was available: the management cone. Managing embassy operations was
critical work, but I had already managed budgets, personnel, and planning
schedules in my advertising job. As much as I had enjoyed it, I was joining
the Foreign Service to do something different.

Unfortunately, doing something different wasn't one of my options, so I
faced a tough choice: take the management job or wait and see whether my
score would be high enough to snag a political cone slot in the next round.
I quickly learned that waiting would be a big gamble. Congress had just
passed the Gramm–Rudman Balanced Budget Act, and there were rumors
that the State Department could soon face a hiring freeze. If I held out for a
better offer, I could end up being stuck in advertising for a very long time.

I decided not to let the best be the enemy of the good. Even though the
management job wasn't what I wanted, it would at least get me back overseas, to another adventure. And I'd be on the team. Maybe I wasn't going to
be negotiating treaties, but I'd be supporting important work. I learned that
there was at least a theoretical opportunity to change cones in the future. It
was a bit of a catch-22 — I'd need to get two years of political experience to
make the switch, and it wasn't clear how a nonpolitical officer could accomplish that. But ever the optimist, I thought I'd be able to figure it out. And I
told myself that I wasn't committing to a career, just to the first tour, and if
the thrill was gone after that, I would quit and do something else.

JOINING THE FOREIGN Service felt like my own personal declaration of independence. My parents were of two minds, however. They would have preferred me to marry and put down roots near them with a brood of children they could spoil. But Mama, who had left her own family behind when she sailed off to Canada at just about the same age, understood my decision. In time Papa came around too. Having been denied choices for so much of their lives, my parents supported me in making my own.

In February 1986 I left my advertising job and got ready for several months of training in Washington, D.C., and my new life in the Foreign Service. As I surveyed my apartment, my overthinking seven-year-old self reemerged. I knew I was making the right choice, but I was nervous. Then I came across the black apron I'd worn while waiting tables. The apron had helped put me through college and survive my first months in New York. I hadn't needed it in a couple of years. But on some level the insecurities born of the displacement that my parents had experienced had become my insecurities as well. Our parents had taught André and me to reach for our dreams but to be prepared for the worst. So even as I looked forward to my new and exciting career, I packed my black waitress apron, just in case my new dream didn't work out. Every move since then I've made the same decision. That black apron is still in my bureau drawer today.

I ARRIVED in Washington on a sunny Sunday in March. I had no idea where in the world I'd end up going for my first posting, but I was eager to start my new life. I woke up the next day, put up my hair in a serious-looking bun, and dressed in my most conservative attire: a straight skirt with a boxy jacket. I wanted to look the part, and back then we thought that looking professional meant dressing like the men did. There was a limit to what I could do on that front, but I did my best.

Perhaps I should have realized sooner from the fact that our training took place in a nondescript suburban Virginia office building, a full river away from Foggy Bottom, as the State Department's Washington, D.C., home was known, but I quickly learned that my anticipated master class in American diplomacy was not happening. We didn't study geopolitics, the art of diplomacy, or even how to negotiate. The fifty of us in my Foreign Service class, destined to serve in every cone and every part of the world, were treated to a multiweek introduction to the bureaucracy of the U.S.

government, and our instructors programmed us with endless lectures on time sheets, pay schedules, vouchers, and per diem payments.

The average age of our orientation class, known as A-100, was thirty-one; our youngest class member was still finishing up his last college credit. Despite the fact that only a high school diploma was required, most of my classmates had advanced degrees, and there was the usual handful of lawyers among us. After hearing the Foreign Service described as "pale, male, and Yale," I was expecting my peers to be mostly White men with Ivy League degrees. I was only partly wrong. Our class was equally split along gender lines. But most of my classmates, like me, came from elite academic institutions, and the class lacked significant diversity with respect to either race or ethnicity — a challenge that the Foreign Service continues to struggle with today.

As I got to know my colleagues, I discovered that they had joined the Foreign Service for the same reasons that I had: an interest in foreign affairs, a wish to serve our country as nonpartisan professionals, and a desire to make the world a better place. The excitement of starting off on this journey together created a strong bond, and the many hours in and out of class reinforced it. I had found my peer group, and I was beginning to think that I had made the right career choice.

About a week into the orientation class, we were officially sworn in as Foreign Service officers. The ceremony took place in the Benjamin Franklin State Dining Room on the eighth floor of the State Department. In those days, when Oklahoma City and the World Trade Center indicated only geographic locations, people could usually just walk into federal buildings and move unescorted to their destinations. So I could tell that I was in for a different experience when my family and I had to present identification to the guards and then follow an escort to a special bank of wood-paneled elevators, programmed to stop only at the eighth floor.

When the doors opened, we left institutional Washington behind and entered the diplomatic reception rooms, where the secretary of state meets with and entertains foreign dignitaries. Early American artwork graced the walls, and historically significant furniture, such as the desk that was used at the signing of the Treaty of Paris, which ended the Revolutionary War, filled the rooms. Even my brother, André, then a blasé college freshman, was impressed.

A small, temporary dais had been placed on one side of the hall, and my classmates and I sat in front of it with our guests behind us. Our guest of honor was Diego Ascencio, former U.S. ambassador to Colombia and Brazil. The only thing I remember about his remarks is his account of negotiating his own release after the M-19 guerrilla group held him hostage in Bogotá for sixty-one days a few years earlier. Ascencio said he wasn't going to allow armed terrorists to write the ending to his story. Sitting in the audience, I hoped that I would be that skilled — and that fearless — in the challenges ahead.

Ambassador Ascencio then administered the oath of office. Raising our right hands and swearing that we would "support and defend the Constitution of the United States against all enemies, foreign and domestic," was not just our promise to the American people, it also reminded us of the responsibilities that we were about to undertake.

Once we were official, we mingled and congratulated each other as we ventured out to the balcony that offered sweeping views of the capital city, from the Washington Monument to the Lincoln Memorial and across the Potomac River to the Pentagon. It was breathtaking — especially to this newly minted diplomat.

AFTER THE POMP and circumstance of our swearing-in ceremony, it was back to the real world, with more lectures on rules and regulations and a lot to learn about Foreign Service culture. Like every organization, the Foreign Service has its own norms and beliefs, customs and conflicts. It was a whole new world, and very little was intuitive.

It was also a world in transition. A 1980 reform law had attempted to convert the Foreign Service from an old boys' network, where success frequently depended on who you knew and which schools you had attended, into a merit-based, professional service corps. The changes aimed to give previously underrepresented groups an equal shot at success. But many old-timers were bristling at the reforms, which they saw as unnecessary and unfair.

As if to underscore that parts of the Foreign Service were only very slowly joining these modernization efforts, a representative from the Protocol Office came to one orientation session to instruct us on State Department etiquette. One piece of advice solely for the female members of the class focused on how to utilize calling cards. Calling cards — as distinct from business cards — offer just your name and provide you with some-thing to leave at the door (or with the butler!) when a person you visit is not "at home." Very Jane Austen. We were more bemused than outraged at the suggestion that we women would have the time our male counterparts lacked to pay social calls during the day. At the time women were inured to such slights; if we'd gotten mad at every one, we couldn't have done any-thing else. But when I caught up with my A-100 classmates years later, every woman in the class remembered that presentation.

One of the most valuable A-100 sessions was the Myers-Briggs Type In-dicator test, which assesses which of sixteen personality types test-takers have and how they generally see the world and make decisions. I turned out to be an INTJ (introvert, intuiter, thinker, and judger), a result I learned ap-plied to nearly 50 percent of FSOs but only 1 percent of all tested Americans. Maybe I had found my home.

I found the exercise useful, because despite Psych 101 at Princeton, this was the first time that I had internalized that others might come to an issue with a completely different psychological makeup from my own. It gave me a framework to think about how to approach problems and was especially useful in dealing with people from different cultures — not just those from other countries but also fellow Americans who represented other U.S. agen-cies. As I later came to learn, there were vast gulfs of experience and per-spective among the many different U.S. agencies charged with our national security. Learning how to navigate them became essential to doing my job.

We spent a lot of time learning how to protect ourselves and our work from the many risks we'd face as Americans working abroad for our govern-ment. Our instructors made sure we understood that foreign intelligence agencies would likely scrutinize every aspect of our lives to exploit our vul-nerabilities. My time in Moscow had already exposed me to the concept of being surveilled, but I hadn't been a U.S. government employee with a se-curity clearance and secrets to hold close. How, I wondered, would I keep classified and unclassified information separate in my brain so that I didn't inadvertently say the wrong thing to the wrong person? I was relieved when our teachers assured us that compartmentalization would become second nature, and it quickly did.

It was clear, though, that we had to be careful — a fact that our trainers emphasized, sometimes in ham-fisted ways. In one session agents from the Diplomatic Security Bureau, tasked with keeping diplomats safe and classified information secure, showed us grainy training films to underscore the security risks of befriending foreigners. I was offended at how it portrayed women as excessively needy (and therefore more likely to spill secrets to any man who tossed us a compliment) and depicted Asian-Americans as untrustworthy due to alleged mixed loyalties. Indeed, the only Asian-American member of our class much later told me that he almost quit after that session. This security briefing also left me with the odd feeling that at least some in the State Department, the U.S. agency charged with advancing relations with other countries, didn't really want us to engage with citizens of other countries. Change may well have been coming to the State Department, but this session underscored that it was often at a glacial pace.

PARTWAY THROUGH the A-100 class, we finally got started on what we all considered to be the main event: figuring out where we'd be going for our first postings. Unlike most people entering new careers, Foreign Service officers don't know where they will be living and working until after they've started the job — but they do know that they are destined to move repeatedly over the course of their career. The Foreign Service believes that its workforce performs best when officers change jobs every two or three years. The constant change ensures that officers get broad experience in different places with different problems, and that the challenge of working in difficult or dangerous environments is evenly distributed. Regular rotations also aim to keep diplomats from getting too attached to any particular country. As Secretary of State George Shultz used to make clear to newly appointed American ambassadors, when U.S. diplomats say "my" country, they should mean the U.S. and not the country to which they are assigned.

For a single twenty-seven-year-old, it was exciting to think that I could end up anywhere in the world. Bogotá, Hong Kong, London, and Mogadishu were some of the cities on the Xeroxed list we were given. Each locale was different and thrilling in its own way, and jobs were posted for every cone.

We were told to rank our top choices, an experience that reminded me of being back in college and choosing courses. So many possibilities, so little time! But instead of picking a subject to dip into for a few months, we were selecting a job in a foreign country — a place full of new customs and challenges — for a full year and a half (first rotations back then were shorter than later tours).

I decided to rank Somalia as my top choice, because the job in Embassy Mogadishu included both management and political work. I thought I had stumbled onto the jackpot — a way to start immediately gaining the political experience I needed to support a cone switch. Plus I had never been to Africa. This was an opportunity to make an impact while also seeing the world. Somalia was listed as a hardship tour, a posting with substantially more difficult conditions than those at home. But I couldn't think of anything more extraordinary than going to a historically nomadic country on the Indian Ocean. It would be an adventure, I told myself.

WE CALLED the last day of A-100 "Flag Day," because our teachers gave each of us a small flag to reveal our destination. I received the blue-and-white Somali flag and reveled in the thought that my wish had been granted. My triumph didn't last long, however. I quickly learned that the job I thought I was getting had been changed and I would be spending my entire tour doing management work. I wouldn't have the opportunity to rotate into the political officer role after all.

I was disappointed and angry, and it didn't feel like I was off to a very good start in my new employment. But there was nothing I could do about it. This was my first but not my last experience with the somewhat arbitrary nature of the State Department bureaucracy, and I received the same vague explanation for it every time: "the needs of the service." It was a setback, but I gave myself a pep talk. I would turn these lemons into lemonade.

As I contemplated the move to Mogadishu, I was exhilarated and apprehensive in turn. I was excited but also wondered whether I was putting myself into a situation I wasn't up to handling. I would later discover that these same feelings would accompany me at the beginning of every tour, no matter how many times I took up a new job.

I had a lot to learn before I left. I enrolled in a department training course on management of embassy operations. I had thought I knew a lot about management from my work in New York, but embassy management turned out to be a completely different animal. It would require me to follow countless government rules, many of which were far from instinctive. I took a lot of notes during classes that gave new meaning to the word "dry."

My big takeaway was that I could go to jail for breaking procurement and spending laws — a scary prospect for a rules-follower like me. Bottom line: I needed to stick to the regs and make sure that I was a good caretaker of U.S.

government funds. I was okay with that but worried that I could get tripped up in the complex and seemingly endless rules of a bureaucracy that was, as I'd just discovered, also capable of surprising capriciousness.

MY FAMILY was starting to realize that we wouldn't see each other — or even have much contact at all — for a year and a half. My apartment in Mogadishu wouldn't have a phone, and I could make an international call only at the embassy and only by appointment. Letters — the single reliable means of communication in the days before cell phones, home computers, the Internet, and social media — would take three months round-trip via the State Department pouch. In every sense Mogadishu was very far away.

So we held on to each other for a little longer. Papa took the train down from Connecticut to D.C. to help me finish my packing before putting me on a plane to Frankfurt. Mama was working on her second master's degree in Germany, so I met her in Wiesbaden, where she spent two days introducing me to her hometown. As we walked around, Mama retold the stories of her youth, and I was transported back to both of our childhoods, remembering not just the tales she had told but also the way they made me feel about her as a child: my pride in her accomplishments as well as my hope that I had inherited at least some of her strength and resourcefulness.

From Germany I took a night flight to Nairobi, arriving tired but full of anticipation in the very early hours of the morning. Before the late-afternoon flight to Mogadishu, I put on a green floral Laura Ashley dress, very much in vogue at the time. I thought the light cotton outfit would be perfect for Somalia's heat and that it would look just right — not too formal yet appropriate for the environment.

As I waited to board the flight to Mogadishu, I felt like the adventure was already starting. Airport personnel herded all the passengers, struggling with heavy luggage, onto the tarmac. We awkwardly passed our suitcases up to baggage handlers, who were stooped precariously in the hold. I had never seen anything like that before, but it was comforting to know that my luggage had actually made it onto the plane.

As I waited to board, I breathed a sigh of relief that I hadn't ripped my dress while wrestling my suitcases over my head and into the hold. I wanted to make a good first impression when I arrived.

Part II

Postings

1986–2016

3

Somalia

A S WE DESCENDED toward Mogadishu, the late-afternoon sun illuminated a spectacular sight: an intensely blue ocean, an unspoiled coast-
line, and sprawling, sunbaked structures. Once we touched down, though,
the experience was less dazzling. Airport workers wheeled up rickety mo-
bile stairs, and we disembarked into a wall of heat and onto a dusty, pockmarked runway.

Waiting for me at the bottom of the stairs was the embassy's Somali "expediter." Embassies hire local expediters to assist in countries where Americans find it challenging to navigate byzantine airport procedures on their
own—and where they might face the possibility of an expensive shake-
down. I felt like a character in a Graham Greene novel as the expediter took
my passport and luggage tags and nodded toward the man who would serve
as my immediate supervisor throughout my time in Somalia.

My boss introduced himself. A middle-aged man of medium height with
a complexion that didn't agree with the equatorial sun, Roger Sullivan held
the title of supervisory general services officer, a position that put him in
charge of three Americans, including me, and hundreds of Somalis. Roger
came across as a Foreign Service veteran whose five tours had left him somewhat cynical. He was polite, if rather curt, and I gathered that small talk
wasn't his thing. It was disconcerting, but I told myself that airport intro-
ductions are always a little awkward. I tried to make the best of it by soak-
ing in my new surroundings.

As Roger and I were clumsily chatting, the expediter set off to get me
and my belongings out of the airport. There was no discernible line for
passport control, just a heaving mass of people elbowing each other aside
to get the required entry stamps. Retrieving the luggage was a full-con-

tact sport too but one the expediter told me to watch from the sidelines. I pointed him to my bags, and once he recovered them, we made our way to the exit of the cavernous one-room terminal. It was clear that some of those not so fortunate as to have an expediter had to "tip" the customs officials to avoid luggage inspections, paperwork obstacles, and other completely avoidable delays.

I didn't know it at the time, but Roger had taken one look at me and decided I wasn't going to last a month. Apparently my carefully chosen dress, with its lacy white collar, made me look young, naive, and untested. And my wide-eyed reaction to the airport scrum did little to change his first impression. Fortunately Roger didn't share that vote of no confidence until I was departing from Mogadishu for good. By that point I could admit that I hadn't had a clue about what I was getting into, and that if I had known what lay ahead, I would probably have gotten right back on the return flight to Nairobi.

WE CLIMBED INTO a big Chevrolet Suburban for the fifteen-minute drive to the American residential compound that I'd call home for the next eighteen months. Named K-7 for the number of kilometers from the center of Mogadishu, the compound was surrounded by high walls and protected around the clock by guards, like every other U.S. property in the city. It housed roughly a dozen bungalows and a small apartment building. I was thrilled to learn that I would have a room with a view — an apartment on the top floor.

When I got up early the next morning and ventured out, I got my first real look around, and every one of my senses told me that I was far from home. Even at sunrise the dry heat seemed to make every color starker: the hot yellow sun, the cloudless blue sky hanging over the darker blue ocean, the flamboyant pink bougainvillea growing wild on the streets. Above all there were endless shades of white — fading whitewashed walls, the dirty white of the desert sand reclaiming the dusty and barely paved roads, and the hospital white of the traditional sarong-like clothing many Somali men wore.

When the city awakened, a cacophony of sounds arose with it. Many sounded surprisingly rural for a metropolis of about one million: roosters crowing; goats and sheep bleating as they ambled off to graze; donkeys, mules, and horses braying; and the occasional camel bellowing as it carried its cargo. But there were city sounds too: the hum of conversation mixed with the din of buses and cars in various stages of disrepair, struggling to keep going as drivers leaned on their horns to warn people and livestock to move out of the way.

The smells were no less overwhelming. Animal odors mingled with the stench of burning garbage, the only way most people could get rid of their refuse. Countering those unwelcome fumes were the sweet smells of breakfast emanating from open-air kitchens and the ever-present scent of frankincense, used to freshen up clothing in a place where water was at a premium and washing clothes was an all-day chore.

It was a vibrant but completely foreign landscape for me, alien except for one sensation, which greeted me with welcome familiarity that first morning. The sound of the muezzin offering the Muslim faithful the first of five daily calls to prayer had roused me from bed. Although I'd never heard it before, I knew exactly what it was, and I smiled to myself as I remembered the Kent School chapel bells summoning us to services a world away. The sounds were different, but the ritual was the same. An auspicious start, I thought.

WHEN I ARRIVED in Somalia in 1986, it was still possible to understand why some long-ago tourism promoter had advertised Mogadishu as the "White Pearl of the Indian Ocean." The influence of long-gone Arab, Persian, and Indian traders gave the Somali capital some cosmopolitan luster. Italianate villas, many with ocean views, lined the main streets of the city center. Still five years in the future were the events that would make Mogadishu infamous in the United States: the country's descent into civil war and chaos, which ultimately led to the horrific deaths of eighteen U.S. servicemen in the city's streets. Although that tragedy was unimaginable during my time in Somalia, the country was poor and divided, and its authoritarian ruler, Mohamed Siad Barre, was driving a country already on the edge further into poverty and disorder with his mismanagement and corruption.

To some degree the country's challenges were inevitable. When the Republic of Somalia gained independence in 1960, its borders better reflected the region's colonial past than traditional Somali lands. Somali clans found themselves scattered across the adjacent nations of Kenya, Ethiopia, and Djibouti. As a result, many often felt greater kinship to fellow clan or subclan members living on the opposite side of an arbitrary international line than to the new Republic of Somalia.

When President Barre seized power in a military coup in 1969, he tried to forge a unified Somali identity and championed his own form of socialism. He allied with the Soviets and benefited from their help through much of the 1970s. That changed beginning in 1977, when Barre invaded the Ogaden region of Ethiopia, the birthplace of his mother and an area populated primarily by ethnic Somalis. His army initially saw great success, but Somalia's defeat became inevitable once the Soviets switched sides, sending arms and Cuban troops to support Ethiopia. The loss left Somalia with tremendous debt, many refugees, and the makings of future civil conflict.

Barre responded to the Soviet betrayal by playing the U.S. card. At the time the U.S. was engaged in an epic competition for global influence with the Soviet Union, now firmly ensconced in bordering Ethiopia. Barre wagered that we would jump at the chance to gain a foothold in his strategically important neighborhood, perched right on the critical shipping lanes that led to and from the all-important Suez Canal.

Barre's bet paid off big. By the time I arrived in the mid-1980s, the United States was pouring economic assistance into Somalia. Our military was training Somali troops and had access to ports and airfields in Mogadishu and Berbera. The State Department was about to start construction on a shiny new embassy to accommodate our growing staff and send a signal about the importance of the bilateral relationship. The United States was fully committed, despite the warning signs about its new partner.

Barre's nationalization of key industries, poor governance, and rampant corruption led to a failing economy and an increasingly dissatisfied population. A member of the Darood clan, Barre turned increasingly to his closest kin to maintain his grip on power. He consolidated his political base in Mogadishu by installing loyal clan members in government positions, which they then used to collect bribes and plow government revenue into their personal accounts rather than public services. When infrastructure and services deteriorated and resentment among other Somali clans grew, Barre started cracking down. Smelling weakness, Somali fighters backed by Ethiopia launched a guerrilla war for independence in the country's north. The harsher the measures that Barre deployed to repress opposition, the greater the resistance to his rule, both in the north and in Mogadishu. It was a downward spiral with no easy solutions in sight.

REPORTING ON THESE developments and analyzing their significance for our partnership with Somalia was precisely the kind of work I had envisioned when I joined the Foreign Service. What I would be doing instead was dealing with their practical impact as I tried to provide logistical support for the embassy.

My office was at the embassy's administrative compound, about half a mile past the K-7 residential compound on the main road out of town. The administrative compound also was the future site of our embassy, but until the new building was completed — something that wouldn't happen until after my tour ended — the ambassador and the political section would continue to be situated about twenty minutes away, at the existing embassy in the center of Mogadishu.

It was disappointing to be so far from the action, but I tried to make the best of my situation and threw myself into my dauntingly long list of responsibilities, all of which served to keep the embassy up and running. If embassy staff needed to transport anything into or out of Somalia — whether bringing in supplies for the new embassy or shipping out personal belongings for an employee returning home — it was my job to arrange the packing and unpacking, coordinate the transportation to or from the port, organize the shipping, and deal with the paperwork. If one of the many generators we relied on to supplement the intermittently functioning city electricity grid broke down, it was my job to get it fixed — and fueled. And if anyone needed a vehicle for official business, it was on me to dispatch the ride, and to ensure that our huge fleet was in working order.

It was quite an irony. I had learned to drive just before joining the State Department, when it had suddenly occurred to me that I might get assigned to a city without good public transportation. Now I was in charge of all the embassy's vehicles, not just the many SUVs that our staff used for official business. My wheels included a special truck to deliver water to embassy residences, a tow truck to rescue the American vehicles that frequently broke down in the sand, a fuel truck to fill the generators, and a garbage truck to pick up the trash. In a country lacking a well-functioning government, the embassy had to provide nearly all basic services to American staff. We were a city within a city.

Fortunately I had an experienced team of locally employed staff (LES) to help me with my responsibilities. Like most U.S. missions abroad, Embassy

Mogadishu relied on a vetted local workforce to fill most of our support jobs, a necessity owing to the high cost of sending and maintaining American workers overseas.

I couldn't have done my job without them, but I could tell from the start that it was going to be a challenge to supervise the sixty or so Somali men working in my department as drivers, dispatchers, and mechanics. They came from a society that generally viewed women as inferior and rules as inconveniences. It was a culture clash from the get-go. I could do nothing to change my gender, and I wasn't going to ignore my obligations. But I had to figure out a way to make it work, because my value-add was to ensure that my staff followed U.S. policies and regulations and were good stewards of taxpayer money.

My first meeting was with the motor pool dispatcher, Hajji Koshen, a distinguished man who had earned his honorific by making the hajj, or pilgrimage to Mecca. Attired in traditional Somali dress, Hajji Koshen opened the conversation by declaring that he had been working at the embassy for longer than I had been alive. It was a not-so-subtle hint that I should keep my nose out of his business, and it left me with the distinct feeling that if the meeting had lasted one minute longer, I would have received a pat on the head and an admonition to run along.

Yassin, the senior LES in charge of shipping, presented a different challenge. He was wiry and energetic and eager to move things along. As soon as we met, he gestured to my desk, barely visible under the neat stacks of papers awaiting my signature, and asked me to sign them. My predecessor had left several months before my arrival, which meant that most papers requiring an American signature had atrophied in my in-box. My Washington training kicked in. I knew I needed time to get my bearings and do this right. I declined the request to rubber-stamp the papers, which Yassin accepted with his usual good grace but just a touch of exasperation as well.

My staff all tried to be polite, but there is no doubt that my job would have been easier if I had been a man. The Somali employees just didn't know what to make of me. I was single, had no children, and soon after arriving started dating one of the Marine security guards. By the age of twenty-seven, most Somali women had been married for many years and had several children at least. I was an anomaly.

From day one my employees all called me Mr. Mash (from my nickname, Masha). They knew I was in a position of authority but apparently couldn't reconcile that fact with traditional Somali views about the role of women. So they gave me a man's title, and I occupied a third category, "honorary man" — clearly female but male in the position that I occupied. My counterparts in the Somali government also treated me as an honorary man. I later learned from female colleagues that this was a common experience for women diplomats working in Muslim countries.

On the very rare occasion that I was invited into a Somali home, I was treated as an honorary man there as well. I sat with the men on cushions in the living space while the women stayed in the kitchen. The women prepared the food and waited on the men (and me), and they would eat later — if we had left any food. The first time this happened, I went into the kitchen to say hello and offer to help out, just as I would at home. But what I saw as politeness the women saw as an unwelcome intrusion. I didn't want to be the Ugly American, so I stopped.

The obvious impact of my gender on the Somalis with whom I interacted made me uncomfortable too, but I didn't really know what to do about it, or who to ask for advice. There wasn't a single woman in a position of authority at the embassy, and it felt awkward to raise it with my male colleagues. Undoubtedly they had neither encountered nor considered the prospect of their authority being questioned because of their gender; it was unlikely that they would ever be treated as an honorary woman. I couldn't imagine that they would have good advice about how to handle this challenge.

Also, I was still at the phase in my career when I was doing my best to ignore my gender rather than embrace it. The climate may have forced me to opt for cotton dresses rather than boxy suits, but I still wanted to present just like one of the boys. I especially didn't want to draw attention to gender differences which might be perceived as weaknesses. So I kept these issues to myself.

FOR BETTER OR WORSE, I couldn't dwell on the gender challenge, because beginning almost immediately upon my arrival in Somalia I found myself dealing with an urgent work challenge, one that drove home to me Somalia's endemic corruption: the Somali government was holding all American cargo hostage at Mogadishu's port in an effort to extort large payments from the embassy.

Under international law, sovereign governments may not tax each other. And under U.S. law, Americans are barred from paying any kind of bribe, whether to U.S. or foreign officials. When operating abroad, our government and its staff pay fair fees for normal services, just like at home. Agreeing to anything more would put us at the mercy of foreign officials and fly in the face of international norms.

A couple of months before I arrived, Somalia's Ministry of Revenue had jacked up legitimate port fees for the U.S. embassy to extortionate levels. The embassy pushed back, but the Somali Clearing Agency, which controlled Mogadishu's seaport, refused to process any shipments to and from the embassy until we paid up. As a result, containers holding vehicles and supplies, construction materials for the new embassy building, and the personal belongings of newly arrived staff (including mine) all just sat at the port, inaccessible and undeliverable. Staff and their families were understandably unhappy, and projects such as the new embassy construction could not proceed.

It was clear what was going on: Somalia was broke, and the government was looking for revenue wherever it could find it. On top of that, high-level officials, who were almost all Barre's clansmen, wanted a cut of the money coming into their agencies and inflated the price for all services within their purview. And on top of *that*, lower-level customs officials pushing paper at the port weren't receiving a salary sufficient to support their families and were expected to make up the difference in whatever "fees" they could collect on the side. The system had completely broken down, creating the perfect conditions for corruption at all levels to flourish.

From a local perspective, the U.S. embassy offered a rich target: we imported and exported at a large volume, and we had money. From the U.S. perspective, however, Somalis had to play by the rules. In the gap between these viewpoints lay one of my first lessons as a diplomat. I had seen how brazen the acts of petty corruption were at the airport when I arrived. Now I was seeing how corruption played out on a much bigger scale. This wasn't something that a new junior officer, or even her immediate supervisors, would be able to resolve; only the highest level at the embassy could work with government ministers to fix this situation. Indeed, weeks after I arrived, the chargé d'affaires, the embassy official then in charge because of a vacancy in the ambassador position, was finally able to secure an agreement that would enable us to resume normal operations at the port.

In theory, implementation of the agreement should have been straightforward: all we had to do was take the paperwork to various government offices, get the right stamps and signatures, pay the newly negotiated fees, and pick up the shipments. In practice, however, it was a completely different matter. Despite what the embassy viewed as a comprehensive agreement, my Somali counterparts at the port acted as if it weren't game over. I didn't know whether top Somali officials just hadn't really reached consensus among themselves and were still battling it out behind closed doors, or whether the working level had decided to get entrepreneurial and see what they could get away with. Either way, the initial result was the same: no shipments were released.

Along with Yassin, the most senior member of the locally employed staff responsible for shipping, I spent hours and days trudging from office to office trying to get our cargo released. Sometimes we were downtown at the Ministry of Revenue. Mostly we were at the seaport. Yassin acted as my guide and interpreter. He knew the port like the back of his hand and had known our counterparts for years. Ordinarily I wouldn't have been going to the port to talk about individual shipments, but I was the American, the enforcer signaling that the U.S. embassy meant business.

Not that I was throwing my weight around; quite the opposite. We spent a lot of time standing around in dusty anterooms bereft of chairs and filled with other, mostly Somali petitioners waiting for an audience. A fan was usually moving overhead, but it didn't seem to make a difference in the heavy air. Often my counterparts would be mysteriously absent when I arrived. And often I would tell the gatekeeper that I would just wait, knowing that all the endless cups of industrial-strength espresso and chai would eventually force my counterpart out of his office where he (always a he) would have to deal with me. I have always believed in the power of persistence.

I am also a believer in finding common ground with people, no matter how different from me they may seem to be. Since many of my counterparts had been educated in Moscow when Somalia was aligned with the Soviet Union, I was able to surprise them by chatting in Russian and try to build rapport based on common — and not always positive — experiences in the USSR.

Shipment by shipment, we got each Somali bureaucrat to realize that we were serious and that he couldn't outwait us. It required cajoling, arguing, sweet-talking, a couple of strategic meltdowns, and most of all patience. But by midautumn, after more weeks of beating our heads against the wall, shipments were moving forward at a normal pace. That was cause to celebrate, because the flow of building materials for the new embassy resumed. Even more important to me, all the way at the bottom of the embassy food chain, I was now springing loose people's personal shipments and vehicles. I felt that I could finally show my face at embassy events without risking an interrogation about the delivery status of a colleague's car or baby supplies.

DESPITE THE CHALLENGING work environment, life in Somalia frequently provided just the kind of adventure that I had imagined when I had bid on the post back in my orientation class. Mogadishu hosted a vibrant expatriate community comprised of embassy employees, aid workers, teachers, and businessmen. On Saturday mornings I often met friends at a restaurant on the outskirts of town where outdoor tables were encircled by a fence made of thorn tree branches. Overhead, the tall thorn tree itself shaded us from the morning sun. There was only one item on the menu: sautéed goat liver with french fries. Liver isn't high on my list of favorite foods, but when in Somalia, I did as the Somalis did, and it was delicious.

Embassy friends and I frequently took camping trips in the bush as well. As we drove, the blue sky, the blazing sun, and the hot white sand seemed to stretch out forever in front of us. Somalia's beauty was harsh and stunning.

We often came across Somalis in the interior still living a traditional nomadic existence. They were so isolated that when one group of children touched my face and hair with curiosity, I realized that they had never seen a person as light-skinned as me before. Another group of kids reacted to the ice cubes in our coolers with such wonder that it made me think about frozen water in a whole new way.

Most of our travels ended with a trip to the beach. Along with friends from the expatriate community, I had the luxury of exploring the pristine beaches near Mogadishu. My favorite spot was close to Merca, about an hour's drive south from the capital city. We were always able to find an empty expanse of untouched white sand, and after we'd had our fill of sunbathing, we grabbed lunch at a seaside café in the thousand-year-old fishing village of Merca.

Although Mogadishu had its own small stretch of sand, it was crowded with people and filled with trash. Even worse, when the Soviets had built a fish processing plant nearby, they had damaged the reef that protected the city waters. As a result, when plant workers threw unused fish parts back into the ocean instead of disposing of them properly, they attracted sharks close to where people were swimming. That was enough to keep me away, but without transportation or air conditioning, many Somalis didn't have any other option for beating the heat. Tragically, Mogadishu's beaches saw weekly shark attacks, often on children.

I rarely ventured into the ocean, as sharks sometimes visited Merca's idyllic beaches as well. Others weren't so cautious, and on more than one occasion a shark attacked an expat. The lack of adequate medical facilities in Somalia made these events particularly horrifying, especially after an embassy spouse who volunteered at the local hospital shared graphic stories of the unsanitary conditions there. Her reports seemed right out of a Stephen King novel, and I couldn't shake the image of a stray kitten wandering into the operating room and licking the human blood pooling on the floor.

I used a safer option for my swimming. The K-7 compound where I lived housed a small employees' association with a pool and a snack bar. It wasn't fancy, but it was cheap to join, and I loved it, because it was the only time in my life that I was able to come home from work and jump right into a pool. But even that small oasis was not immune from trouble. A White couple from apartheid-era South Africa managed the association and supervised its Somali staff. Soon after I arrived, it became clear that the staff was unhappy with how they were being treated. They went on strike, and a meeting between the staff and the pair ended with threats against the South Africans. The next day I went home to a closed pool and a compound that was off-limits to all but residents.

The day after that my boss pulled me into the drama, probably because I was the only American working late that day at the administrative compound. The hostile exchange had caused embassy leadership to conclude that the couple could no longer safely run the employees' association, and it was decided that they should leave the country. Roger's plan was to drive them to the chargé's residence, considered the safest place for the South Africans until they could leave Mogadishu the following day. Roger didn't know what to expect on the drive over, and he didn't know what the sympathies of our local drivers would be if there was trouble en route, so he wanted an American driver. And he wanted to separate the couple into two vehicles to lower the risk. He'd drive one car, and I would drive the other, he said.

He phrased his explanation as if he were offering me a choice, but there was only one right answer. Of course I would help drive the couple, I replied. I hoped I had my game face on. But I hadn't taken the class that trains diplomats on how to drive in dangerous environments, and I hadn't quite gotten the hang of the stick shift on my newly acquired jeep. I was worried that I'd choke.

Driving our separate cars, Roger and I picked up the couple. Roger took the husband and I took the wife. Roger left before I could ask him for directions, but as he roared off, he yelled to me to *make a left at the third garbage pile after the embassy building and then go up the hill.* Those directions sounded crazy to me, but they were probably the best anyone could have done. Most roads in Somalia did not have names, much less street signs, and GPS for civilians was still a long way in the future. But Roger had not given me nearly enough to go on. I knew the well-worn half-mile path between K-7 and the administrative compound, but I was less familiar with the drive into town, and I had never been to the chargé's house.

I am sure I looked stricken, because my South African passenger told me she could navigate, and so off we went. As I ground through the gears of my jeep, I apologized so often that my copilot, who was no doubt much more stressed than I was, snapped at me to stop.

We drove on in silence. It felt like an eternity, but thirty minutes later we were there, with the chargé and his wife graciously welcoming the couple. There had been no incidents along the way, and no one had followed us.

Even at the time I thought it was odd that two administrative officers, not security officers, had managed this exit. Thankfully it had worked out, but what if it had gone wrong? Everything was still new and strange to me, so I just told myself that this is what it meant to be a Foreign Service officer, ready and able to do any job. But the thought nagged at me: What would I have done if someone had tried to stop the jeep? Even then it seemed to me that this episode was symptomatic of how anomalous everything was — not just in Somalia but at Embassy Mogadishu.

AS I GOT deeper into my tour, the wide-eyed girl in the green flowered dress was becoming more cynical. The airport shakedowns and the multi-level extortion scheme at the seaport, along with sundry dealings with officials at all levels of the local bureaucracy, made me realize that corruption was a pervasive and inescapable fact of life in Somalia. There were no constraints — no checks or safeguards to prevent people with power from putting their own interests ahead of those of their country. Rather than just serving as a distraction, a drain on the local system, corruption had *become* the system, and that didn't bode well for Somalia's future. How could a Somali build a successful business, for instance, if any profit would end up going to Barre relatives extorting cash for "protection"? Who would invest in such a climate? And without investment, how could life for regular Somalis ever improve? I was shocked by a report describing Somalia's economy: agriculture and livestock were important sectors, but the country's primary economic activity was remittances from Somalis working abroad and international assistance. As far as I was concerned, that spoke to a *lack* of economic activity more than anything else, and it underscored how bleak the situation was under Barre.

As insulated as we were at the embassy, we too experienced the spillover effects. Despite our best efforts at vetting our staff, our Somali employees reflected the environment around them, and sometimes we discovered an employee pilfering U.S. government property or shirking his duties. I understood the gulf between the Somali and the U.S. systems, but we treated our Somali staff according to American norms and paid them well. In return we expected them to conform to U.S. workplace rules. There was the principle of the matter. But there was also a practical aspect: if we didn't stop small and petty acts of theft, we could expect more — and more consequential — theft. But three incidents made me realize that not all of my American colleagues came down on these issues in quite the same way that I did.

Despite numerous warnings over a period of months, one of our local employees continued to manipulate the time clock, causing us to pay him for more hours than he worked. After he once again ignored our admonitions and lied about his hours while Roger was away, I recommended firing the man in response. It seemed obvious to me that an employee who repeatedly commits fraud has to be let go, not just to stop him from stealing but to set an example. Inexplicably, the higher-ups in the embassy disagreed. Fortunately Roger took my side when he returned, and the employee was eventually, if belatedly, fired. Roger didn't share with me the closed-door discussion on this issue, although at that point I was just glad that the issue was finally settled.

But when another incident occurred around the same time, Roger took a different position. One morning I went to work two hours early to finish a project. At 5 a.m. I expected to find a quiet compound with the gate guard at his post, other guards on the perimeter, and a single driver on call in case of emergency. It was still dark as I honked the horn to let the gate guard know that I had arrived. Usually the guard would respond immediately. But the guard didn't come. I was worried that there was a problem.

There was a problem, but not the sort that I had expected. I got out of the car, peered through the gates, and made out a number of people clustered around the gas pump. It didn't take a genius to figure it out: the guards were helping the on-call driver siphon gas from the pump. After the gate guard let me in, a full fifteen minutes after I had arrived, no one would answer my questions. But the numbers on the fuel pump didn't match with the amounts recorded in our books.

I thought that we had no choice but to dismiss the driver — the only one of those involved who fell under Roger's and my direct supervision — especially since I had witnessed the act. I sent Roger a memo to that effect, also noting that the guards, who did not report to us, had left their posts unattended for over fifteen minutes, typically a firing offense. This time both Roger and embassy superiors disagreed with me, and the gas thieves kept their jobs.

To this day I cannot understand why no disciplinary action was taken. Given what I knew then (and now), I still agree with my first-tour instincts and decisions. But if I was wrong, it could have been a teachable moment. I'm the first to admit that I was very green back then and probably sticking too strictly to all the rules I had been taught in my D.C. training. Rules provide a necessary framework, but good judgment and some measure of empathy are also important — qualities that usually come with experience. But neither Roger nor his boss, the head of the Embassy Management Office, gave me an explanation. So I was left to wonder: Was there not enough proof? Was I just plain wrong about what I thought I had observed? It would have been useful to know why a different decision was taken, especially one that cut the legs out from under me. And the lack of any explanation from my superiors for disregarding my recommendation left me feeling not just angry and disempowered but aggrieved and lonely at the far edge of the world — and longing for the relative predictability of New York.

As upsetting as that experience was, the third incident was even more troubling, because it involved Americans only. One of my embassy colleagues asked me to help his private recreational club save money. He wanted me to sign papers claiming a container of the club's imports as U.S. government property so the club could avoid paying Somali import taxes. I turned down the request, but the request kept on coming back — and from increasingly senior officers.

I am sure that none of the coworkers who approached me thought these requests were out of line. They probably thought that they were just helping out their club. But to me it wasn't even a close call: the shipment wasn't for the embassy, so we'd be falsifying paperwork if we said it was. And we'd be using our positions of privilege to benefit connected individuals at the expense of the Somali people.

Beyond the questionable nature of clearing this one shipment, I worried that it wouldn't be a one-time event; once word got around that I was open to signing phony documents, other organizations would likely ask for similar help. And I wondered what price the Somali Clearing Agency would extract once it caught on, not to mention what kind of example I would be setting for our local staff, who undoubtedly would notice that they were assisting in clearing items not meant for the embassy. It was crystal-clear to me that the right thing in this case was also the smart thing, even if it was unpopular.

I never signed the papers, but I worried nevertheless, and I took a copy of the file documenting my actions to my next post. A year and a half later, investigators from the State Department's Inspector General's Office interviewed me about the issue. I don't know who tipped them off, but clearly I wasn't the only one who thought something questionable was going on. I kept the file until the new embassy building in Somalia was ransacked and gutted in 1991 and our Mogadishu mission was closed. I figured that no one would be asking me about it after that.

EVERYTHING IN SOMALIA — its infrastructure, its economy, its people's ability to peacefully coexist — deteriorated significantly during my eighteen months there. The worse conditions got, the bolder Somali officials seemed to grow in their corruption. For me, the effects were most visible as I tried to ensure a sufficient supply of fuel for embassy operations.

U.S. government agencies working in Somalia required enormous amounts of fuel to run all of the vehicles and generators, and it was my job to get it. This was not easy, as Somalia did not produce fuel domestically, and a variety of factors (civil war, a closed border, the rainy season) made it challenging to import anything over land. Several months before my tour ended, the local pumps went dry, and we at the embassy were down to a critical one- to two-week supply. Fortunately a shipment the embassy had previously ordered soon arrived, giving us some breathing room for the next couple of months — or so I thought.

As it turned out, the Somali military had a fuel problem as well. Knowing about our shipment, the defense minister asked the recently arrived U.S. ambassador if we would share the wealth. The minister claimed that the Somalis needed the fuel to participate in Operation Bright Star, an upcoming regional military exercise led by the U.S. and Egypt. The minister knew how invested we were in the success of the joint exercise, which formed a key part of U.S. efforts to counter Soviet influence in the Horn of Africa and beyond. His gambit worked: after weighing the embassy's need for fuel against our larger strategic interests and the US. military's desire for Somali participation in Operation Bright Star, the ambassador told us to provide the Somali military with the requested fuel.

I could see the big picture — I understood why we wanted to keep the Somali military onside — but I worried that giving the Somalis fuel wouldn't leave us with enough fuel for our own needs, especially given our own military requirements for Operation Bright Star. I also suspected that the notoriously corrupt Somali military had invoked the joint exercise as a pretext and that they were really just planning to turn around and sell our fuel for profit.

When I raised these concerns, my supervisors didn't disagree but said it was a policy call and told me to follow the ambassador's instructions. I couldn't let it rest, however, and I asked to make the case directly to the ambassador. At a minimum I thought that he should be fully informed of the impact of his decision on his embassy's operations. My supervisors were as surprised as I was when the ambassador agreed to see me. We were not surprised that he did not change his mind. I saluted and delivered the fuel to the Somali military.

Two weeks later the city of Mogadishu was awash in fuel, even though no new deliveries had been received at the port. It was clear we had been played.

I remember this incident not just because it was one of the few times I met with the ambassador, but also because of the dog that didn't bark: I don't recall any conversation after the event about the Somali military's unabashed act of theft or whether it affected our bilateral relationship. Maybe I was just too junior to be included in those conversations, but I never heard anyone frame it systemically, talk about changing it, or discuss helping the Somalis move along a different path. I don't think we even officially protested the misappropriation of U.S.-purchased fuel.

Although I wasn't thinking about these tensions in as sophisticated a way as I would later in my career, I worried that in prioritizing our military interests over everything else, the U.S. was showing a gullibility that the Somalis would feel empowered to continue to exploit. We were opening ourselves to more of the same from a regime that seemed to view us as just another target of opportunity. Looking back at this episode through the prism of America's Cold War mentality, policymakers probably believed we had a binary choice: accept that poor governance and corruption were the cost of doing business with Barre's regime or risk losing a partnership that advanced our strategic objectives. But that calculation ignored an important point: it worked only if Barre was going to call the shots forever.

Barre was deposed three years after my departure, and U.S. support for his regime eventually cost us both the partnership and American lives as we belatedly tried to intervene in Somalia's civil war. The irony was that all of this happened just as partnerships like Barre's were becoming less important to the U.S. Mikhail Gorbachev had already launched the political and economic reforms — glasnost and perestroika — that would usher in the end of the Soviet Union. There was simply no need any longer to prop up a dictator like Barre — if there ever had been.

AS MY POSTING neared its end, even basic order in Mogadishu seemed to be growing increasingly tenuous. When I had arrived, I had been completely comfortable driving around in my jeep, listening to music, my window open to catch the ocean breeze. But one year into my tenure, crime had become so rampant that a man felt free to reach through my open car window to try to pull an earring off my ear as I sat waiting at a traffic light in broad daylight. I kept my earring (and, thankfully, my ear), but after that incident I drove with the windows up and the doors locked to keep the outside world at bay. The local people, of course, couldn't keep the real world out. They had to put food on the table, and as the economy kept on nosediving, that was becoming harder to do.

The civil war in the north was escalating, and reports of military casualties became more frequent. The two commercial planes that traveled to Nairobi twice each week also served as military transportation to the north, and a colleague told me how sobering it was to head off for vacation on a plane with bloodstained seats. Conscription became increasingly frequent and was accomplished at the barrel of a gun: soldiers rounded up young men on the streets, loaded them into trucks, and shipped them north. Parents found out only when their sons didn't come home in the evening. I remember one of our drivers being absent for days as he tried to locate his son. He eventually brought his child home, but only after he found the right people to pay off. Many families could not afford to do so, meaning the unpopular war was increasingly being fought by the poorest of the poor.

As the security situation in the north deteriorated and political pressure on the regime increased, Barre ruled with a heavier hand. Any trust between the government and the people had long since disappeared, but it now seemed that Barre was cracking down on even the rumor of any dissent and that he doubted the loyalty of his own security services. Like so many authoritarian leaders, he started to rely even more exclusively on his closest kin. He also began to use violence as a tool on the home front as well as on the front lines.

Barre had established an elite regiment to control security in Mogadishu, and he appointed his oldest son to lead it. At the embassy we called them the Red Helmets, and the ambassador, an experienced Africa hand, instructed that if we ever encountered them, we were to do whatever they demanded. They were armed and dangerous and acted with impunity.

Never having lived under such an oppressive regime before, I didn't really understand what these developments could mean for me. One night I found out. As I was driving home from dinner at a restaurant, I encountered a roadblock. Stopping at the end of a long line of cars, I saw wooden sawhorses barricading the road up ahead and Red Helmets with Kalashnikov assault rifles slung over their shoulders interrogating the driver at the front. It didn't feel right. My spider sense was on alert as I debated what to do. The rules-abiding girl in me thought, I have done nothing wrong, I have a diplomatic ID card, there is nothing they can do. The survivor in me thought, I am a woman alone in a foreign land, late at night, with a security force that is undisciplined and unaccountable. I am far away from them and they have not seen me yet. The survivor won out. I turned the wheel sharply left, drove over the median, and headed the other way. Maybe the Red Helmets didn't see me, or maybe they saw the diplomatic plates and decided not to follow me, but one way or another, no one came after me. I got home safely, if not via the most direct route. It felt like a close call, and I wondered what would have happened if I had been a Somali and not a privileged diplomat.

AS THE END of my tour approached, the walls I counted on to protect me from the regime's lawlessness seemed to break down even further. One afternoon a Somali man I didn't know appeared in my office and proceeded to aggressively ask me out. I repeatedly declined his invitation and eventually got him out the door. Given the compound's multiple layers of security, it was unusual for a stranger to show up at my office unannounced, and I asked my Somali staff who he was. Clearly uncomfortable, they avoided eye contact as my questions became more pointed and their answers more vague.

A bit later Yassin came into my office and quietly let me know that my would-be suitor was President Barre's nephew. When I asked how the nephew had gotten past our guards and into the compound without a business reason, he shrugged. Our Somali gate guards weren't going to tangle with such a close relative of the president's — not then or ever.

Over the next couple of weeks the nephew dropped in on me several more times. It was disturbing, but I told myself it was manageable. Then I woke up late one night to the sound of banging on my apartment door. It was the nephew, drunk and persistent. I was furious — and frightened. I lived on the top floor of a multistory apartment building in a secure, guarded compound that housed dozens of other Americans. For the nephew to get to my door, he had to first be admitted by the gate guard and then, even more troublingly, be told where I lived. At that moment I experienced just a tiny portion of the powerlessness routinely experienced by Somalis in the face of the Barre family.

I kept my reinforced door locked, and the nephew finally went away. But it was clear to me that the man was not stable and that he didn't plan to take no for an answer. I didn't want to make waves, especially on this kind of issue, but I knew I had to ask for help. I went to the embassy security officer to request his assistance. His advice in those long-ago days before

#MeToo: *Don't encourage him.* That was the reaction I had feared, and it's why I hadn't spoken up sooner. It infuriated me. How could anyone consider this to be my fault?

I left, pretty sure that my concerns had not registered. Thankfully, I found out a few days later that I was wrong. A colleague who worked with Somalis close to the Barre family pulled me aside and said that he'd take care of it. He was as good as his word, and I never saw the nephew again. But I couldn't shake my residual discomfort or the realization that if this had happened to me, it was undoubtedly happening to other women in Somalia, women who weren't fortunate enough to have the resources to push back.

ON TOP OF the Red Helmet incident, my encounter with Barre's nephew made me glad that I would soon be leaving Somalia. Crime was worsening by the day as people became more desperate, and the war in the north felt increasingly close, at least psychologically. Somalia's broken infrastructure was affecting not only our work but all aspects of our lives. For months the city's power grid could produce only three to four hours of electricity a week, making me anxious about the toll on the generators and our fuel reserves and making all of us hot and cranky.

The unhealthy environment was a constant concern too, even for someone young and fit like me. I found it wearing to keep debating the relative risk of catching malaria versus taking a preventive drug and chancing the very serious side effects. And a persistent open sore on my calf from the unclean bathing water was painful, unsightly, and just plain weird. I wondered whether it was ever going to go away.

I might have been able to manage all that if I had liked my job or found anything about it rewarding, but I didn't and I couldn't. I had joined the Foreign Service to work on foreign policy. Yet here I was, in a challenging and unsafe environment thousands of miles from home, working hard at a job that didn't match my interests and with no support from my bosses.

If I had thought I was learning something, I might have been ready to stay on a little longer. I knew I could have learned a great deal about how to be a better leader and manager, skills useful in any job. But neither Roger nor his superiors seemed interested in taking the time to make me a better officer. With no other reference points, I was sure that my future bosses in the Foreign Service would behave the same way.

I was particularly discouraged by one conversation in which my boss mocked me for making a proposal that he considered "*so* stupid." Instead of explaining why he thought I was wrong, he told me that if I didn't drop the idea, he would send the suggestion to Washington with the information that the crazy idea came from me. I was taken aback by the unprovoked ridicule and wondered what message Roger was trying to send me. Maybe he was trying to tell me I wasn't right for the job, but the message I took away was that this job was not right for me. If this was what a career in the Foreign Service was going to be like, I thought, then I was going back to New York. I had promised myself in the beginning that when the thrill was gone, I would go home. And the thrill was definitely gone.

I couldn't afford to be unemployed while looking for a job in the private sector, so I decided to bid on a post that would most easily enable me to interview for jobs back in New York: London. Our embassy there had a huge staff, with plenty of vacancies for junior officers from all cones to help process the enormous volume of visa applications. Still, I wouldn't even have tried for the London post if I had listened to Roger and his boss. They counseled me that it wasn't worth the effort, since so many FSOs wanted to go to London. That seemed like dubious advice to me. Someone had to go to London; why not me? The downsides were nonexistent. The only sure thing was that if I didn't try, I wouldn't get the assignment. So I was especially elated when I learned I got the London posting.

They say that what doesn't kill you makes you stronger, and as I left Mogadishu, I certainly felt that I was stronger. But I wasn't thinking about how my experience in Somalia — managing the challenges, the characters, the corruption — would serve as a foundation for the rest of my diplomatic career. Quite the contrary: I just wanted to get on with the next chapter in my life. As so often happens, the next chapter didn't turn out the way I thought it would.

4

The United Kingdom and the United States

I WENT TO LONDON so I could search for a job in the private sector. Instead I found a career in the State Department. For me, London ended up being everything Mogadishu wasn't, but even more importantly, the American embassy in London taught me how wrong I had been to assume that I'd find every posting as limiting as my first. I found bosses who wanted to mentor me, opportunities open for anyone willing to work for them, and a succession of three impressive ambassadors, each with his own style but all skilled and successful in his own way. They showed me that diplomacy was anything but a one-size-fits-all profession.

Even London itself seemed to be signaling that I was in for a fresh start. I arrived in May 1988 to a glorious springtime, every park green and every flower blooming. I quickly settled into my embassy-provided apartment, just a stone's throw away from the spot where the Beatles strode across Abbey Road for their iconic album cover. My building's preprogrammed security code, 1776, was one that every American could easily remember — but not my British cousin, who didn't catch the date it referred to when she came to visit me in my new digs. Clearly British schools don't emphasize the American Revolution in the same way we do in the U.S.

That anomaly served to remind me that while everything was familiar, there were differences too. I recalled that old truism that Britain and the U.S. are two countries separated by a common language. I knew that "tube" meant "subway" and "lift" meant "elevator," but I learned the hard way that "pants" meant "underwear." And who knew that "trump" meant "fart"?

But the differences between the U.S. and the U.K. were not nearly as noticeable as the differences between the U.K. and Somalia. For sure, I had to learn my way around a new city and remind myself to look right before stepping into the street, but I was grateful to find that I no longer had to spend time thinking about whether I should take my malaria pills, and the open sore on my leg finally started to heal.

Even better, I was getting to know Mama's family. In the U.S. I had just my tight nuclear family of Mama, Papa, and André. In the U.K. I had Oma, assorted aunts and uncles, and eight cousins to spend time with. We might have grown up an ocean apart, but we had a common past, and it was fascinating to hear familiar family stories refreshed with details I hadn't heard before. My presence in London also gave Mama an excuse to make several long trips, and I got to see her in a new light: as the second-eldest sibling navigating our complicated extended-family dynamic. Mama's example taught me a lot about diplomacy.

Even as I reveled in the warmth of my family, though, I realized how fortunate I was that Mama had chosen to leave London. As wonderful as it was, Britain in the 1980s remained a society in which social class often determined one's options. As the daughter of two stateless refugees, I would probably not have had the opportunity to represent the U.K. as I was now representing the U.S.

AS EXPECTED, MY job in the London consular section had me reviewing applications of people who wanted to visit the U.S. Back in those days, even the British needed visas to vacation in the States, and our job was to facilitate legitimate travel to the United States while keeping out criminals, terrorists, and others with questionable intentions. It was frequently tedious work, but we also knew that it was critically important for us to make the right call, even as we slogged through hundreds of visa applications a day.

A few weeks into my new assignment, a call went out for volunteers to work on President Ronald Reagan's farewell visit to the U.K. At the end of his eight years in office, Reagan wanted to honor the "special relationship" between the two countries, as well as his close working partnership with Prime Minister Margaret Thatcher. Mama always said that 99 percent of life is showing up, so I raised my hand to help out. It sounded like a far more exciting opportunity than visa processing, and I was sure to learn a lot.

Presidential visits are momentous events and require a lot of people, both in Washington and at the embassy, to plan the complicated logistics that come with a visit from not just a head of state but the hundreds of ac-companying staffers, security personnel, and members of the press. The advance team arrived from the U.S. to nail down all the details, and daily countdown meetings started about two weeks before the visit. We reviewed the president's schedule, minute by minute and in excruciating detail, so that everything would proceed smoothly. Days before Reagan arrived, transport planes flew in his limo, known as "the Beast," and his helicopter, Marine One. The preparation was intense. Nothing could be left to chance.

I was put in charge of organizing embassy vehicle movements and seat-ing manifests. This was a huge operation and far beyond anything I had organized in Mogadishu. The leap in responsibility was made all the more stressful when a senior management officer pulled me aside. Even if a sum-mit yields a historic agreement, he told me, what becomes lore for those in-volved are the logistical mishaps. Not enough rooms at the hotel, invitations going astray, the motorcade getting lost — these are the things that people remember. I got the message: don't screw it up.

I wasn't sure how I would pull this off. I didn't even know my colleagues yet and still needed a map to get around London, but here I was being put in charge of organizing a presidential motorcade. Fortunately, I quickly found out, the embassy had an experienced British staffer who had performed this drill many times; all I had to do was listen and learn. We reserved every ve-hicle in the embassy motor pool and hired every available car and driver in London. We choreographed every movement from one destination to the next and ensured everyone expected had a seat. I prepared to trail the mo-torcade in a spare vehicle in case of a breakdown or other emergency.

On June 2, 1988, I waited at Heathrow Airport as Air Force One, carry-ing President and Mrs. Reagan, touched down. It was the first time I had seen Air Force One in person. Standing on the tarmac, I felt a rush of pride and patriotism as the blue-and-white plane taxied up the runway, the words "United States of America" drawn in large letters on its side getting bigger and bigger as the plane approached. But I didn't have much time to indulge my feelings. I needed to make sure that the hundreds of people in the presi-dential party made it into their vehicles and on their way into London.

The arrival went smoothly, as did the visit itself, except for one small hitch. During the Reagans' stay, Prime Minister Thatcher hosted a dinner in the president's honor at 10 Downing Street, the home and office of Brit-ish prime ministers since 1735. Tired after the long trip, the Reagans left a little early, taking the motorcade with them. I quickly realized that this meant our ambassador, Charlie Price, didn't have a way home. I had never met Price, a political appointee and an old friend of President Reagan's, and although I had heard that he was down-to-earth, I had a fleeting worry that this could be the screwup I had been warned not to let happen.

I scrambled and wheeled up the only vehicle still in reserve: a brightly colored four-door MG. The contract driver didn't know where the ambassador's residence was, so I introduced myself to the ambassador, piled into the front seat with my trusty map, and navigated us to his residence. Not the usual way our ambassador to the Court of St. James's gets around, but it worked, and Ambassador Price thought it was funny — and fun.

When it came time for the Reagans to leave, Ambassador Price accompanied them to Heathrow and then flew back to his residence on the president's helicopter. The senior management officer had told me that it was my responsibility to designate the helicopter seats on the return trip and that I should include myself in case something went wrong. I wasn't sure what that last part meant, but I was only too happy to comply. What a thrill it turned out to be to see London by air, on one of the most famous helicopters in the world, and so soon after my arrival. Mama's advice about showing up was "spot on," as the British would say.

I WASN'T BACK at my day job processing visas for long before another, even better opportunity to show up presented itself. The State Department was looking for a Russian-speaking officer to process visas in Moscow for a month until someone permanent was assigned. Soviet leader Mikhail Gorbachev's policies of openness and reform had started to loosen up his notoriously closed country. Without fanfare, ordinary Soviets were now allowed to travel abroad. Pent-up demand had doubled the number of eager visa applicants at Embassy Moscow in just two months, and the embassy needed a dedicated officer to handle the load. My senior management asked whether I would go.

I wanted to seize this chance to go back to Moscow at what seemed like a historic moment. But having been warned at my original security clearance interview that my family ties to the Soviet Union put any posting there off-limits, I didn't think I could accept. When I told my boss, he responded with laughter and some disbelief at my naiveté. The needs of the service urgently required a Russian-speaking officer in Moscow, and there weren't that many people who fit the bill. Washington was requesting me by name. How soon could I travel? This rules-abiding girl was taken aback but thrilled. And I was happy to learn that the "needs of the service," which had been the reason given for the bait and switch that landed me in a management-only job in Somalia, cut both ways.

Less than a week later I was back in the USSR. My head was spinning. I had worked in the visa section in London for less than three months, yet here I was, in charge of processing visa applications for Soviets who wanted to visit the U.S. Granted, it was a section of one officer (me), but I felt lucky to be able to see firsthand the changes that Gorbachev was bringing to the Soviet Union. It wasn't just that Soviets were finally being allowed to travel. There was a lighter feel in the air. It was easier to meet Muscovites. There was more open discussion, and even criticism of the regime was tolerated. Furthermore, to my delight, a number of private restaurants were popping up around the city.

Although I spent most of my month in Moscow buried in the visa section, a colleague and I squeezed in a short trip to Estonia, Latvia, and Lithuania. The Soviets had occupied these nations during World War II, but the U.S. and other countries never recognized their incorporation into the USSR. The three Baltic states were now peacefully agitating for greater freedoms, and the Soviet authorities weren't eager for foreigners to witness any of that political ferment up close. Perhaps that's why the Soviets gave us a reality check: permitting us to travel but not authorizing hotels for us. They probably assumed that the lack of lodging would stop us from going.

The bureaucratic roadblock just piqued our interest. Instead of spending a leisurely weekend in one Baltic republic at a nice hotel, we reconfigured our trip and managed to see all three over a long weekend. We took night trains from Tallinn to Riga to Vilnius, arriving early in the morning in each republic's capital.

Our first stop each morning was the *banya*, the public bath where people could wash up, take a sauna, swim, have a massage, and improve skin circulation by beating themselves with dried birch or eucalyptus branches (no joke). You could make a day of it with friends and refreshments of all kinds, especially the alcoholic kind. For us it was a novelty, but for many Soviets it was the best way to keep clean, as communal housing often offered inadequate bathing facilities. After freshening up each morning, we then toured the city of the day, stopping in grocery stores to see what was obtainable, checking out cafés, and talking to as many people as we could. Since the State Department was interested in the mood in the Baltics, I drafted a note for the embassy's political section, which I was thrilled to learn got incorporated into reports back to Washington.

It was a short but important month for me. With the Soviet Union on the brink of major changes that would likely ripple outward, it was clear that Moscow was where the action was. I wanted to go back for a full tour, this time in the political section, if I could figure out how to swing it. I wanted to be "present at the creation," to borrow a phrase from Dean Acheson, secretary of state under President Truman and one of the chief architects of the post–World War II international order. In that summer of 1988, I didn't foresee that the Soviet Union was about to implode, but I could see that changes were afoot that would require recalibration and the diplomacy to match. I wanted to be there for whatever was coming next.

I put on pause the idea of the private-sector job hunt that I had been planning when I left Somalia. In my four months at Embassy London, I had been afforded two chances to do something different, both of them exciting and rewarding. The Foreign Service, especially in large embassies, offered opportunities that I had been completely unaware of in Mogadishu. People in London were looking out for me, and I felt I was learning. Plus I was having a great time.

SHORTLY AFTER I returned from Moscow, yet another opportunity came along, this one working for Ambassador Price as his staff assistant. It was a junior position and the hours were long, but the job came with exposure to just about everything the ambassador did. I decided to go for it and was happy to be selected for the position. Turns out Price had liked that flashy ride home in the MG.

The position required me to arrive early in the morning to review the overnight messages from Washington and then stay late to complete all the required follow-up and organize the next day's papers. In between, I got to sit in on many of the ambassador's meetings and events, an exposure rarely available to junior officers. In a place like London, which deals with virtually every foreign policy issue that comes before the U.S. government, I got a very broad view. The word "interesting" didn't begin to do the job justice.

Sadly, my new position was also — and very quickly — marked by tragedy. I started in the front office on December 19, 1988. Two days later Pan

Am Flight 103 exploded over Lockerbie, Scotland, killing all 259 people on-board as well as 11 on the ground. One hundred and ninety Americans lost their lives, including 35 college students who had been heading home from a study-abroad program. It was devastating for the families of those lost on the plane and in the small town of Lockerbie.

The embassy scrambled as the news trickled in on the evening of December 21. The ambassador called in his top advisors from every U.S. agency represented at the embassy. They shared what they could learn from their British counterparts and contacts back in Washington, and they started to plan our response. Most importantly, we revved up to assist the grieving American families, who we knew would want help in bringing their loved ones home and would expect to be kept updated on the progress of the investigation. We didn't yet know the reason for the explosion, but terrorism was at the top of the list.

Ambassador Price decided that he should immediately go to the crash site. He wanted to make sure that the families, the horrified American and British publics, and our adversaries knew that getting to the bottom of what happened was of the highest priority. With no commercial flights available at that time of night, he requested a U.S. military plane stationed at a nearby British base to fly him to Scotland.

Watching the embassy team swing into action and so quickly anticipate the needs of both the families and our government back home reinforced my decision to stay in the Foreign Service. I realized that night that I wasn't going back to the private sector. The U.S. government didn't do everything right during the Pan Am 103 crisis or the long investigation — and much longer quest for justice — that followed. But what I observed in the first twenty-four hours and during my remaining time in London, even from my junior vantage point, was individuals and agencies who wanted to do the right thing, for our national security and for the families, and who worked hard to make that happen. This work mattered. This was what I had been looking for when I joined the Foreign Service.

In the ensuing days and weeks, I realized how lucky I had been to land in the London Embassy's front office. Ambassador Price wasn't a career FSO, but he taught me how essential people skills are in diplomacy. A blunt businessman from Kansas City and a member of Reagan's kitchen cabinet, Price was outgoing, unpretentious, and charming. He knew who he was and what he had to do. He was able to leverage his close ties with President Reagan and Prime Minister Thatcher to the benefit of both countries. He was a master at forging genuine connections with the Brits, whether they were blue-blooded lords or blue-collar workers. He wasn't a stereotypical diplomat, but he produced results. I found it amusing to watch some of the embassy team try to make him conform to their idea of what an ambassador should be, even though he was doing just fine being his authentic self.

As eye-opening as it was, I knew I'd never be able to replicate Ambassador Price's success. Much of his influence relied on his ability to call Reagan directly and say *It's Charlie* with the confidence that the president of the United States would know who was on the other end of the phone. As an FSO with my background, it was unlikely I would ever have direct access to the president. So when Price left at the end of the Reagan administration, I was glad to work for his temporary replacement: Ray Seitz, a senior FSO and someone whose career path was closer to the one I could hope to follow.

A diplomat's diplomat, Seitz was elegant, erudite, and more British than the British. He knew the special relationship inside out and was able to advance our interests through his intellect and his vast network of contacts in both London and Washington. He taught me how important mastery of the substance was — and that it wasn't enough. You also needed to be able to communicate your view and persuade others that your view is the right one. His example made me realize that hard work and determination could take you to the top of the State Department even if you were starting at the bottom rung of the FSO ladder. Seitz later became the only career FSO ever appointed ambassador to the Court of Saint James's, a testament to both his skills and his savvy.

My good-boss karma continued when political appointee Henry Catto arrived. A close friend of President George H. W. Bush, Catto was a Texas straight shooter. He shocked the British when his wife didn't accompany him to London because she had her own career in the U.S. He shocked them again — and left a lasting impression on me about what leadership looks like — when he refused to go to a men-only club in London to deliver the traditional American ambassador's address on U.S.-U.K. economic ties until the club reversed its decision to bar his female economic counselor from attending. The times were changing, but it took more than women demanding their rights to make it happen; it also took men like Ambassador Catto to act on principle and support them.

The twelve-month period during which I worked for the three embassy heads in London, observing how they handled different personalities, different challenges, and different opportunities, was pivotal for me. There were few women to emulate, and until then I had thought I needed to model myself on an imagined stereotype of a straitlaced male who never showed emotion. But I realized that wasn't the case after working for three successful men with big, distinct, and very different personalities. They were comfortable in their own skin. The embassy staff, the Brits, and Washington responded to that.

Together these three bosses taught me a powerful lesson. I didn't need to be something that I wasn't in order to succeed, whether it was a mini-man in a boxy suit or a person trying to adopt a persona that wasn't my own. I could be myself and still be effective. It was liberating.

LONDON PROVED TO BE the turning point of my early career, but there was a lighter side to life in the front office as well. New ambassadors present their credentials to the head of state, and in the U.K. that is Queen Elizabeth. No country can out-pomp the U.K., and for this avid *People* magazine reader, it was fun to work through the details with the Foreign Office. Picture this: the embassy staff sending off the ambassador, dressed in top hat, black tie, and tails, in one of the Queen's horse-drawn carriages to present his credentials to Her Majesty at Buckingham Palace. Somewhere I have a photo of myself complying with instructions from British protocol and feeding the horses sugar cubes and carrots.

I wasn't senior enough to attend that ceremony, but I did get to go to the Queen's annual Diplomatic Ball. "If you have a tiara, wear it," a British friend advised in her clipped upper-class accent when I asked her for advice on attire. I had no tiara, of course, and it also turned out I didn't even have the right dress. My very limited formal wardrobe consisted of one black dress, but the instructions accompanying the invitation indicated that black, reserved by the royal family for mourning, was unacceptable. Happily, I found a Rent the Runway–type store and was able to wear a fabulous purple ball gown, which I matched with newly purchased amethyst earrings.

The night of the ball I joined a group of colleagues in splurging on a catered dinner to tide us over until the very late supper we'd be offered at Buckingham Palace. To drive to the palace, we double-splurged on the ultimate ride, a chauffeur-driven Maybach—a snooty car this country girl had never heard of. It felt like a senior prom night on steroids.

Ambassador Catto presented us to the Queen, Prince Philip, Prince Charles, and Princess Diana. It was among the most memorable sixty seconds of my life. The Queen impressed me as a tiny woman with an enormous presence, and although I had been instructed that American diplomats do not bow to royalty, I couldn't help but give a little bob of my head. Prince Philip, known to be a bit bawdy, did a double take when Ambassador Catto introduced me as his staff assistant. Deadpan, he inquired whether I assisted in holding the ambassador's staff, leaving all of us at a complete loss for words. Prince Charles didn't make much of an impression, but I vividly remember how everyone in the room, including me, was riveted by Princess Diana. Her glamour made me think she was from a different world, and then I noticed that her nails were bitten to the quick, just like mine.

There was dancing, a buffet dinner, the world's most valuable private art collection to admire in the grand corridors, and all that history permeating the walls. I felt like Cinderella at the ball and had to pinch myself, just so I'd know it was real.

AMBASSADOR CATTO KNEW that I wanted to be a political officer, so when my year in the front office ended, he moved me to the political section for my last five months in London. I didn't have a set portfolio, but in some sense that made it all the more interesting.

Embassy London dealt with all the many international issues on which the U.S. and the U.K. collaborated, resulting in a very busy political section, especially as the people of Eastern Europe began to throw off autocracy and the Soviet yoke. Some of the more senior political officers needed assistance, which made me feel as close to the center of the action in London as I had felt detached from it in Somalia. I was thrilled when Ambassador Catto flagged for the personal attention of President Bush a cable I wrote on British thoughts on impending German reunification—a real confidence-booster for me.

As my time in London wound down in the spring of 1990, I hoped that my next posting would be just as stimulating. I was pretty sure it would be: Ambassador Catto had recommended me for a job in the State Department's Operations Center, the nerve center of the department and a place considered an important stepping-stone to higher-level jobs. The job was based in Washington, and I would start in June.

FSOS USUALLY RETURN to the U.S. for their third tour to get Washington experience. I was ready. I loved living in London, but after almost four years abroad it was good to come home and reconnect with family and friends. I rented a house with a friend from my Mogadishu days and settled back into my American life as though I had never left.

My new job on "the Watch," however, was as novel as my surroundings were familiar. The department had established the Operations Center in 1961 after President Kennedy couldn't get a phone call answered at the State Department one night during the Bay of Pigs crisis. At first the center consisted of one guy, a phone, and a cot. By the time I got there in 1990, it had become the department's communications and crisis management hub — the central node of a vast network that kept watch over the world 24/7. Working in teams on eight-hour shifts, Watch standers, as we were called, fielded phone calls and cables reporting urgent information from around the world and made sure that everything of import quickly made its way to the department's leaders.

Just as my time in the London front office had given me an overall perspective on the work of an embassy, this job pulled back at least a part of the curtain on how things worked at Foggy Bottom's highest levels. I saw the most important issues of the day and how department leadership responded. It was heady stuff. A young woman ran the day-to-day operations of the Watch, and she was a highflier who said what she thought and wore brightly colored clothes. In London I had seen men succeed being themselves. At the Ops Center, my boss gave me my first example of a woman doing the same. I wasn't ready to push the dark, boxy suits out of my closet, but I started jazzing them up with colorful tops, scarves, and the craft jewelry that I loved.

Two months into my time on the Watch, in early August 1990, Iraqi president Saddam Hussein invaded Kuwait. Iraq had been steadily amassing thousands of troops on its border with Kuwait, a small country with large oil and gas reserves. We had known what was coming. Nevertheless, it was a shock to pick up the phone and hear our ambassador to Kuwait, Nathaniel Howell, telling me that Iraqi troops had crossed the border. I followed our protocol, calling the team to attention to tell them that Iraq had invaded

Kuwait, which triggered a slew of calls informing department leaders of the news. That night we helped set up the emergency task force to coordinate the State Department's response for the duration of the crisis. We tracked the fast-breaking news and provided updates to those at the top.

Over the months that followed, President Bush and Secretary of State James Baker built the thirty-five-nation coalition that would launch Operation Desert Storm the following January and push Saddam out of Kuwait. Part of our job on the Watch was to arrange and then patch through calls for the secretary with world leaders as they coordinated their response to Saddam's aggression. Events were so fast-paced that Watch standers were drafted to listen in and draft memoranda of Baker's phone calls. All of a sudden I had a front-row seat to history.

I met Secretary Baker only once — for a photo opportunity. A wily political operator, consummate Washington insider, and close friend of President Bush, Baker had already served as treasury secretary and White House chief of staff under President Reagan. When he had started at State, department personnel had found him cold and aloof, and the media reported that he didn't trust the career folks. Maybe so, but it was clear immediately that he was a master of diplomacy. It was fascinating to observe how he managed each relationship and hear which arguments he advanced. There were lots of pragmatic, realpolitik reasons to move forward with a military response to Saddam's invasion of Kuwait, but I was surprised and gratified by the idealism that Baker sometimes conveyed. I found it reassuring that our foreign policy wasn't just about our interests; as I had hoped during the Grenada episode some ten years before, it was also about our values.

THE FALL FLEW BY as the diplomatic and military preparations for Desert Storm progressed. Then another crisis emerged, one that unexpectedly caused my past to collide with my present.

After my departure from Mogadishu, the civil war in Somalia had intensified, eventually dragging the country into total chaos. On January 1, 1991, our ambassador reported that it was no longer safe for American staff to remain in the country. The embassy had to evacuate.

With U.S. troops massing in the region in anticipation of the imminent launch of Desert Storm, we had resources not too far away that would enable us to carry out an evacuation of Embassy Mogadishu. The Ops Center established another task force in one of our conference rooms to monitor the situation in Somalia as the military began to plan the challenging operation. As Watch standers, we provided support to the task force and got regular briefings in order to keep department principals up-to-date on the plans to bring our people home.

By this point the military could no longer use the most efficient means to evacuate: fixed-wing military aircraft picking up embassy staff at Mogadishu's airport. The Somali government, to the extent that it still existed, could not guarantee safe passage for our people from the embassy to the airport. That left helicopters landing at the embassy compound itself as the only way out. But helicopters have substantially less range and seating capacity, meaning that the military had to move ships carrying the helicopters close to the Somali coast before launching rescue operations.

As two warships steamed southwest to Somalia, the security situation in Mogadishu deteriorated even further, and the ambassador sent a message urgently requesting immediate evacuation. Armed militias were in the streets. There was fighting outside the embassy compound, and Somali government forces could no longer keep order. Only the usual six-person contingent of Marines, augmented by the embassy's unarmed local security force, guarded the embassy. The situation was dire.

I could only imagine what was going through the minds of my American colleagues waiting at the embassy, and I couldn't escape the thought that it might have been me trapped in the compound instead of them. Anyone paying attention knew that we needed to act quickly, but the coming war with Iraq was — understandably — taking up virtually all of the U.S. government's bandwidth.

I probably felt the situation more acutely given my connection to the embassy, and I couldn't get my mind off the great risk even minimal delay posed to our people on the ground in Somalia. From the start the Foreign Service tells its people that it prizes good judgment and initiative above everything, and even though I was very junior, I felt I couldn't just stand by. I marched up to my shift supervisor and urged him very strongly to escalate the issue to department leadership and press for immediate action.

No doubt others were doing the same in their channels. However it happened, the logjam broke, and the next morning two large helicopters set off on the 450-mile flight with a sixty-man detail to establish a secure perimeter around the embassy until the evacuation could go forward. The ships were still so far away that the helicopters required in-flight refueling — risky under any circumstances, but especially when approaching what was effectively a war zone. But time was running out, and waiting for the ships to get closer before launching the operation was no longer an option.

Back in my seat in Washington, I answered a call from the Pentagon's version of the Operations Center to hear a startling question. I was told that a Marine participating in the rescue operation was warning that the choppers were flying to the wrong location. He had worked at Embassy Mogadishu a year earlier and insisted that the rescuers were following outdated maps and going to the former embassy site in downtown Mogadishu rather than the current American embassy, five miles away. The Pentagon needed immediate confirmation: Where should the helicopters go?

Although I am sure the Pentagon was getting corroboration in other ways as well, it felt like providence that I was the one who answered that call. I was the only one in the Ops Center who could have confirmed the Marine's information immediately. What were the odds of that?

The helicopters rerouted to the new embassy compound, and they arrived not a moment too soon, scaring off about a hundred Somalis who had been putting up ladders to scale the compound walls. The U.S. military ultimately evacuated 281 people from Mogadishu — 61 Americans and much of the rest of the international presence there, including 12 ambassadors and 4 chargés d'affaires from foreign nations that had no other way to extract their people. Reflecting the warming relationship with the Soviet Union, the passengers include the ambassador and 38 additional Soviet diplomats. Before the month was out, Siad Barre too had fled Mogadishu, and anarchy engulfed the country.

I played only a small role in the Mogadishu evacuation, but I was proud of my work, especially when my employee evaluation read: "Her decision to force immediate action at the highest levels of the Department, the Pentagon, and the White House saved lives."

JOBS ON THE WATCH last just one year, so I was bidding on my next assignment almost as soon as I arrived. Emboldened by my run of good luck since I had left Somalia, I decided to throw my hat in the ring for a political job in Leningrad.

Coming from the management cone, I would usually have had no chance at the job, but I had spent much of the past three years doing jobs with political components and had the support of Ray Seitz, who was by then the assistant secretary for Europe. But my experience and Ray's recommendation weren't enough. A political cone officer wanted the job as well, so it went to her.

I was stuck in a catch-22: I couldn't get a posting to a political section job because I wasn't in the political cone, and I couldn't switch to the political cone without two years of political cone experience. I had performed some political work in the course of my post-Somalia postings, but switching cones was such an opaque process that I couldn't even get a clear answer on whether any of my assignments would count as political experience, since they were not all demarcated as political cone jobs.

My supervisors on the Watch and mentors in the European Bureau were looking out for me, however. They suggested that I bid on a one-year assignment working on the Regional Political-Military Desk in the department. The job focused on European security policy and arms control, and I hoped it would give me a grounding in security issues and count as political experience when I next applied for a political cone job.

I spent much of that next year working on efforts to ratify the Treaty on Conventional Armed Forces in Europe, which limited troops and conventional weapons in Europe, making a surprise attack or full-scale war less likely. It represented a huge step forward in increasing security for our European allies and the U.S. I was grateful to find myself involved in such globally critical events.

But this was another one-year assignment, meaning that once again as soon as I started my job I was immediately bidding on the next one. I was fresh out of ideas on how to become a political officer. Assuming that the department calculated my political cone experience in the most conservative way possible, I would have at most seventeen months of political experience after my current assignment ended, well below the twenty-four months required to apply to change cones. I was on the verge of giving up when a helping hand reached across a generational divide to set me on my path.

SEXISM AT the State Department had a long history, and I had certainly experienced it, although fortunately not the worst aspects. But from the strange lesson on calling cards for the women in my A-100 class to the paucity of female role models at the department to the infuriating suggestion in Somalia that I had somehow encouraged Barre's nephew to harass me, I had seen, firsthand and from the very beginning, the attitudes and obstacles that women in the Foreign Service contended with every day. Nonetheless, I had been fortunate to find a measure of success, and like many women of my generation, I figured that the chauvinism of the disgruntled old guard was the price of being a woman in the 1980s workforce in America.

It's not that the discrimination didn't bother me. It's just that I tried to brush off the belittling comments, sexual and otherwise. But it was hard to unhear the opinion that married women couldn't be "real" political officers, the implication being that their husbands' careers had to come first. And in the "you can't make it up" category, every day I encountered porcelain testaments to the State Department's failure to adapt to the increasing number of women it employed. Unbelievably, from the day I started in 1986 to the day I retired in 2020, many of the women's restrooms at Foggy Bottom contained urinals. It took me two decades to complain about it, and the response I received from a male facilities staffer was even more absurd than I would have expected: "Some women," he insisted, "prefer them." It was such a startling assertion that I checked with my female friends to make sure that I wasn't missing something. I wasn't. To the contrary, as one friend colorfully put it, the urinals stand as a "big fuck you" to women every time they see one in a Foggy Bottom restroom.

It didn't occur to me that these slights were part and parcel of more consequential barriers that had placed and kept me in the management cone until I learned about a class action lawsuit brought by a courageous, crusading FSO named Alison Palmer. Palmer had joined the State Department in 1955, three years before I was born, at a time when the challenges facing women were far greater. The Foreign Service rarely employed women back then, and those who succeeded in getting hired as FSOs faced a career in which certain assignments were explicitly off-limits and in which, until 1971, the choice to marry brought the mandate to leave the service. Against all odds, Palmer became an FSO, only to find herself pigeonholed into positions traditionally viewed as suitable for women. She was displaced from other assignments by men of lower career rank because, the reasoning went, they needed the job more than she did. That was the way it was. But Palmer didn't think that was the way it should be.

Palmer fought back and sued the State Department for discrimination. She won her case and then in 1976 launched what turned into an epic, decades-long class-action lawsuit aimed at reforming a system that stymied women in ways less obvious than the blatant discrimination that had thwarted her own career. The lawsuit exposed systemic bias in the way the department tested female applicants for admission to the Foreign Service, how it assigned women to the various cones, and how it promoted women. I hadn't realized it at the time, but when I first applied to the Foreign Service and was placed in the management cone, the system was stacked against me.

The Palmer case brought many important changes to State's personnel system, phased in over a number of years. One of these changes took effect just when I needed it most. To remedy discrimination in the assignment of cones, the department agreed to offer fourteen female FSOs who had been placed in the consular or management cones the opportunity to move to the political cone and to choose their next assignment. I competed for one of the slots and in December 1991 received an early Christmas gift: an assignment to work in Embassy Moscow as a political officer.

It felt like I had won the lottery: I was going to be doing the kind of work I most wanted to do in the country I most wanted to go to. But while I was beyond excited, I also felt the irony. I knew that I had received this opportunity because multiple court judgments had determined that the department had discriminated against women like me and had ordered the department to make it right. After working hard, garnering support from many mentors, and trying every possible avenue to move into the political cone, I received my big break not through Plan A (volunteer for a rotation in Somalia that included a year of political work), Plan B (take every opportunity to volunteer for political work wherever I was), or even Plan C (the Hail Mary pass for the job in Leningrad). I got my big break because I was the right gender at the right time.

Of course, it wasn't quite that simple. I wouldn't have received this opportunity if I hadn't been among the women who had faced the systemic discrimination Palmer had proved. Even more importantly, I would not have been selected as one of the fourteen — or continued to move up after my time in Moscow — if I had not proved my merit at every stage of my career. But as always I was conflicted. On the one hand, I felt — and still feel — tremendous gratitude to Alison Palmer for fighting for me and so many other women. Her tenacity made the department take steps well beyond the ones that benefited me to level the playing field for women — and men.

On the other hand, I knew of the opposition to the lawsuit among many senior officers, and that number included some of the men that I worked for. I was still carrying my childhood insecurities, and I still believed that the standards that the male old guard applied were the ones that counted. I wanted to succeed or fail on the merits, not because I was a woman benefiting from the lawsuit. I hadn't fully realized that "merit" is a meaningless term if it's not judged on a level playing field.

So I didn't tell anyone. I decided that no one needed to know that I was a beneficiary of the Palmer court case. It just seemed safer that way, and I kept silent for decades. I'm sharing this story now only because I think it's important to understand that sometimes persistence and hard work aren't enough. Sometimes we also need an iconoclast, an Alison Palmer, willing to risk it all in the fight to make our institutions live up to our ideals.

IT WAS DECEMBER 1991 and I was on the way to fulfilling my dream of going back to Moscow. But not quite yet. First I had to finish the six months left in my current assignment and then spend a year improving my Russian. Or at least that was the plan.

In April, in a sign of the fast-moving times, I was tapped to go as a political officer to one of the new countries that had sprung out of the 1991 dissolution of the Soviet Union. Turning on a dime, the U.S. had to establish embassies in eleven of the countries that emerged from the former Soviet Union and in the three Baltic states; only Russia already had a U.S. embassy. It was a mammoth task. Eager to establish beachheads as quickly as possible, State sent small teams of FSOs on six- to eight-week missions to temporarily staff makeshift embassies in each country while the department figured out the longer-term arrangements. In April 1992 I joined one such team and traveled to Uzbekistan to help lay the foundations for a diplomatic relationship between our countries.

I had barely heard of Uzbekistan, a double-landlocked Central Asian nation of roughly 21 million people. Settled by Scythians and ultimately conquered by the Persians, the Mongols, and then the Russians, Uzbekistan had been enriched by all these influences, as well as by the impact of the Silk Road traders. The Uzbeks had brought the world important advances in astronomy, trigonometry, and geometry.

But for all that history, Uzbekistan had been an independent country for only eight months when I arrived, and the U.S. embassy in the capital, Tashkent, was just one month old. I was unsure of what to expect but had been warned that food might be hard to come by. So in addition to my suitcase full of clothes, I took a duffel bag containing ninety pounds of ramen noodles, peanut butter, energy bars, and other food.

The Uzbeks were eager to establish a bilateral relationship with the U.S. and hopeful that we could help balance the influence of powers such as Russia, China, Turkey, and Iran. This was my first taste of Central Asian hospitality, and U.S. diplomats were warmly welcomed. Suddenly I was getting paid to do what I would have done for free: talking to everyone in Tashkent, from high-ranking ministers to students to opposition leaders, then writing it up for Washington along with my analysis of what it all meant. I was the lone political officer, and it was fascinating. It was also important, as we tried to help the Uzbeks establish an independent country.

Our makeshift embassy was in the former Communist Youth League building, where a bust of Lenin still presided in the first floor's main hall. There was no setback, no wall, not even a Marine guard standing between Embassy Tashkent and the rest of the city. In fact, our small team of Americans took turns sleeping in the embassy to guard our communications equipment.

The risks of this arrangement became clear a couple of weeks into my stay. I was hard at work on the second floor when a man sprayed the building with gunfire, jumped through a large window, and then barricaded himself in one of the ground-floor offices, taking our Uzbek accountant hostage. In the pandemonium I ran to the window and shouted urgently in Russian to passersby to call the police. Within minutes Uzbek security forces poured out of an adjacent building and surrounded the embassy. I was mightily impressed by their responsiveness until I realized that they had been there all along, undoubtedly to surveil us. I just hoped they weren't trigger-happy; Soviet-trained troops were not known for their skill or their discipline, and bystanders like me could pay the price for a soldier's recklessness.

As the minutes ticked by, I knew that I had to get to my boss, the chargé d'affaires, who was just down the hall. We needed to figure out how to bring this disaster to a peaceful conclusion. But getting to him was no easy task. Our offices fronted onto an interior balcony hallway overlooking the first floor. If the shooter stepped out of our accountant's office, he would be able to see — and shoot at — anyone walking on the balcony.

So I crawled along the balcony floor to the chargé's office, and we got to work. The chargé called Washington to get authorization to negotiate with the man, and I called the Ops Center in D.C. to brief them on what was happening. When the Watch stander — no doubt imagining a well-fortified embassy — asked why we had allowed the gunman in, I realized that there was little understanding back home of just how expeditionary our mission was. But recalling some of the silly things that I had said when I was on the Watch, I simply reported back to the chargé that it didn't look like Washington would be able to do anything in the short term. We were on our own.

In the end, after several tense hours, the crisis was defused by the Uzbek commander who had responded so promptly to my cries for help. After talking the gunman down, he told us that the shooter was angry about the Uzbek army's treatment of his son. We never learned why he chose our embassy as the venue to air his grievances, but I've always assumed that he was just one of the many individuals all over the world who believe in the power of America and our ideals and conclude that even in a foreign land we can somehow right the wrongs done to their people.

AFTER MY TIME in Uzbekistan, I spent a long, hot, and absolutely fascinating summer in Rome, supporting international efforts to broker peace in the war in Nagorno-Karabakh, a historically ethnic Armenian enclave but legally part of Azerbaijan. I was working on issues that mattered to me and seeing the world — and feeling grateful that the Palmer remedy had transformed my career possibilities.

After Rome, it was off to the Foreign Service Institute for a year of language training in anticipation of my move to Moscow. Improving my Russian-language proficiency was a great way to prepare for my upcoming assignment, as we read the news, watched TV, and discussed current events, all in Russian. Even from the vast remove of my ivory tower, I could see the multiple crises enveloping Russia, and I wondered what my next tour would bring.

In August 1993 I set out to discover just that. After seven years in the Foreign Service, I had reached my goal of becoming a political officer. And I was doing it in the place I had wanted to return to since my short 1988 stint in Embassy Moscow. It seemed too good to be true. But my first year there made me recall that old saying: be careful what you wish for.

5

Russia

Wᴴᴇɴ ɪ ʀᴇᴛᴜʀɴᴇᴅ to Moscow in mid-August 1993, I found a country fundamentally altered by the end of the Cold War. From the U.S.
perspective, the consequences of the Soviet Union's 1991 dissolution were
being reasonably well managed. Negotiations to consolidate the far-flung
Soviet nuclear stockpile and safeguard it in Russia were proceeding constructively. The Warsaw Pact, a mutual defense alliance of the Soviet Union
and its satellite states established to counter NATO, had been disbanded.
The Iron Curtain had lifted, and most of the countries that had emerged
from the breakup of the USSR, as well as most of the Warsaw Pact countries,
expressed interest in becoming democracies with free-market economies.
They didn't necessarily know what that would mean in practice, but it gave
us hope that President Bush's vision of a Europe "whole and free" would become a reality. At the same time, Russia was too busy with its own problems
to interfere much in the affairs of the other eleven republics that had made
up the Soviet Union and that, like Russia, were now tackling the task of establishing themselves as independent states.

Moreover, the United States had developed a strong and positive relationship with Russia, especially at the top levels. President Boris Yeltsin had
taken Russia's helm when it had still been part of the Soviet Union and was
now trying to steer the newly independent country toward a democratic
political system, a free-market economy, and better relations with the West.
That was precisely what we had hoped the end of the Cold War would bring.

What we didn't fully appreciate was how devastating the changes were
from a Russian point of view. Many saw the collapse of the Soviet Union as
an existential humiliation, an overnight loss of a great empire. Even worse,
millions experienced it as an economic disaster. Although there had been

no self-determination under communism, to say nothing of the severe repression that many Russians endured, a sizable percentage of the population mourned the predictability and the guarantees of the past: the state-provided education, jobs, apartments, health care, and child care. They may not have studied what they were interested in, gotten the jobs they wanted, or even lived in the cities of their choice, but they had been provided for all the same. Up against post-1991 uncertainties, the old social contract seemed preferable to many Russians.

But that deal had been swept away with the USSR's demise, and Russia's new leaders offered little to replace it beyond the abstract promise of greater political and economic freedom. In the meantime, steps aimed at improving Russians' lives just seemed to be making things worse. Transitioning to capitalism meant that workers were losing their jobs as many formerly subsidized state-owned enterprises went out of business or were privatized. The public suffered through the abolition of price controls, high inflation, and the resulting loss of any savings. The situation was so dire that the U.S. was flying humanitarian shipments to Russia, including surplus wheat and chicken thighs (known in the region as "Bush legs" in honor of President Bush). Two years in, millions of Russians were desperate to have their old lives back and apprehensive about the changes still ahead. Elderly Russians talked about the curse of being young in communism and old in capitalism.

Not everyone was suffering, however. While many Russians were sinking, a prescient few embraced — and exploited — the opportunities brought about by the Soviet Union's demise. When the USSR had owned and operated virtually everything, there had been no reason to develop a comprehensive body of laws and regulations controlling private ownership of property or companies; neither had there been a need for a robust set of contract and employment laws. The Communist Party had decided everything, and if employees, tenants, or others had a problem with party decision-making, they were out of luck. That became an issue when Russia initiated the privatization of previously state-owned companies without first establishing companion laws to govern the country's newly unleashed commercial activities and protect those at risk of exploitation. Every Russian citizen received vouchers to buy shares of the privatized companies. But with no understanding of how capitalism worked and no laws to watch out for them, hungry workers ended up selling their vouchers on the cheap, allowing the nimble, the strong, and the ruthless to accumulate significant ownership interests in lucrative companies.

In fairness, the Russian leaders were building the plane while they were flying it. But the result was that Russia in the early 1990s frequently resembled the wild wild West. Party bosses, factory managers, middlemen, criminals, and those in the security services often won big. They were the insiders who knew which state assets were valuable, and they worked the system to ensure that they would gain control of them. Others didn't even bother pretending to work within the system. Criminals and security service personnel had their own ways of convincing rivals to step aside. Assassinations and shootouts in broad daylight testified to the high stakes.

Although the appropriation of resources in this era mostly wasn't a crime, there *were* victims: the Russian people. They saw valuable state enterprises fall into the hands of a small cohort of their fellow citizens as they themselves struggled to make ends meet. By the time I returned to Moscow, millions of Russians felt worse off than they had been two years earlier and had concluded that if this was what capitalism was all about, then we in the West could keep it. Their newfound freedoms — to speak openly, travel abroad, live where they wanted — weren't enough to make up for their economic struggles. Many pocketed the positives and looked back with nostalgia, choosing to ignore the downsides of the former system.

And those downsides didn't magically go away in 1991. They continued and contributed greatly to Russia's problems even after communism had been left in history's dustbin. Most striking, as I had seen during my first stay in Moscow, was the resigned acceptance of many Russians of the arbitrary nature of their life under the Soviet regime. The rule of law — the idea that the same defined, transparent, and enforceable standards governed everyone in the society equally, no matter their position — had been quite literally a foreign concept. The Communists had preached the theory that all citizens were equal, but in reality Communist Party members had always been more equal than others, and the higher up the ladder they climbed, the more equal they became. Prosecutors and judges weren't independent of the party, and ordinary people had no recourse other than to accept the inherent unfairness of this allegedly egalitarian system.

Regular Russians saw the Communist Party leaders appropriate for themselves scarce consumer goods, the best apartments, and places at elite

universities for their children. Those lower down in the pecking order —
that is, the vast majority of Russians — got what was left.

Communism also stymied the Soviet Union's growth and prosperity as it
sapped both ingenuity and productivity. Centralized planners couldn't possibly match supply and demand correctly for every product needed in the
entire Soviet Union, so the command economy inevitably failed at getting
the right products to the right places at the right times. As I had experienced during my student days in Moscow, and again during my posting to
Embassy Moscow in 1988, shortages of everyday items and lines for everyday services were commonplace.

With not enough to go around, the result had been preordained: systemic corruption infused every Soviet institution and virtually every aspect
of Soviet life as people did what they needed to do to get by. Corruption at
the highest levels in large part caused the problems, and it then became the
lubricant that made the failing system workable at the ground level. A phy-
sician might find necessary but scarce medication for a patient in exchange
for a "financial consideration." A place in the long line to get a telephone
might be fast-tracked with a "tip" to the right person in the state telephone
monopoly. Placement in a better school could be arranged for a "gift."

Yeltsin had promised to change all this and deliver a better life for Russians when he became president. His team worked valiantly to establish
a functioning economy and the rule of law, but those kinds of systemic
changes take time to put in place and generations to take root. In the meantime the Russian people still needed to get by. With corruption endemic in
Soviet culture, it should not have been a surprise that Russians continued to
fall back on what they knew as the surest way to survive in uncertain times.

By the summer of 1993, Yeltsin's heroic image — the strong leader standing on a tank in August 1991, defying attempted coup plotters and taking
Russia into a new era — had faded. He still garnered significant support,
especially among pro-reform, pro-Western, small "d" democrats, but he
also faced significant opposition. The center of that opposition was Russia's holdover parliament, or Duma, dominated by old-guard members who
had been elected before the USSR's breakup. A combination of Communists, nationalists, and others, they opposed the Soviet Union's dissolution,
democratic and economic reforms, and Yeltsin himself. With an array of
grievances — Russia's wounded pride, the impoverishment of its people,

and what they claimed was Moscow's subservience to the West — Yeltsin's opponents had a lot to work with.

I WAS INTRIGUED by the prospect of helping our government navigate these challenges, and I was grateful to be working at Embassy Moscow for a Foreign Service legend: Thomas Pickering, a seven-time ambassador whose experience in hot spots around the world made me confident in his leadership and certain that I would learn from his example. Wickedly smart, Ambassador Pickering had a phenomenal memory and seemed to have a system for just about everything, on the policy side or otherwise. For staying awake during boring meetings, he recommended digging your nails into the palm of your hand or chewing on the inside of your cheek — techniques I found painful but effective. Pickering seemed to work around the clock, and rumor had it that he had so mastered the skill of power-napping that he required only a few hours of sleep a night. Well over six feet tall, he was a man in a hurry, and I quickly learned that I wouldn't be able to keep up unless I wore flats so that I could trot along beside him.

The embassy compound was located in the middle of Moscow and housed our offices, a cafeteria, a small store, a recreational area, and homes for many American employees, mostly families. Senior management lived there as well, except for Ambassador Pickering, who occupied a historic residence nearby.

Above the compound towered the unoccupied eight-story shell of what was supposed to have been our new embassy, a replacement for a long-outdated and outgrown building located in an adjacent compound. The U.S. had halted construction on the new embassy in the mid-1980s, after discovering Soviet listening devices built into the support structure. Staff originally continued working at the old embassy, but a 1991 fire had so damaged that building that most had to move to makeshift offices in the new compound. For me, that meant sitting cheek by jowl with the rest of the political section in a repurposed section of the garage. Work conditions were not ideal, but it was Moscow, I reminded myself.

Beyond the compound walls lay a whole city to be explored. The Kremlin was a twenty-minute walk away along a main boulevard. A five-minute stroll in the opposite direction took me to the Russian White House, home to the Duma. Facing the American compound entrance across a narrow lane were apartment buildings, as well as a church that my friends and I called "Our Lady of Perpetual Observation" in honor of the Russian security services we assumed camped out on the premises to keep eyes and ears on American diplomats.

Kiosks had popped up along the streets, selling just about everything — proof of a newfound middle-class entrepreneurism. But there was also evidence of the desperation so many now felt. Impoverished pensioners lined the busy metro entrances, offering passersby a heartbreaking array of goods for sale: chipped plates, a bouquet of homegrown flowers, a grandfather's military medals. In the new post-Soviet reality, some people did not even have a few kopeks for a loaf of bread. Once again I felt grateful that my grandparents had made the choice to leave the Soviet Union so many decades earlier, and that their children, my recently retired parents, were now enjoying a comfortable life in the United States.

The embassy had arranged housing for me about a fifteen-minute drive away from the compound, in a building that the Russian government rented out to foreigners. My living room windows overlooked October Square, which still featured a big statue of Lenin marching forward into some unseen future. The central location often served as the rallying point for demonstrators — another sign of how much things had changed since my first time in Moscow.

WHILE I WAS getting settled, Yeltsin and the old-guard parliament continued to clash. On September 1, just two and a half weeks after I arrived, Yeltsin escalated matters by suspending his vice president, Aleksandr Rutskoy, who enjoyed significant support among the legislators. Although he had partnered with Yeltsin in the aftermath of the Soviet Union's demise, Rutskoy, a decorated former general, had broken with Yeltsin by 1993, challenging the president's programs as "economic genocide." Members of parliament objected to Rutskoy's suspension, arguing that Yeltsin lacked the constitutional authority to remove him — and it appeared that they were right.

As this conflict was brewing, embassy leadership wanted to get a sense of how it was playing outside the capital, so two colleagues and I took an overnight trip to meet with local officials in a region south of Moscow. The morning after our arrival, we were preparing to leave our hotel for our first meeting when we heard the bombshell announcement that Yeltsin had ordered the parliament dissolved and called for new parliamentary elections in December. Russia's Soviet-era constitution didn't give him the authority to take those actions either.

I called to confirm our appointments with the region's top officials, but their aides could tell us only that our counterparts were conferring behind closed doors. An hour later a nervous official informed us that our meetings had been canceled. It was clear that no one wanted foreigners around, least of all American diplomats.

There was no point in staying, so we headed back to Moscow, where we learned that the parliament had quickly impeached Yeltsin and named Rutskoy acting president of Russia. Defiant deputies, fearful that Yeltsin might attempt to arrest them or take over the parliament if they left the White House compound, decided to hunker down and move in. They brought food, blankets, and weapons and settled in for what they expected could turn into a long standoff. Their supporters formed a protective buffer outside, filling the area around the building and in the adjacent park. Large crowds demonstrated by day, and a hard core of activists maintained a vigil overnight. Yeltsin responded by sending his forces to surround the area and establish control over who entered and departed from the White House grounds.

Because our embassy compound was so close to the White House, we ended up inside the security perimeter, and watched as it hardened each day. At first a couple of pimply young policemen with black-and-white batons lounged casually at the top of the lane that led to the embassy and on to the White House. The next day they seemed more alert, asking for identification before letting us pass. Soon wooden sawhorses barred vehicles and the idly curious from entering. Then the boys were replaced with hard-faced men from the security services.

I noted the changes, but perhaps because they happened over the course of a number of days — or perhaps because of my own inexperience — the ratcheting up of force didn't trigger an alarm, at least not for me. Also, I was too busy to be nervous. While Yeltsin's forces strengthened their grip on the White House perimeter, we were gathering information and assessing the situation for Washington. I went to the White House every day to talk to the pro-Rutskoy deputies and their supporters and to mediators from the Russian Orthodox Church, which had sway with both sides.

About a week into the crisis, though, events forced me to confront how serious the situation was becoming. During one parliamentary session at which I was present, Duma guards interrupted and instructed everyone to shelter in the basement. I joined hundreds of legislators and visitors slowly descending the stairway and found myself next to Communist Party head Gennadiy Zyuganov. As we chatted the lights flickered and went out, and I overheard Zyuganov mutter to no one in particular, *And so it starts.* The lights came back on quickly, but the moment had sobered me. I decided that discretion was the better part of valor and left the White House as soon as I could.

But I didn't stay away for long. There was an insatiable demand for information in Washington, and I was more energized by the political action than I was afraid of the potential for violence. I was finally doing exactly what I had joined the Foreign Service to do, reporting on historic change and trying to make sense of it so that Washington could make the best policy choices. Now that I finally had the chance, I was anxious to prove myself. I returned to the White House the next day.

Yeltsin continued to ratchet up the pressure on the parliament, ordering the electricity, heat, and water turned off in the White House. Concertina wire went up around the building, and trucks with water cannons appeared. Hundreds of troops, ready to be called into action if necessary, were staged in buses on the side streets, including on the lane outside the embassy. Police with loudspeakers urged the White House defenders to give up their arms. But the parliamentarians inside and the demonstrators outside showed no signs of giving up. In fact both camps were digging in, and Yeltsin didn't seem inclined to help the parliamentarians find a way out.

On the eleventh day of the standoff, a Friday afternoon, Ambassador Pickering determined that the situation had become too dangerous for embassy staff to continue going to the White House. In those pre–cell phone days, he sent someone in to tell me and a colleague to leave immediately. I returned to my desk, wrote up what I had, and went home for what I hoped would be a restful weekend. In retrospect, I can't help but wonder whether the ambassador knew what was coming.

THAT SUNDAY AFTERNOON, October 3, I was visiting with Russian friends from my postcollege days in Moscow. I was happily sitting in their cramped kitchen nursing my tea when someone knocked on the door. A neighbor slipped in to report that there was shooting at the White House and people were gathering at the Kremlin to support Yeltsin. She was heading there herself and wanted to know whether we would join her.

Yeltsin was a flawed man, an alcoholic whose best days were probably behind him. Like just about everyone else who had the chance, he played fast and loose with Russia's constitution and laws. But the vestiges of the past arrayed against him — first and foremost, the parliament and the Communist constitution — were obstructing Russia's future. True, Yeltsin's extralegal acts aimed to keep him in power, but he also seemed to want to use that power to put Russia on the path to democracy, a market economy, and positive relations with the West. Indeed, when Yeltsin had dissolved the Soviet-era parliament in September, he had called for swift parliamentary elections and a referendum on a new constitution in December, thus leaving it to the Russian people to decide who would represent them and how they would be governed. No question, Yeltsin's actions were controversial, but my friends, ardent democrats, believed that Yeltsin was far preferable for Russia than Rutskoy and his ilk. They immediately decided to go to the Kremlin to show support for the president.

I knew I couldn't go; this turn of events undoubtedly meant I had work to do. I had to get in touch with the embassy right away. The problem was, there was no obvious way to accomplish that. We always assumed that the Russians were monitoring embassy phone lines, and I felt I couldn't risk exposing my friends at such a politically volatile moment by calling the embassy from their apartment. I thought about driving straight to the embassy but realized that the fighting around the White House might make it impossible to reach the compound. Plus I was mindful that an A-100 classmate had returned from a tour in Haiti with a number of bullet holes in her car, and I didn't want to risk damaging mine. I decided to drive home to my apartment, about forty-five minutes away from my friends' place in southwest Moscow, and call from there.

It was a disconcerting drive. On the streets I saw nothing out of the ordinary. It was a beautiful autumn day, and the late-afternoon sun still gave off both light and warmth, even as the Russian winter approached. Everywhere I looked, people were taking advantage of the weather and going about their daily business.

But my car radio broadcast an entirely different sort of day: pro-Rutskoy demonstrators had marched from October Square near my apartment to the White House. They had swept through the streets and knocked over the barricades that Yeltsin's forces had erected around the parliament complex. Duma Speaker Ruslan Khasbulatov was urging the crowd to occupy the nearby mayor's office and, even more significantly, the Ostankino television tower, so they could control the airwaves and communication across Russia's eleven time zones.

Yeltsin's security forces were trying to regain control of the situation, and pitched battles with Rutskoy supporters took place around the White House and in the Ostankino area. I thought back to my brief time in Warsaw in 1980, when everything had been calm in the capital even as people in Gdansk were setting in motion a chain of events that would soon transform Poland. This time I understood that a lack of activity on the streets where I was driving did not in any way diminish the consequential nature of the events underway elsewhere.

When I got to my apartment, I ran to the phone and called the embassy. And called. And called. Probably just like every other American in Russia. It seemed like an eternity before a Marine guard finally answered. When I identified myself, the Marine responded that he couldn't talk; "we" were evacuating. Then he hung up.

I didn't know who the "we" was and whether it was supposed to include me, but I knew I didn't want to be left behind. With all the fighting at the White House, I didn't think I could get to the embassy safely, so I dialed my boss, Tony Brooks, one of the deputies in the political section. He told me that the evacuation was on hold and that Ambassador Pickering and others were working out of the embassy and keeping an open line to Washington. Tony and a small group of colleagues were going to the ambassador's residence, Spaso House, to set up a secondary location in case the embassy was overrun. I should join him there, he directed.

Spaso House was within walking distance of the embassy but outside the immediate area of conflict. It was also relatively close to my apartment. But since it was already dark and I didn't know if armed men were in the neighborhood, I decided to take the metro rather than walk. I put on a pink parka that screamed "American," deciding that this was a rare circumstance in which it was probably better to be a foreigner than to blend in. In my pockets I packed my notebook, a pen, and some power bars. It didn't occur to me that a change of clothes and a toothbrush might be needed too.

On the metro I was relieved that no one gave me a second glance, and when I hustled to Spaso House, all seemed normal. The guard let me in the gates, and I entered the residence to find a small group of Americans already assembled there. While waiting for a possible evacuation of the embassy, we did what we could to supplement the efforts of our colleagues there. We tried to get in touch with our Russian contacts to help us understand the situation, but we didn't have much success. We couldn't even watch the news, because the fighting at the Ostankino television tower was so fierce that TV and radio stations had been forced off the air.

With little to do and the hour getting late, I went upstairs, found a spare bed, and tried to get some shut-eye. I expected that the next day would be momentous, and I needed to be as well rested as possible. But sleep didn't come easily, and I finally gave up trying at first light.

In the crisp Moscow morning, I joined a couple of colleagues on a wide balcony facing in the direction of the White House. Buildings obscured our view, and we couldn't see the tanks that had moved in overnight to surround the parliament. But almost as soon as I stepped out onto the balcony, we heard the thunder of their guns, felt the building shaking, and saw black smoke rising. "Son of a bitch, he actually did it," one of my group said of Yeltsin's decision to attack the parliament building.

A minute later we watched in shock as Russian security forces pursued a group of armed, balaclava-clad men as they ran down the street toward Spaso House. A firefight started, and then *we* were running — into the house and down into the basement. The rest of our colleagues soon joined us.

We turned out the lights and drew the shades on the window wells so that no one could see us. About ten in all, we sat on the concrete floor, leaning against shelves holding the ambassador's canned goods. There wasn't a lot of small talk, and as I listened to the sound of sporadic street fighting outside, I thought about how I had ended up here, just six weeks into my tour. My boss, Tony, was quietly arguing with another embassy staffer about what to do next, and the tension between them didn't increase my confidence that anyone was actually in charge of our small group.

At around noon I was startled when the ambassador's chef came down and asked us what we would like for lunch. I hadn't realized that the locally employed household staff had arrived for work as usual that Monday morning and were doing their chores upstairs while we Americans were huddling in the basement. I felt ridiculous. But as I was contemplating lunch, I looked up and saw the silhouette of a man crouching in the window well, holding a long gun. I was facing the window and could easily see how a bullet meant for the gunman could pass through the glass and hit one of us. I didn't know whether the gunman could hear us, so I whispered to the others that we had company.

As the others discussed what to do, I decided I wasn't going to wait for instructions. I voted with my feet and ran up the stairs. I could hear the others following. We settled in the library on the top floor, and soon the chef arrived with pasta and peas in a cream sauce. That delightful meal during the fighting outside amounted to one of the more incongruous moments in my Foreign Service career.

Although the library was considerably more comfortable than the basement, we couldn't relax. Yeltsin's security forces had mounted a house-to-house search for opposition supporters, and although I doubted either side would actually try to enter the U.S. ambassador's residence, we continued to hear frequent shooting and worry about wayward bullets. So when the ambassador sent word that he was coming to the residence and needed Russian-speakers to return to the embassy with him, I was ready to go. The embassy was arguably in a less secure spot, but I had faith in Ambassador Pickering—and I wanted to do something, anything, other than simply sit and wait for the fighting to find me.

THE AMBASSADOR soon arrived in an armored Cadillac with his driver and security officer, all in helmets and body armor. Pickering took a quick shower, grabbed a sleeping bag, and came back down. Tony and I both were returning to the embassy with the ambassador, but there was only one additional helmet and bulletproof vest, which, without discussion, went to Tony. I wasn't happy about that, but I couldn't very well insist on a coin toss or wrestle the protective gear out of his hands. I could have stayed behind rather than risk the dangers on the street, but I figured it was only a five-minute drive. I hoped that I was calculating the risk correctly.

It turned out that the most dangerous part of the journey was right there at Spaso House. With bullets still flying outside, the embassy security officer, whose most recent posting had been Beirut, told us how to get to the limo—and to do it fast. After the driver pulled the car up to the side entrance, Tony would jump into the back seat, followed by the ambassador, then me. As the one without body armor, I was to lie on the floor.

The limousine pulled up, and the ambassador and Tony dived in as planned. But when it was my turn to go, the fighting around us escalated. Three times the security officer signaled for me to run the few steps to the car, but twice he pulled me back because tracer rounds were streaking past the residence entrance. The third time was the charm. Once we were all in the Cadillac, the residence guards quickly opened the gates, and we sped toward the embassy.

The ambassador leaned over me, in part to protect me and in part so he wouldn't be visible through the windows. There is nothing more disorienting than crouching on the floor of a moving vehicle with action you can't see going on all around you. As the vehicle slowed down to enter the embassy gates, I pulled up my head to see what was happening. Ambassador Pickering gently pushed my head back down, reminding me that this was no time for idle curiosity.

The limo drove into the underground garage. One of our Marines was there to let us in, and it was jarring to see him not in the usual dress uniform but wearing what looked like full combat gear. Even though I was with the ambassador and the Marine surely knew the circumstances of our arrival, I presented my identification as usual. Ever the rules-abiding girl, I guess I was hoping for some semblance of normality.

Tony and I went to the political section's makeshift space and I joined another political officer in drafting reports for Washington. Yeltsin's forces had regained control of the television tower overnight, and TV stations were broadcasting again. We monitored the news and talked to the few contacts we could get on the phone. We also took turns at the shredder, destroying classified documents in case we had to abandon the building. Shredding our files was never something that anyone had thought would be necessary here. Maybe at high-threat posts like Embassy Tehran and Embassy Beirut, but Embassy Moscow? It was hard to believe that the capital of America's once-mighty competitor had become a war zone.

Colleagues told me that I had missed a harrowing twenty-four hours at the embassy. Fighting on the streets surrounding the compound had been intense on Sunday afternoon. The ambassador had ordered all compound residents — hundreds of people, including many children — to shelter in the partially underground recreational area. The management staff had immediately started exploring an evacuation for family members to Frankfurt, Germany, but almost as quickly had had to rule it out; an evacuation required an assurance from the Russian government that our people could safely travel from the embassy to the airport, but when the ambassador tried to reach his counterparts for help that Sunday, he literally found nobody home. Like the rest of Moscow, the Russian leaders were enjoying one of the last warm weekends of the season at their dachas outside town. When they finally resurfaced, they said that they could not guarantee safe passage: the Russian security services did not control the streets around the embassy compound. Those were chilling words, and I recalled that we had heard something similar during the Mogadishu evacuation. I added this to the rapidly expanding list of things I had never expected to experience in Moscow.

Meanwhile, embassy staff and their families — many outside the compound on that beautiful Sunday afternoon — had urgently tried to find each other. A friend told me that she had been at the old embassy building when her twelve-year-old son, at home in the new embassy compound, phoned to say, "Mama, Mama, come quick, the shooting has started." Crushingly, she couldn't go: it was too dangerous to make even that short walk. Only several hours later, during a brief lull in the fighting, did she literally make a run for it. Skirting pools of blood and clutching the hand of a colleague for moral support, she raced to her children.

My friend emerged unscathed, but not everyone connected to the embassy was so lucky that day. A Russian sniper, who I was told was positioned in the bell tower of Our Lady of Perpetual Observation, had shot one of our Marine guards. It was probably a case of mistaken identity, but the guard would have died if not for the quick action of one of his fellow Marines, who compressed the wound. Such a story made me realize again just how dangerous the situation had been.

MOST OF THE FIGHTING ended that Monday, with Yeltsin victorious and Rutskoy, Khasbulatov, and many others under arrest. Reliable casualty numbers were hard to come by, but the Russian government put the totals at 187 dead and 437 wounded. The dead included two Americans, a journalist and a lawyer; the latter was shot while trying to help wounded Russians caught up in the fighting around the television tower.

For days afterward we heard wild stories, including that parliamentarians and their supporters had fled via underground tunnels from the White House and that hundreds more had perished or remained unaccounted for. Whatever the truth, Russian security services systematically conducted

door-to-door searches throughout the area, looking for opposition supporters, unexploded ordnance, and booby traps. It wasn't at all clear that the
fighting was over, so my colleagues and I spent that Monday night sleeping
under our desks. In the morning I went to the cafeteria, which miraculously
was offering a big breakfast — luckily for me, since that magnificent lunch
at the ambassador's residence was now a distant memory. We churned out
another report for Washington, by which point — it was now Tuesday afternoon — Yeltsin's forces had regained control of the streets and the security
crisis, as distinct from the political crisis, had begun to wind down.

I hadn't been home for two days, but I left the familiarity of the American compound reluctantly. I was unsure of what I would find outside our
walls, and the blood I saw staining the street when I first ventured from the
embassy compound only unsettled me further. Beyond the immediate vi-
cinity of the White House, people were shopping, chatting, picking up their
kids from school, as if it were just another beautiful fall day. That was unsettling too, because as I made my way home that afternoon, it felt as if nothing was ever going to be the same again. For many nights afterward I would
wake up to the sound of gunfire. Nobody else heard it, so I guess it was just
a series of bad dreams.

But the physical reminders of the fighting were evident for all to see. Not
only was the parliament building destroyed, but it seemed that every plate-
glass window on Moscow's version of Fifth Avenue, Novyy Arbat, was shattered. By Wednesday, when all the American staff who had sheltered outside the embassy compound had made their way back to work, we found
the compound walls full of bullet holes and the embassy kids busily competing for who could collect the most bullets.

My political section colleagues and I embarked on a different sort of
hunt, fanning out to discover what the past week's events meant for Russia's future. We had to work hard to find many of our usual contacts. Some
were in hiding, while others weren't around because their offices had been
destroyed in the fighting. Midlevel government officials were reluctant to
talk to us, since they didn't know what to say. We pounded the pavement to
get a picture of what would happen next, sometimes literally running into
Russian counterparts on the streets as they too were looking to reconnect
with each other.

Both sides of Russia's political crisis may have been shaken by the violence, but it had only served to further harden their positions. The opposi-

tion had been beaten and its leaders were in jail, but it wasn't destroyed, and it certainly wasn't giving up. But polling in the immediate aftermath of the fighting gave Yeltsin's supporters, known loosely as "democrats," reason to think that the tide of history was on their side; most Russians, it appeared, blamed the Communist legacy and the personal ambitions of Rutskoy and Khasbulatov for the violence and found Yeltsin's actions justified.

For this first-time political officer, the whole thing was very sobering. I wasn't privy to the high-level U.S. policy conversations that no doubt were going on about how we should react to the events in Russia, but I had no trouble forming my own opinion. We could have publicly condemned Yeltsin's actions, but doing so would have accomplished nothing beyond alienating Yeltsin. Yeltsin had countless flaws, but rule by a combination of Communists and nationalists who were seeking to eject him would have proved disastrous for Russia, and would have torpedoed U.S. hopes for a closer commercial, political, and security relationship with this post-Soviet republic. But that didn't mean that the decision to back Yeltsin was risk-free.

In foreign policy often there aren't good choices. The U.S. just has to make the best of it. In the fall of 1993, Yeltsin seemed to be the least bad option. But as in Somalia, we would be paying for this tradeoff for a long time to come.

NEEDLESS TO SAY, politicians from both sides of Russia's widening divide were throwing all their energy at the December parliamentary elections and concurrent constitutional referendum. We had some sense of the political discussion in Moscow, but the actual votes would come in from every corner of Russia's vast expanse. We needed to get out of the Moscow bubble and find out what the voters thought — or at least what was going on in the heads of the provincial leaders, who would in turn influence the voters in their districts.

For me that meant hopping on a plane to Omsk, Siberia. Flying domestically in Russia at the time could be hazardous, and we always traveled in pairs in case something went wrong. The country's Communist-era airline, Aeroflot, was spinning off into separate, regional "baby flots," most of which had aging and poorly maintained fleets. Fuel was not always available, and safety didn't seem like a high priority. I was a white-knuckle flier anyway, so it was with some trepidation that I joined the only female in the Defense Attaché Office on a long flight east in early November.

Omsk had been a so-called closed city in the Soviet era — a place off-limits to foreign travelers — and even after its "opening," its remote location meant that foreign visitors were still few and far between. Although it was technically still autumn, winter weather had long preceded our arrival at the Siberian city. When we climbed down the rickety stairs from the plane to the tarmac, we found banks of high snow everywhere and a temperature of forty below zero.

The news that American embassy representatives were arriving brought a reporter from the local television station to greet us. Upon seeing two women deplane, though, all the journalist could manage was a stunned *Are you here on vacation?* The thought of two female diplomats apparently was more incongruous to him than that of two Americans vacationing in freezing cold Siberia. We quickly set him straight, but he was shocked again when I tried to break the ice by sharing that my father had been born (relatively) nearby, in Chita, by Lake Baykal. The possibility that an American diplomat could come from Siberian stock was another anomaly that seemingly was too hard to process.

During our meetings officials told us about their challenges and shared their generally anti-Yeltsin views. They were guarded, however. And they wouldn't say anything about Sergey Baburin, a prominent nationalist deputy from Omsk, who had been one of the leaders of the White House revolt. He had disappeared after the October 3 events, and we thought he was probably hiding in his native city. We wanted to find out what he had planned, beyond running for a parliamentary seat. If there was going to be a reprise of the armed resistance, Baburin would be in the thick of it.

Near the end of our three-day visit, one of Baburin's former staffers followed us out of a meeting and handed me a piece of paper with Baburin's number. When I called, Baburin immediately agreed to meet with us but insisted on doing so in his Soviet-style jeep, presumably so we wouldn't know where he was staying and our conversation couldn't be overheard. Baburin drove us all over Omsk, giving us an opportunity to admire the turn-of-the-century wooden buildings painted in pastels and frosted with the snow that was blowing hard that cold morning. It felt like a scene out of *Dr. Zhivago.* All that was missing was the sleigh.

Charismatic and defiant, Baburin insisted that we stop alongside the road and do a shot of vodka — at ten in the morning — so he would be able to trust us, he said. We chased the vodka with salo, rendered pork fat in the shape of a big fat white slug and just about as appetizing. I choked it down but decided I wasn't going to be making this particular sacrifice for my country again.

In the end, despite our roadside heroics, Baburin shared very little of consequence with us. But I left Omsk that November with the distinct impression that the democrats would have an uphill battle in the parliamentary elections and beyond.

That impression turned out to be right. On the day of the election — Sunday, December 12, 1993 — the embassy mounted an all-hands observation effort and watched as the Russian people turned out in force to cast their votes. They seemed to split the vote. Yeltsin, not himself on the ballot, got his desired post-Soviet constitution, which hugely expanded his powers. But in the parliamentary contest, his supporters, the democrats, did poorly, making the electoral outcome seem like a repudiation of Yeltsin's reform agenda. The biggest winner was Vladimir Zhirinovskiy, a right-wing, nationalist showman who had never held elected office before. He promised to grow Russia's economy without painful reforms, blamed Russia's problems on the West, and amused a weary public with his outrageous antics. Thirteen other parliamentary groups also won seats, making it difficult for any one party to control the legislative agenda.

Yeltsin had hoped that the December elections would consolidate his power, but they seemed to do just the opposite, at the same time exacerbating the divisions in the country. Yeltsin's confrontations with parliament would continue throughout his time in power, although thankfully there was no return to the violence of October 3. But the seeds of discord that were sown during this period would bear bitter fruit in the years and decades ahead.

UNDERSTANDING WHAT ALL of these epic events meant for Russia was critical to my job. I wanted Russia to succeed, and I firmly believed that its success was in U.S. interests. But my concern over Russia's fortunes went deeper than that. It was also personal: I wanted the family my grandfather had left behind to benefit from the freedom and prosperity that reforms could bring to Russia.

I hadn't been in touch with my Moscow relatives since my student days more than a decade earlier, but I had a chance to see the impact of events firsthand when I reconnected with them. My great-aunt Vera, the only one who had been willing to meet with me when I first visited Moscow, in 1980, had died, but Vera's fiftysomething daughter, Ksenya, welcomed me with open arms. So did her family, which I took to be a sign of how much things had changed.

Ksenya's daughter, Aleksandra, my second cousin, was in her late twenties, a little younger than I was. Looking at her, I could imagine what my life might have been like if my grandparents had remained in Russia. Aleksandra shared a one-bedroom apartment with her husband and their two kids. Like everyone else, it had been hard for them to transition from communism; both were happy that they still had jobs and the health care and other benefits that came with them, but they joked that "they pretend to pay us, and we pretend to work." Their salaries were so modest that Aleksandra's husband had to supplement their income with outside work. Like so many others in Russia, they did what they had to do to get by.

For my extended family, as for other Russians, the fall of the Soviet Union had proven hardest for the older generation. In Soviet times both Ksenya and her husband, Anton, had joined the Communist Party, which facilitated professional advancement. Anton was still a true believer, especially after the past two years of inflation and its catastrophic effect on his pension. At the beginning of the October standoff, Anton had demonstrated at the White House in support of the old guard, although he stopped when the confrontation escalated.

Anton had mixed feelings about me, an American and a diplomat and therefore someone he saw as complicit in these unrelenting hard times for Russia. He didn't buy that the U.S. really believed that a prosperous, democratic, and secure Russia was in U.S. interests or that we were trying to reach out a hand to help. His was a zero-sum world, and he railed at me that I was a tourist, looking at Russians like they were "animals in a zoo." That hurt — and I hoped that he would eventually understand that he was wrong. I hoped that the reforms would kick in and improve Anton's life. He deserved better. All Russians did.

BACK AT THE EMBASSY, I had been working flat-out and, like all my colleagues, was exhausted. But that's not what I found most draining. Despite working what felt like 24/7, I could seemingly do no right by my boss.

Tony supervised about ten of us in the part of the political section called "internal." We covered domestic affairs in Russia, as distinct from the foreign policy and security issues covered respectively by the "external" and political-military divisions of the political section. I was looking forward to working in other parts of embassy political sections in future assignments. But first I would have to prove myself, starting with my current boss.

Tony was a Soviet hand with many tours under his belt; he probably had forgotten more about the USSR and Russia than I would ever know. He didn't suffer fools gladly, and he seemed to think that everyone junior to him — especially those who didn't look like him — was a fool. A product of the prereform Foreign Service, Tony had told me two things at our first meeting in Washington. First, because I was single, he would keep me at work later than my married colleagues, who had families to go home to. Second, I shouldn't expect to take Thanksgiving and Christmas vacations, since that was family time. I didn't mind working late — I always did anyway. But on the second point I pushed back, telling him that I had a family too. He didn't say anything in response, but the smirk on his face spoke volumes.

There were other warning signs. When I asked Tony at that first meeting what my responsibilities were going to be, he replied, *We don't really have portfolios. I like people to fight for things.* This did not bode well for me. I don't thrive in a cutthroat environment; frankly, I don't think many people enjoy battling it out with their coworkers, nor do they do their best work in that kind of atmosphere.

I had arrived in Moscow while Tony was on vacation. True to his word, he had not left any instructions for me. Even after he returned two and a half weeks later, his only guidance came when he announced at a staff meeting that *as Masha now knows, he who comes late to the assignments process gets what's left.* I wasn't sure what he was talking about, since I had arrived in Moscow right on schedule. I flailed for the next couple of weeks and mostly occupied myself by catching up on the section's recent reporting.

The increasingly serious standoff between Yeltsin and the parliament threw me a lifeline. The events required everyone to pitch in, and my willingness to go to the White House all of a sudden meant I had my work cut out for me. But although we had literally been under fire together, my crisis performance wasn't good enough for my boss. After the October events, Tony pounced. Rather than raising any concerns privately, he unexpectedly asked me during a staff meeting, *What are you producing for internal? What real work are you doing?* I found his treatment humiliating.

When I went on vacation in late January (having bowed to the greater good so that my colleagues with families were able to take leave over the holidays), Tony took the opportunity to remind me of something three months off: *You want me in a good mood when I write your evaluation,* he said. That made me worry about my evaluation the whole time I was away.

Mama and Papa came to visit a few months later. As a rules-abiding girl, I did what I thought was expected and invited my supervisor over for dinner to meet them. While I was out of earshot in the kitchen, he shared his view that *women don't belong in the Foreign Service. They can't do the job.* Surprised and concerned, my parents naturally pressed him. He grudgingly allowed that maybe they could work in the internal political section, but in external, he proclaimed, *they are a disaster.* When my parents later told me about the conversation, I didn't know what to do. I finally was on a career path that I wanted to pursue in the long term and in all its aspects, but my first boss on my first political tour didn't think women could really do the job.

At one point Tony told me that of those who had reported to him over the years, *only the women and minorities had ever later made it into the senior ranks of the Foreign Service.* I could have interpreted that statement positively, as almost a guarantee of promotion, since I too was a woman working for Tony. But it came across as a grievance, a statement that White men were getting a raw deal. In that moment, and many thereafter, I was glad that I had not told anyone — and particularly not Tony — that I was in the all-star Moscow political section courtesy of Alison Palmer's class-action lawsuit.

It turned out that I had been right to worry about my evaluation. Tony gave me the worst review I have ever received, going so far as to disparage my work throughout the standard five-page questionnaire rather than keeping it to the area the form designated for criticism. I worried that I'd never get promoted with that assessment in my file, so I went in and talked to him, and then after that didn't go well, I talked to his boss. His boss didn't want to get involved, and Tony's response was to edit the evaluation to make it even worse, something my colleagues, who had their own issues with Tony, had warned me he would do. I stopped digging that proverbial hole, but I was angry at the unfair treatment and my own sense of powerlessness — and also because, for a time at least, Tony pushed me into the trap of believing the worst about myself.

Fortunately, there was a light at the end of the tunnel: Tony was rotating out of Moscow that summer. I just had to wait him out. In the remaining time I did what I always do, which is to keep my head down, keep working, and do the best I can. But even as I did, I allowed myself the fervent hope that better management would replace him, especially when, as a parting gift, Tony gave me an extra, out-of-cycle evaluation covering the four months before he left. It was just as bad as the first evaluation.

Tony's boss, the political section head who had refused to intervene in Tony's evaluation process, had already transferred out of Moscow, so I asked the deputy chief of mission whether he would write a review statement for me in the evaluation. Without calling Tony out, the embassy's second in command, who had observed my work, contradicted everything Tony had written. I felt redeemed.

I like to think that despite everything, I did a decent job that first year in Moscow, but I only really blossomed when the new management team arrived. On paper my new boss, Tom Graham, had the same pale, male, Yale profile as Tony. Tom was also a Russia expert with many Foreign Service tours under his belt. But as far as I was concerned, that's all they had in common. Tom wasn't just a big brain but also a great manager. He defined our responsibilities, established work goals, provided guidance, and shared information freely. Tom trusted the people who worked for him, and he made me feel like I was a valued member of the team. I was learning again, and the joy of work had returned.

My luck continued when, shortly thereafter, Bill Burns arrived to take over as the new head of the political section. His reputation as the most gifted diplomat of his generation had preceded him. With astonishing consistency, Bill could read a room, deploy the right argument, and get the desired result. I was pretty sure that he was always the smartest person in the room, but he had the gift of making his officers — and every other interlocutor — feel that their views counted. Genuine humility and respect for others were (and remain) increasingly rare attributes in Washington, and Bill had both in spades.

Observing how Bill and Tom, not to mention the other Tom (Ambassador Pickering, as I called him), worked with the Russians to advance our foreign policy goals was the best apprenticeship in diplomacy-for-results that I was ever going to get. I felt privileged to be on the team.

Over the next two years I was not only productive but happy. If I hadn't known it before, I learned then the power of working for a good manager and a good leader. A great job can destroy you if you have the wrong boss, and a sleepy posting can end up being your most important career experience if you have the right boss. Being in Moscow, which felt like the center of the universe to me, with three incredible role models was an exceptional experience.

IN MY LAST two years in Moscow, I worked on two presidential summits and covered several more Russian elections, the most consequential of which was the 1996 presidential race. The Russian people by then had a five-year record on which to judge Yeltsin, and we expected their judgment to be harsh. The economy was failing, the brutal war against separatists in the republic of Chechnya in southern Russia was taking a toll, and Yeltsin seemed increasingly erratic after surviving a series of heart attacks. In the prior year's parliamentary elections, the Communist Party, which campaigned on a nostalgia platform of returning Russia to its Soviet glory, had tripled the number of seats it controlled. Zyuganov, the head of the Communist Party, seemed poised to win the presidency.

Yeltsin knew that he had to shake things up if he was to have any chance at victory. If he lost power, he could well face legal charges or worse under a Communist regime, which would view many of his policies as not just wrong but treasonous. A group of Russian businessmen also shared his interest in maintaining the status quo. They feared that if the Communist Party won, it would seek to renationalize Russian assets, costing the tycoons much of their wealth and inviting unwelcome scrutiny of how they had acquired it. The solution was to join forces.

Together, Yeltsin and the businessmen devised a scheme called "loans for shares." The businessmen loaned the government money and in return received shares in some of the most lucrative oil, gas, and mineral companies still owned by the Russian government, at a fraction of their real worth and in an auction widely regarded as rigged. In theory the businessmen would return their shares after the government repaid the loans following the elections.

There was good reason to question how it would all turn out in the end, but in the short term the plan worked as intended: the Russian government received an enormous cash infusion, which Yeltsin immediately pumped into the economy to support his populist presidential campaign. As a bonus he got glowing coverage from the media outlets controlled by the tycoons, which billed the race as a choice between Yeltsin and a return to totalitarianism. And the businessmen enriched themselves by acquiring Russia's resources for a song. It was a win-win — except for the Russian people, who lost the long-term benefits that could have accrued to them through a transparent deal or well-managed government control of many of Russia's natural resource companies.

From my junior perch at the embassy, I watched these developments with wide eyes. I knew that Yeltsin was a better president for Russia and partner for the U.S. than Zyuganov, his Communist challenger, ever would be; besides rolling back economic and political reforms, Zyuganov might well return Russia to an antagonistic footing with the U.S. But regardless of who was behind the scheme, loans for shares clearly was one of the biggest heists in history.

U.S. policy in Russia, as in other former Communist nations, was predicated on the inherent value of capitalism and democracy and on their potential to bring positive change to countries that adopted them. We had assumed that once the concept of private property became ingrained in Russia, the business community would push for the rule of law and independent courts in order to protect their assets. We thought the commercial sector would become invested in creating a level playing field and a system that was predictable and fair, which would benefit all Russians as well as Americans wanting to do business in Russia.

That was the theory, at least. But loans for shares seemed to be moving Russia in the opposite direction. The transfer of such wealth to a handful of rich Russians drove that group to continue to bend the law to protect their personal objectives. Because the handful of men who benefited from the loans-for-shares scheme knew that the process was at best questionable, they did not wait for the questions to come. Like corporate raiders the world over, they stripped the assets of their new holdings and fired employees. They also placed much of the resulting profits — which could have been reinvested in Russia — into offshore bank accounts safe from Russian justice should questions ever arise. In so doing, these men not only unjustly shaped Russian law to benefit themselves but also sabotaged the rule of law itself. Once again the Russian people paid the price.

Not having been privy to the Washington policy discussions at the time, I can only ask myself in retrospect whether the U.S. and the international community could have done more to nudge Russia onto a more positive trajectory. No doubt it would have been tough under any circumstances to convince Yeltsin not to pursue the scheme. The reality is that when the stakes are political survival, leaders are rarely swayed by outside voices. In Washington, Yeltsin, despite his flaws, was seen as a pro-Western reformer, the better president for Russians, and the better partner for the U.S. I also assume that the default was to ensure that we did nothing that could help the Communist Party take back power.

The U.S. and the rest of the West took the less bad option, but I wonder whether there was a way we could have threaded the needle and signaled our concern about the course that Yeltsin was charting. It might have increased U.S. credibility in the eyes of the Russian people, who by this point were skeptical of both the U.S. and the benefits of capitalism. To this day Russians are continuing to live with the adverse impacts of both the badly implemented voucher privatization programs and the loans-for-shares scheme. Russia has a wealth of natural resources — resources that rightfully belong to the Russian people — but insiders and crooks were able to game the system and scoop up sovereign assets for well below their worth. In so doing, they cheated the Russian people out of a better future.

Yeltsin won a second term on July 3, 1996. The government never paid back the loans, and the businessmen got to keep the energy and commodities assets. They went from being millionaires to being billionaires. And then they became known as oligarchs. The people's wealth had been redistributed to benefit a small handful of Russians. It might not have been illegal, but it sure as heck was corrupt. To this day I wish that the U.S. had been able to stop it.

I LEFT MOSCOW eight days after Yeltsin's reelection. My three years there had been jam-packed, both for Russia and for me. I had finally achieved my goal of becoming a political officer, and I had gotten hard-won experience to prepare me for my next posting. If I had any regrets, it was that I had never found the time to go to Papa's birthplace, Chita, and discover more about his past. I did, however, have the opportunity to welcome Papa back to Russia for the first time since he had left as a toddler.

During their two visits, Papa and Mama reveled in the country's culture and its spiritual life. And Papa, who often felt like an outsider in his adopted home despite having lived in the U.S. for almost half his life, found that all those years in America had made him an American. When he walked down the street in his chinos and sneakers, Russians didn't see one of their own; they saw an American coming. When he conversed in Russian, Papa spoke the language differently, sprinkling it with prerevolutionary vocabulary that had been preserved only in the émigré community. My Russian friends loved talking to him, because Papa opened a window for them into an earlier era. But Papa had to stay out of political discussions with Mama's relatives, because he wasn't going to accept criticism of the United States from Anton or anybody else.

THE REGION WAS in my blood, and now it had captured my imagination as well. What could be more interesting and important than serving in a country in transition, with all the hope and heartbreak that entailed? But our mission in Russia was all-consuming, and I needed a break from the unrelenting pace. So once again I followed in my parents' footsteps — this time to Canada.

I spent the next two years representing my adopted country in the country of my birth, learning more about political-military affairs while enjoying Canada and my newfound proximity to family in the United States. While I was in Ottawa, President Bill Clinton named the first female secretary of state. Madeleine Albright was qualified and capable and brought her own style to diplomacy, communicating American values and interests through the persuasiveness of her rhetoric as well as the power of her pin collection. She not only made the women at the State Department proud, she empowered us. While in Ottawa I was recruited to return to Washington and spent two years as a deputy director on State's Russia Desk. The pace was familiar, but the issues were new: the 1998 Russian financial crisis; the ensuing political crisis and four changes of government in a year and a half; Yeltsin's abrupt resignation on New Year's Eve 1999, paving the way for Vladimir Putin, a relative unknown, to ascend to the Russian presidency; and of course the war between the Serbs and the Kosovar Albanians, which considerably raised U.S.-Russia tensions when NATO intervened militarily on the side of the Kosovars against the Russian-backed Serbs.

Throughout these momentous events, I was moving up. Unlike in my foreign postings, I was now actually participating in the foreign policy debate, albeit at the lowest levels. I was advising decision-makers and getting important experience in executive management, not only by managing the process by which an idea becomes U.S. policy and then gets implemented but also by managing our small staff of ten on the Russia Desk.

At the end of those two years I felt ten years older and (I hoped) ten years wiser too. I wanted to be able to reflect on what I'd seen and done over the past fourteen years, so in 2000 I went back to school for a master's degree from the National War College in Washington. The State Department encourages midcareer officers to participate in the Defense Department's many institutions of higher learning so that we get an intellectual grounding in the challenges before us, as well as exposure to our partners in national security — especially our colleagues in the U.S. military.

The program I entered aims to educate military officers and civilian officials for leadership roles. We argued about the Kosovo war from our different points of view, studied the concept of homeland defense (new to me in those innocent, pre-9/11 days), and sparred with classmates from other agencies, including the Department of Defense, USAID, and the Commerce Department, about the relative merits of our different agency cultures. I decided to broaden my knowledge and took a yearlong course on India, Pakistan, and Afghanistan, as well as a course on ethics. The year was an eye-opener, and I left feeling that our military and our government were in good hands with my classmates as our future leaders.

AFTER THIS HIATUS I was ready to get back overseas. When I looked at the possible posts, no place seemed more interesting to me than Ukraine, another former Soviet republic on Russia's borders and Europe's eastern edge. In fact, of all the postings available at the time, I couldn't imagine going anywhere else. Ukraine was in the region that I knew the best, and it was facing many of the same trials as Russia. I knew that it would be a challenging but fascinating posting.

I had worked with the U.S. ambassador to Ukraine, Carlos Pascual, when I was on the Russia Desk. In another stroke of good fortune, he selected me as his deputy chief of mission, the second in command of the fifth largest embassy in Europe. It was a big jump up. I should have been thrilled. But now that I was close to getting the job I wanted in the country I most wanted to serve in, I was characteristically nervous. I was also unsure that I actually could do the job — thanks in part, I'm sure, to the amplification of my long-standing insecurities which had been further deepened during my first year in Moscow, but thanks also to more subtle and pernicious pressures.

Like many women, I struggled with imposter syndrome, something that would dog me throughout my career. Despite successes, I often wondered whether I was good enough to do my current job; whether people at the next job would finally find out that I was just lucky, not talented; and whether working harder than anyone else would be enough to overcome my weaknesses or I would be revealed as not having the right stuff, just like Tony said.

So before I accepted the offer of a posting in Ukraine, I canvassed friends and colleagues: Did they think I could do the job? Every single one of my female friends understood exactly what I was asking. They reassured me, catalogued my strengths, reminded me that not only had I competed for the job, I had also been selected by someone who knew me and respected my work. My male friends just laughed. They couldn't understand what the issue was. I was smart and successful and I had beaten the competition. Of course I could do the job.

It was a revealing set of conversations, in that it laid bare how so many men often perceive a promotion as a right while women often fear that it is somehow undeserved and that they won't be able to measure up. The advice and support of my women friends — and the reality checks from my male friends — saved the day. I swallowed my fears and took the post.

As soon as I accepted the job offer, excitement started competing with my usual preposting nerves. There was a third feeling as well. I had spent five years within easy reach of my family. Returning to the former Soviet Union would take me an ocean and a continent away from my parents, who were in relatively good health but aging.

Nevertheless, it was time to resume my travels, and as I prepared to leave for Ukraine, I thought I knew what to expect. Like just about everyone else, though, I was stunned by the black swan that almost immediately swept onto the global stage, reshaping our thinking, upending our priorities, and transforming the U.S. and the world.

6

Ukraine

I ARRIVED IN UKRAINE in August 2001 to take up my new position as deputy chief of mission at Embassy Kyiv. It was a huge leap in responsibility. As DCM, I'd be in charge of the day-to-day management of the embassy's seven-hundred-strong staff and would frequently stand in for the ambassador. I was excited by the challenge and ready to get to work on the many issues facing the country. But as ever, the future had other plans in store.

On September 11, I was in Kharkiv, a city of roughly a million and a half on the Russian border, to inaugurate an American cultural center. About thirty Ukrainian-Americans from the Cincinnati-Kharkiv Sister City Project, which had helped sponsor the project, were present for the ceremony. When my turn at the podium came in the late afternoon, seven time zones away from Manhattan, I forgot to turn off my cell phone. Midway through my remarks, my phone started ringing, and it kept ringing and ringing. It was so distracting that I finally had to pause and silence the phone.

When I completed my remarks, I stood to the side as the ceremony continued and called back Stella Speris, my assistant in Kyiv. She gave me the news that a plane had crashed into one of the towers of the World Trade Center in lower Manhattan. I hoped that it was a terrible navigational error, but minutes later Stella called back with the news that another plane had hit the second tower. I asked her repeatedly whether she was absolutely certain, and when she said she was, I asked her again — and again. It wasn't that I couldn't process the news; it's that I didn't want to. If it was true, this was an act of terrorism, and the implications of that were more than I could comprehend at that moment.

The inauguration of the new center continued, interminably. I tried to look interested in the proceedings as I worried about whether any of my friends who worked in the financial district had been in the Twin Towers. Stella kept on calling with updates and soon told me about a third plane attacking the Pentagon. That hit me even harder than the news about the Trade Center. With no further information yet, I thought of all the Defense Department colleagues I had worked with over the years. Any one of them could have been at the Pentagon that day.

I couldn't deal with my emotions, so I stayed in work mode. As soon as the event concluded, I gathered the American citizens who were present so I could provide as much information as I had, including the additional news of a fourth plane crashing in Shanksville, Pennsylvania, and the update that U.S. airspace had been closed. Understandably, they had lots of questions that no one had the answers to yet, from the global to the personal: What had happened? Would there be additional attacks? When would American skies reopen so they could go home? What about their plane tickets? Where would they stay? What would happen next? I mustered as much reassurance as I could, which wasn't much when it came to their understandable desire to know whether there was more to come. At least I was able to connect them with the embassy's American Citizen Services section, which assists Americans abroad. Over the coming days and weeks that section would do yeoman's work helping not only the Cincinnati group but thousands of other Americans stranded in Ukraine that September.

Several hours after the event ended, I took the overnight train back to Kyiv. I arrived at the embassy early on the morning of September 12 to find the compound's outer walls heaped with flowers. Small votive candles, a testament to the spontaneous outpouring of Ukrainian sympathy the previous night, had lost their flames but not their force. Even in faraway Ukraine, people understood that this was an attack not just on the United States but on free people the world over. I had felt very alone on my sleepless train ride, but now I was grateful to realize that I wasn't alone — and neither was our country.

Inside the embassy the tension was palpable; we didn't know whether more attacks might be coming. The State Department, which typically sends out a stream of instructions on every conceivable topic, was silent. Foggy Bottom had been evacuated in a hurry, normal channels of communication had been severely disrupted, and it was still not even business hours in Washington yet.

In the absence of immediate guidance from home, we all looked to the ambassador. Carlos Pascual was a Cuban refugee who had flown to freedom as a young child on one of the last shuttles to Miami before Castro shut them down. Carlos was brilliant, energetic, and committed to helping Ukrainians achieve their dreams, just as his own family had been able to do. He also proved himself to be an invaluable source of stability for embassy staffers in a time of overwhelming uncertainty.

As soon as everyone had arrived for work, Carlos assembled the staff. There was no room big enough to hold everyone in the embassy, so he called an impromptu meeting in the foyer. People crowded into the hallways, up the stairs, and even outside in the entryway. Once we had all gathered, Carlos acknowledged our fears, reassured us of America's resilience, and underlined the values that make us strong. He didn't need instructions from Washington, because he knew what the American people are made of and what our country stands for. It was inspiring and a formative lesson in leadership.

Over the next days Carlos stayed in close touch with the Ukrainian government, which had been quick to declare public support for the United States. Ukraine was then holding one of the rotating seats on the UN Security Council and joined the call for an emergency meeting to condemn the attacks and show the international community's support for bringing those responsible to justice. After it became clear that the attacks had originated in Afghanistan and that the U.S. would respond militarily, Carlos knew that Ukraine's strategic location on the flight path to Central Asia made it likely that we would be asking the Ukrainians for air space clearance and base access. He prepared the Ukrainians so that when the requests arrived, they responded rapidly, granting the U.S. military overflight and refueling clearances and providing the use of three Ukrainian airfields as well.

At the embassy we started to harden our security. We asked the city to close off the quiet residential street in front of our compound, a measure that happened immediately despite the objections of neighbors. We updated and drilled our emergency phone tree. We reviewed our emergency protocols, including the triggers for an evacuation.

Adding to the uncertainty and anxiety and hard on the heels of the 9/11 attacks, an unknown assailant began mailing a powder containing the deadly toxin anthrax to several American news organizations and U.S. senators' offices, ultimately killing five people. At the embassy we received an envelope containing white powder, which we eventually determined was not toxic, but not before our mailroom staff underwent a thorough and distressing decontamination process. We moved mail processing out of the embassy and added new mailroom protocols to our growing list of security procedures.

September passed into October, and like all Americans, we were still on edge. Then, on October 4, Siberia Airlines Flight 1812 exploded over the Black Sea while en route from Tel Aviv to the Russian city of Novosibirsk, killing all seventy-eight people aboard. With the 9/11 attacks so fresh in our minds, we asked ourselves the unthinkable: Was this another terrorist attack?

Within hours of the event, the top official for Ukraine at the State Department, Steve Pifer, called the embassy. Carlos was out of the office, so Steve said he needed to talk to me immediately on a secure line. I ran up to the vault where our one secure phone was located. A little out of breath, I listened as Steve told me that the U.S. had evidence that the Ukrainian military, which had been conducting an exercise in the area, had shot down the plane.

We assumed that the shootdown was not deliberate, but we needed to make sure. Our defense attaché reached out to the Ukrainian military, and Carlos, having returned to the office, called the Ministry of Foreign Affairs and the office of Ukrainian president Leonid Kuchma. We encouraged the Ukrainian government to be as forthcoming as possible. This was no time to stonewall, but it took nine days for the Ukrainian government to publicly acknowledge its terrible mistake and admit that a Ukrainian surface-to-air missile had been responsible for downing SibAir 1812.

The entire incident was disheartening. Bad news does not improve with time, and the Ukrainian leadership's inability to promptly own up to what had happened hurt them in Washington. It was the first of many occasions when I saw the degree to which present-day Ukraine had failed to shed its old Soviet habits: there was no transparency, no accountability. This led to a lack of trust of the government, not just among its own citizens but also among the nations of the West that Ukraine was hoping to court as new partners.

THE SOVIET LEGACY lived on in other ways as well. Although Ukrainians had celebrated the independence that had resulted a decade earlier from the dissolution of the Soviet Union, they found that not much had changed at the top once the dust had settled. Former Communist Party bosses, reared in the Soviet way of doing business, had remained firmly in control of Ukraine's government — and seemingly its future.

Ukrainian leaders hadn't spent the late 1980s clamoring for change, nor did they nurture the emergence of a generation of reformist leaders in the 1990s. In part their relative complacency was a result of the privileged status that the republic had enjoyed in the USSR. Ukraine had been second only to Russia in both population and economic output, providing a substantial part of the empire's food supply and supporting its productive mining and manufacturing sectors. The largely Slavic leadership in Moscow had even trusted their fellow Slavs in Ukraine with a significant portion of the Soviet nuclear arsenal and allowed the Ukrainians to develop a vast and sensitive defense production sector.

But Ukraine's past privilege didn't protect it from the economic disruptions caused by the Soviet Union's disintegration or from Moscow's neo-imperialist aspirations. Once a cog in the greater Soviet machine, Ukraine had to establish its own freestanding economy virtually overnight, and under the leadership of those without any experience in or inclination toward free markets or accountable and transparent governance.

Like Russia, Ukraine struggled mightily. It adopted many of the same reforms, with many of the same free-for-all results. It launched a voucher program similar to the one employed in Russia, with the goal of equitably distributing the country's wealth by enabling all citizens to own shares in formerly state-owned companies. But as in Russia, workers did not understand the concept or potential of stock shares. They opted for the bird in hand and sold their vouchers on the cheap, which allowed the connected to accumulate significant ownership interests in lucrative companies.

When I arrived in Kyiv in the late summer of 2001, President Kuchma, a former Communist factory director, was in his seventh year of leading the country. His election had marked the first peaceful transition of power in the post-Soviet space, something that, combined with his promise to reinvigorate Ukraine's sluggish economy, had given Ukrainians cause for some optimism. But despite Kuchma's assurances, the country had closed out the twentieth century with an economic output of less than half of its 1991 level.

Kuchma's leadership contributed to Ukraine's hardships in other ways as well. The president had not only failed to improve the lot of ordinary Ukrainians, he had also presided over the explosion of high-level corruption, a curse that only further diminished the country's prospects.

As in Russia, the rise of the oligarch class in Ukraine was something relatively new: a handful of men taking advantage of the lack of a comprehensive legislative and regulatory framework for a free-market economy and the absence of a rule-of-law culture to openly enrich themselves at the country's expense. These newly minted oligarchs then solidified their status by buying politicians and media outlets. Some ran for parliament to take advantage of the immunity from prosecution that Ukraine's constitution provided to all national legislators — a huge plus for those whose businesses were on the shady side.

In Russia, by 2004, Putin and his former KGB coworkers had effectively neutralized the oligarchs, ensuring that Russia's economy and politics were completely under their purview. In Ukraine, in contrast, that did not happen, at least not as of this writing. The oligarchs would become richer and stronger, consolidating their grip on the country's economy and politics. Neither path fostered the transparency and rule of law essential to developing democracy and a market economy, and the people of both countries would suffer greatly as a result.

The writing was on the wall when I got to Embassy Kyiv. In Kuchma's Ukraine, the institutional corruption that had pervaded all aspects of life in the Soviet era continued unabated. Kuchma kept the Soviet system of "telephone justice," where politicians picked up the phone and told prosecutors and judges what to do. Tax audits, civil suits, and criminal investigations were weaponized against political adversaries and even businessmen, embroiling them in costly and time-consuming legal battles and often causing them significant public embarrassment.

Watching Ukraine struggle while corruption flourished, I couldn't help but think of my Mogadishu days. As in Somalia, corruption extended all the way down the line. People paid to get certain government jobs, because working as a customs official, policeman, or judge could make them wealthy. They could collect bribes from businessmen to wreak havoc on their competitors. Or a businessman under investigation for a real or imagined crime might pay them to look the other way. Officials in lower-level jobs would send off-the-book payments to everyone up their supervisory chain, an insidious system called *potik,* "the stream." With no level playing field and no rule of law, legitimate businesses struggled to take root, and foreign companies — and even wealthy Ukrainians — had little incentive to invest in Ukraine.

Despite all this, Kuchma had won a second term in 1999 — a reelection made possible by his willingness to deploy the full powers of his government to influence the outcome of the elections. By the time he was reelected, there was widespread unhappiness with his policies and his failure to address the unrelenting corruption in the country. But the Ukrainian people could do little to express their displeasure democratically, because their country still didn't yet have a fully mobilized civil society.

"Civil society" — the people or groups who take an interest in issues of public concern and advocate for their preferred outcomes — is a term we don't hear much in the United States. That's because we take its omnipresence for granted. The vast majority of Americans belong to some type of civil society group, whether a business association, a PTA, a veterans' organization, a gardening club, a church, the Girl Scouts, or a group of demonstrators. In the Soviet Union, in contrast, any effort by individuals to join together independent of the government was brutally stamped out, leaving citizens in the new countries without the experience or the skills to advocate — and if necessary agitate — for their interests.

Ukraine's civil society may not have been robust enough to affect the outcome of the 1999 election, but change was afoot. Brave citizens and independent journalists had taken some steps to uncover and expose malfeasance in the government and hold Kuchma and others accountable. It was dangerous work. In September 2000, roughly one year before I arrived in Kyiv, investigative journalist and frequent Kuchma critic Heorhiy Gongadze had disappeared; in November his headless body was found in a forest outside the city.

Gongadze's murder shocked the nation. And Ukrainians' horror turned to outrage when audio recordings emerged of Kuchma speaking before Gongadze's disappearance and indicating that somebody needed to deal with the journalist. There were about a dozen recordings that dealt with Gongadze, more than enough for many to conclude that Kuchma had ordered Gongadze's murder — although Kuchma, of course, denied the charge.

By December 2000 protests had begun under the banner "Ukraine Without Kuchma." Thousands of Ukrainians ultimately joined in, continuing to call for Kuchma's ouster, until March 2001, when the security services

forcibly ended the demonstrations and arrested over two hundred partici-
pants. Civil society was stirring in Ukraine, and although it didn't succeed
in dislodging Kuchma that spring, it foreshadowed a future of greater involvement by the country's citizens in their own governance.

When I arrived five months later, the prevalence of corruption in daily
life hit me almost immediately as soon as I moved into an apartment in the
center of Kyiv that the embassy had found for me. Within a week armed
guards, hired to protect a wealthy and disreputable neighbor downstairs
from me, tried to shake me down. They told me I needed to pay up, since
I was "benefiting" from their presence. I was stunned. I told them what
I thought, and not very diplomatically: my security was not enhanced by
the presence of Kalashnikov-toting thugs; in fact, their presence put me
at greater risk. It was their turn to be stunned; the guns they packed usually ensured that people didn't talk to them that way. That was the end of
it, as my diplomatic status deterred them from pursuing the matter further.
It was a small insight into the constant petty shakedowns ordinary Ukrainians faced, except that many Ukrainians wouldn't have been able to push
back. In Kuchma's Ukraine, just as in Barre's Somalia, people could reasonably fear that the connected — and their hired gunmen — could get away
with just about anything.

As with Russia, the U.S. believed that we could help Ukraine transition
toward a democratic political system and adopt a free-market economy,
and we believed that doing so would serve the interests of both the United
States and the people of Ukraine. We saw it as a win-win: countries with
functioning economies and accountable and responsive governments are
usually better at meeting the needs of their people, lifting their people out
of poverty, and alleviating civil strife. They also make more reliable partners for the U.S., because democracies are less likely to cause trouble for
their neighbors and are more likely to share our values and interests. Plus
their predictable and rules-based playing field creates business opportunities for Americans.

From what I saw when I arrived, the Ukrainian people shared our views
and wanted the benefits of reform. We joined with other countries in warning Kuchma both publicly and privately about the importance of addressing his government's corruption and paying more than just lip service to
democratic norms if Ukraine wanted closer ties with the United States and
the European Union, as Kuchma stated he did. While Kuchma often said

the right things, his lack of follow-up suggested that he was counting on us to view Ukraine's strategic location as of greater value than concrete steps toward reform.

Granted, he had some reason to take that bet. Second in size only to Russia on the European landmass, Ukraine borders four NATO allies and straddles the Black Sea and its critical shipping routes south to Turkey and the Mediterranean. Just as importantly, it lies between Russia and much of central Europe, home to some of our closest allies.

But in the summer of 2001, ten years after the dissolution of the Soviet Union, the threat from Russia still seemed to be manageable. Vladimir Putin had been president of Russia for a little over a year. In the West we weren't quite sure what to make of him yet, but we were ready to try to work with him. Weeks before I arrived in Ukraine, President George W. Bush had met Putin and famously said of their encounter, "I looked the man in the eye. I found him to be very straightforward and trustworthy . . . I was able to get a sense of his soul." Bush wanted to work cooperatively with Russia in important areas, especially strategic stability and counterterrorism. In 2001, Putin was talking a democratic game, and although he was starting to consolidate power domestically, we hoped that he would use his dominance to benefit the Russian people while expanding Russia's cooperation with the United States.

We didn't fully understand then that Putin was acting in his own interests and those of his inner circle — mostly colleagues and friends from the KGB, Putin's earlier place of employment. Nor did we fully understand then how ruthlessly Putin and these closest advisors would seek to expand Russia's control over its neighbors in the years ahead. For centuries imperial Russia had treated Ukraine as a colony, using it as a buffer zone with its European adversaries to the west. And Putin and company seemed to follow in that tradition; they saw maintaining sway in Ukraine in particular as critical to Russia's own security.

Even if we didn't at the time see Putin's Russia as the malign force we now know it to be, it was hard to discount Ukraine's location between the democracies of Europe and the historically expansionist Russia. It was in Europe's interest, and therefore in ours, given our economic ties and treaty commitments with Europe, to show Ukraine the value of embracing closer relations with the democracies to its west. With the Cold War over, we rejected the concept of spheres of influence, where a regional power like Russia would have veto power over its neighbors' foreign policy choices. We weren't asking Ukraine (or any other country) to choose the U.S. over Russia. Rather, we believed that sovereign nations like Ukraine should be free to determine their own futures, and we had faith that if given the choice, they would choose freedom and prosperity over subservience and stagnation.

That didn't mean that Russia should be left out in the cold. For the U.S. at least, geopolitics wasn't a zero-sum game. Ever since Gorbachev had ushered in reforms in the Soviet Union, we had been hoping for a "Europe whole and free," as the first President Bush had said in 1989. In this regard at least, our definition of Europe included Russia. We were transparent about our efforts to work with the former Soviet republics, and in the early years Russia was the main beneficiary of those efforts, in terms of the high-level attention of our leaders, assistance dollars, and inclusion in organizations that bolstered the international order. We wanted to have constructive relations with Russia, but we were mindful throughout that the relationship could worsen. We "tended the garden" with Russia, working each day to solidify and sustain a good relationship between our countries, and we did the same with Ukraine. We knew that if our relations with Russia deteriorated, a Western oriented Ukraine would provide Europe with one of its first lines of defense against a bellicose Russia.

So Kuchma pursued a "multivector" foreign policy, balancing between Russia and the West and trying to gain the most from each partner. It's a common tactic for smaller countries caught between giants: they seek friendship with all countries but also play off the giants against each other to get what they can from each. Nevertheless, Kuchma's lack of interest in meaningful reform and indecisiveness regarding a closer relationship with NATO made U.S. policymakers wonder whether he had a genuine interest in a European future for his country.

THE STAKES IN Ukraine were high, and the agenda was long. We were busy, so busy, and I quickly found myself working harder even than I had in Moscow, because in Kyiv I was involved in virtually everything the embassy did — and we did a lot.

Embassy Kyiv handled the same day-to-day issues that were fundamental to the operations of every U.S. embassy in Europe. We provided emergency services for American citizens, advocated for American companies that did business in Ukraine, liaised between the U.S. military and the Ukrainian government with respect to the war in Afghanistan (and later Iraq), and partnered with Ukraine on law enforcement issues, such as stopping Ukrainian businesses from stealing the intellectual property of American businesses. These tasks alone would be enough to keep any embassy staff busy day in and day out. But in addition to all that was an agenda unique to countries in transition: helping Ukraine become a secure and prosperous democracy, with functioning institutions that responded to the will of its people.

To that end, Embassy Kyiv administered a large assistance program of about $280 million in fiscal year 2002 alone. Contrary to popular perception, this didn't mean that the U.S. Treasury wrote Kuchma's government a check for nearly $300 million; the U.S. rarely gives foreign governments or independent organizations cash. Rather, foreign assistance dollars typically fund programs — usually staffed by Americans — to implement goals we negotiate with the foreign government or organization. Often the money is used to buy American goods or hire American experts. In Ukraine's case, the assistance budget enabled U.S. government agencies, as well as private-sector organizations, to help their Ukrainian counterparts as they sought to develop and strengthen their transitioning country.

The embassy provided energy experts to help Ukraine restructure an energy sector dominated by a state-owned conglomerate where Soviet-style corruption still flourished. We imported American legal experts to help educate Ukrainian prosecutors and judges about the rule of law and how to establish a fair and accountable legal and judicial system. We brought in scientists, managers, and equipment from our nuclear laboratories to help Ukraine manage mitigation at Chornobyl, the site of the 1986 nuclear disaster. And we enlisted military experts to help Ukraine's legacy army transform its Soviet doctrine and practice into one that could better interface with NATO.

Aside from keeping track of all our assistance programs and troubleshooting with staff whenever difficulties arose, I helped implement the broader U.S. policy agenda. But perhaps most importantly, now that I was in the front office, I was also responsible for managing embassy operations. Nothing, including my management experience dealing with logistics at the line level in Somalia, prepared me for the task of overseeing a seven-hundred-person enterprise. Embassies aren't for-profit businesses, but at the top they frequently look like them. The ambassador is the chief executive officer, setting objectives and strategy. As DCM, I was the chief operating officer, tasked with managing personnel and resources and making sure the ambassador's plans got implemented. Just like in the business world, the roles overlap and in the best case are mutually reinforcing. That's how it worked for me in Ukraine, not least because I was fortunate to be working for an ambassador who trusted and relied on me.

With so many employees to manage, Embassy Kyiv was a quantum leap for me, one for which I had received little training. The State Department's two-week DCM course was heavy on touchy-feely — lots of climbing rope ladders to make you realize that you couldn't succeed without the help of others. It was useful, but it just wasn't enough. I was looking for concrete skills and for guidance on the bigger picture.

I got some of that at a conference I attended partway into my tenure. Beth Jones, the assistant secretary in charge of Europe and someone who would later become both an important mentor and a friend, convened the DCMs from all over Europe and gave us the vision that I had found lacking in the DCM course. Think big, she told us. We had the opportunity to set the tone for the entire embassy — to change policies that we thought made no sense and to create the embassy that we would have liked to serve in when we were junior officers. Hearing that, I was all in. I felt empowered thinking of my job as not just enforcing the rules that others set but creating a workplace where our employees could thrive. I didn't want others to feel as embattled as I had in Mogadishu and in my first year in Moscow. I'm not sure I succeeded, but that was my goal.

Embassies are a microcosm of America, and our employees brought to the workplace their own experiences, outlooks, and political inclinations. Most were federal workers from the many U.S. government agencies other than State represented at the embassy: military officers coordinating security cooperation, economists from the Commerce Department helping American businesses promote trade, Justice Department lawyers and FBI agents working on international law enforcement issues, and USAID employees providing governance and economic assistance, to name a few. All added their own agenda and agency culture to the mix, but it was my job to help the ambassador coordinate and ensure that all worked from the same policy page and spoke with one voice.

Everybody felt the pressure that our enormous policy agenda imposed, and it was sometimes hard to find a way to decompress. American government workers serving overseas represent our country 24/7, regardless of whether we are on the clock. We have to show respect for our hosts, reflect well on our country, show a united front as one Team America, and leave no opening for foreign intelligence services to take advantage of us. That means no sharing of our personal political preferences with host-country citizens and no questionable personal behavior — an expectation that applies not just to American employees but to their spouses, partners, and children as well. At least that is the ideal we strive for.

As you can imagine, not everyone easily internalizes that the code of conduct changes at the water's edge. What might be a private matter in the U.S. can become a political liability overseas. Even relatively small transgressions can reflect poorly on the U.S., creating international incidents and ending careers in the process. During my second year in Ukraine, for instance, a prank by an employee's teenager endangered some Ukrainians, led to police action, and resulted in the employee and the family being sent home. We couldn't keep an employee whose family member gave rise to conflict with our host country, but it was nonetheless sometimes difficult to accept that what would be a private family matter in the U.S. could blow up an employee's career if it happened overseas.

We had high expectations across the board, not just regarding personal conduct. In Ukraine circa 2001, those expectations could sometimes seem nearly impossible for our embassy employees to meet. We had never fully recovered from Secretary of State Baker's decision a decade earlier not to seek extra money to help the department set up the fourteen new embassies in the Baltic states and the former Soviet republics. Imagine if a company decided to establish more than a dozen new branch offices overseas without fully funding them. We were working with one hand tied behind our back.

Our premises were a case in point. When I arrived, embassy staff worked at five different sites in various states of disrepair. The geographic challenge made it difficult to unify the mission. At the main site, employees who worked inside the actual embassy building were jammed into whatever workspaces we could cobble together, just as I had experienced in Embassy Moscow. There we had been forced to work in the garage; in Kyiv the solution was more elaborate. At some point enterprising individuals had repurposed six cargo containers to give us more office space in the compound's back yard. They built three separate structures by welding two containers together, one on top of the other, cutting out doors, and adding a set of metal stairs for those in the top row. The makeshift offices surely didn't meet the public's idea of a glamorous embassy life, let alone U.S. workplace safety requirements. During the long, icy Kyiv winters, I worried that someone would plunge off the slippery stairways, which seemed precarious even at the best of times.

Our long to-do list was taxing, especially since our resources were inadequate for the task. But meeting Washington's high expectations — and our own — was even more challenging, because just like me, everyone at Embassy Kyiv was punching above their weight. When the new embassies were established, the State Department was still thinking about the new countries as satellites of Moscow, so the positions that were authorized were too few and often too junior. Ten years later the department still hadn't adjusted. We had section chiefs who had never supervised before and first-tour officers working directly with high-level government officials on critical issues. It was a great opportunity for all of us, but the responsibility came at a price: the worry about whether we were getting it right, the long hours to get the work done, and the constant need to coordinate with Washington after hours.

It was tough for everyone on the personal side too. Embassies are not just workplaces. They are also communities, with our coworkers serving as our extended family and social networks for the length of our stay. There were perennial issues that affected almost every post: the lack of employment prospects for spouses, the quality of the expatriate schools, the availability of good housing. And in Ukraine there was something else: even though seventeen years had passed since the world's worst nuclear accident, the Chornobyl nuclear plant still posed a concern to those living barely eighty miles away in Kyiv. We never fully shook the fear of ambient radiation — a particular worry for employees whose children had come with them to Ukraine.

In short, there was a lot to be stressed about, and people streamed into my office with all kinds of problems. There were so many tears that my conference table featured a box of tissues and a small Zen garden, the kind with sand, tiny rocks, and a miniature rake that offered people something to do with their hands while discussing difficult subjects. Because there was no bright line between work and home life, we dealt with everything from personnel issues to substance abuse, domestic violence, child abuse, illness, and even death. The State Department psychiatrist assigned to our region was on speed dial and told me that if the psychiatric issues were physical diseases, Embassy Kyiv would be considered in the grip of an epidemic.

I wasn't immune from the stressors and their toxic effects. I worked crazy long hours. I developed a habit of reading briefing papers while walking to and from the car, not looking up in the hallways or as I got into the vehicle. I felt I had no choice, because it was the only time to prep for whatever meeting I was about to attend. But one of the junior officers called me on it. She told me I never greeted people and was radiating tension as I ran from one thing to the next. That was a painful moment, a clear mistake for someone trying to lead by example. I tried to look up after that and focus on better channeling the advice of George W. Bush's secretary of state at the time, Colin Powell: never let them see you sweat.

Learning to manage my own insecurities had always been one of my biggest challenges. Although I like to think that I got better at projecting confidence, I don't think I ever really succeeded in quieting the voice in my head that questioned whether I was up to the job. Everything was new for me, and there was never enough time. I remember my assistant once chasing me into the ladies' room to take a phone call from Washington and my exasperated feeling that surely, surely I could have just five minutes of privacy.

On the bright side — and in the best Foreign Service tradition — I got a tremendous amount of on-the-job management training. It was humbling to learn that I usually wasn't the smartest person in the room, but empowering to discover that I didn't need to be. I realized that my team could accomplish way more if I trusted the subject-matter experts to take the lead. I was pleased to realize that I had the ability to recognize the best ideas and the skill to lead teams in implementing the heck out of those ideas. I learned that success at the top was about growing other people's talents rather than trying to make myself the indispensable person in the room.

Good leadership was also about empathy, something that Carlos, as I called Ambassador Pascual, modeled for me time and again, and which he also made a priority for our work within the embassy. We worked hard to balance the workload for our employees, lighten up the pressure, and create a better sense of community. At the end of year two there was a general consensus that the working environment had improved. And the day I was told that I should "declare victory" on that particular issue was a very good day.

The worst day, by contrast, was when I got word that our much-beloved consul general, Greg Hulka, and his ten-year-old daughter, Abby, had been killed in a car accident on the way to a wedding outside Kyiv. I received a call from our nurse practitioner and security officer informing me of the accident early on a Saturday night in November 2001. As on September 11, I kept on asking for more information. I finally had to admit to myself that the facts were not going to change. I called Carlos, and we went together to inform Greg's wife — now his widow. To this day it is one of the hardest things I have ever done.

The family was shattered, and so was the embassy community. But we rallied together to support the Hulka family. Carlos gave a heartbreaking eulogy and threw a rousing wake to celebrate Greg and Abby. Everyone in the community contributed food; it was important for people to be able to provide support to the family. Abby's schoolmates painted eggs — a Ukrainian tradition known as *pysanky* — and turned them into permanent ornaments to hang on our Christmas trees in her memory. Six moves and twenty years later I still have that beautiful maroon egg, and every year I hang it on my Christmas tree to remember Abby and Greg.

The way Carlos handled the Hulka tragedy was one of my most important leadership lessons: genuinely caring, demonstrating respect, looking out for his people, and celebrating the best in us. Whether he was listening — really listening — to human rights advocates under threat, taking the time to hear one of our staffers in need, or kneeling next to an individual in a wheelchair so he could converse at eye level, Carlos modeled the behavior we should all emulate.

Carlos wasn't my only role model when things got tough. When I was in a jam, whether it was policy or personnel, I would often think back to my childhood and ask myself, What would Mama and Papa do? The lessons my parents taught me, especially to treat everyone as we want to be treated, often rang in my ears.

I also found helpful the ethics class I had taken at the War College the previous year. While we studied the work of many great philosophers, it was the more mundane lessons that really stuck with me: the *New York Times* test and the grandma test. If I'd be embarrassed to defend a decision that made its way to the front page of the newspapers, I told the team we needed to find a different route. Likewise, if I couldn't explain our actions to Oma, chances were high that we needed to rethink what we were doing.

HOWEVER ALL-CONSUMING my responsibilities on the management side were, I also had policy work to deal with. One of the most challenging issues arose when another shocking audio recording of President Kuchma emerged in early 2002, capturing a two-year-old conversation between the Ukrainian president and Valeriy Malev, the head of Ukraine's arms export company. In the conversation Kuchma authorized the sale to Iraq of a highly sophisticated early warning system produced in Ukraine known as Kolchuga.

If the recording was authentic, this was a huge problem. Both at the time the tape was recorded and when it came to light, U.S. and British planes were patrolling Iraqi skies to enforce a no-fly zone established in the aftermath of the 1990–1991 Gulf War. The Kolchugas would enable Iraq to track the aircraft and potentially shoot them down, putting our air crews at risk. In addition, if Ukraine had transferred the Kolchugas to Iraq, it would contravene UN sanctions on Iraq and probably also U.S. law prohibiting weapons sales to that nation.

Just as importantly, the recording again raised concerns about whether Kuchma was a trustworthy ally for the United States. He professed a desire to partner with the U.S. and further develop Ukraine's relationship with NATO. He had been asking to meet with President Bush to solidify the relationship. But if Kuchma really had authorized weapons sales to Iraq, it was clear we couldn't trust him — not if his priority was profiting from illegal arms deals that put our people at risk.

It took some time, but finally in August 2002, U.S. government experts concluded that the voice on the tape was indeed Kuchma's. Washington policymakers decided to respond with a pointed message: the suspension of $55 million in assistance slated for the Ukrainian government programs we thought Kuchma cared about most. But when Carlos and I confronted his chief of staff about Kuchma's actions in late September, he denied not just that Ukraine had sold the Kolchugas to Iraq but also that Kuchma had ever authorized the sale, despite the clear evidence on the recording.

The story exploded into public view with a *New York Times* story on September 24, using unnamed U.S. officials as sources and citing excerpts from the recordings. The Ukrainian government responded with a press release that repeated the denials it had made to Carlos and me and added that it was "open to verification by the relevant international bodies, including U.S. experts." "Trust but verify" is an old proverb in the region. Since at this point there was no trust in the U.S. toward the Kuchma administration, we were more than ready to accept the invitation to verify the Ukrainian claims.

Carlos had been planning to use a previously scheduled public event on September 25 to explain our position to the Ukrainian public, many of whom were understandably concerned about the impact of this latest scandal on the bilateral relationship, as well as about the loss of aid. At the last minute, though, the Ukrainian government preempted Carlos by scheduling a meeting of key foreign ambassadors to reinforce the Ukrainian contention that the U.S. and Britain (which had also suspended an aid program and joined us in our push for the truth) were wrong.

Clearly Carlos had to attend the government meeting so that other countries had the facts. But we weren't going to allow the Ukrainians' maneuver to prevent us from getting our position out to the public. That meant that I would be doing the public event, which quickly turned into a press conference.

It was an important moment in my career development. I had very little experience dealing directly with the press until then, and I had never held a press conference on even a minor topic, let alone on an issue with this kind of international profile. We had been working on the Kolchuga affair for months, so I knew the facts cold. Nevertheless, I was being thrown in the deep end without warning — never ideal.

Carlos and I had a few minutes to confer before we went our separate ways. Although he was as supportive as ever, I could tell that he was worried for me as we reviewed the material. Nervous, I snapped at him that I could handle it. It was not my best moment, and I told myself I needed to calm down.

When I got to the press conference, it was standing room only; every media outlet in Kyiv seemed to be in attendance. The impatience of the assembled press corps was palpable. My nerves hadn't abated, but I recalled Papa's advice to do the best I could.

The questions came fast and furious. Ukrainians were worried that the scandal would cause the U.S. to turn its back on their country. What had happened? they wanted to know. How did we know? What were we going to do? What would it mean for the relationship? It was the first time that I was the person out in front representing the U.S. rather than the behind-the-scenes supporter. A misstatement would have made its way into both Ukrainian and American press reports. It was a lot of pressure for my first time out, but when the press conference ended, I felt I had done a good job of explaining the U.S. position and had earned my spurs. For the next seventeen years, through three ambassadorships, that press conference was still the first item that came up whenever I Googled myself. Only in the final months of my career would it be displaced by other information.

That October the Ukrainians kept their word and hosted a U.S.-British team of experts to review what had happened. Despite promises of transparency, they did not fully cooperate, which for us raised the question of why, if it wasn't Kuchma on the recording and if they hadn't sold any Kolchugas to Iraq, the Ukrainians weren't forthcoming. It was the same Soviet legacy of stonewalling that had taken place after the Siberian Air shootdown. This action had potentially put members of our armed forces at risk, and as a result produced intense anger and distrust at the highest levels of the U.S. government. The only silver lining was that with the help of the U.K. and Poland, Ukraine committed to reforming its export control system, adopting systems that would make it harder for illicit sales of this sort to occur in the future.

The U.S.-Ukraine relationship had already been tense because of Kuchma's lack of progress on moving democratic reforms forward, but the Kolchuga scandal brought it to its lowest point yet. NATO canceled a summit with Ukraine and President Bush refused to meet with Kuchma — humiliating slights for Kuchma, but also missed opportunities for Ukraine to move its agenda forward with Europe and the U.S.

In January 2003, Washington held a policy review on Ukraine. Carlos briefed the Ukrainians and listed some of the steps they could take to get the relationship back on track. Ironically, it was our request for help in Iraq — of all places — that began the process of mending the relationship. The Bush administration wanted as many nations as possible to participate in the coalition preparing to launch Operation Iraqi Freedom in 2003. Ukraine responded with a battalion specializing in nuclear, biological, and chemical weapons and ultimately provided approximately 1800 troops. It wasn't enough to turn the relationship completely around, but it was a good start.

U.S. forces did not find Kolchuga systems during Operation Iraqi Freedom, which has caused some Ukrainians to claim that we made the whole thing up. Kuchma's son-in-law later suggested that after initially approving the sale, Kuchma may have changed his mind. There are additional possible explanations: the sale fell through for other reasons, the Kolchugas were destroyed before we found them, or maybe they're still in a cave somewhere in Iraq. To this day I don't know what happened to them. But I have no doubt that Kuchma authorized the sale and that we were right to conclude that his willingness to put our air crews at risk and undermine our Iraq policy was more than enough to suggest that he was not a reliable partner.

I learned a lot from this episode: the importance of verifying facts, since they will be disputed vigorously; the imperative to move forward even with imperfect knowledge; the importance of trustworthiness in international relations, since we can't partner fully with countries and individuals we don't have faith in; and the importance of acting with allies — in this case, the British, the Poles, and other NATO countries — because we are stronger when we work together.

I also learned, once again, the importance of transparency, accountability, and strong institutions, including a functional legal system. The Ukrainian arms export company was a government monopoly, with a few men making all the decisions behind closed doors. The tools to dissuade them from pursuing an illegal but presumably personally lucrative deal did not yet exist in 2000, when Kuchma authorized the sale, or even in 2002, when we discovered his duplicity. Ukraine did not have governmental oversight institutions or an independent court; it did not have a parliament free of oligarch influence (especially since in Ukraine oligarchs and politicians were often one and the same); it did not have a powerful civil society or a fully free press. Ukraine did not have any of the mechanisms to expose wrongdoing, and even if wrongdoing came to light, there was no expectation that the powerful would be held accountable. Bottom line: there was no rule of law.

IT'S A LONG, hard road to establish the rule of law or democracy in a country where it does not exist. I had seen this firsthand in Russia, and I was reminded of it again in Ukraine. Less well-intentioned politicians worried that changing the status quo meant that they and their patrons, the oligarchs, would lose out on sweetheart deals worth millions. Even those who had a vision of a better future worried that with the people in charge in a real democracy, they would be voted out of office if they did the right thing, fixed the economy, and triggered the short-term pain that reforms bring in exchange for long-term benefits.

That was the situation in Ukraine. But we didn't give up. Instead we tried to create incentives for reform as a counter to the tremendous inducements for inertia and graft. We deployed a large arsenal of carrots — positive incentives — from offering to increase assistance programs to inviting leaders to the U.S. for high-level meetings. But because our interests were at stake, not just Ukraine's, sometimes we deployed sticks as well.

Sometimes sticks are our only option. We had to use them, for instance, when we found out that Kuchma had authorized the Kolchuga sales to Iraq. Canceling assistance programs and high-level meetings hit Kuchma where it hurt. Presidential-level meetings and American assistance are affirming, and leaders — not just in Ukraine — use them to show their people that they have world standing and are getting results for their countries.

Using sticks can be risky. We had been warned by Kuchma allies that by signaling our displeasure, we risked "losing" Ukraine by pushing Kuchma closer to Russia, which again made us wonder how committed Kuchma really was to a different path. In the end, however, those sticks got Kuchma's attention, and we were able to work with the Ukrainian government to start building back the relationship with the U.S.

One stick we fortunately did not have to use in the Kolchuga affair was the deployment of sanctions, although we wondered whether we might have to. The U.S. tries to apply sanctions surgically, so that the people of a country aren't harmed just because their leaders need a strong incentive to change their behavior. Late in my tenure in Ukraine, President Bush employed a new tool, issuing an order barring anyone "engaged in or benefiting from corruption" from coming to the United States. In a place like Ukraine, where plenty of questionable oligarchs relished visiting and doing business in the U.S., the Bush order gave us a lever to pull. I worked with embassy staff to draft the justification for closing America's doors to a prominent Ukrainian oligarch, Hryhoriy Surkis, who had deep ties to the Kuchma administration but who didn't hold a government position himself. We hoped that barring him from the United States would send a signal to corrupt oligarchs that dirty money wasn't welcome in the U.S. and neither were the people who wielded it. We wanted to show them that their actions had costs — and that if they wanted to enjoy the delights of Disney World or the bright lights of Manhattan, they needed to clean up their act.

Yet during my time in Kyiv as deputy chief of mission, neither Bush's order nor any of the other diplomatic tools available to us seemed to work. It
was hard to escape the conclusion that Ukraine under Kuchma was not going to make progress toward more accountable governance. But Ukraine's
strategic location and size, natural resources, and vast commercial potential made it too important to write off. We concluded that we would have
to redouble our efforts to work with progressive government officials and
civil society groups (as well as bringing along Kuchma and the less reform-
minded elements of the government) to help them make the small changes
that we hoped would lay the groundwork for transformative change later.
At the embassy we left no stone unturned in our efforts to help Ukraine
continue to develop its democracy and economy.

But we had to be in it for the long haul, because it was clear that Kuchma
and what he represented were not going away anytime soon. The parliamentary elections in March 2002 turned out to be as challenged as the
presidential elections in 1999. The two most important parties — the pro
Kuchma For a United Ukraine Party and the opposition Our Ukraine Party
of former prime minister Yushchenko — battled it out, but Kuchma again
commandeered government resources and personnel to help his supporters.* Surprisingly, his machinations resulted in only a one-seat majority for
his party, a sign that perhaps the Ukrainian people had finally had enough.

Ambassador Pascual departed in the summer of 2003, and his replacement, Ambassador John Herbst, arrived in September. My own tour was
due to end in the summer of 2004. The new ambassador and I spent much
of my last year in Ukraine continuing U.S. efforts to promote democracy
and economic reform, but without much success. When it came down to it,
Ukraine's elites — its politicians and oligarchs — were willing to reform only
if the new laws, regulations, and institutions didn't touch their interests.

International goodwill and international assistance were proving to be
insufficient in moving Ukraine forward. We were able to help democratically minded Ukrainians make change on the margins but not the kind of
fundamental change that would have meant a better life for ordinary Ukrai-

---

* After independence, many post-Soviet countries introduced a government structure with both a president and a prime minister. Their responsibilities and power
vary, but usually the president is the dominant official and handles defense and foreign policy issues, and the prime minister manages economic and social issues.

nians — and not the kind of changes that we were hoping for, the kind of transformational changes that would cement Ukraine's place in the West. In part, it has to be said, it was because we weren't dealing with the elephant in the room. We hadn't yet realized the extent of the toll that corruption was taking on the country's development. As a result, we were not as focused on combating corruption in Ukraine as we would be later on. The carrots we offered were insufficiently tasty and the sticks we deployed insufficiently large. Ultimately it would take an action of the Ukrainian people themselves to transform Ukraine.

Kuchma announced that he wouldn't run again in elections scheduled for the fall of 2004, leaving the field for his preferred candidate, current prime minister Viktor Yanukovych, to face off against former prime minister Viktor Yushchenko. It was a clear choice: Russia and the increasingly corrupt and undemocratic ways that it represented (Yanukovych) or a Western path of liberty and reform (Yushchenko). But would the next electoral process be any more fair than the ones that had kept Kuchma and his allies in power in the past? That remained to be seen.

MEANWHILE, MY TIME in Ukraine was winding down, and new opportunities were beckoning. My tour was set to end in July 2004, and I had been asked the previous summer whether I'd be interested in going to the Baltic state of Latvia *as ambassador*. The offer came as a happy surprise, and this time I didn't need to canvass my friends before accepting the invitation to put in my papers for the job. Three years as DCM had given me the confidence to believe that I was both qualified and ready for the task.

I did, however, reflect again about how merit is usually not enough to be considered for opportunities such as this: you also need to be lucky. When, in my long-ago London days, I had first decided to focus my career on the Soviet Union, the State Department had needed just one ambassador for the region. Now there were fifteen U.S. embassies scattered throughout the former Soviet Union and the Baltics, all of which needed ambassadors. That was one stroke of luck. Another was that in 2003, Beth Jones, the diplomat in charge of European policy, wanted to increase the anemic number of female ambassadors, and she supported my candidacy. I filled out the mountains of paperwork, and then, knowing that it would be a many-month selection process, put the whole thing out of my mind as I focused on the work in Kyiv.

I also needed to devote attention to what matters most: family. Papa had survived a battle with cancer while I was living in the U.S., but as the winter of 2004 turned to spring, he suffered a relapse and began deteriorating rapidly. In late May, Mama called me in the middle of the night to tell me to come home. I dropped everything and flew to North Carolina, where my parents had been enjoying their retirement. A harrowing couple of weeks followed, filled with anguish at Papa's suffering, uncertainty about whether we were doing the right things for him, and lots of love. Although he was very ill, Papa was still his same old self, and when I whispered that I was up for an ambassadorship, he beamed. His will to live was still as strong as ever, but at eighty-two his body was betraying him. We finally moved him to a hospice in the countryside, with French doors that opened onto a field of flowers. When he looked outside, Papa, a green thumb who could make anything grow, beamed once more.

I was fortunate that I got to say goodbye; many who serve overseas are not so lucky. I am also fortunate that I don't have many regrets about my relationship with my father, or his passing, although I do regret that I didn't spend more time asking him about his first forty years. His life was a testament to the power that each one of us has to persevere against the toughest of circumstances and to survive with our integrity intact. He never lost his faith, his hope, or his ability to love. Those qualities are what made him the man I and so many others loved and admired. Once he was gone, many details of his stories were lost to me, but his example continues to guide me.

WHILE WE WERE at the hospital with Papa that terrible June, I got a call informing me that President Bush had decided to nominate a political appointee to the Latvia post. I was so worried about Papa that I barely registered the news. But Carlos was still looking out for me, and he knew of an open position in Washington working for the under secretary for political affairs, the number three at the State Department. The paperwork moved swiftly, so at least I didn't have to worry about the next job.

The best part of the new job was that I'd be working in the U.S. and could help Mama adjust. After we buried Papa that June, I flew back to Kyiv for a week to pack out. It was an abrupt end to my tour, but Ambassador Herbst threw me a beautiful farewell party. Once again I at least had a chance to say goodbye.

After I departed, Ukraine held presidential elections. They were marred by irregularities and scandal, including the mysterious and near-fatal poisoning of Viktor Yushchenko, the leading reform candidate. International observers found the second-round runoff to be anything but free and fair. Russian president Putin had made no secret about who his candidate was, and he publicly congratulated Yanukovych before the results were announced. Ukraine's election officials soon called the elections for Yanukovych, but the exit poll, funded by the U.S., told a different story: 54 percent for the pro-Western candidate, Yushchenko.

This time the Ukrainian people had finally had enough; armed with the facts, they did not accept the results and took to the streets during a bitterly cold November and December. The world watched to see if Kuchma would deploy the security services to quash the protests, as he had in late 2000 following the release of the recording which appeared to implicate him in the murder of journalist Heorhiy Gongadze. Using his bully pulpit, Secretary of State Powell weighed in, making it clear that the U.S. could not accept the election results and urging Kuchma not to attack his own people.

Democracy prevailed. In early December the Ukrainian Supreme Court ruled the election results invalid and ordered another runoff. Held on December 26, the election delivered victory to the reformer, Yushchenko, who was officially declared the winner. Kuchma's refusal to deploy force against his fellow Ukrainians and his facilitation of a peaceful transfer of power were the biggest contributions he made to Ukraine's democratic development.

The Orange Revolution — so called because orange was the color of the Yushchenko election campaign — became the stuff of legend: Ukraine appeared to be on the way to a real democracy without a shot being fired. It seemed that all the work over the past thirteen years since independence — work we often worried was for naught — was actually paying off. It was gratifying to watch Ukraine's victory, especially since it came just a year after the Rose Revolution in Georgia, another former Soviet republic. We thought that the arc of history was bending toward democracy.

I was overjoyed to witness Ukraine's achievement, even if it was from afar. And I had another reason to celebrate as well. After the Latvia ambassadorship fell through, Beth hadn't given up. In the summer of 2004 the European Bureau at the State Department put me forward for the ambassadorship to another former Soviet republic, the remote and landlocked Central Asian nation of Kyrgyzstan. I was pretty sure that a political appointee wouldn't edge me out for that posting, which wasn't the kind of prestige assignment most political appointees want.

That winter I learned that President Bush had agreed with State's recommendation and had decided to nominate me to represent my country as ambassador. When the Senate confirmed me in late June 2005, even my sorrow that my father wouldn't be able to see me sworn in as ambassador couldn't diminish my excitement.

I knew enough about my new posting to understand that it was going to exercise many of the same muscles that I had developed in Ukraine. Kyrgyzstan had initially seemed like fertile ground for a democratic form of government; the country had a nomadic culture and a long tradition of decentralized and communal decision-making, and its first post-Soviet president, Askar Akayev, had impressed Washington policymakers. But perhaps we were just hearing what we wanted to hear, because as in so many other former Soviet republics, Kyrgyzstan moved only in fits and starts toward establishing a democratic political system and a reformed economy.

By 2005 it had become clear that Akayev and those closest to him were prioritizing their own power and pocketbook above the progress of the country. In March of that year, political protests erupted after parliamentary elections that were plagued by vote-buying, deregistration of candidates, closure of independent media, and a discredited appeals process. To everyone's surprise, by the end of the month Akayev had fled to Vladimir Putin's Russia, where he would find sympathy for his undemocratic tendencies.

The Tulip Revolution, as it was called, turned Kyrgyzstan into front-page news around the world. The demonstrations and Akayev's dramatic departure, the hasty establishment of an acting government, the July 2005 presidential elections, and the subsequent formation of the new government: these dramatic developments all made one thing clear as I prepared to leave for Kyrgyzstan that summer. It may have been a small post, but there would be more than enough to keep me busy.

7

Kyrgyzstan

Bishkek, the capital city of Kyrgyzstan, is nestled in a valley of the Ala-too mountain range. When I arrived, the distant peaks were snow-topped and stunning even in the intense August heat. The 2005 Kyrgyz Independence Day festivities immediately awaited, and I spent two hot hours reviewing a military parade before attending a formal dinner at the Presidential Residence. It was the kind of event — in any country — that is so long and boring that you start hoping a colleague might call you about a crisis that forces you to leave early. That is especially true for me, an introvert, much happier one-on-one, in a small group, or alone.

Making the event particularly memorable, Foreign Minister Alikbek Jek-shenkulov approached me with a plate filled with Kyrgyz delicacies. "The baby pony is delicious," he said. "You must try it." All I could think of was the long-ago TV series about a pony, *My Friend Flicka*. With no emergency phone call to the rescue, I put a forkful of Flicka in my mouth. To my surprise, it wasn't bad, but Flicka was still front of mind. I am sure that some of the foods that we eat in the U.S. might generate a similar reaction from someone visiting from Kyrgyzstan, but still, I was relieved when the foreign minister moved on and I could put the plate aside.

The following day I attended a game of kok-boru, Kyrgyzstan's national sport. Kind of like polo if it were mixed with rugby, kok-boru features players on horses but without mallets, doing whatever it takes to grab and carry a decapitated goat carcass into the goal. There didn't appear to be any rules, and by the end of the match the goat was literally a bloody mess. On the upside, this was a game of speed, strength, skill, and stamina, which I duly noted to the assembled members of the Kyrgyz media, who were wondering what I thought of the match.

To myself, I thought that everything was going to be different here. I recalled what one of my predecessors had told me about Kyrgyzstan: it may not be the end of the world, but you can see it from here.

To be sure, in some respects Kyrgyzstan seemed remarkably recognizable: it shared the same Soviet past and was governed by the same type of Soviet-educated leaders as Ukraine and Russia. It also faced many of the same post-Soviet challenges, most significantly corrupt government institutions in serious need of reform and an economy that benefited just a favored few. On the plus side, like Ukraine, it had a developing civil society that was pushing for reform, although with the same mixed results.

Added to this familiar mix was a new and unusual element, at least in the former Soviet Union. Kyrgyzstan hosted a U.S. military installation, the Manas Air Base, which provided logistical support for Operation Enduring Freedom in nearby Afghanistan, less than two hours' flight time from Bishkek. Ensuring continued access to that base — and easing the tensions its presence created with the Kyrgyz — ended up consuming an inordinate portion of my time in Kyrgyzstan. This task was made all the more difficult by the efforts of Kyrgyzstan's president, Kurmanbek Bakiyev, to exploit the base for his own profit.

PRESIDENT BAKIYEV HAD negotiated the original agreement with the U.S. for its use of the Manas Air Base in December 2001, while he had been serving as former president Akayev's prime minister. He and Akayev parted ways six months later, and by late 2004 Bakiyev had become the head of a new opposition party in the Kyrgyz parliament. He soon helped lead the demonstrations that turned into the Tulip Revolution and took over as acting president following Akayev's ouster in March 2005. The month before I arrived, Bakiyev won the presidency in his own right in an electoral landslide.

Although he had ridden into office on a reform wave, Bakiyev quickly demonstrated that he wasn't a believer in the cause. He institutionalized corruption on a huge scale, virtually ignoring his mandate to reform the government. He installed his two sons and multiple brothers in key positions, a level of nepotism that rankled the Kyrgyz people, especially as the economy worsened, utility and staple costs rose, and unemployment rates and emigration to Russia accelerated. People joked that at the next elections they would vote for the candidate with no brothers.

Chaos soon became what passed for the governing principle of Kyrgyz-stan's new administration. Ministers and staffers rotated in and out, and loyalty seemed to be the most important qualification for a government job. The infighting among politicians was intense: over government revenue streams that could be diverted into private pockets, over who would control lucrative government companies and contracts, and over positions that could generate payments for personal gain. Bakiyev offered neither leadership nor stability, and organized crime quickly took advantage of the power vacuum. Beyond Bakiyev himself, Kyrgyzstan didn't have enough money to support a true oligarch class of the type I had seen in Russia and Ukraine, but criminals can find a way to profit even in the poorest of places. They partnered with politicians to the financial benefit of both and sidelined or if necessary killed parliamentarians and rivals who got in their way. In the absence of effective government services, they often provided for the people who lived in their home areas, just like Robin Hood — or Pablo Escobar. And just like those outlaws, they engendered loyalty, often more loyalty than the Kyrgyz felt toward their government.

This situation was personified by a crime boss named Rysbek. His full name was Rysbek Akmatbayev, but organized criminals, like divas, often go by only one name. A couple of months after I arrived, Rysbek's brother was killed while visiting a prison in the middle of an inmate riot. Rysbek blamed Prime Minister Feliks Kulov, a rival of President Bakiyev, and brought thousands of paid demonstrators, many of them criminals, to Bishkek's main square to demand Kulov's head. They set up yurts and blocked off main streets for about a week, impeding parliamentary business and pretty much everything else. Even in the face of being held hostage by a criminal, the government, riddled with individuals who were either on Rysbek's payroll or simply enemies of his enemies, wouldn't take action to end it.

Colleagues in other countries had shared stories about this sort of thing, but this was the first time that I had personally observed mobbed-up criminals threaten the stability of a state by bending politicians and decision-making toward their own ends. Seeing it up close, I was horrified by how destabilizing it was. The government had ground to a halt, businesses in the city center had been forced to shut, and the international community had little confidence in Bakiyev's abilities to manage the situation, let alone govern. Something needed to be done.

Following a well-publicized meeting between Bakiyev and representatives of the international community, I asked to see Bakiyev in private. I bluntly told him that international donors and investors wouldn't put money into a country run by criminals. Whether because of international pressure, a side deal with Rysbek, or some other factor, Bakiyev finally did end the demonstrations shortly thereafter — although notably, he did so without uttering any public defense of his embattled prime minister. It was hard for us to figure out what was really going on, but it was clear that a storm was raging in Bishkek and that the whole country was feeling its effects.

THE DEMONSTRATIONS and unrest in Bishkek reminded me of my tour in Moscow in the early 1990s, although Bishkek seemed even more violent. It certainly felt closer to home. Maybe that was because the Kyrgyz capital was smaller and I had quickly come to know a number of the affected politicians, businessmen, and journalists. No question, the bloodshed made them fearful. For protection, many had enormous, semiwild dogs roaming their properties and didn't leave their compounds without a bodyguard or a gun — frequently both. When they visited me at my home, their bodyguards had to stay outside, and guns were checked at the coat closet. As a diplomat, I didn't feel personally threatened by the violence around me, although I too had armed guards and an armored vehicle. No dogs, though. At least, not at this time — and it was unlikely that the cockapoo I adopted a number of years later, Scout, would have scared anyone off anyway.

I'd be the first to tell you that if Washington had known everything that was going to go down in Kyrgyzstan, they would have sent someone more experienced. But there I was. I was thrilled, of course, but being an ambassador was a big leap for me. Serving as the number two in Embassy Kyiv had prepared me well, but having the buck stop with me gave me an entirely new perspective.

Part of the challenge was that the embassy in Bishkek was even more chronically understaffed than the one in Ukraine. As usual, the State Department hadn't provided a lot of guidance before I left the U.S. During the two-week class for new ambassadors (fondly known as "Charm School"), one speaker bluntly told us that Washington would provide support when we needed it, but we were being paid to solve issues and keep them off Washington's plate. I was ten time zones away from Washington, which meant that we were already done with our day when Washington was starting up — and I no longer had Ambassador Pascual or Ambassador Herbst to run big decisions by. It reminded me in some sense of my first tour, in Somalia — of being thrown in the deep end and being forced to sink or swim. So, as Papa always told us, I did the best I could.

I was lucky to have a crew that was hardworking and effective. I was also lucky that Mama visited twice for extended periods. At seventy-eight, she was as energetic and adventurous as ever, and, after Papa's death, free to travel. She embraced life in Bishkek, starting a knitting club and learning how to swim for the first time. When a USO tour came to the base in Bishkek, Mama was eager to attend the show, to the dismay of the base leadership. Kid Rock was coming, and the brass feared that the f-bombs that were sure to come with him would upset a septuagenarian. Mama didn't even blush. Kid Rock called her "Grandma," and my photo of the two of them served as my screensaver for at least a year.

Mama was quick to adapt in other ways as well. In the late hours of a Fourth of July event at my residence, she encountered an unexpected visitor when she wanted to go to bed: a Kyrgyz special forces sniper was posted at her window to ensure the safety of the guests below. She shrugged it off and slept in my bedroom that night.

Mama served as a force multiplier during those visits. She both humanized me to the embassy staff and extended what I was capable of doing. Most ambassadors bring their spouses wherever they go. Very unfairly, the mostly female spouses often assume a number of unpaid responsibilities. I didn't have a spouse to impose upon, but when Mama came to visit, she took on many of those duties: managing the household staff, working out menus, attending embassy events that I couldn't go to, and serving as a strong American presence in the international women's organizations that are still a staple of diplomatic life. People told her what they were thinking — frequently with the expectation that she'd funnel the information to me, which she often did. She also told them about me, making me more approachable.

On a more personal level, it was just wonderful to have her warm and loving presence with me in such a faraway place. I was still the same over-thinker that I had always been, and I worried all the time. Even though I was in my late forties, Mama's presence was reassuring.

In my defense, there was a lot to worry about in early 2000s Kyrgyzstan. It was an uncertain time, and I could understand why many Kyrgyz, like their counterparts in Russia and Ukraine, looked back nostalgically to the more predictable and less blatantly corrupt days of the Soviet Union. If that were the extent of Russia's influence in post–Cold War Kyrgyzstan, it would have been a relief. But Moscow clearly was taking a renewed interest in its former empire — occasionally to our benefit, but often not.

WHEN THE U.S. had first sought military bases in Kyrgyzstan and neighboring Uzbekistan to support Operation Enduring Freedom in Afghanistan in late 2001, Russian president Putin, in office for a little over a year, had blessed both arrangements. It was, we thought then, a sign of progress: Cold War rivals coming together to fight the global threat of terrorism. But by the time I arrived in 2005, Putin had had a change of heart. Having consolidated power in his own country, he was pushing to eject the United States from Russia's self-proclaimed sphere of influence in Central Asia. In July 2005, Kyrgyzstan joined with other countries in the region — most notably Russia and China — in calling for the U.S. to set a timetable to close the Manas Air Base.

But it wasn't clear what that statement meant in practice. In keeping with his view of governing as a series of transactions benefiting himself, Bakiyev tried to leverage the U.S. base, not just to play us off against Russia but to line his own pockets. Right after the timetable announcement, he asked the Department of Defense to review the base agreement, which we understood as code for "You can stay if you give me more money." When Uzbekistan, in retaliation for American criticism of the Uzbek government's massacre of hundreds of protesters earlier in the spring, unilaterally closed the only other U.S. air base in the region, Bakiyev thought his hand was strengthened. But he misjudged: the U.S. expected Kyrgyzstan to live up to its commitment to host the base and was not prepared to renegotiate the agreement.

Six weeks into my tenure, Secretary of State Condoleezza Rice made a lightning visit to Kyrgyzstan. I set up two meetings for her: one with President Bakiyev and another, less formal one with both Bakiyev and prominent civil society activists. Bakiyev initially agreed to the joint meeting with the activists but then canceled his participation, probably because someone in his camp realized that the activists might use the meeting to criticize his nepotism and corruption. Then the Bakiyev team registered that not being there might make Bakiyev look even worse; after all, just a few months earlier he had led a popular revolution with these same people, yet now he appeared to be afraid of what they might say in front of Secretary Rice. Bakiyev's people thought they could solve the conundrum by pressuring both the embassy and our Kyrgyz invitees to cancel the event altogether.

It was easy for me to withstand the pressure but more complicated for the activists. Defying a request from their president could bring on anything from retaliatory tax audits to physical violence. But individuals fighting for reform against a repressive regime are a special breed. These were the advocates demanding freedom of the press, shining a light on corruption, and holding the country's leaders accountable. They had helped create the change that put Bakiyev in power. They wanted to share information with America's leadership, and we wanted the secretary to hear directly from these smart, engaged Kyrgyz about how they were helping to transform their country and what challenges they faced.

We explained this to the Bakiyev government, even as the State Department was getting nervous that going through with the meeting might offend Bakiyev and make tensions over the base more challenging to defuse. But I urged the department to stand firm, and the meeting stayed on Secretary Rice's schedule.

With the program set, I focused on ensuring that Rice's visit would be worth the long trip by making it what we call an "action-forcing event." Principals—a cabinet secretary or a president—don't normally meet with their counterparts unless they know that they will have something to show for it after the meeting. What we wanted to show—the action that we wanted to force—was a joint statement enshrining Kyrgyzstan's commitment to host the base and hopefully ending the swirling speculation about its future.

With Secretary Rice's plane winging toward Bishkek, I was finalizing the text of the base statement with Miroslav Niyazov, Bakiyev's national security advisor. But he was stonewalling, and we were running out of time. I had to get to the airport to welcome Secretary Rice. Niyazov could see me sweating—never a good look in any kind of negotiation—and he seemed to be enjoying prolonging the discussion. That is, until I stood up and told him I was going to the airport. Bakiyev would have to work out the statement with the secretary, I said. And good luck to Bakiyev, I thought to myself.

I raced to the airport in half the time it usually took, getting there just as the landing lights of the secretary's plane became visible in the distant sky.

As the secretary deplaned, the Kyrgyz foreign minister and the American commander of the Manas base joined me in greeting her, as did Kyrgyz girls offering bread and salt (a traditional sign of hospitality in the region) and a falcon with his handler (a cultural point of pride in Kyrgyzstan). The secretary stopped to thank the hundreds of U.S. troops assembled to welcome her, and we quickly departed for Bishkek.

First on the agenda, the meeting with the civil society activists — without Bakiyev. As I had expected, the secretary had a great dialogue with them and left the meeting energized, telling me, *The Kyrgyz people deserve to succeed.*

Then on to the meeting with President Bakiyev. The mere presence of the secretary seemed to disarm Bakiyev, who assured us that the base was welcome as long as it was necessary for operations in Afghanistan. I was pleasantly surprised by — if skeptical of — Bakiyev's sudden agreeableness, but not everyone in the room shared my reaction. Bakiyev's staff appeared concerned, probably because he was contradicting the July call for a firm exit date for American troops. They pulled Bakiyev aside to confer privately. But when he came back, he reiterated what he had said before. The two staffs quickly finalized the joint statement in two languages.

As Secretary Rice and Bakiyev were about to announce their agreement to the press, an embassy staffer gave my arm a tug and said that the Kyrgyz had changed their text and that the new language undermined the Kyrgyz commitment to the base. We told Bakiyev, and Bakiyev told his staff to fix it. A few minutes later my staff came back with the same concern about the "revised" version. The secretary confronted Bakiyev, who again ordered the changes made. This time the Kyrgyz text came back right.

There was no possibility that Bakiyev's staff had somehow changed the agreed-upon wording of the statement behind his back, and the episode created a terrible impression that the president was just trying to slip things past us. Later on Secretary Rice turned to me and asked whether Bakiyev wanted her to ever come back — a rhetorical question, but the meaning was clear. If Bakiyev was going to play games, meeting with him was a waste of her time.

At the joint press conference, Rice and Bakiyev announced that the U.S. would have access to the base until the mission of fighting terrorism in Afghanistan was concluded. Secretary Rice used the opportunity to give a shout-out to the democracy activists with whom she had met earlier in the day, emphasizing that our relationship with Kyrgyzstan was much broader than security cooperation and Bakiyev.

In the end we got what we wanted — for the moment — just as the Russians had temporarily gotten what they wanted in July. But I was nonetheless personally disappointed. When you serve in a country, you become invested. I had wanted the Kyrgyz president and his new government to shine in this first encounter with Secretary Rice. Not for the last time, I was disappointed to see that Bakiyev's tendency to play both sides against the middle was stronger than my aspirations for the Kyrgyz people, their country, and their relationship with the United States. For the rest of my time in Bishkek, I would be reminding Bakiyev of his commitments on the base. For all three years the scenario of promises made and promises broken would repeat.

I UNDERSTOOD THAT the base issue was a complicated one for the Kyrgyz, and not just because of Bakiyev's greed. Bakiyev also had to deal with pressure from Russia, which wanted to keep the "near abroad," as the Russians called the other former Soviet republics, in their sphere of influence.

Russia and Kyrgyzstan shared a long history dating back to the pre-1917 Russian empire. After the dissolution of the Soviet Union, Russia was one of Kyrgyzstan's most important trading partners. While I served in Bishkek, approximately one fifth of the Kyrgyz people worked in Russia. By 2008 total remittances, most of which were from Russia, accounted for almost 24 percent of the Kyrgyz GDP. On top of that, the two countries continued to be connected by a web of personal, business, government, and military relationships, including Russia's own military base in the town of Kant. The Kyrgyz relationship with Russia was complicated, multifaceted, and very unequal. Like a number of other former Soviet republics, Kyrgyzstan relied on Russia for so much that it had no obvious path to self-sustainability.

The United States, for its part, wasn't competing for primacy in Kyrgyzstan. We weren't asking Kyrgyzstan to choose between the U.S. and Russia. And we repeatedly assured both the Kyrgyz and the Russians that we didn't want a permanent base in the country. We were committed to supporting Kyrgyzstan's transition to a secure, stable, and democratic state, but Kyrgyzstan was too small and too far away for the U.S. to see it as a location for a permanent military presence or even a significant commercial partner.

But sometimes when you say what you mean, people look for other motivations anyway. What's more, Russia often holds up a mirror to itself and based on that vision makes conclusions about U.S. intentions and actions. With Putin now firmly in control, the Russians had reverted to playing a zero-sum geopolitical game. Putin believed — as did many Russians — that the Soviet Union's demise, the loss of Russia's client Serbia to the NATO-backed Kosovar Albanians in the 1990s, and NATO's expansion eastward in 1999 and 2004 had cost Moscow not only its empire but also its pride.

The Russians didn't like having U.S. military bases in their neighborhood, even if they had agreed to it after the shock of 9/11. They didn't like the successive democratic revolutions in Georgia, Ukraine, and Kyrgyzstan. They found the so-called colored revolutions and our programs supporting civil society profoundly threatening. After all, if democracy started flourishing in a former Soviet republic such as Kyrgyzstan, the Russian people might start getting ideas.

The fact that we had neither interest in nor, frankly, the ability to supplant them in the region didn't seem to matter to the Russians. They still played every card from the old Soviet deck to try to undermine our standing with the Kyrgyz, especially vis-à-vis our continued access to the Manas base.

Disappointingly, Bakiyev let Russia wage this shadow campaign without protest. He probably thought it was in his personal interests even if it was detrimental to the interests of the Kyrgyz people. He may well have thought he had no choice but to acquiesce to Russian manipulation, whether because the Kyrgyz government was still thoroughly penetrated by Russian operatives or because Kyrgyzstan was so economically dependent on Russia, or perhaps because he and his family were on the Russian payroll and the Russians had so much compromising material on him, his dirty dealings, his corrupt family, his Russian wife, and his Kyrgyz mistress. Whatever the reasons, in Kyrgyzstan the Russians operated in a permissive environment, which allowed them to get away with whatever they wanted to in terms of harassing our personnel and undermining our efforts.

Perhaps most damaging, the Russians deployed "political technology," a term widely used in the former Soviet Union and in Russia today to mean manipulating the political process and influencing the outcome of elections. There were many ways to exploit politics and public opinion against the U.S. One of the most effective was also one of the simplest: the Russians would make up something negative about U.S. plans or the actions of a particular embassy employee, spread the falsehood via the media and online, and then watch it get picked up repeatedly until its origins were so obscured that no normal person could be expected to figure out that it was a lie. Some of these lies even got picked up by U.S. outlets: for example, the charge that the U.S. could be storing nuclear weapons at the Manas base.

There were many tools in the Russians' disinformation arsenal, honed and sharpened throughout the Soviet period, and for the most part they were inexpensive, risk-free, completely deniable, and very effective. For instance, sometimes a Russian surrogate would establish a GONGO, an Orwellian acronym for a government-organized nongovernmental organization. Appearing to represent concerned Kyrgyz citizens, the GONGO might call a press conference and level accusations at us originated by the Russians. Sometimes the GONGOs knew they were a Russian front and sometimes they were unwitting dupes, but the cutouts allowed the Russian government to plausibly deny that any of it was their doing.

The Kyrgyz embraced this "technology" as well, both helping to spread Moscow's lies and originating disinformation themselves. The symbiosis was such that it was often hard to discern where Russian action ended and Kyrgyz action began.

The biggest lie that we battled throughout my three years as ambassador was that the U.S. was behind the 2005 Tulip Revolution and that we had masterminded former president Akayev's ouster. It was a crazy assertion, especially if you consider that there was no percentage in sponsoring a revolution in a country where a U.S. military base is located. But the lie persisted despite the complete absence of evidence, and it persists at the time of this writing. To this day Akayev, retired in Moscow, periodically pleases his hosts by accusing the U.S. of launching the revolution that deposed him.

Disinformation campaigns don't need to be internally consistent in order to be effective, and the deployers of the anti-American "technology" also peddled the claim that we were working to depose President Bakiyev, the man the U.S. supposedly installed after we tired of Akayev. We weren't, of course, but the rumors played into Bakiyev's deep insecurities about his hold on power. Those insecurities were on full display when he heard about my meetings with people who did not support him. Just as foreign diplomats in the U.S. meet with Republicans, Democrats, and thought leaders of all stripes, the embassy staff and I met with a wide array of Kyrgyz. Some supported Bakiyev and others did not. Meeting with Kyrgyz of all viewpoints was necessary in order for us to know what people were thinking and to be positioned to protect our interests no matter who was in power. But Bakiyev, like all strongmen, was very sensitive about his status, and he had started confusing his personal interests with Kyrgyzstan's. If we met with any of his critics, he seemed to believe that we were plotting against him — and by extension his country.

I met with Bakiyev frequently to assuage his concerns. But the "technology" fed constant whispers to him about alleged U.S. activities against him, and he always seemed to believe the last person in the room. Sometimes I wished I could staple myself to his side. Bakiyev's suspicion of the U.S. always lingered and often flared. His skepticism of U.S. actions and intentions remained a constant theme in our conversations, just as the base and its future remained a perpetual subject of debate. It felt like a Russian hand was guiding Bakiyev's suspicions, but it was hard to pin down and impossible to fight.

BAKIYEV MAY HAVE committed to Secretary Rice that we would have continued access to the Manas base, but he wasn't giving up his quest to get more money out of the arrangement. The Kyrgyz people weren't happy about the base either, but they had different reasons.

The Manas Air Base and the thousands of coalition service members who cycled through were not popular in Kyrgyzstan, and the Kyrgyz people's concerns weren't entirely without merit. When the base had first opened, some of the troops had behaved in ways the Kyrgyz regarded as disrespectful toward Kyrgyz women. The military had tried to resolve that issue early on by severely limiting time off-base and imposing strict fraternization rules, but a bad taste lingered. The Kyrgyz also complained that our planes dumped excess fuel over the mountains to make landings safer, a practice they believed polluted their water and caused the crops to fail. The air force explained that dumping at high altitude disperses the fuel, but the Kyrgyz remained unconvinced. To make matters more complicated, the Kyrgyz also harbored the fear that the very presence of the base made Kyrgyzstan vulnerable to attack if America's adversary Iran was looking to strike a nearby American asset. But all of those concerns seemed secondary to the real problem for most Kyrgyz: they saw the base as a source of illegitimate profit for the privileged few and of no benefit to the rest of the country.

While the Kyrgyz did have some legitimate concerns, they were also being manipulated. Hard-to-pin-down sources in Russia and Kyrgyzstan planted negative, exaggerated, and sometimes downright false stories in Kyrgyz media. The embassy spent significant time and energy trying to address the criticism, but it was difficult to convince regular Kyrgyz that the base was worth the perceived downsides.

I asked my military counterparts to host a series of open houses, to which we invited everyone from parliamentarians to the press, businesspeople, and nearby villagers. We encouraged them to ask us whatever they wanted about our operations. The base commander and I took a VIP group up in a tanker to observe in-air refueling. I escorted a group of Kyrgyz officials to Afghanistan so they could hear from President Hamid Karzai about how the sixty-nine-country coalition that Kyrgyzstan was participating in and the Manas Air Base contributed to Afghan, Kyrgyz, and regional security interests. But there was only so much impact we could have when public opinion was already against us, and when the country's president wasn't supporting our efforts. Bakiyev seemed to view the base not as a strategic asset in the global war on terror but rather as a bargaining chip in a purely transactional relationship with the United States.

Bakiyev had agreed that the base could remain, but that didn't mean that he wouldn't try to take advantage of the fact that he had something the world's richest country wanted or that he wasn't going to attempt to make us pay for his alleged willingness to stand up to Russian pressure. The domestic political environment fueled by general Kyrgyz dissatisfaction with the base encouraged Bakiyev to play hardball. After Secretary Rice's visit, Kyrgyz appeals for greater base compensation came fast and furious. For months the U.S. told the Kyrgyz that an agreement was already in place — the one that Bakiyev, as prime minister, had negotiated in 2001. Back then Bakiyev had fended off those on the Kyrgyz side who had tried to take advantage of the situation. Now he was the one trying to take advantage, and we would soon find out that no one was standing in his way.

In February 2006, Bakiyev, fresh out of a meeting with Putin, announced that the U.S. and Kyrgyzstan had reached a deal to increase the rent for the base for exponentially more than the $2 million in the existing agreement. In fact no such deal had been struck. In April, Bakiyev tried again, this time issuing a public ultimatum: either the U.S. would pay Kyrgyzstan $200 million or the base was out. From Bakiyev's point of view, there was no downside to this gambit. If it succeeded, Kyrgyzstan would receive more compensation, much of which he undoubtedly planned to pocket for himself.

If it failed, his domestic stature would rise nonetheless as a result of going toe-to-toe with the world's most powerful nation, and he'd get credit from Russia for talking tough to the Americans.

Bakiyev's tactics angered all of us, but at the embassy we realized that the dynamics had changed. The U.S. couldn't continue to stonewall; we had been doing so since before I had arrived in Kyrgyzstan, and that string had run out. The U.S. needed to respond or be prepared to lose the base. The Department of Defense later reached the same conclusion, and in the spring it officially agreed to revisit the question of compensation for the base.

But we still had a problem. Bakiyev was dug in deep with a very public demand for $200 million in cold cash, while Secretary of Defense Donald Rumsfeld wasn't willing to pay anything approaching that king's ransom for base access. It was an epic culture clash. Bakiyev saw a rich country that he believed had the money to pay big for something he thought was essential to its war effort. The U.S. saw Manas as a symbol of the U.S.-Kyrgyz partnership and thought that both parties benefited from the base's continued operation. We believed that Kyrgyzstan had a stake in ejecting terrorists from its neighborhood and that providing the base — for which we paid fair compensation — was Kyrgyzstan's contribution to that war effort

At the embassy we started strategizing on how we could help bridge the divide between the Kyrygz and U.S. positions, and we established a small team focused on the base negotiation, composed of DCM Don Lu, Defense Attaché Tom Plumb, and political officer Liam O'Connell. One thing became clear right away: whatever final number Rumsfeld landed on for the rent payment, it was going to appear so humiliatingly far away from Bakiyev's demand of $200 million that presenting it to Bakiyev as our counteroffer would risk sending the Kyrgyz leader straight into Putin's arms to announce that the base was closing. We needed to figure out a way to dress up our proposal.

At the same time, it seemed to me that Bakiyev had mistaken an "important" base for an "indispensable" base. He didn't seem to understand that although the Pentagon wanted to keep the base, the U.S. military always has other options; no doubt it would be disruptive, but we could walk away from the Manas Air Base if we needed to.

But even if the military could move on, I didn't want to see that happen for broader reasons. I worried that if we closed the base, U.S. interest in Kyrgyzstan would decline, and what progress Kyrgyzstan had made in developing an active civil society, in encouraging the kind of reform that would make the country a better partner for the U.S., and in being a willing participant the next time we called on it could be jeopardized. Even worse for both us and the Kyrgyz, Kyrgyzstan would be left to Russia's not-so-tender mercies. These negotiations had to succeed.

We needed some creative thinking about how to close the gap between the two sides. I had been stumped, but luckily for me, more innovative minds were at work. Don and Liam suggested that we redefine the terms of the negotiation and frame our offer in the context of the totality of the U.S.-Kyrgyz relationship. After all, there was so much more to the bilateral relationship than the monetary compensation we gave the Kyrgyz for use of the base, which was Bakiyev's fixation. We had a large assistance program that added up to about $43.5 million a year; the U.S. government was one of the country's biggest employers; and we pumped a huge amount of money into the local economy through the goods, fuel, and services purchased by the embassy and the base. In all, they calculated that the U.S. had infused over $150 million into Kyrgyzstan every year for the past several years — much of which would be lost if we vacated the Manas base. That number, plus a modest increase in our rent, would bring us close enough to $200 million that it might prove a face-saving way for Bakiyev to climb down from his untenable opening position. The idea was far from perfect, but it was the best one out there. I asked Don and Liam to fine-tune their thoughts, and then we reached out to the base negotiator, Jim MacDougall, DoD's top official for Eurasia policy, in the hope that he would see the wisdom of this gambit too.

There can sometimes be a difference in how diplomats at the embassy and our Defense Department colleagues from Washington view a situation. At the embassy we were responsible for the full breadth of the bilateral relationship. We lived and worked in Kyrgyzstan and met with Kyrgyz from all walks of life. The DoD negotiators, in contrast, were responsible solely for the military equities — in this case, the base agreement — and they flew in for a couple of days for the negotiations. It fell to the embassy team to help Kyrgyz and DoD negotiators better understand each other's positions as well as the environment in each country. That didn't always make us popular with either.

But Jim was an experienced regional hand and a great partner. He had an understanding of the headwinds blowing against the base and agreed that under the circumstances, Don and Liam's suggested approach was the best available to us. So when Jim came to Bishkek at the end of May 2006 for an initial, informal round of discussions, we presented the proposal to the Kyrgyz.

Bakiyev had appointed as his negotiator National Security Advisor Niyazov, the same official who had resisted finalizing the joint statement in the hours before Secretary Rice's visit. Over a day and a half, Jim and I and our small team from the embassy met with Niyazov and his staff in his office in the presidential office building. Not surprisingly, the Kyrgyz weren't thrilled by our presentation. It wasn't at all what Bakiyev had in mind, and I could almost see the gears going in Niyazov's mind. He must have been wondering how he would explain this to his mercurial president. But we persevered, explaining that Bakiyev's maximalist position was a nonstarter and that our proposal would provide Bakiyev with a reasonable deal, more rent for the base, and a face-saving way to sell the result to his people.

Bakiyev wasn't in the room, but his was the only opinion that counted. He didn't make it easy for us — or for Niyazov. True to character, Bakiyev would insist on a point only to rescind it, leaving Niyazov flat-footed and guessing what the boss wanted. But eventually, after a lot of shuttling between his own office and Bakiyev's, Niyazov reported that Bakiyev was interested in continuing the conversation under our proposed framework.

We had made more progress than I had expected, and as Jim headed back to Washington we agreed to reconvene for a formal second round of negotiations in July. At the embassy we continued to tweak the presentation. But as often happened in the post-Soviet world, an unrelated crisis was developing that in time threatened to upend our hard work and progress on the negotiations.

IN APRIL 2006 a GONGO no one had ever heard of held a press conference to denounce one of our political officers, William Hodges, accusing him of funneling money to Kyrgyz NGOs to overthrow the Bakiyev government. The false charges were concerning enough, but it was the kind of accusation we had become used to in the former Soviet Union and knew how to handle.

Far more unusual — and worrisome — was an article that came out in late May alleging that William had trained commandos to kill the crime boss Rysbek, whose paid demonstrators had shut Bishkek down the previous year. Rysbek had been assassinated earlier that month while running for a parliamentary seat. He had until the end remained at the nexus of Kyrgyz crime, corruption, and politics, and we had no way of knowing whether his followers would believe the ludicrous story about William and try to retaliate. The head of embassy security was so concerned that he recommended that William curtail his assignment in Bishkek and return to the U.S. But I didn't think we should give in to the "technology." I worried that if we caved to these tactics, we'd never see an end to this kind of harassment. So we wrapped William and his family in a 24/7 security bubble, going so far as to drive his three-year-old daughter to her ballet class in an armored Suburban. However upsetting for all involved, especially William's family, we found the situation manageable, at least for the time being. Then, on the eve of the second round of base negotiations in July, Bakiyev escalated.

We didn't know whether Kyrgyzstan, Russia, or rogue elements in one or both governments were behind the original disinformation campaign against William, but Bakiyev took advantage of the audacious work of fiction to set the embassy on its heels and distract us from focusing on the negotiations. Foreign Minister Alikbek Jekshenkulov called me in and nervously announced that Kyrgyzstan was declaring William Hodges persona non grata — diplo-speak for "we're kicking him out of the country." For good measure, the Kyrgyz were also PNGing Liam O'Connell, who was integral to our base negotiation team and whose name had not previously been associated with the anti-Bakiyev or Rysbek rumors. The charges against both officers were completely unfounded, but I didn't think it was a coincidence that the Kyrgyz had improperly thrown a red card at William and Liam just as the negotiation was getting underway. But I had to remind myself that if this was a game, it wasn't polo, football, or even rugby — the Kyrgyz were playing kok-boru, the game with no easily discernible rules.

Jekshenkulov falsely claimed that our two officers had engaged in activities not in keeping with their diplomatic status, which in plain English meant "they're spying." In fact William and Liam had simply been doing what all political officers all over the world do: openly meeting with all elements of Kyrgyz government and society and reporting back, so that Washington policymakers would have a good understanding of the country.

Jekshenkulov trotted out the same old lies about the U.S. undermining the government and paying the opposition. He didn't go so far as to bring up the Rysbek rumor — that would have been hard for even Bakiyev's people to push with a straight face — but he did come up with a new tall tale, accusing our officers of sneaking into saunas and taking photos of Kyrgyz leaders frolicking with young ladies.

This allegation too was absurd. Our political officers weren't in the business of trying to compromise their counterparts, but since Jekshenkulov had left the realm of diplomatic niceties, I saw no reason not to do the same: I asked whether that was what Kyrgyz leaders were up to — frolicking with young ladies in saunas. That sent Jekshenkulov into orbit, a place he often inhabited. When he landed, I told him that Kyrgyzstan had made a grave mistake — the U.S. was not going to accept this. William and Liam had done nothing improper, and I was furious that the Kyrgyz government would make such accusations. I needed to see Bakiyev immediately.

While waiting for Bakiyev's response, I drove back to the embassy so I could consult with Washington. I was fuming. The Kyrgyz move was extraordinary, completely out of bounds. Countries almost never PNG each other's diplomats — not without firm evidence of wrongdoing and not when the country is the recipient of millions of dollars in assistance from the other country. I didn't think it was likely that little Kyrgyzstan would have overstepped normal diplomatic practice without some active coaching from the Russians. Nor did I think the timing was an accident. I told my bosses in Washington that if the U.S. didn't fight back, our embassy in Bishkek would face endless bullying and risk losing its effectiveness. I also told them that I thought I could get Bakiyev to reverse the PNG decision, but only if we were steadfast.

The State Department backed me to the hilt. Senior officials in Washington called the Kyrygz ambassador into Foggy Bottom for a "full and frank discussion," as we say in diplomatic circles. The ambassador quickly reported to Bakiyev that the PNGs would cause a rift in relations. I met with Bakiyev to stress the same point and had a series of late-night meetings with his top officials as well. Bakiyev was taken aback by our refusal to accept his decision, and as he always did, he wavered. I thought I could bring him around.

As we tried to work through the diplomatic standoff, the pressure on William, Liam, and their young families was real and continuing. The Kyrgyz security service was monitoring their homes and their movements — something our officers could handle but which was a strain on the families. I made the decision that all of them needed to leave — temporarily, I hoped

— to lower the tension. On their last day in Bishkek, I received a call saying that Bakiyev had agreed to let the two officers and their families remain in Kyrgyzstan. Given the strain on the families, we didn't want to cancel their travel plans just as they were about to leave, although I knew that once they left the country, the Kyrgyz might not allow them to return. It was a gamble, but under the circumstances I didn't think there was another option.

Just in case this was a final farewell, DCM Don Lu threw the two officers and their families a big blowout party. I went to the airport at 1 a.m. to see them off with bottles of champagne. I wanted the Kyrgyz security service to report that our folks were flying out in style, heads held high.

The formal second round of negotiations on the Manas Air Base agreement began later that morning. I hoped that all the work we had put in over the past few months was about to pay off.

THE JULY NEGOTIATIONS took place at the Kyrygz Ministry of Defense in a large conference room that was both sunny and antiseptic. In contrast to the small-group configuration of the first round, it seemed that every ministry and department had sent a representative to this one. It was standing room only. The lead negotiators — Jim and Niyazov — sat with their closest advisors at a long table, backed up by experts perched on rows of chairs lining the walls and ready to provide additional information or whisper advice.

The meeting opened, and each side presented more polished versions of the same proposals we had discussed in May. The Kyrgyz highlighted a long list of grievances and demands that the U.S. make them right, while we showcased the comprehensive approach that Don and Liam had conceived. Although Niyazov (and Bakiyev, who was monitoring the negotiations from his office) knew our position and much of what we were going to say, Bakiyev was so unpredictable that it was hard to know how he would react to the $17.4 million that DoD announced it was ready to pay for rent. Would he accept the almost ninefold increase in rent payments, even though it was very far from the hundredfold increase he had been seeking? Would he instruct his team to haggle as if we were in a Central Asian bazaar, even though our team told them up front that it was a take-it-or-leave-it offer and we had no mandate to increase our offer? Or would he instruct them to do something dramatic and counterproductive?

The volatility of the situation made me nervous, but this was one time

when Bakiyev defied my expectations for the better. The negotiations concluded successfully on July 13 with no surprises, and the following day Jim
and Niyazov signed a protocol formalizing the agreement. The day after the
negotiations wrapped up, I received the news that Bakiyev had once again
changed his mind and decided that the PNG decision would be reinstated.
This time it proved final.

The hurried middle-of-the-night departure of the Hodgeses and O'Connells had been their last goodbye to Kyrgyzstan. The impact on these families was profound: they had planned to spend a full tour in Bishkek but now
found themselves unexpectedly back in the U.S., where they had to quickly
figure out where they would live, what work assignments were available to
them, what schools their kids would attend, and where their spouses would
find employment. With the rushed departure, most of their belongings
were still in Bishkek. Strangers had to pack them out. But I had the honor
of returning the most valuable cargo. Three months later I accompanied
the O'Connells' cat back to the U.S. for a happy reunion with the children.

MANAS BASE ISSUES took up more of my three years in Bishkek than everything else I worked on combined, but my heart was drawn elsewhere:
to supporting the courageous Kyrgyz who were trying to transform their
country into a flourishing democracy. I wanted to help them make the most
of our large assistance program, which focused on transforming opaque
and frequently unaccountable institutions — everything from the legislature to the judiciary to the tax system — into ones that served Kyrgyz citizens according to the rule of law. We funded programs to teach parliamentarians how to make sure the public had access to their decisions and
proceedings and to help local governments improve service delivery. We
brought judicial experts from the U.S. to teach Kyrgyz jurists how to instill trust by adhering to clear rules and meting out impartial justice. And
we worked with Kyrgyz election authorities to improve the organization of
elections. It was exciting — and important.

I was especially invested in the programs that we developed to support
Kyrgyz women. Every country needs the full economic potential of its entire population, not just the male half, but traditional societies frequently
don't focus on developing the talents of women and girls. Our goal wasn't
to change gender relations in Kyrgyzstan but to help the Kyrgyz take small
steps toward bettering the lives of the women who lived there. We part-

nered with the American University of Central Asia to get professional Kyrgyz women to serve as mentors for roughly seventy-five female students. Some of the mentorships were wildly successful and others atrophied after a single meeting, just like in the U.S. We eventually built out the program with three regional universities. At a meeting a year later, one of the young students fervently thanked us for organizing the opportunity and told us that the students could assume leadership of the program themselves. I wanted to stand up and cheer. In the assistance field, working yourself out of a job is the ultimate success story. I was proud — proud of the young women and proud of our staff who had made this happen.

I hoped that my presence and the example of Zamira Sydykova, the Kyrgyz ambassador to the U.S., could encourage young women in their aspirations. Surprisingly, I was the third woman the U.S. had sent to Kyrgyzstan as ambassador during the country's fourteen-year existence. On the one hand, that was probably some sort of record, and I was grateful to be in that number. On the other hand, I uncharitably attributed it to Washington's desire to pump up the anemic numbers of female ambassadors while not sending us to the "big" countries. But the important things to me were that the Kyrgyz accepted me and that I could make a difference. Even though I was probably the first female ambassador most of my American staff had worked for — my two immediate predecessors were men — it didn't seem to be an issue for them either.

Every once in a while, though, something would come up that reminded me that the United States, like Kyrgyzstan, still had a way to go. Within weeks of my arrival, I was preparing to do my first TV interview, a coming-out of sorts that would introduce me to the Kyrgyz people. We were filming it at my home for a personal touch. When I arrived, everything was set up and the press team — all male — thought they had a great plan: the first footage would be me coming down the staircase with a plate of cookies to offer the reporter.

Seriously? The U.S. ambassador as Betty Crocker?

I couldn't believe it. Inarticulate with anger when presented with the idea, I was literally unable to explain to the press attaché in charge why I couldn't do this. I said I needed a break and went upstairs to collect myself.

A timid knock on my door a few minutes later alerted me that time was up. I went downstairs. We did away with the cookies. I did the interview.

Afterward I tried to explain to the head of the press team why this had been such a bad idea. I asked him whether he would ever have suggested that my male predecessor descend a grand stairway with a plate of cookies. He looked puzzled and replied, "Of course not." Exactly, I said. I thought I had made everything clear. It turned out I hadn't. His wife did that night. The following morning this good man came in and said his wife told him he needed to apologize. I think for both of us it was a lesson in what it's like to be in someone else's skin.

SIMILARLY, THE KYRYGZ soon knew what it was like to be in our skin when they PNGd our two diplomats. In diplomacy, reciprocity is a bedrock principle, which is why in August 2006 the U.S. PNGd two Kyrgyz diplomats. I hoped that with this necessary action behind us and the renegotiated base agreement in place, we would be able to get the bilateral relationship back on track.

But my hope was short-lived. Although framing the base payments to take account of our large assistance package and the many contributions of the base to the Kyrgyz economy enabled us to get to yes with Bakiyev, the Kyrgyz people were left disappointed by the deal. Bakiyev's bluster had led them to expect an additional infusion of $150 million into public coffers. When that didn't happen, they thought Bakiyev had stolen it. When more of the details became public, the Kyrgyz people just felt deceived — by Bakiyev, but also by the U.S.

Then a series of unfortunate events occurred in quick succession that decisively galvanized Kyrygz opinion against the base. First, in early September, U.S. Air Force Major Jill Metzger vanished while shopping in downtown Bishkek. Needless to say, the disappearance of an American service member during the height of the war in Afghanistan raised alarms right up to the secretary of defense. I told the Kyrgyz leadership that no stone could be left unturned in the search for Major Metzger, and I went on Kyrgyz television to make an appeal in Russian for any information as to her whereabouts. Embassy and Manas base security officers pushed Kyrgyz law enforcement hard, which led the Kyrgyz to feel disrespected by what they felt was a heavy-handed U.S. approach that did not respect their sovereignty. Thankfully, Metzger reappeared four very long days later, reporting that she had escaped from her kidnappers. Despite the best efforts by the air force, the FBI, and Kyrgyz investigators, her captors were never found, and the hard feelings engendered by the incident among the Kyrgyz far outlasted the disappearance itself.

Just a few weeks later a Kyrgyz passenger jet taking off from Manas airport struck one of our KC-135 refueling planes, which had just landed. Thankfully, no one was killed or seriously injured, but both planes were damaged. Even worse, the Kyrgyz plane turned out to be the one that President Bakiyev used for his long-haul trips — his Air Force One — making it a very personal issue for the president.

Under the terms of the base deal, both sides had agreed to self-insure for accidents like this one, but the Kyrgyz sent us a bill anyway. The U.S. Air Force declined to pay, and so this accident became another one of the many irritants surrounding the base, even after an investigation found that Kyrgyz air traffic control bore primary responsibility. Bakiyev refused to let the issue go, and it took months of effort on the embassy's part to convince the Defense Department that it was best to provide the Kyrgyz with some financial compensation so that Bakiyev could claim victory and we could put the issue behind us.

The third incident, a terrible tragedy, happened one evening in early December 2006. An American airman named Zachary Hatfield fatally shot a Kyrgyz truck driver who was delivering fuel to the base. Hatfield claimed that he had seen the driver, Aleksandr Ivanov, pull a knife. The public outcry in Kyrgyzstan was immediate and ferocious. Ivanov was a local family man and well respected. No Kyrgyz believed that he had been armed and threatening the airman.

By seven the next morning I was at the base to be briefed and to walk the gate area where Ivanov had been shot. My visit was cut short by a message from Bakiyev, demanding that I come to his office along with the base commander, Colonel Joel Reese. I wanted to ensure a serious discussion about this tragedy, not a public spectacle, and I wanted to be as precise as possible in what would surely be a difficult meeting. So my office called ahead to be sure that there would be no press and that the embassy interpreter could attend. We got agreement on both counts.

But when the base commander and I got to the presidential offices, Kyrgyz aides barred our interpreter from entering and ushered us into a meeting room where a television crew was already in place. Bakiyev swept in and proceeded to lambast us for twenty minutes or so with the camera right in our faces. He then allowed me to express our condolences. It was an impossible situation. Bakiyev felt he had to be seen to be defending his citizens, and he was going to accomplish that by making demands and dressing us down on national TV. I understood what he was doing, but he was treating us like pawns for his ratings rather than as partners who would do whatever we could to make it right.

I knew this was going to be a supercharged issue for a very long time, but it was also on the verge of becoming a complete circus. Before that happened, I wanted to reach out to Ivanov's family and express my condolences personally rather than over the airwaves. Accompanied by Colonel Reese, I went to the wake at the Ivanovs' modest apartment. When I introduced myself to Mrs. Ivanova, she appeared shocked that we had come. She hugged me, and for that one moment and only that moment we were just two women, one in deep grief and the other trying to console her. She showed us where Ivanov lay in an open coffin, and Colonel Reese and I each placed two white carnations in the coffin, as is customary in the Russian Orthodox tradition. It was gut-wrenching.

The Kyrgyz government quickly issued a raft of demands: they wanted to conduct a joint investigation, they demanded that we turn Hatfield over to Kyrgyz justice, they wanted compensation for the family, they wanted assurances that this wouldn't happen again. It was completely understandable, but other than reviewing and changing the gate protocols to prevent another incident, it didn't seem doable. Under the base agreement — and U.S. practice — the U.S. military alone investigated and prosecuted its people. On the compensation issue, which I had thought would be straightforward, I learned that the Defense Department paid the kind of compensation Kyrgyzstan was seeking for the death of civilians only in certain countries, presumably places where active war zones make such incidents more common. Kyrgyzstan wasn't on the list. That meant the air force had no authority to give Mrs. Ivanova the compensation Kyrgyzstan was demanding.

I was stuck trying to find common ground between the U.S. military, which was adhering to the rules, and a Kyrgyz government and public that believed we did not value Kyrgyz lives. Unable to give the Kyrgyz what they wanted, I told the military that we needed to do whatever we could — to share as much information as possible, include the Kyrgyz in as much of the investigation as possible, and find a way to offer some compensation to Ivanov's widow. In the interim, embassy staff organized a collection for

Mrs. Ivanova, to which a number of base personnel contributed as well. We were able to quickly give her $1000 out of our own pockets, but, unsurprisingly, it did not quell her anger, and the court of public opinion was firmly on her side.

As with the damaged plane, it took months to move forward on compensation for Mrs. Ivanova. An enormous bureaucracy engaged on the American side: the base, the U.S. Air Force, the Office of the Secretary of Defense, U.S. Central Command, the State Department, the embassy — the list went on, but the Department of Defense stuck to its position that it couldn't compensate Mrs. Ivanova because Kyrgyzstan didn't appear on the list of countries where that was authorized. When I asked how to get Kyrgyzstan on the list, I was told there was no procedure.

It was a maddening catch-22, and as the months passed, the Kyrgyz were getting angrier by the minute. We were the only superpower left, and yet we couldn't seem to cut through the red tape to make a simple humanitarian gesture. Even more concerning, the rumblings about canceling the base agreement were resurfacing, not even a year after we had renegotiated it. For a very long time the Ivanov issue came up in every Kyrgyz meeting, whether with the government, civil society, or the press. The failure to offer compensation was damaging the standing of the base, and more broadly the U.S. I started looking into whether the chronically underfunded State Department could identify discretionary funds to provide compensation, even though this should have been in DoD's purview to fix.

I was relieved when the military unexpectedly ponied up a payment of $55,000 for Mrs. Ivanova in 2007, although to the Kyrgyz it proved that there had been a path to a payment all along and the U.S. just hadn't wanted to find it. But to my frustration, the matter wasn't finally resolved until the summer of 2009, three years after Mr. Ivanov's death and a year after I had left Kyrgyzstan. The U.S. military decided to give Mrs. Ivanova an additional $250,000 — at the same time as they informed the Kyrgyz government that they had dismissed the criminal charge against Hatfield. From a Kyrgyz point of view, the good news didn't cancel out the bad. In a country where people already thought the U.S. military was overstaying its welcome, the large sum came too late to change the ingrained impression that the U.S. did not respect Kyrgyz life. The tragedy badly damaged our interests in Kyrgyzstan, including our military interests.

This was all taking place against the backdrop of an increasingly resur-

gent Russia, ready to exploit any American misstep to get us out of Kyrgyzstan. In February 2007, in an address to the Munich Security Conference,
Putin listed a litany of Western sins and declared that "the U.S. was overstepping its borders in all spheres." The U.S. was taken aback, but at the
time, overwhelmed by the war on terrorism, we did not fully understand
Putin's words as the threat they turned out to be.

PUTIN AND HIS inner circle were growing more and more determined to
evict the United States from the region. Once again Putin was pulling out
the old KGB playbook to plot his next move. And once again he was finding that one of the easiest methods was to corrupt other politicians in the
neighborhood.

In late 2005 the Kremlin reached out to Kyrgyzstan's fellow former Soviet republic Ukraine with a deal regarding the country's gas supplies. If
Ukraine agreed to use an intermediary, RosUkrEnergo, a company half
owned by Ukrainian oligarch Dmytro Firtash, then Russia would continue
to send Ukraine gas at a preferred price. Usually sovereign governments
don't utilize intermediaries, since they serve no function, but if Ukraine did
not agree, the price would steeply rise and highly placed government insiders in both Ukraine and Russia would lose the eye-popping kickbacks they
were sure to glean from the $2 billion-per-year profit that the deal would
pull in for each government. To underscore the point, on New Year's Day
2006, during a very cold winter, the Russians turned off the gas.

Yushchenko quickly acquiesced and never looked back. From Moscow's viewpoint, the RosUkrEnergo deal must have seemed like an excellent investment, especially since Yushchenko's rival — Kremlin favorite Yanukovych — was installed as prime minister seven months later. Beyond
the corrupt gas deal, reforms stalled, as did integration with the European
Union and NATO. Just like that, the promise of the Orange Revolution died.

The broad outlines of that gas agreement were public knowledge at the
time, and it made me wonder whether the Russians were doing something
similar in Kyrgzstan. Despite a Russian ban on the export of fuel for other
nations' military use, as far as anyone could tell, Russia was the only country in the region that could supply the large quantities of fuel required for
Operation Enduring Freedom. The U.S. military was buying fuel through
contractors, and it was widely suspected that the contracts were held by private companies that were controlled by or at least working with the family

of the Kyrgyz president: first Akayev, then Bakiyev. So it appeared that the Russians therefore controlled the profits going to the Bakiyev family.

That was troubling enough. Even more troubling was the fact that if this was truly where our contractors were getting the fuel, then the Russians could turn off the fuel supply for Operation Enduring Freedom at a moment's notice, just as they had done in Ukraine.

Given the business climate in Bakiyev's Kyrgyzstan, it's not surprising that allegations of fraud, corruption, and self-enrichment abounded. Many of these allegations were directed at us. To the average Kyrgyz, it looked like the U.S. was actively enabling the Bakiyev family to corruptly profit from a base most Kyrgyz didn't even want in their country — when that is exactly what the Russians were doing.

I tried to raise a flag about the fuel contracts, which were the subject of so much Kyrgyz speculation. Were we exercising due diligence regarding our partners and their fuel sources? Was there real competition for these enormous contracts? Were we paying a corruption tax? But when I raised the issue, I was told that "the sanctity of the procurement process" made it inappropriate to ask these kinds of questions. I'm not sure why I accepted that brushoff, except that this was my rookie ambassadorship and I had plenty of other issues to deal with.

I should have kept on pushing. In 2010, two years after I departed, the second Kyrgyz revolution deposed Bakiyev, and a new president came in with an agenda to get rid of the base. Later that year the House of Representatives issued a scathing staff report that roundly criticized the Department of Defense and the State Department and found that "real and perceived corruption in the fuel contracts has now been linked to two revolutions and seriously strained U.S.-Kyrgyz relations."

There was lots of blame to go around, and when I read the report I regretted that I hadn't followed my instincts. Like a three-legged stool, good governance, prosperity, and security reinforce each other. However, in Kyrgyzstan we consistently prioritized our security interests over all others, which had the effect of undermining all our interests. This included our security interests: Bakiyev's successor ultimately closed the Manas Air Base in 2014.

As I had seen in Somalia so many years earlier, we had mistakenly believed that winking at a corrupt leader would strengthen our national security. It worked for a while, but in neither place did it create the stable partnership necessary to secure our interests over the long term. Moreover, in Kyrygzstan it created an opening for greater Russian influence and the undermining of democracy, as the Bakiyev dynasty used its ill-gotten gains to rig elections, buy off the opposition, and intimidate and undermine civil society.

BY THE TIME my tour ended in the summer of 2008, I was ready to leave. Despite the challenges, concerns, and disappointments, I was proud of the supporting role that I had played in the War on Terror and of the progress we helped the Kyrgyz make on the margins on rule-of-law and civil society issues. But three years is a long time to try to work with a leader like Bakiyev. His unapologetic greed in one of the world's poorest countries was nothing short of unforgivable to me. I had come to regard him as an unprincipled buffoon, a prodigious drinker, a man so weak he couldn't keep his word to the U.S. or Russia, or even to his own people.

My view was validated when Secretary of Defense Robert Gates, Rumsfeld's successor, visited Kyrgyzstan. He said that his meeting with Bakiyev was the worst he had ever had with a head of state in his decades of meeting with international leaders. In a part of the world famed for its hospitality, Gates noted the insult of not even being offered a cup of tea. If someone with Gates's experience had that reaction, even this overthinker couldn't blame herself for some of the challenges we faced in Bakiyev's Kyrgyzstan.

I was ready for a change of pace, but I was deeply ambivalent about the new posting that had appeared on the horizon. While still in Bishkek, I had been approached about going to the Republic of Armenia after the Kyrgyz posting ended. I was honored by the relatively rare prospect of a second ambassadorship, and normally such an offer would have given me cause to pop a champagne cork. But this one was far too complicated to warrant such a quick celebration.

8

Armenia

THERE WERE NO ILLUSIONS at the State Department about the U.S. ambassadorship to Armenia. Everyone knew that it was a demanding position. If that hadn't been clear before the previous ambassador's exit, it certainly was by the time I was asked if I would be willing to replace him.

Ambassador John Evans had left his post as U.S. ambassador to Armenia in September 2006, after deliberately breaking with Bush administration policy and publicly using the word "genocide" to describe the Ottoman Empire's massacre and deportation of one and a half million Armenians. Although this tragedy had occurred nearly a century earlier, the issue of whether to call it genocide had in recent years become a challenging domestic and foreign policy issue for the United States. On one side, the Armenian-American community was organized and united in demanding that the U.S. use the word "genocide." On the other, Turkey, successor state to the Ottoman Empire and a NATO ally, not only denied the historical facts but also feared that the U.S. classifying the events as genocide could bolster Armenian hopes for reparations.

Turkey had long made clear to the U.S. that our bilateral relationship, including our very important military partnership, would suffer great damage if we uttered the word "genocide" when describing the atrocities. From the first President Bush on, successive Republican and Democratic presidents had made a purely realpolitik call and deferred to Turkey, concluding that the value of our geostrategic alliance with that country outweighed accommodating the aspirations of the small Armenian-American community. It's not that U.S. administrations denied the facts; each one issued a statement commemorating Armenian Remembrance Day that recalled the tragic events, memorialized those lost, and pledged to support modern Ar-

menia. But every April, to the despair of the Armenian-American community, the U.S. proclamation had accommodated Turkey by avoiding the
term "genocide."

In February 2005, Ambassador Evans, without consulting Washington,
decided to buck U.S. policy and use the word during public meetings in the
U.S. with Armenian-American groups. Understandably, the diaspora was
not just gratified but encouraged and energized. So when Evans departed
from his post early and retired as a result of the uproar, one of the diaspora
groups urged its allies in the Senate, which confirms all ambassadorial appointments, to put a hold on any proposed replacement for Evans unless
administration policy changed.

A number of people in the State Department supported a policy change,
but the decision about using the term "genocide" was reached at the highest
levels of the White House. There can be only one foreign policy: the president's. No one was going to be nominated who didn't agree to put aside personal views and follow the official policy once the decision was made.

To replace Evans, President Bush named Dick Hoagland, a capable and
qualified career Foreign Service officer who was then serving as ambassador to Tajikistan. As all American ambassadors must, Dick did his job and
upheld the president's policies during the confirmation process. As a result,
Senator Bob Menendez blocked the vote to confirm Dick as ambassador in
an attempt to pressure the Bush administration to change its mind on the
genocide issue. Dick was dragged through the mud and excoriated for declining to repudiate a policy over which he had no control. His nomination
languished for more than a year, the policy didn't change, and Armenia remained without a U.S. ambassador. It wasn't clear to me, watching from
afar, how any of this helped Armenia — or the U.S. Eventually the administration decided that it had no choice but to withdraw Dick's nomination.

Then the State Department asked me whether I would be willing to put
my head in the lion's mouth.

IT WAS PAINFUL not to jump at the opportunity to represent the United
States as its top diplomat in Armenia. In many respects this posting would
be right in my wheelhouse. Armenia was a former Soviet republic, and the
main job of the U.S. ambassador there would be to do just what I had done
in Russia, Ukraine, and Kyrgyzstan: support the country's ongoing transition to a rule-of-law democracy with a market economy. But if I accepted

the offer, I would have to do just what Dick had done: acknowledge all the facts of the ethnic cleansing at what was likely to be a difficult confirmation hearing while refusing the senators' inevitable admonitions to call the events genocide. If I was confirmed, I would have no choice but to hew to that script every time an Armenian-American challenged me on the policy.

I didn't want to put myself in this position. It was clear to me that the Ottoman Turks *had* committed genocide, and I didn't relish the notion of not characterizing it as such. What's more, given my own very different but still painful family history, I understood why Armenian-Americans wanted the tragedy that had befallen their parents and grandparents to be recognized for what it was. And I certainly didn't want to be attacked the way Dick had been.

Somewhat melodramatically, I told Assistant Secretary of State Dan Fried that the department was offering me a poisoned chalice. But even as I said it, I could feel the tug of duty. The chief-of-mission position at our embassy in Yerevan, the Armenian capital, had by that point been vacant for a year, although the very capable deputy chief of mission, Joseph Pennington, was standing in as chargé. But someone had to take up the ambassadorial position, and I had long experience in the region and had been confirmed by the Senate relatively recently. Dan assured me that he would work with the diaspora to try to repair the relationship and do his best to ensure that my confirmation process would be less vitriolic than the one Dick had endured.

I told myself that I could do this — that I could follow our policy of not using the word "genocide" even if I thought the description accurate. It wasn't my call whether our strategic interests in Turkey justified not verbalizing our values on a horrific tragedy that had occurred one hundred years ago. This was the president's call, and as a career and nonpartisan Foreign Service officer, I was obligated to implement it.

That's not to say that I would have blindly implemented any policy; I had an obligation to my conscience and the Constitution. If an issue was so antithetical to both that I couldn't work within the system to change it, then I would have to resign. But I concluded that this didn't reach that level. I agreed that Turkey needed to come to terms with the Ottomans' actions and that the U.S. should help in that reconciliation process, but there was nothing we could do to change the past. Leaving the post vacant — the inevitable result if no one agreed to take the position — would change nothing; it would just deprive Armenia and the U.S. of high-level representation there.

After a lot of soul-searching, I decided to accept the nomination. I told myself I could make a positive contribution in Armenia and advance our interests in the region. The bottom line for me, as for all of us in the Foreign Service, was this: when your country calls you, you go.

THE SENATE HEARING room was packed on June 19, 2008, when four colleagues and I took our seats for our joint confirmation hearing. The other ambassadorial nominees were up for postings in Kosovo, Macedonia, Moldova, and Russia, countries where lots was going on. But the audience was there for me. They wore buttons that read "End the Gag Rule," meant to shame the administration into letting me say the word "genocide." Diaspora groups had bused in so many Armenian-Americans that spectators had to rotate out of the hearing room periodically to give everyone a chance to attend.

As is the custom, my family accompanied me to the hearing. Usually these are occasions when your family can bask in the glow of your accomplishments, but I didn't think that was going to be the case this time. I had told Mama and André to expect anything and to keep quiet. But Mama was irrepressible — and slightly deaf. When she saw all the buttons, she asked loudly what they said. When I whispered an explanation, Mama couldn't catch it and more loudly asked again. I was praying she wouldn't ask for a button. The hearing hadn't even started yet, and it wasn't going well.

I had asked former Senate majority leader Bob Dole to introduce me to the Senate panel. I had met him when he had visited Kyrgyzstan, and I knew his backing would be meaningful to the Armenian-American community, with whom he had long-standing ties. He more than delivered, giving me a blush-inducing endorsement before the crowded hearing room. I appreciated as well his admonition to the senators to focus on Armenia's present challenges and not to fixate on the past.

One other, perhaps even more important person was there to support my nomination: Tatoul Markaryan, the Armenian ambassador to the U.S. He had a nonspeaking role, but his presence spoke volumes, underlining the point that the government of Armenia wanted a U.S. ambassador in Yerevan. Behind the scenes Markaryan quietly made that clear to the diaspora — and to the senators.

After we were all introduced, each nominee gave an opening statement. In mine, I referred to the atrocities that began in 1915 as the Medz Yeghern, the term Armenians use to describe the genocide and which roughly translates as "the Great Calamity." Saying that had required permission from the White House, because it pushed the envelope. But the Bush administration had okayed that language, and I hoped that it would be welcomed by the community.

Then the questions started. More of the hearing time was devoted to grilling me about the genocide issue than was used to question any other nominee. I received only one question that wasn't about the genocide, despite the fact that, as Senator Dole had pointed out, Armenia had a host of pressing problems, as did the countries my colleagues would be going to. Senator Menendez, a former prosecutor, interrogated me as though we were in a courtroom. Wanting to show their constituents that they were on the case, he and six other senators who later submitted similar questions in writing pushed me to break with the president's policy and say the word "genocide." It wasn't going to happen, and everyone knew it. It was pure Kabuki.

Despite the acrimonious hearing, the message got through: it was counterproductive to leave Armenia without a chief of mission. I was easily confirmed in August and arrived in Yerevan in September 2008. I knew that the Armenian community in the U.S. was still skeptical of me, but after Ambassador Markaryan's efforts, I had reason to expect that my reception in Armenia would be warmer. Thankfully, my hope was rewarded.

AFTER A TWO-YEAR GAP between ambassadors, I was received in the Armenian capital with open arms. There was the usual swirl of introductory meetings and a large welcome event at the big U.S. embassy compound. The property boasts the best view in Yerevan of Mount Ararat, the fabled resting place of Noah's Ark and the national symbol of Armenia, despite its location across a closed border in what is now Turkey.

Notwithstanding the success of the Armenian-American diaspora in concentrating the confirmation hearing on the genocide issue, no Armenians raised it with me upon my arrival in Yerevan. I had been told this would be the case, but it still was a relief. Armenians living in the country cared very much about the issue but were more concerned about the present: the sluggish economy, the violent aftermath of recent presidential elections, and the ever-present tensions between Armenia and its neighbor Azerbaijan over the contested territory of Nagorno-Karabakh (N-K for short). The U.S. was concerned about these things as well. In the 1990s we had seen how age-old ethnic rivalries in the Balkans could embroil our country in present-day conflict. Similar ethnic tensions had been flaring for decades in N-K, and we saw it as in our interests to promote regional stability among Armenia and its neighbors — and historical antagonists — Turkey and Azerbaijan.

The Armenians are an ancient people and have inhabited the same general area in the Caucasus and the Middle East for almost three millennia. Empires have come and gone, but the Armenians, bound by a common church, language, and culture, have survived and thrived. After the cataclysms of World War I and the genocide (a word I can use now, since I no longer speak for the government),* President Woodrow Wilson proposed boundaries for an Armenian state that would encompass not just Armenia's current territory but also some of the historically Armenian lands of central and eastern Turkey as well as the Black Sea port of Trabzon. But history overtook the Wilsonian map: the U.S. Senate would not ratify the mandate, and the Ottoman Empire was racked by a civil war that eventually produced modern-day Turkey. Armenia ended up confined to mountainous lands smaller than the state of Maryland, encircled by Turkey, Azerbaijan, Iran, and Georgia, with no access to the sea and with borders that separated ethnic Armenians from their kin. For many Armenians, the Wilsonian map became a symbol of all that Armenia had lost at the hands of the Ottoman Empire and its successor state, Turkey: over a million and a half souls murdered or forcibly deported during the genocide and then much of the areas historically inhabited by Armenians (including Mount Ararat and the lands around it) turned over to the Turks.

Armenia enjoyed only a brief independence before it was incorporated into the Soviet Union. Stalin redrew internal borders and turned N-K, a mountainous area in Azerbaijan populated mostly by Armenians, into an autonomous region of Azerbaijan, an ethnically Turkic republic. Stalin's manipulation of N-K was a way to stoke grievances and keep everyone

---

* In the spring of 2021, as I was writing this book, President Joe Biden recognized the Armenian genocide and used the term "genocide" in his 2021 Armenian Remembrance Day statement.

bickering with each other and dependent on Moscow for solutions. During the next seventy years, the border-drawing policy did exactly that.

But Stalin's handling of the N-K issue did not change the loyalties of its people, who eventually became swept up by the same winds of change that would blow down the Soviet Union. In 1988 the 80 percent of the N-K population that was ethnically Armenian overwhelmingly voted yes on a government referendum asking whether the region should secede from Azerbaijan and reunite with Armenia. Neither the Soviet Union nor the Republic of Azerbaijan recognized the referendum as legitimate, since N-K could not hold a referendum according to Azerbaijani law. But it left no doubt that the majority of N-K's residents wanted out of Azerbaijan. Tensions continued to simmer until, in 1992, a full-scale war broke out between the newly independent nations of Azerbaijan and Armenia over N-K. Despite the international community's efforts to end the fighting, the war continued for two more years, until Russia finally succeeded in negotiating a ceasefire. By the time the shooting stopped, Armenia controlled not just all of N-K but seven provinces around it, amounting to 9 percent of Azerbaijan. Tragically, the war produced not only significant casualties but also hundreds of thousands of ethnic Armenian and Azerbaijani refugees.

Armenia had won the war, and both Armenia and Azerbaijan assumed that Russia would back Armenia if the war resumed. After all, although the Russians had long ties to both sides, there was a greater affinity with the Armenians, who came from a similar Christian tradition, were highly educated, and had held important positions in Moscow under the Communists. Notwithstanding Russia's continued willingness to sell arms to Azerbaijan, the military relationship between Armenia and Russia was growing increasingly close.

But in many ways Armenia's victory in the war masked the fact that it hadn't won the peace. The international community continued to recognize N-K as part of Azerbaijan, despite Armenia's control over an area populated by people who largely wanted to join Armenia. Moscow, meanwhile, was content to let the tensions between Armenia and Azerbaijan fester, as it did in a number of other areas in the former Soviet Union. This kept the countries off-balance, more focused on security issues than democracy-building, and looking to Moscow for assistance. As a result, the hot war between Armenia and Azerbaijan morphed into a so-called frozen conflict, a term coined to describe the state of tension that isn't all-out war yet isn't peace either, in certain parts of the former Soviet Union.

Having agreed only to a ceasefire, not a peace treaty, the parties' competing claims to N-K remained unresolved. That meant that Armenia still had to ensure a robust military presence in N-K. Over the years there were periodic skirmishes along the line of contact, as the dividing line between Armenian-Karabakhi and Azerbaijani forces was called, and the casualties continued to mount. The fighting might not have made international headlines, but this war was frozen only in name.

Despite the success of its military effort, moreover, Armenia suffered terribly both during and after the war. The Turks closed the border with Armenia in 1993 to show solidarity with the Muslim and ethnically Turkic Azerbaijanis and never reopened it. With effective blockades at both the Turkish and the Azerbaijani borders, Armenians were unable to import crucial supplies, most importantly fuel. There was virtually no gas, electricity, central heat, or even city water. Transportation, telephone, and even hospital services were all adversely affected, with surgeries and childbirths often carried out by candlelight. Factories closed. Almost every tree in Yerevan was chopped down and burned for fuel, and virtually every park and city bench ripped up to heat homes during subzero winters. A writer I met years later told of how he burned all his books to keep his children warm during this period; he was still full of remorse when he described his desperation to me more than a decade afterward.

Armenia had other challenges as well. A 1988 earthquake in the country's second largest city, Gyumri, had killed between 25,000 and 50,000 people and wreaked hundreds of millions of dollars' worth of destruction. Even six years later the heartbreak and expense of reconstruction were daunting.

Armenians call the years from 1992 to 1995 "the cold, dark years" and compare this period to World War II and the genocide. Those who could leave did so, and the population dwindled. It was a searing experience, and began to end only in 1995, when the Armenian government recommissioned the Metsamor Nuclear Power Plant, which had been mothballed after the Chornobyl disaster.

As it emerged from this grim period, the new state of Armenia had to manage the aftermath of the war as well as an economy in shambles. Although Armenia had made progress in rebuilding its economy by the time of my 2008 arrival, it still had a lot to overcome, and decades of Soviet mismanagement made the challenge even greater. Armenia still hadn't become a fully functioning democracy, and corruption and mismanagement flourished. The country did have a small and burgeoning group of activists who advocated for transparent and accountable government, but as in the other post-Soviet states, those in charge had no experience in good governance, rule of law, or accountability, and it was questionable whether — despite a lot of lip service — they were interested in establishing these hallmarks of democracy in Armenia.

I hoped that I would be able to help. But if my time in Kyrgyzstan and Ukraine had taught me anything, it was that progress wouldn't come easily or quickly.

ARMENIA HAD HELD presidential elections in February 2008, roughly seven months before I arrived. President Robert Kocharyan was term-limited, so he endorsed his ally, Prime Minister Serzh Sargsyan, to replace him. The U.S. congratulated Armenia on "active and competitive elections," but noted "significant problems with electoral procedures" and urged that recounts be managed "comprehensively and transparently" and that allegations of irregularity be investigated. Armenia's Central Election Commission, set up to be an objective and professional organization responsible for all elections, ignored the charges of vote count fraud, voter intimidation, and other issues and called the race for Sargsyan, claiming that he beat his closest rival, former president Levon Ter-Petrosyan, known as LTP. Displaying uncommon courage, two of the twelve commissioners refused to sign off on the results.

Joseph Pennington, the chargé d'affaires leading Embassy Yerevan in the absence of an ambassador, headed the U.S. election monitoring team and observed firsthand some of those irregularities. At one precinct he watched with disbelief as the chair of the vote-counting committee took each ballot, looked at it, then passed it *facedown* toward the committee member responsible for keeping a particular candidate's votes. No one else saw the ballots. Needless to say, Sargsyan's committee member received the lion's share of the ballots and Sargsyan won that precinct in a landslide.

Joseph later tried to attend one of the precinct-level recounts ordered by the Central Election Commission. When he and one of our local employees arrived at the polling station, they waited for hours for the recount to begin. When they sought an explanation for the delay, they were first told that one of the committee members had been rushed to the hospital. Then it was lunchtime, and then a host of other excuses followed. By about 4 p.m. no votes had yet been counted, but a convoy of SUVs pulled up to the polling station and toughs in leather jackets got out and started milling around in a menacing manner. Concerned for their own safety, our team didn't wait to see what would happen next. But they later learned that the recount had proceeded as soon as they were out of the way. Unsurprisingly, the new count affirmed the original vote count, and that precinct too was declared in favor of Sargsyan.

LTP refused to concede and called for demonstrations to protest the fraudulent results. The protests began the day after the elections. President Kocharyan falsely alleged that the peaceful demonstrators had amassed a weapons cache, and he declared a state of emergency that banned public gatherings. Early on March 1, he directed security forces to disperse the crowd by force, leaving at least ten dead, dozens injured, and more than one hundred under arrest, including LTP.

Kocharyan's reaction to the 2008 protests was all too typical of governments in countries trying to transition from authoritarianism to democracy. In such countries, power, money, and personal security are often interlocked. If you or your allies are out of power, you can easily lose your businesses, your wealth, and even your freedom. Your family and associates might also suffer the consequences. These unhappy prospects incentivize some leaders to do whatever it takes to stay in power and perpetuate the downward spiral to authoritarianism. That ruthlessness makes them look strong for the moment, and sometimes that moment can last for a very long time.

The United States, which was providing support to Armenia, was concerned by the backtracking in a country that had thus far shown some potential for democracy and which had a powerful domestic lobby back home. So the U.S. and the international community sharply criticized Kocharyan's refusal to allow peaceful protests and the eventual violence that resulted from his policies. Right after Kocharyan's brutal crackdown, the U.S. also warned Armenia that it could lose some of our assistance funding unless the government held those who had harmed demonstrators accountable and released people who had been wrongfully jailed. With so many dead, injured, and in jail, we told them, it was hard to make the case that Yerevan was committed to political rights or civil liberties, key criteria for eligibility to receive funding from a Bush administration initiative known as the Millennium Challenge Account. The program, created as a tool to incentivize countries' reform efforts, was providing assistance to help Armenia promote economic growth and reduce rural poverty via new infrastructure and other improvements.

Armenia was far from the only post-Soviet republic where the U.S. was worried about backsliding during this period. About a month after Sargsyan took office, in May 2008, former Russian prime minister Dmitriy Medvedev was inaugurated to the presidency in his country. Putin was still very much on the scene, having been appointed prime minister in Medvedev's place, but we hoped that Medvedev's ascent signified that Russia would return to a more liberal path after the Putin years. Then in August, less than two months after my confirmation hearing, Moscow invaded Armenia's neighbor, the former Soviet republic of Georgia. The five-day war ended with unilateral Russian recognition of Georgian regions South Ossetia and Abkhazia as independent countries, almost 200,000 displaced persons, and yet another frozen conflict in the region. It was not an auspicious start for Medvedev's young presidency.

When I arrived in Yerevan that September, nerves were palpably frayed from the war next door. The unresolved political situation following the Armenian presidential elections and our warning about the assistance money fostered ongoing tensions. Sargsyan, Kocharyan's prime minister and ally, was ensconced in the president's office. Key opposition members remained in jail or in hiding. LTP was under house arrest, with the government still doggedly claiming that the opposition had tried to illegally seize power by force.

Clearly Armenia needed to find a better path, and it was not going to find a role model in the dominant regional power, Russia. In order for Armenia to move forward domestically and stay in good standing with the U.S. and other international stakeholders, Sargsyan and his government needed to deal with the political-prisoner issue, hold accountable the killers of the protesters, and recommit to good governance more broadly, including political rights, civil liberties, control of corruption, and rule of law. It was my job to try to help them get there.

Behind closed doors I held a series of sensitive discussions with Sargsyan and the general prosecutor (Armenia's equivalent to our attorney general), encouraging the new administration to act. The government needed to ad-here to the rule of law and be accountable to its people, I said; democra-cies permit their citizens to have a voice and a vote, and Armenia's leaders needed to ensure the sanctity of the ballot box and the safety of those citi-zens, regardless of their views.

I was trying to catalyze a discussion of the country's path forward, and my efforts extended well beyond these early conversations with the Sargs-yan administration. I raised the subject of the political prisoners and gov-ernment accountability for the ten deaths at almost every high-level meet-ing. Coming to expect this, the general prosecutor responded by bringing to each meeting three-by-five index cards, one for each prisoner, ready to be consulted when I raised the issue. To me it revealed a heart-wrenching disconnect every time he produced them: imagine having your life — and liberty — reduced to an index card. I would remind him that each card rep-resented a person being held for politically motivated reasons, with a fam-ily deprived of that person's presence. I emphasized that democracies allow political opposition, and if Sargsyan and his general prosecutor were in the opposition, they would want their rights protected, too.

Despite our steady and sometimes spirited dialogue, I don't think that Sargsyan really believed that the U.S. would follow through on our threats to withhold assistance over these matters. He seemed to assume that dias-pora supporters would keep U.S. funding intact. And for a time they did. But eventually even diaspora pressure wasn't enough to overcome U.S. un-willingness to ignore the government's violent and antidemocratic actions. After making virtually no headway in our discussions with the Armenian government, the U.S. announced in June 2009 that we were withholding $58 million from the $235 million Millennium Challenge project meant for reconstruction and repair of about six hundred miles of Armenian rural roads, critical to help those areas of the country develop economically.

Although Sargsyan never acknowledged it, I believe that our action sent him a wake-up call. Later that same month the Armenian government of-fered a general amnesty for prisoners being held for nonviolent offenses and sentenced to fewer than five years. The amnesty was a face-saving way for Sargsyan to finally release dozens of political prisoners.

It was a start, I told myself, but some of the most prominent political prisoners remained behind bars, and Sargsyan was painfully slow in freeing these remaining demonstrators. In fact the final political prisoner was not released until nearly two years later. For the most part the security forces who had killed the demonstrators, and the leaders who had ordered force to be used against them, have largely escaped justice as of this writing.

Questionable election practices continued to plague Armenia, and the 2009 Yerevan municipal elections were rife with irregularities. I joined colleagues in observing the polls. I saw thugs hanging around the voting precincts intimidating voters and the same busload of voters being transported to multiple polling precincts in order to vote multiple times, a practice called "carousel voting." It made me wonder what was going on out of an ambassador's eyeshot.

THE PROBLEMATIC 2008 and 2009 elections stiffened U.S. resolve. We needed to keep working with both Armenia's government and its civil society in order to help reform the country's electoral system before its 2012 parliamentary elections and 2013 presidential elections. I hoped that with the right electoral framework in place, Armenians could avoid repeating the events of 2008. I realized, however, that simply changing the country's laws or imposing paper penalties for violating them wouldn't be enough; successful electoral reforms also would depend on the government's political will to actually implement the changes.

So as I worked with the Sargsyan government, I also tried to support the efforts of Armenian activists fighting for greater freedom and against corruption. As in Kyrgyzstan, the U.S. wanted to highlight their accomplishments to help create space for their work in a difficult environment. Armenia, like Kyrgyzstan and other post-Soviet states, was nothing if not precarious for people brave enough to speak truth to power.

Having seen in other countries how protective international recognition can sometimes be for activists, I had created a local "woman of courage" award when I served in Kyrgyzstan and then replicated the idea in Armenia. I modeled it on an award established by the State Department to recognize brave women around the globe who risk all to advocate for justice and human rights. I was gratified to see the immediate results that flowed from the embassy's decision to give the award to a young activist, Mariam Sukhudian, who had publicized sexual and other abuse at an Armenian school. Sukhudian was precisely the kind of person we wanted to honor and protect. For defending children who could not defend themselves, she had been charged with false denunciation, a crime that could land her in jail for five years. The charge was dropped the day after she received the award.

I got a similar reminder of the power of diplomacy at an event for the Armenian Freedom Defender Award, which we gave to three judges who had bravely ruled against the government and done their part in defending Armenian freedoms. I had invited the prime minister, a technocrat and reformer, to speak on the importance of a strong and independent judiciary. He was brilliant, making the high-profile audience a little uncomfortable with his boundary-pushing.

At the end of the evening, in a private aside, Armenia's police chief—a man who did not easily embrace reform—asked me whether policemen were eligible to receive the award. I told him we would very much like to see the police defending freedom and would recognize them for it if they did. That was a win, I thought when I went home that night, and it underlined for me the subtle strength of U.S. ambassadors. Despite our sometimes uncomfortable conversations, the police chief wanted U.S. recognition, and we wanted to provide it—but it had to be earned.

As in Kyrgyzstan, I encouraged my team in Armenia to find small wins, since systemic change didn't come easily. We found them in programs aimed at bettering the lives of disenfranchised Armenians, with the hope that empowering individuals also helped the country. We again established a mentoring program for female students. If we could move the needle on women's issues in the Armenians' self-described traditional culture, it would not only strengthen the fabric of society, it would jump-start the economy by helping to move more women into the workforce. No country, I would often repeat, can afford to sideline half of its economic potential.

Although I wished that we could have been more successful in bringing justice to the ten slain protesters and their families, I was proud of the work my team and I did to free the political prisoners. I was especially gratified when the State Department recognized our accomplishment by giving me the Secretary's Diplomacy for Freedom Award in 2009. Most host governments would have ignored the American ambassador receiving such an award, since it did not place the country in a positive light. But President Sargsyan congratulated me, and it seemed to me that he was at least listening to our concerns, although his apparent, polite receptiveness didn't always translate into action.

The secret in diplomacy — perhaps any business — is knowing how hard to push. Since the U.S. provides generous assistance, the White House and congressional members often want to see immediate results. All of us want countries like Armenia to be secure, prosperous democracies — yesterday. Most of us forget that reform is always difficult and that transformational change takes time. What is the right balance between pushing and patience? Especially when too much pushing could compromise some of our other equities, or send a country's leaders over the edge and into the arms of our adversaries.

I spent a lot of time urging Washington — and our own embassy team — not to give up or get cynical just because we didn't see systemic change on our own timeline. Sometimes the best that the embassy can do is socialize ideas, provide training that will be put to use only in the future, and help reform-minded lawmakers draft legislation that won't become law for a very long time. We were helping reform-minded Armenians in civil society and in government lay the groundwork for change at some future point when the country would be ready for it. I called it the "hitting your head against the wall" school of diplomacy. It might be painful, but if we kept at it, eventually there would be an opening, even if we personally weren't there to see it.

In the years since, I've thought a lot about whether we did enough in Armenia, especially to help gain justice for those killed and imprisoned for their roles in the 2008 protests following the presidential election. We pushed hard, but diplomacy, to borrow a phrase, is the art of the possible. Getting Sargsyan to hold his friends and allies fully accountable for the violence and the deaths that ushered in his rule was probably never in the cards for foreign governments.

But in 2018 the Armenian people took these tasks into their own hands. That year's so-called Velvet Revolution forced Sargsyan's resignation and brought to power Nikol Pashinyan, one of the political prisoners whose case we had championed when I was ambassador. Belatedly I allowed myself to feel that we may have helped Armenia to make some progress on the truth and reconciliation front after all.

WHILE PROMOTING INTERNAL reform was important, it was not our only objective in Armenia; of equal importance to us was advancing the cause of regional stability. This is an important U.S. goal everywhere in the world.

If countries have serious disputes or are at war with their neighbors, every-thing else — their political systems, their economies, their reliability as U.S. partners — is at risk. In the case of Armenia, this universal goal was more urgent than most.

The hostile relationships that existed between Armenia on the one hand and Azerbaijan and Turkey on the other had both destabilized the Cauca-sus and severely stunted Armenia's economic and political development. Fighting still flared periodically in the standoff between Azerbaijan and Ar-menia, and young men died along the line of contact every year. Peace-fully settling the Nagorno-Karabakh conflict with Azerbaijan, opening Ar-menia's borders, and establishing Armenian relations with Azerbaijan and Turkey were critical goals for both Armenia and the United States. I was not alone in worrying whether the frozen conflict could turn into a proxy war, with Russia backing Armenia and Turkey championing Azerbaijan. Because Turkey was a NATO ally, it was unlikely but not completely incon-ceivable that a war between Turkish and Russian client states could lead to broader tensions between Russia and NATO.

Armenia and Azerbaijan were dug in deep. Over the years an interna-tional effort launched in 1992 known as the Minsk Group had worked to re-solve the N-K conflict. Cochaired by the United States, Russia, and France, it had successfully negotiated a number of ceasefires, with the goal of even-tually producing a comprehensive peace settlement. But most of the Minsk Group's meetings were spent talking about the talks, in this case the princi-ples that would serve as the framework for negotiations. Azerbaijan insisted on the primacy of territorial integrity, meaning that it wanted its land back. Armenia defended equal rights and self-determination of peoples, mean-ing that it wanted the ethnic Armenians who populated N-K to decide for themselves who governed them, despite living in what Azerbaijan and the world saw as Azerbaijani territory. Armenians argued that Azerbaijanis had been able to determine their independence by referendum in 1991, so why couldn't the Karabakhis do the same? Each insisted that its preferred prin-ciple take precedence, and neither side seemed fully committed to a third critical principle, nonuse of force.

Armenia seemed to think that the status quo wasn't so bad. It had won the war in 1994, not only capturing N-K lands populated by ethnic Ar-menians but also occupying a buffer zone of seven Azerbaijani provinces around N-K. The Russian relationship with Yerevan was as strong as ever.

Russia had kept its military base in Gyumri, on the border with Turkey, and most Armenians assumed that Russia would come to Armenia's military aid if necessary.

But the status quo did not work for Azerbaijan, which had lost not just N-K but also a chunk of undisputed Azerbaijani territory. Its president, Ilham Aliyev, believed that the Minsk Group was stacked against his country, because the cochairs all had large Armenian diasporas. Aliyev had chosen not to integrate the ethnic Azerbaijanis who had fled N-K more than a decade and a half earlier into the rest of Azerbaijani society. Instead he kept them isolated in refugee camps and turned them into living, breathing symbols of the loss of N-K. Aliyev used them as a political rallying cry, but at some point he would need to deliver or lose all credibility. Whether that would occur through negotiations or renewed hostilities was the question.

Armenia arguably should have exhibited more urgency at the negotiating table. Although it had fielded a capable military in the early 1990s, Armenia's comparative advantage had begun to disappear as Azerbaijan's oil and gas sector had grown. Azerbaijan plowed its profits into developing its military and adroitly played the energy card internationally. U.S. energy companies were doing a booming business in Azerbaijan, and Azerbaijan's supply of gas to Europe supported our goal of weaning Europe off its dependency on Russian gas. The U.S. military also partnered closely with Azerbaijan, particularly with regard to facilitation of U.S. military supply flights to Afghanistan. Although advocates for these commercial and military interests hadn't yet succeeded in swaying U.S. policy, I worried that the longer Armenia delayed, the more it was tempting fate.

But domestic politics severely limited Armenian leaders' options. Any Armenian leader who showed a willingness to make concessions on N-K risked his political career — and potentially his life. Disagreements over N-K policy had played a large role in the resignation of Armenia's president in 1998 and in the 1999 assassinations of its prime minister, parliamentary speaker, and other officials. The message was clear: Armenian leaders compromised on historically Armenian lands at their peril.

For the three years that I was in Armenia, the Minsk Group negotiators shuttled back and forth, bringing the presidents of Armenia and Azerbaijan together, issuing statements to prod progress, and brokering ceasefires when necessary. Their efforts didn't produce any game-changers, although they did create a process for the two countries to talk to each other, which was better than the alternative. Still, if there was hope for stabilizing the relationships among these longtime rivals, it seemed to be not in the Minsk Group's domain but rather in another diplomatic channel that was active at this time.

BEFORE I HAD departed for Yerevan, I had been briefed on then-secret negotiations that the Swiss were conducting between Turkey and Armenia. The goal was to reestablish full diplomatic and economic relations between the two historical enemies and to reopen the border that Turkey had closed in 1993 out of solidarity with Azerbaijan. The Swiss idea was to shift the focus of diplomatic efforts: instead of putting energy into the seemingly intractable N-K issue, they would tackle the apparently more straightforward problem of Turkey-Armenia reconciliation. At least in principle, establishing formal relations and an open border between these two countries, which required a discussion of border policies, trade agreements, and the like, could be disaggregated from the two big issues that colored their relationship: Nagorno-Karabakh and the genocide. With those two problems left for another day, the Swiss hoped that normalization could transform the political, economic, and security environment, not just for Armenia and Turkey but for the region. Perhaps *this* would be the game-changer and ultimately catalyze movement on the N-K issue as well.

It would take political will, however. That's why the U.S. had been brought into the process — to provide superpower backing. We weren't at the table, but we were briefed on every meeting and provided moral encouragement and some judicious arm-twisting when warranted to get Armenia and Turkey to keep talking and moving forward.

Although reaching an agreement on opening a border and normalizing relations was relatively easier than concluding a peace negotiation, it was still challenging. Armenian president Sargsyan and Turkish president Abdullah Gul knew that in the Caucasus, to borrow from Faulkner, "the past is never dead. It's not even past." In Turkey, some would want to tie the talks to a resolution of the N-K issue, out of solidarity with their Azerbaijani kin. In Armenia and the diaspora, meanwhile, there would be grave concern that any moves to reconcile with Turkey would inevitably lead to unacceptable concessions regarding N-K. The Armenian diaspora and a few smaller political parties in Armenia would also strongly object to Armenia talking to its historical enemy before the genocide issue was resolved.

In short, the negotiators would be burdened with lots of baggage that they had to set aside, at least temporarily. If the most fraught of these issues were allowed into the Turkey-Armenia reconciliation talks, they would almost certainly kill that process.

Apart from those complicating factors, the underlying lack of trust between Turkey and Armenia made even a willingness to talk to each other a politically risky proposition for both sides. But you rarely get to negotiate with your friends. If the two countries were ever going to reach a settlement, they would need to reconcile themselves to speaking to their adversaries first and foremost.

Hoping to soften attitudes among their populations, Sargsyan and Gul launched "soccer diplomacy" in September 2008. To both fanfare and criticism, Gul traveled to Yerevan to watch a World Cup qualifier between the two national teams. While the discussions were still secret, it was unprecedented for a Turkish president to come to Armenia, and it signaled a public willingness for greater openness between the two countries.

THE TURKEY-ARMENIA RECONCILIATION process was a priority for the Obama administration, which took office in January 2009. That made it a high priority for me. I was completely committed, and while President Sargsyan might not have been an ideal partner on domestic reform, I found his courage and resolve on rapprochement with Turkey impressive. Sargsyan knew the history and the risks, and he was willing to make the biggest bet of his presidency on reconciliation. It seemed to me that if anyone could get it done, it was Sargsyan, given his unassailable security credentials in both N-K and Armenia.

At its core, diplomacy is about building relationships that enable us to have influence when it's needed. Over the years America had stood with Armenia. But this was a whole new challenge: we were trying to get Armenians to trust not just us but also their historical enemy. So I leaned into the relatively close relationship the U.S. had with Armenia. At difficult stages — that is, at every stage — I encouraged the Armenian negotiators, counseled them when they were overstepping, and advised Washington when higher-level U.S. intervention was necessary. Although I wasn't the one talking to the Turks, I did convey to the Armenians Washington's conviction that the Turks were serious about the negotiations, and I encouraged the Armenians to keep on going.

High-strung Armenian foreign minister Edouard Nalbandyan and I had almost daily conversations, often at a high decibel level. Nalbandyan didn't trust the Turks. He was worried that they were stringing the Armenians along. After all, Turkey had closed the border precisely because of the war in N-K, and if at some point the Turks linked the Turkey-Armenia negotiations to N-K, it would torpedo the talks. He was concerned that once news of the negotiations became public, hardliners in Armenia and the diaspora would train their criticism on him and he would lose his job, his reputation, even perhaps his life, given the violent history around these issues. I sometimes felt that I was practicing psychiatry without a license. Where was my little Zen garden when I needed it?

But after every negotiating round, the Armenians would report that the Turks still hadn't raised the issue of N-K. Having entered the negotiations skeptical, they finally began to allow themselves to hope. As time went by and the negotiations stayed on course, I found myself beginning to hope as well.

BY APRIL 2009, Turkey and Armenia had quietly agreed on two protocols. One would establish diplomatic relations between the two countries. The second laid out a road map for the specifics of how commercial and political relations would be developed. It was nothing short of historic, and we hoped would reverse the past fifteen years of acrimony between the two countries, if not the past century of bad blood.

At about the same time, the newly sworn-in Obama administration was staging another, more widely heralded attempt to improve relations between two countries, this one between the U.S. and Russia. The reset, as it was called, sought to reverse the "dangerous drift" in relations, especially following the Russia-Georgia war. The U.S. hoped to work with Russia on foreign policy goals important to both countries, and the Turkish-Armenia reconciliation talks were one area of cooperation.

On April 22, two days before Armenian Remembrance Day, Armenia and Turkey released the first public acknowledgment of the negotiations. Their short statement offered no details, noting only that the two sides "had achieved tangible progress" on normalization of relations and that "a road map has been identified."

The joint statement ignited a firestorm of speculation. No one outside the negotiations knew what the agreements contained, but that didn't stop lots of people — in Armenia, in Turkey, in Azerbaijan, in the United States, and elsewhere — from expressing strong opinions. Everyone's fears and prejudices were on stark display. As predicted, some Armenians, especially in the American diaspora, staunchly opposed negotiating with Turkey on anything until Turkey acknowledged that the Ottoman Empire had perpetrated a genocide. Armenians everywhere worried that concessions on N-K were part of the deal. For their part, some Turks, egged on by the Azerbaijanis, demanded that Turkey not normalize relations with Armenia while Armenians still occupied Azerbaijani lands.

Protests erupted in Yerevan over the mere fact of the negotiations. One of the parties in the governing coalition departed in protest. The foreign minister and others received death threats. It was unnerving, to say the least. The passion on display set the Armenian leadership on edge and made me wonder whether all our efforts were about to come undone.

By releasing the statement two days before Armenian Remembrance Day, the Armenian government made a clear calculation that prioritized the reconciliation talks. The announcement would make it easier for President Obama to avoid using the word "genocide" in his first Remembrance Day statement.

Obama had been one of the senators on my confirmation committee who had urged me to use the word. As a presidential candidate, he had declared that "an official policy that calls on diplomats to distort the historical facts is an untenable policy." But nowhere is the old adage "where you stand depends on where you sit" more apt than when talking about the move from the hundred-person Senate to the presidency. Obama's comments about the genocide hadn't affected policy at all when he was in the Senate, but using that word as president could alter the relationship with our important NATO ally Turkey, given Turkey's threats of retaliation. Beyond the implications for our own national security, it also could scramble the precarious negotiations between Turkey and Armenia, with possible consequences for wider regional stability.

Armenian agreement to announce the reconciliation process just two days before Remembrance Day gave the White House an out. As a reason to avoid the word "genocide," the Obama administration could point to the ongoing negotiations — negotiations that, if successful, would be far more impactful than a presidential statement.

The decision was so politically sensitive that it was resolved at the highest levels at the White House; the embassy was not a part of the process. We barely got a heads-up before the White House released the president's statement publicly. When it did, we saw that President Obama had made the same strategic calculation as his predecessors: he did not use the word "genocide." To be sure, he went further than previous presidents by using the Armenian term I had employed at my confirmation hearing, Medz Yeghern (the Great Calamity), but his restraint nevertheless was a bitter disappointment for Armenian-Americans.

Although I had harbored a secret hope that Obama would call the genocide what it was, I was not surprised. Avoiding that word was the right call that year, even if it was a win for the Turks — who had dodged a reckoning with their past yet again.

Obama's tough decision had upset a powerful constituency in the U.S., but it had also kept the Turkey-Armenia negotiations on track and given us the space we needed to continue supporting them as best we could, especially now that the news of the negotiations was public. The announcement of the protocols had given us an opening to push for reconciliation between the people of Armenia and the people of Turkey. At the embassy we engaged in retail diplomacy, making the case directly to the Armenian people about the benefits to Armenians of open borders. In Yerevan I tried to socialize the idea of an eventual rapprochement with public opinion leaders through off-the-record discussions as well as in public speeches. I was constantly surprised that so many Armenians were so used to being cut off from their neighbors that they didn't realize the high economic cost of isolation. It was eye-opening for many when I pointed out that the Turks had taken a big risk and signed a trade agreement with the much bigger European Union in 1998, launching the Turkish economic boom. The same could happen for Armenia if it opened up to Turkey.

In the months immediately following the announcement, moreover, I was impressed to see that Sargsyan and Gul were steadfast in their support of the reconciliation process despite the vocal opposition of many in their respective countries. National leadership of this sort could help to sway public opinion much more effectively than any amount of commentary from foreign diplomats.

Although the Armenians and the Turks had publicly acknowledged the negotiations that spring, they had not yet released the protocol texts. At the end of August the Swiss published the agreements, along with a statement that the parties were prepared to sign them following a six-week period of "internal political consultation." Now that the provisions of the protocols were public, the critics had a lot to work with, and flak came from every corner. Still, I couldn't help but take heart from this groundbreaking development and feel hope for what normalization could mean for Armenia and the region in general.

ON OCTOBER 10, 2009, the Swiss foreign minister convened the Turkish and Armenian foreign ministers in Zurich to sign the protocols. The Minsk Group foreign ministers, including Secretary of State Hillary Clinton, joined to provide international and very public support. But at the eleventh hour, Armenian foreign minister Nalbandyan — my high-decibel interlocutor — balked over objectionable language in Turkish foreign minister Davutoglu's statement. All of a sudden it looked like there wouldn't be a signing ceremony after all.

Clinton immediately started working two cell phones, reminding both sides how far they had come. Other foreign ministers also interceded, and Nalbandyan and Davutoglu finally agreed that neither would make a public statement. In a gracious touch, Secretary Clinton invited Nalbandyan to drive together in her limousine to the signing ceremony.

Three hours late, the Armenian and Turkish foreign ministers signed the historic documents. The two protocols were the same that the sides had agreed upon back in the spring: one to establish diplomatic relations and embassies in each other's capitals, and the other to implement a road map with timelines for opening the Turkish-Armenian border and instituting a framework for developing political and economic relations. Importantly, the two sides also formally committed to discuss the "historical dimension" of their relationship — code for dealing with the issue of the genocide.

It was a momentous breakthrough, and back in Yerevan we quietly celebrated. We knew the formal signing of the protocols was just one very important step and that the work of getting both countries' legislatures to ratify the agreements was going to be an uphill slog. But that was tomorrow's problem. That night I was practically giddy with hope for Armenia and the region. My great expectations only made what came next more devastating.

INITIALLY THE SIGNS were positive. President Gul and the Turkish Foreign Ministry continued to assure the Swiss and the U.S. that they could manage their legislative process. Sargsyan seemed optimistic as well for the prospects of ratification in Armenia, since his party had the votes in the parliament. Within days of the signing, Sargsyan traveled to Turkey for round two of soccer diplomacy, and Gul and Sargsyan spoke encouragingly about the future. To be sure, some in Armenia and the diaspora were reacting loudly and negatively to the protocols' failure to deal definitively with the genocide issue. But Sargsyan seemed to think the criticism was manageable.

Turkey's client state, however, was a different story altogether. It didn't take long for the Azerbaijanis to react to the prospect of Ankara reopening its border with Yerevan while Armenia still occupied lands claimed by Azerbaijan. Worried that they would lose the advantage that Armenia's closed border with Turkey gave them, the Azerbaijanis struck back — at the Turks. Baku's Foreign Ministry called the protocols "in direct contradiction with the interests of Azerbaijan" and said that Turkey's signing "casts a shadow over the spirit of brotherly relations" between Turkey and Azerbaijan. Within days Azerbaijan's President Aliyev underscored the point by suggesting that he might end below-market gas sales to Turkey. There were even reports that the Azerbaijanis were removing Turkish flags from the graves of Turkish soldiers buried in their country. It was getting ugly fast.

For me, the Azerbaijanis' surprise was an unwelcome shock. I had understood that the Turks had been keeping the Azerbaijanis informed throughout the process. Clearly something had gone wrong.

Azerbaijan's high-pressure campaign catalyzed an immediate and explosive Turkish response. Backtracking as quickly as possible, Foreign Minister Davutoglu unequivocally restated his country's commitment to "liberating" N-K from Armenian "occupation," and Prime Minister Recep Tayyip Erdoğan, whose party held the majority in the Turkish parliament, explicitly linked the protocols to N-K. The Turks had told us that Erdoğan was on board with the agreements, but if that was no longer the case, Turkish ratification would be impossible.

This was exactly what Sargsyan and Nalbandyan had feared would happen: Armenia's leadership, having risked all, would be left twisting in the wind, with all the naysayers apparently having been proved right. Any officials who had dared to attempt reconciliation, they worried, might well have to pay a steep price, politically and otherwise.

I was almost sick with worry. A lot was at stake. We had worked so hard;

we couldn't give up now. I strongly believed that the U.S. should do what it could to make sure that our ally Turkey—the bigger, stronger power, with far less to fear—stood by its commitment to Armenia. In frequent calls and video conferences I urged our Washington policymakers to push the Turks hard. Armenia had kept its end of the bargain; Turkey, in contrast, had not. The Turks had assured us they could handle Azerbaijan, but apparently Azerbaijan was handling Turkey.

It was no use. Having pressed little Armenia to negotiate with the enemy despite its leaders' legitimate fears, Washington now seemed to be unwilling to spend any further capital to get the Turks to keep their commitment. What I saw was a ring fence around Turkey and our military equities there. I certainly didn't know the full extent of our interests in Turkey, nor do I likely know the full extent of our diplomatic efforts, but as far as I could tell, we weren't twisting Erdoğan's or Gul's arm and telling them they needed to honor the agreement with the Armenians, nor as far as I could tell were we helping them work through the issues with Azerbaijan.

The Obama administration's apparent unwillingness to take on the blowback from Turkey was infuriating for me, especially since it came at a time that our NATO ally was becoming increasingly autocratic, nationalistic, and unreliable as a partner. Our disinclination to push the Turks on this issue seemed at odds with our long-term regional interests—and our values. From my perch as ambassador, I worried that throwing Armenia under the bus surely would hurt our relationship, not only depriving us of future influence in this tumultuous region but also giving an opening to America's on-again, off-again competitor in the region: Russia.

But while I did the best I could to contain my anger and frustration at what I saw as inadequate U.S. action, I also held out hope that the negotiations could be salvaged. Given Erdoğan's comments, the normalization process seemed dead on arrival in the Turkish parliament, but one ray of light remained: even though Turkey had now linked N-K to the protocols, the Turks had not withdrawn from the process. We all assumed that they didn't want to take the blame for abandoning the agreement. As long as they were still in, there was a chance that rapprochement might take place.

Surprisingly, the Armenians weren't ready to give up either, and I spent the next months trying to help keep the Armenians in the game and on message. In January 2010 the Armenian Constitutional Court ruled that the protocols were constitutional, a critical step in the ratification process. That was good news, but the same ruling also noted that the protocols needed to be in conformity with the clause in the Armenian Declaration of Independence that committed Armenia to fight unceasingly for recognition of the genocide perpetrated by the Ottomans. The Turks could have ignored that part of the court's ruling—the court had said that the protocols could go forward, after all—but they chose to be infuriated by it. That didn't bode well.

Nevertheless, in February, Sargsyan submitted the protocols to the Armenian parliament. With no move from Turkey, by March, Sargsyan had had enough. He didn't trust the Turks to come through, and he was facing increasingly serious domestic and diaspora opposition as yet another Remembrance Day was approaching. I wasn't sure whether he would even last as president. I reported back to Washington that Sargsyan was ready to withdraw from the process.

Secretary Clinton intervened. She convinced President Obama to invite Sargsyan to visit Washington in early April. I flew back for Sargsyan's meetings. But after traveling all the way to Washington and sitting down for separate meetings with Secretary Clinton and President Obama, Sargsyan didn't hear the full-throated support he needed. I could see on his face the dawning realization that he was on his own; it did not seem that the administration had any plans to push Turkey to accept the protocols.

As Remembrance Day drew closer—and with it the one-year anniversary of the announcement of the rapprochement process—the pressure on Sargsyan continued to mount. He consulted with the Russians, and separately told me that if the Turks did not move forward with ratification before Remembrance Day, he would suspend the ratification process in Armenia. Under the circumstances, it seemed to me it was the best way forward—it preserved the protocols for a better day, put the Turks on notice, and salvaged some measure of Armenian pride. Secretary Clinton announced publicly that the ball was in Turkey's court, and I was pleased that at least we were clear where the responsibility lay for the disappointing lack of progress.

On Remembrance Day, with the protocols on life support, Obama decided once again not to offend the Turks and declined to use the word "genocide" in his statement. But that year there didn't appear to be a good reason not to deploy the word—at least, not to me.

WE HAD LOST what might have been the best chance for greater stability in the South Caucasus for generations. And Armenia had lost so much more. I had hoped that Turkey-Armenia rapprochement would open up the Armenian economy and provide opportunities for the Armenian people. I had also hoped that ultimately it would transform regional dynamics and make progress on N-K possible. It had been risky, but the status quo was risky too —and now that was all we had.

I felt terrible, because the price of failure was steep, and because I worried that future Armenian leaders would remember this moment and refuse to dare. I also continued to be concerned that our failure to back Armenia would diminish our influence and push Armenia ever closer to Russia. A few months after the protocols stalled, my fears were confirmed.

In August 2010, Russian president Dmitriy Medvedev traveled to Armenia. The trip, a state visit by the leader of the regional power broker, would have sent an important signal of Russian interest under any circumstances, but it soon proved consequential in other ways as well. During the visit, Medvedev and Sargsyan signed an extension until 2044 of Russia's lease for the Gyumri Military Base on the Turkish border, in exchange for which Russia provided security guarantees, arms, and equipment. Russia and Armenia said that the agreement was aimed at guaranteeing peace in the South Caucasus. But my State Department colleagues and I had misgivings about the signal sent by an upgraded Russian military presence on our NATO ally's border, as well as the impact on Armenia's sovereignty. I met with Sargsyan and urged him to consider the risk to Armenia from ceding so much to Russia. His chief of staff told me later that Armenia had no choice. Armenia knew that Azerbaijan would attack N-K one day, forcing Yerevan to defend its vital interest there. If Turkey supported Azerbaijan, he explained, the only force sufficient to stop them would be the Russian troops at Gyumri.

There wasn't much I could say after that lesson in realpolitik. Armenians are survivors, and they knew that if any country would come to their defense, it was probably Russia. Our inability to push Turkey to keep its commitment certainly left Armenia with little reason to believe that the U.S. would be there to protect them. From an Armenian point of view, it was hard to argue that Sargsyan hadn't made the right choice, although we all knew that getting into bed with the bear always comes at a cost. The failure of the protocols had left the region less secure and, with the increase in Russian influence, arguably less free.

AS WITH ALL my postings, the intensity of the work and the workload itself made downtime hard to come by in Armenia. But experiencing other countries beyond their capital centers is one of the best parts of being an FSO. When I could find the time, I would travel out of Yerevan with friends to experience Armenian culture and to unwind. The highlight was almost always a beautiful church made of stone, a silent testament to the many centuries that Armenians have inhabited these lands. Not too far from Yerevan stands the Temple of Garni, a site that goes back almost two thousand years. I loved going there for the history, for the rejuvenating solitude, and because I could always find my favorite musician, Voskan Vardanyan, playing the duduk. In talented hands, that simple woodwind produces a haunting music that evokes the Armenian soul.

As I got deeper into my career, my work life took over my personal life. Even when I went out to dinner with friends and enjoyed the incredible salads, grilled meat, and fresh fruits that Armenia is famous for, the conversation was frequently shop talk. Much of my "free time" was spent with job-related entertaining.

Small talk had always been a challenge for me, but there was one tidbit that seemed to fascinate everyone and provided endless grist for conversation. Martial arts are popular in the former Soviet Union, with President Putin, a black belt in judo, leading the way. By chance my fitness instructor in Kyrgyzstan had been a highly regarded judo practitioner. I did only aerobics with her, but somehow the word got out that I too had a black belt. It wasn't true, but it was too good a story to die, and it gained new life in Armenia. Almost everyone asked me about it, and my denials only stoked the story. Over the course of my career, it's probably the only piece of disinformation that has worked to my advantage.

When I did have a minute off, I retreated to my bedroom, the only space in my house that was mine, and escaped into *People* magazine. It was a relief to read fluff about all sorts of people who had nothing to do with me or geopolitics. For this introvert, it was a great way to escape from the pressures of the job.

Fortunately, I loved my job. Armenia in many ways felt as remote as Kyrgyzstan, but being the boss no longer felt new to me. I knew what I wanted and how to get it. I was still cautious; even with Secretary Clinton urging us to focus on women, I waited almost a year to launch the women's mentoring program. As the first female ambassador representing the U.S. in this male-dominated society, I wanted to establish myself as a serious interlocutor. I didn't want to be the ambassador who was relegated to serving cookies, as had almost happened in that first interview in Kyrgyzstan. When I asked my DCM, Joseph Pennington, whether I had sufficiently established myself to start the women's program, a younger officer standing in earshot didn't understand what I was asking. I took that as a good sign.

Once again I could see that change was afoot in the State Department, brought about by Alison Palmer's class-action lawsuit, three female secretaries of state—Madeleine Albright, Condoleeza Rice, and Hillary Clinton—plus a legion of Foreign Service officers, both male and female, who wanted the department to catch up with the times.

Yet the job never let up, and the responsibility of running the mission—the policy as well as the personnel—was taking its toll. We may not have reconciled the Armenians and the Turks, but I thought that the U.S. was making a difference in helping to inch Armenia to a more open and democratic society. Nevertheless, I was exhausted, and still disappointed about the protocols. In my opinion the U.S. hadn't lived up to our end of the bargain, and it rankled. What was the point of cultivating strong relations with other countries if we couldn't leverage that relationship when we needed to?

I knew it was time to go for another reason. When I had accepted the appointment to go to Armenia, I had thought that it would be relatively straightforward to follow U.S. policy regarding the genocide. But as the years wore on and I met so many Armenians whose families had suffered in those atrocities, it became harder. The cognitive dissonance of our policy exacted an emotional price on me. We are, after all, a nation not just of interests but of values.

And I missed my family, my friends, and my life in the U.S. Six years representing the U.S. as chief of mission was the honor of a lifetime, but I wanted to go home. At the time I assumed that the end of my three years in Armenia marked the end of my run as an ambassador and the twilight of my career in the State Department. I didn't imagine that I would be an ambassador again—and at that point I was quite sure I didn't want to be.

———

I LEFT YEREVAN on Friday, June 17, 2011, and started a new job in Washington the following Monday. My vacation was the long plane ride back to D.C. The new position was a policy-level job in the State Department managing U.S. relations with central Europe, the Baltics, and the Nordics. Eighteen countries, a whole new set of issues, and lots of travel. The following year I moved up to become the ranking deputy in the European Bureau, and when the assistant secretary departed, I warmed the seat for the next appointee for six months. I finally got that ride on Air Force One that I had wondered about as a junior officer in London, and it was every bit as impressive on the inside. Even the M&Ms came in a box with the presidential seal. In an undignified moment, I grabbed as many boxes as I could.

As I passed my twenty-fifth anniversary in the Foreign Service, I started thinking about what I would do next. I decided that I wanted to try teaching, following in my parents' footsteps. I had no experience and wasn't sure I'd be any good at it — or even enjoy it. But there was only one way to find out. I went back to the National Defense University, where I had spent a happy year as a student at the National War College a little over a decade earlier. I taught for a year at NDU's Eisenhower School and loved it, so much that I spent two years after that at the State Department's Foreign Service Institute rounding out my résumé as dean of the Language School. I thought the management experience in an academic setting would set me up for a second career at a university. After years of living abroad, I was ready to discover America. Since I was sure that I was never going to move again when I started at the Foreign Service Institute, I acquired a four-legged companion to go exploring with — a multicolored, silken-haired cockapoo whom I named Scout.

But I was still watching what was happening in the world, especially in places I knew well, like Ukraine. In that country in particular what I saw thrilled and inspired me — and made me want to get back out into the field.

Part III

Homecoming

2016–2020

9

Return to Kyiv

IT HAD BEEN twelve years since I'd finished my tour as deputy chief of mission at Embassy Kyiv, and when the department announced a vacancy in the ambassadorial position, I realized I wanted to go back. Ever since my first posting there, I had loved Ukraine, and in the time since, from a distance, I had admired the persistence of the Ukrainian people in demanding accountable government — not just once but twice.

Since I had left Ukraine, the country had gone through hell. After the 2004–2005 Orange Revolution, President Yushchenko had spent a lackluster five years in office, failing to make good on his promise of reform. Most disappointing, he seemed to have inherited the sticky fingers of his predecessors, something I, at least, had not expected.

In 2010 the Ukrainians traded down and voted in as president former prime minister Yanukovych, the pro-Russia candidate whose effort to claim the presidency in a rigged election had triggered the Orange Revolution five years earlier. Although Yanukovych still advocated for close ties with Russia, he had artfully repackaged his position toward relations with the European Union, a key issue for the many Ukrainians who hoped that closer ties with Europe would bring economic benefits to their country. That wasn't enough to win over a majority of voters, but he received sufficient votes to make him president. This win seemed legitimate, which was about the only positive thing you could say about Yanukovych's rise to the presidency.

Expectations for Yanukovych were low when he entered office, but he wasted no time in sinking beneath them. Given his past, it was no surprise that he, his family, and his enablers rapidly began diverting government funds to their own accounts. Ukrainians seemed resigned to Yanukovych's larceny, but many were bitterly disappointed in November 2013, when their president turned his back on the Association Agreement with the European Union, which would have opened economic opportunities for average Ukrainians. But Yanukovych found that self-enrichment opportunities via the $15 billion loan Russia was offering Ukraine to repudiate the EU Association Agreement were more enticing than the hard work involved in taking the next step toward integrating with the West and improving the lives of his fellow citizens.

Yanukovych's rejection of a closer relationship with the EU and the attendant economic benefits shocked many, even some of his own advisors. When a small group of students protested, the regime responded brutally. Instead of suppressing dissent, the crackdown enraged Ukrainians, and the demonstrations quickly expanded, bringing hundreds of thousands to protest in Kyiv's Independence Square (known as the Maydan) and across the country. Yanukovych shocked Ukrainians again by responding with even greater force, and in February 2014 his security services killed more than one hundred peaceful protesters near the Maydan.

European and Russian negotiators stepped in to try to end the violence and brokered an agreement that allowed Yanukovych to stay in power until early presidential elections in December. But Yanukovych must have realized that this was only a temporary reprieve. He shocked Ukrainians yet again when he fled to Russia within hours of signing on to the February 21 agreement — and took with him roughly $40 billion of Ukrainian funds he and his cronies had embezzled.

Yanukovych's ignominious departure and the success of the 2014 "Revolution of Dignity" in driving him from office set the stage for the hard work to come. Ordinary Ukrainians, tired of watching their leaders ignore their needs and bleed the country dry, had once again demanded to be treated equally and with dignity. They made clear that they wanted Ukraine to look West, not East, and to be governed by the rule of law. And they were committed to ensuring that this time, unlike after the Orange Revolution in 2004, the people's will would prevail.

Ukrainians were free of Yanukovych, a corrupt Russian puppet, who had disappointed them endlessly. But there was no time to celebrate, because even before Yanukovych's flight, Russia was already taking advantage of the turmoil in Ukraine.

———————

PUTIN DIDN'T WANT to own Ukraine, but he didn't want Ukraine to be fully independent either. He had long understood that a Ukraine not under Russia's influence would seek closer association with the European Union and NATO, something that would bring Western values — and potentially Western forces — right to Russia's doorstep. At the same time, he also understood that neither the EU nor NATO would have much interest in admitting a dysfunctional, unreformed country, let alone one at war. Russia had long worked on multiple fronts to keep Ukraine on edge. It had co-opted Ukrainian leaders, undermined reformers, and sowed disinformation, all with the goal of keeping Ukraine a destabilized borderland that could be easily manipulated. With Yanukovych's departure, Putin showed just how far he was willing to go to achieve those goals.

At the end of February 2014, a group of masked and armed men seized control of Crimea, a peninsula on Ukraine's southern Black Sea coast. Crimea is internationally recognized as part of Ukraine but is heavily populated by ethnic Russians, thanks to Stalin's deportation of Crimean Tatars to Kyrgyzstan and Uzbekistan and importation of Soviet Russians. The provisional government in Kyiv had just been established and was unprepared to mount a resistance.

It was hard to figure out what was going on. The masked men wore green uniforms with no identifying markings: Could they really be Russian forces? The Obama reset with Russia was long over, but the international community was nevertheless unsure how to respond and reluctant to call out the Russians on their claim that the "little green men" were not Russian troops — which it soon became evident they were. Russia's effective use of *maskirovka,* or military deception, created confusion, giving it time to occupy the entire peninsula before the West could react.

On March 16, Russia's proxies in the Crimean government organized an illegal referendum, at the barrel of a gun, asking Crimeans whether they wanted to become a part of Russia or gain greater autonomy within Ukraine. Keeping the status quo was not a referendum option, and neither were those who favored the status quo allowed to campaign for it. The "referendum" violated the Ukrainian constitution, the Crimean constitution, and international standards and was not recognized as legitimate by the international community. But Russia hailed the vote as proof that people in Crimea wanted to become a part of Russia, even though earlier public opinion polling had indicated the opposite. Two days later Putin signed a law making it so.

The whole charade was an example of how Putin uses apparently democratic practices to produce undemocratic results, and it was a tactical masterstroke. Crimea was historically important to Russia, but annexing it also served Russia's geostrategic goal of controlling the Black Sea and destabilizing Kyiv. It took almost a full year for Putin to come completely clean about Russia's planning and military involvement in the annexation of the peninsula. By that point Crimea had long been firmly under Russian control.

Within a month of illegally occupying Crimea, Russia struck again. This time the Russians sought control of the Donbas, Ukraine's aging industrial heartland, which, like Crimea, was located adjacent to Russia's western border. As in Crimea, a sizable ethnic Russian community lived in the Donbas, most of whose members had arrived as the area industrialized in the early twentieth century. These factors made the Donbas another natural target for Russian meddling.

In the Donbas, a motley crew of ethnic Ukrainians and ethnic Russians — all of them directed by Moscow — took up arms against Ukraine; they were joined by regular Russian soldiers and mercenaries. Yet Russia once again denied any involvement in the fighting inside Ukraine, implausibly claiming that even the regular Russian soldiers fighting there were simply volunteers who were acting on their own while on vacation. It was clear, however, that the invasion was planned, organized, supplied, financed, and often manned by Russia. In case there was any doubt about who was leading the charge, Russia massed troops and tanks at the border to intimidate the Ukrainian troops and provide reinforcement if needed. To keep it simple, we called the war against Ukraine "Russia-led."

At the outset the Russia-led fighters in the Donbas saw stunning success, taking wide swaths of territory. The Ukrainian military was caught off guard by these initial victories and was still on its back foot. Years of corrupt generals skimming off the defense budget had left Ukraine's armed forces ill-equipped and ill-trained. It fell to ordinary Ukrainians to mount the country's defense. Ukrainian patriots went to war with whatever they could find, frequently just a grandfather's World War II–era rifle. Their courage was awe-inspiring, as was the context in which it was happening: in a matter of months the Ukrainian people had risen up against Yanukovych and chased him out of the country, and then they mounted a second campaign, this time to defend their nation's sovereignty against foreign aggression. The Russian invasion accomplished what the Ukrainian government had failed to do over the past twenty-three years of independence: unify the fractured Ukrainian people into one cohesive nation.

Slowly, as the Ukrainian military regrouped, it began to push back the Russia-led proxies. If conventional military forces massed on the other side of the Russian border intervened, the Ukrainians would have been routed, but as long as Russian "volunteers" and local proxies were the only ones fighting, the government in Kyiv stood a chance.

To increase pressure on Kyiv, Moscow established the so-called People's Republics of Luhansk and Donetsk in the part of the Donbas it occupied. Ukraine's acting government found itself trying not just to defend Ukrainian lands but also to mobilize international support and manage a bankrupt country. Thankfully, the U.S. and our partners levied robust economic sanctions against Russian companies and individuals, which sent a strong and painful signal to Putin that the West was watching.

In May, Petro Poroshenko, a prominent oligarch and politician whose television station had backed the protests on the Maydan, was elected president of Ukraine, replacing the exiled Yanukovych. Ukrainians hoped Poroshenko would provide reform-minded leadership and forcefully resist Russia's incursions into Ukrainian territory. But Ukraine's challenges continued to multiply after his election.

Russia had succeeded in illegally occupying Crimea, but the Russia-led military campaign in the Donbas continued, and was reinforced by the rollout of the vast influence arsenal I had seen in my previous postings. The Russians kept Ukrainians fearful and confused by strategically spreading rumors, deploying misinformation on social media, and engaging in targeted cyberattacks. They even sent texts taunting deployed soldiers and their families, creating untold heartache. Right before the 2014 presidential elections they successfully compromised part of Ukraine's Central Election Commission computer system, resulting in concerns about possible additional attacks. Fortunately that attack did not put the election results in doubt, but other actions were harder to combat.

One rumor that took on a life of its own claimed that Ukrainian troops had crucified a small boy in eastern Ukraine because he was a Russian-speaker — a story undoubtedly crafted to inspire anti-Ukrainian government sentiment among the region's many Russian-speakers. Crazy stories and conspiracies seemed to spread like wildfire, were often believed, and were extraordinarily difficult to battle. In short, Russia utilized disinformation to chip away at any confidence Ukrainians had in their democratically elected, Western-oriented government. Putin thought he could convince them that an authoritarian regime like Russia's provided a better option — stability and predictability — than the unruliness of democracy.

In the Donbas the Russian military was getting bolder. In July 2014, two months after Poroshenko's election, a Russian surface-to-air missile struck a Malaysian passenger jet as it flew over Donbas, killing all 298 people aboard. It was probably a tactical miscalculation by men on the ground, but Russia never acknowledged responsibility, instead offering over twenty different explanations — a classic disinformation gambit aimed at confusing the public rather than revealing the truth.

Then, in August, with Ukraine regaining lost territory, Russia gave up any pretense that it wasn't involved in the war. Putin wanted to retain enough hold on the Donbas to keep Ukraine's future uncertain. Reinforced with heavy weaponry, Russian forces surged across the border into Ukraine. Russia called the line of troops, trucks, tanks, and artillery a "humanitarian convoy," but no amount of spin could cover up what was happening.

Ukrainian forces were no match for the Russian army, and Kyiv quickly lost its momentum. Even in battles where the Ukrainians waved a white flag, the Russians continued the carnage, in one case massacring up to four hundred Ukrainian soldiers as they retreated after the Battle of Ilovyask. That was the official count, but eyewitnesses claim considerably more perished.

With Ukraine losing badly and casualties mounting, Poroshenko had no choice but to accept international mediation. Over the next six months, Ukraine, Russia, and Russia's two proxy entities in the Donbas, the Luhansk and Donetsk People's Republics, agreed to two protocols. Known as the Minsk Agreements, they called for a ceasefire and formed the framework for a resolution to the conflict. But neither that nor subsequent ceasefires held, and the fighting settled into a World War I trench warfare standoff, with Ukraine suffering several casualties on a nearly weekly basis. Even at the time of this writing, the Minsk Agreements are only partially implemented, and Russia continues to illegally occupy roughly 7 percent of Ukrainian territory, including Crimea. Most observers credit international sanctions for preventing Russia-led forces from pressing farther west and causing further Ukrainian losses.

As the forces in the Donbas became locked in a stalemate, the war by other means continued unabated. Every day Russia launched thousands of cyberattacks on Ukrainian infrastructure. Ukraine's cyber defenses held against most but not all of them. In December 2015 a cyberattack on Ukraine's electrical grid plunged about a quarter of a million people in western Ukraine into darkness for up to six hours. It could have been a lot worse, but the significance of the event was not lost on the international community. Nations had feared an attack on their electrical grids for decades, but this was the first time it actually happened. Ukrainian experts quickly concluded that Russia was to blame. This was a wake-up call, not just for Ukraine but also for any country with reason to fear a hostile Russia.

The hybrid war had many prongs. Russia launched a campaign of targeted assassinations, eliminating senior Ukrainians who stood in Russia's way. Many of these killings were carried out by highly sophisticated explosions with almost no collateral damage, even on the streets of central Kyiv. It was a message from the Kremlin to the leaders of Ukraine: we know where you are, and we can reach right into the heart of your capital to get you.

It was also a message for Russia's opponents. Russia was using Ukraine as a testing ground, trying out new military equipment and tactics in the Donbas and experimenting with different kinds of cyberattacks and new ways of trolling the public. Those methods would later resurface in Syria, the U.S., and Europe, underscoring our view that we needed to robustly support Ukraine against Russia's attacks. The U.S. understood that it was in our interest to help the Ukrainians turn their country into a proving ground, the place where Western values, strategy, and technology would prevail against Russia's hybrid war.

It wouldn't be easy to counter these Russian tactics, and in some ways it would be impossible to repair the damage. By the summer of 2016, the war in the Donbas had cost the lives of more than 10,000 souls. It was considered another frozen conflict in the former Soviet Union, but for the Ukrainians, who saw fighting on their eastern front almost every day, it was hard to see it as anything less than a hot war.

Not surprisingly, the death and destruction had left Ukraine in desperate straits, especially when added to still-present challenges of remedying a country racked by years of mismanagement and corruption. When Yanukovych fled to Russia, he left a looted treasury, government services on the verge of stalling, and a country dependent on Russia for its energy needs. The Revolution of Dignity may have succeeded, but the country was at risk of collapse. Ukrainians needed help, and they looked to the West for that support. Fortunately a committed and coordinated international community of donors was ready to come to their aid. Besides the U.S., Ukraine had supporters in the European Union, our fellow G7 countries (the UK, France, Germany, Italy, Canada, and Japan), and international institutions such as the International Monetary Fund, the World Bank, the European Bank for Reconstruction and Development, and the UN. These donors understood how critical Ukraine's security, stability, and success were to our collective interests. They understood that Ukraine was literally the front line between the West and a newly aggressive and militaristic Russia. If we could help the Ukrainians build a new Ukraine, we could ensure that this strategically located country would not become a destabilized Russian satellite in the center of Europe but rather a democratic nation that was prosperous, secure — and a good partner. Russia's multivector attack on Ukraine, its unilateral decision to change international borders, and the implications for the U.S. and the rest of the world increased the urgency of the task.

In the U.S., Vice President Biden led an interagency team to focus U.S. policy and assistance to help Ukraine. He personally engaged with Poroshenko to encourage him to implement reforms that would build confidence in democracy and create sustainable economic growth for *all* Ukrainians. He also provided top cover for the embassy to insist that the Ukrainian government keep its commitments.

But while the U.S. and the other donors wanted to help, the international community had been down this road before and insisted on putting conditions on the assistance. Ukraine had to show that it would use taxpayers' money responsibly and not divert it to the pockets of oligarchs or sink it into bloated and opaque bureaucracies. The specific conditions were negotiated with Ukraine, of course; the international community could no more dictate terms than Ukraine could insist on support. It was a delicate balance aimed at helping the country to reform without undermining Ukrainian public support. Push too hard on reforming the economy, for example, and the most vulnerable would fall through the cracks while the most dissatisfied could create civil unrest. But push too little and entrenched corrupt interests would keep holding on, appropriating government resources for themselves, and ignoring the needs of the vulnerable and the dissatisfied alike.

In theory Poroshenko had no problem agreeing to political and economic reforms in exchange for international assistance. After all, eradicating corruption and establishing rule of law were key demands of the Revolution of Dignity, which he had ridden to power, and progress in these areas would do much to improve the lives of ordinary Ukrainians. Ukraine was fighting a two-front war: a war for territorial integrity and a war for what kind of a country it would become. The Ukrainians had to prevail in both fights to secure their future.

In the two years since the Revolution of Dignity, Poroshenko's government, Ukraine's activists, and the international community had worked together to produce some remarkable achievements: a stabilized economy; significant reform of the banking system; and energy independence from Russia. But change never comes in a straight line, and it almost always brings with it a lot of pain. As I watched these events from afar, I was impressed by what Ukraine had accomplished — and concerned by the obstacles it still had to overcome.

FOR ME, an ocean and a continent away in Washington, the Revolution of Dignity and the Ukrainians' defense of their homeland from Russian aggression were inspiring. With the ambassadorial post in Kyiv about to open, I found myself pulled toward Ukraine, a country where change seemed possible and the first place I had assumed a leadership role. I wanted to play a part in these momentous events. With perhaps some hubris, I thought that I was uniquely qualified to help the Ukrainians in this historic moment.

But two things held me back. For one, I wasn't really eager to move back overseas. I liked living in the U.S., and I liked having my privacy back. In Yerevan and Bishkek, I had felt on display, my every action monitored and commented upon. And then there was Mama. At eighty-eight, she was still the life of the party, but she was slowing down. She was living independently in the North Carolina community that she and Papa retired to, but she had the occasional medical emergency that often comes with age. I could take care of her from Washington, but not from Kyiv. If I went to Ukraine, Mama would have to come too.

We discussed it, and Mama, always game for an adventure, blessed the decision to throw my hat in the ring and agreed to go to Ukraine if I got the job. At least, that's my version of the story. I later learned that she told her friends that she was going to Kyiv because I would have a tough job and I needed her support. Mama always taught us that we needed to take care of each other, and that's what we were doing.

MY UKRAINE CONFIRMATION process was as uneventful as the Armenia confirmation process had been dramatic. As in Armenia, I would be the first woman in the role of ambassador, and it would be a level jump in terms of visibility and importance of my mission. I felt I was ready for it, and I wanted to do a good job. On July 14, 2016, I got the welcome news that I had been confirmed by voice vote in the Senate. Mama and I worked fast to move her out of her apartment in North Carolina and me out of my house in Virginia. Five weeks later we were in Ukraine.

We arrived in Kyiv on a hot and dusty Monday in late August 2016, just in time for the country's Independence Day celebrations on August 24, as the Ukrainians had requested. We had no time to settle in before I started drinking from the firehose. Within days I presented my letter of credentials to President Poroshenko, whom I had known slightly during my last time in Ukraine. He welcomed me back warmly, and — in the first sign of how much had changed — he brought up the challenge of corruption unprompted. The last time I had served in Kyiv, corruption wasn't mentioned in polite society, let alone in the president's presence. I took it as a good sign: you can't fix things if you can't even talk about them.

Two years after the Revolution of Dignity, corruption was still an ongoing and urgent problem, one made infinitely more challenging by the fact that not everyone wanted change. The people with the most power — namely, the oligarchs — were especially resistant. It made for a two-steps-forward, one-step-back process.

To be sure, progress was visible, thanks to reformers in the government and the legislature working with enterprising civil society activists. Necessary and major structural economic changes had been achieved, but serious challenges remained. Most Ukrainians didn't yet feel like they were better off. They were grappling with inflation, tariff hikes, falling incomes, and a government that still wasn't providing the necessary services. People had a lot to be disappointed about. Prosperity hadn't reached most households. Justice had not been served for "the Heavenly Hundred" who had perished near the Maydan. And not a penny of the stolen assets that former president Yanukovych had taken with him to his Russian exile had been recovered.

Even worse, the pace of reform seemed to be slowing, and Ukrainians openly wondered whether Poroshenko's commitment to reform was waning as well. There was widespread grumbling that the president, who had promised to sell his companies if elected, was still operating his wide-

Papa, handsome in a Yugoslavian military uniform circa 1940, shortly before the Nazis invaded and sent him to a POW camp in Germany.

The Theokritoff family before a feared meeting with the Gestapo. Mama, with braids, is standing on the far left. While the children seem unperturbed, the grim look on Oma's face telegraphs how worried she was.

The Yovanovitch family in Kent, circa 1980.

With Mama and André at my swearing-in as a Foreign Service officer, March 1986. We are standing in front of a bust of Ambassador Ben Franklin, our country's first diplomat.

Wearing my green floral dress in Wiesbaden, en route to Mogadishu, 1986.

In Mogadishu circa 1987, with some of our locally employed staff—the backbone of every U.S. embassy operation—who provide local knowledge, continuity, and expertise.

Cinderella in my kitchenette, on the way to the Diplomatic Ball at Buckingham Palace, 1989.

The scene during Russia's 1993 constitutional crisis, after President Yeltsin ordered the army to fire tank rounds at the Russian parliament. The nearby U.S. embassy is not quite visible behind and to the lower right of the burning building.

At the Vorontsov Palace in Crimea, Ukraine, circa 1994, twenty years before the Russian invasion and when Americans could still travel to Crimea. Churchill stayed here when he, Stalin, and Roosevelt negotiated the Yalta Agreement and decided the future of eastern Europe.

Election monitoring with Ambassador Pascual (standing to my right) during Ukraine's 2002 parliamentary elections.

In 2005, Under Secretary of State Nicholas Burns swearing me in as ambassador to Kyrgyzstan in the Treaty Room at the State Department. Zoë did double duty, holding the Bible and checking to make sure that Nick was getting it right.

In 2008, Under Secretary of State Bill Burns swearing me in as ambassador to Armenia in the same room, with Zoë reprising her role.

In 2016, Deputy Secretary of State Tony Blinken swearing me in as ambassador to Ukraine. The photos document Zoë growing up — and me getting older.

OATH OF OFFICE

I, *Marie L. Yovanovitch*

DO SOLEMNLY SWEAR

THAT I WILL SUPPORT AND DEFEND

THE CONSTITUTION OF THE UNITED STATES

AGAINST ALL ENEMIES FOREIGN AND DOMESTIC

THAT I WILL BEAR TRUE FAITH

AND ALLEGIANCE TO THE SAME

THAT I TAKE THIS OBLIGATION FREELY

AND WITHOUT ANY MENTAL RESERVATION

OR PURPOSE OF EVASION

THAT I WILL WELL AND FAITHFULLY

DISCHARGE THE DUTIES OF THE OFFICE

ON WHICH I AM ABOUT TO ENTER

SO HELP ME GOD.

Marie L. Yovanovitch   *Nicholas Burns*

August 5, 2005

DEPARTMENT OF STATE
WASHINGTON, D.C.

Text of the oath of office that I took when I entered the Foreign Service and each time I became ambassador. It is simple and direct: our role is to "support and defend the Constitution of the United States."

With base commander Colonel Joel Reese and Kyrgyz president Kurmanbek Bakiyev at the Manas Air Base for the fifth anniversary of the 9/11 attacks. I had hoped that this event would help smooth friction over the base.

With Kyrgyz deputy minister of defense General Kubanychbek Oruzbayev on a U.S. helicopter over Afghanistan, circa 2007. The high-level Kyrgyz delegation heard firsthand from the Afghans how important their contribution was to the War on Terror.

With jazz great Stanley Jordan and famed Armenian guitarist Armen Blbulyan in Yerevan, circa 2009. Cultural diplomacy is one of the most effective ways to win hearts and minds.

In 2009, President Obama invited Armenian president Sargsyan to Washington to signal support for Turkish-Armenian rapprochement. The physical distance between the two delegations symbolized to me the gulf between the two sides. Secretary Clinton and I are on the right.

Talking with the press the morning after the U.S. presidential election in 2016.

With Ukrainian ambassador Chalyy, Foreign Minister Klimkin, President Poroshenko, President Trump, Vice President Pence, and National Security Advisor McMaster in the Oval Office, June 20, 2017.

Ukraine's general prosecutor, Yuriy Lutsenko, sought an alliance with President Trump's personal attorney, Rudy Giuliani, which precipitated my recall as U.S. ambassador to Ukraine.

Ukrainian oligarch Ihor Kolomoiskyy, who owned and who has been charged with systematically looting Ukraine's biggest bank. In 2021 the U.S. government sanctioned Kolomoiskyy for corrupt activities.

Ukrainian oligarch Dmytro Firtash, living in Austria since 2014 as he fights U.S. extradition efforts on bribery charges. Information emerged that Firtash was apparently working with Lev Parnas and Igor Fruman to remove obstacles to his energy business in Ukraine, which included me.

Head of the National Anti-Corruption Bureau of Ukraine (NABU) Artem Sytnyk and head of the Special Anti-Corruption Prosecutor's Office (SAPO) Nazar Kholodnytskyy. The U.S. government strongly supported these institutions.

Lev Parnas, along with Igor Fruman, worked with Ukrainian general prosecutor Lutsenko and Rudy Giuliani to dig up dirt on Vice President Biden in Ukraine and to remove me from my post.

Igor Fruman, who was arrested along with Lev Parnas two days before my closed deposition in October 2019.

Rudy Giuliani, former mayor of New York and Trump's personal lawyer, worked with Fruman, Parnas, and Lutsenko to launch investigations in Ukraine with the goal of maligning Vice President Biden, helping President Trump in his reelection campaign, and removing me.

On the front line of Russia's war against Ukraine on New Year's Eve 2016, with Senator Klobuchar, Senator McCain, President Poroshenko, and Senator Graham. A picture is worth a thousand words, and this one conveyed strong bipartisan support for Ukraine.

With Ukrainian navy commander Admiral Ihor Voronchenko on a Ukrainian Gyurza-M class gunboat in the Sea of Azov just one month before Russian forces seized three Ukrainian vessels and twenty-four Ukrainian sailors.

One of my first stops when I arrived in Ukraine in August 2016 was at this wall honoring Ukrainian soldiers killed in the Donbas. When I departed in 2019, the war had taken the lives of around 13,000 Ukrainian soldiers and civilians.

With former Ukrainian detainee Ihor Kozlovskyy, a historian and religious scholar. Political officer Chris Anderson is behind me with other former detainees. It was a U.S. embassy priority to help free the hundreds of Ukrainians held by Russia-led forces.

At a July 4 reception in Kyiv, toasting U.S. independence with DCM George Kent. George's Nalgene water bottle and bow tie, made famous during his impeachment testimony, did not make an appearance at this event. Mama is visible at lower left.

Presenting a plaque posthumously honoring Kateryna Handzyuk as Ukraine's Woman of Courage for her work as a journalist and anti-corruption activist to her father, Viktor Handzyuk. In 2018, Kateryna was attacked with acid, and she died in excruciating pain months later.

In every country where I served as ambassador, I supported efforts to create mentoring programs for girls and women. In Ukraine, I worked with British ambassador Judith Gough (to my right) and French ambassador Isabelle Dumont (to my left) to champion and celebrate women. Next to Isabelle is Oksana Markarova, the minister of finance, who later became the Ukrainian ambassador to the United States.

Team America: with Republican senators John Barrasso, Mike Crapo, and John Kennedy at the meeting with Ukrainian foreign minister Pavlo Klimkin. The senators presented a united front, vigorously defending me after the Lutsenko interview was published in *The Hill*.

The week after Deputy Secretary Sullivan informed me that I was being removed as ambassador to Ukraine, the National Defense University honored my work with the military. Ambassador Dan Smith is on the left and NDU president Admiral Fritz Roegge on the right.

With lead counsel Larry Robbins at the witness table before the impeachment hearing, November 15, 2019. Behind us are seated (left to right) John Naland, Grace Kennan Warnecke, Beth Jones, André, Laurie Rubenstein, Rachel Li Wai Suen, and Larry's law partner, Dick Sauber (focusing the cell phone).

With Zoë, André, Fenway, and Scout after the closed-door deposition on October 11, 2019. Our happy relief is evident.

ranging business empire. Worse, people couldn't understand why he was still holding on to his firm in Russia, a country at war with Ukraine. It made people wonder whether he was working in their interests or his own.

Even the corruption that the 2014 revolution had initially seemed to tamp down was creeping back. After the revolution, Ukraine's oligarchs had kept their heads down, fearing the loss of their extensive holdings — or their liberty. But so far no oligarch or high-level government official had been prosecuted, much less convicted, for corruption. This constituted a clear and egregious failure to meet the core demand of the Revolution of Dignity: to treat everyone as equal before the law. The Ukrainian people could see that some people were still more equal than others, and it rankled, contributing to their growing doubt about Poroshenko's government. If the government wasn't trustworthy, how could it hold the oligarchs accountable, given their symbiotic relationship with those in power?

One thing was becoming clear: the oligarchs were back, if they had ever left. And I was about to find out just how powerful they were.

I FACED my first crisis very early in my posting. The Ukrainian government had over $2 billion on the line in financing from the U.S. and other international donors, including the International Monetary Fund (IMF) and the European Bank for Reconstruction and Development (EBRD). The various forms of financing would enable Ukraine to fund the government, purchase enough heating gas to make it through the winter, and raise additional capital in international markets to continue paying for the country's needs. But the money was conditioned on a number of reforms, and shortly after I arrived in Kyiv, it became clear that Ukraine wasn't going to qualify.

One key reform required the installation of independent supervisory boards to oversee Ukraine's large government-run companies; this took business decisions out of the hands of politicians and placed them with experts looking after the best interests of the company. As a legacy of communism, Ukraine still owned and operated many enterprises, such as the railroads, an enormous defense conglomerate, and Naftohaz, the country's gas and oil company. These companies had billions of dollars sloshing around, murky business practices, and no oversight of any kind. Someone needed to make sure that laws weren't being broken, that funds weren't disappearing, and that these state-owned enterprises were generally being run in a way that benefited the Ukrainian people rather than the people in charge.

Establishing independent supervisory boards in accordance with accepted international business practice would mark a sharp break with the past. The international community insisted that board members be qualified, compensated well enough to attract talented candidates, and selected by a panel composed of Ukrainian government officials, Ukrainian activists, and international officials. Going through the motions wasn't going to cut it if Ukraine wanted the donor community to trust it with other countries' money. We meant business.

A related and equally important reform focused specifically on Naftohaz, Ukraine's largest company, and was known as "unbundling." A conglomerate of Naftohaz's size and reach could not be reformed if it continued to control all aspects of the business, in which opaque and unsupervised transactions between various subsidiaries were the norm. Millions of dollars could get lost to private pockets in these transactions, and routinely did. Most importantly, Ukraine needed to separate gas production and supply on the one hand from the gas transmission system on the other. The separation was crucial to stop rampant corruption and help create a competitive gas market based on market principles.

Previously oligarchs aligned with Naftohaz officials had been able to steal from the company and its owners (the Ukrainian people) by making undisclosed and inflated deals among the various subsidiaries. Unbundling Naftohaz into different companies, still owned by the Ukrainian government but separated and managed and overseen according to international best practice, would make this type of self-dealing much more difficult to pull off.

New Naftohaz management, appointed in 2014, had embraced this reform mandate and aggressively embarked upon the mammoth task of transforming the company. Their work was so successful that Ukraine had been able to end government subsidies to Naftohaz, which had ballooned to 7 percent of the country's GDP. By March 2016 Naftohaz had its supervisory board in place — three British oil and gas executives with almost one hundred years' experience among them plus two individuals selected by the government — to oversee the company. It even turned a profit in 2016, a huge win for the nation's finances and its citizens.

But it was still too easy to funnel Naftohaz money into the pockets of the oligarchs and corrupt insiders. Although the top level of the company was moving in the right direction, some of its constituent parts were trying to continue business as usual — most glaringly at UTH, Naftohaz's gas transmission subsidiary. Indeed, UTH and its patrons in the Ukrainian government were showing such resistance to reform that they had suddenly and seriously jeopardized those billions of dollars' worth of international financing.

In the late summer of 2016, not long after I took up my new post, the Naftohaz supervisory board members decided to take action and fired the head of UTH, Ihor Prokopiv, on suspicion of corruption. The Ukrainian government objected vigorously, and when the board remained firm, the government took the decision out of the board's hands. They transferred UTH from Naftohaz control to the Ministry of Economy, with Prokopiv still in charge. The order came from the top, the result of an emergency dead-of-night cabinet meeting called by Prime Minister Volodymyr Groysman.

Ukraine's government justified the action by calling it unbundling. Of course, true unbundling would have required more than just moving UTH from one place to another; it would have involved creating a business model that ensured a well-managed divorce from Naftohaz, efficient and separate management, better customer service, and transparent practices. There was no business plan to ensure any of this; this was just a slick maneuver to save Prokopiv's head and ensure that the corruption could continue. Moving UTH to the Ministry of Economy put the company under the oversight of Stepan Kubiv, a man said to have strong ties to the same man that Prokopiv was allegedly connected to: the exiled Ukrainian oligarch Dmytro Firtash.

Linked to Russian organized crime, Firtash had made his name in the early 2000s as a middleman for the Russian state-owned company Gazprom and then through a company called RosUkrEnergo. Leveraging his Moscow connections and Ukraine's heavy reliance on Russian fuel imports, he had bought gas from Russia and sold it to Ukraine in an extortionate scheme that I had watched from afar with some concern during my time in Kyrgyzstan. The billions in ill-gotten gains were kicked back to Russian and Ukrainian oligarchs and government officials, with a healthy portion kept for Firtash himself. Everyone was a winner, except the Ukrainian people.

More recently Firtash had been making money on internal gas distribution. Ukraine subsidized household gas purchases but expected businesses, including the many owned by Firtash, to pay market rates. Firtash took advantage of the difference in price and purchased subsidized gas for his companies by claiming that it was going to households. There were various other schemes to profit illegally, including just pocketing the proceeds and never paying UTH for the gas supplied. Amazingly, Firtash got away with it. For years. Clearly reform and transparency in the gas sector would have disrupted the Firtash business model.

Shortly after Yanukovych's 2014 ouster, Firtash was arrested at U.S. request in Vienna, Austria. At the time of this writing, he is still there, fighting extradition to the U.S. to face charges of bribery, racketeering, and money laundering. Yet neither U.S. indictment, nor his exile in Austria, nor even his ties to Russia — a country at war with Ukraine — stopped Firtash from continuing to hold outsized influence in his homeland.

After his March 2014 arrest, and as Ukraine's first post-revolution presidential election approached, Firtash had summoned to Vienna then-candidate Poroshenko and his main opponent, world heavyweight boxing champion Vitaliy Klychko. Klychko emerged from that proverbial smoke-filled backroom meeting to announce that he would run for mayor of Kyiv, leaving the presidential field clear for Poroshenko. Everyone in that meeting says something different about what happened, but you have to wonder why candidates running for president in Ukraine would take the time to travel to a different country when they could have met more easily in Kyiv. What influence did Firtash have over the men who ultimately became president of Ukraine and mayor of Kyiv in 2014?

What influence, for that matter, did Firtash have over Ihor Prokopiv, the embattled head of UTH, and his new boss, Economy Minister Stepan Kubiv? As with so much else in Ukraine's nontransparent energy world, it would have been difficult to prove that Firtash was behind the decision to move UTH to the Ministry of Economy or that Prokopiv and the economy minister were his lackeys. But it was clear that Firtash stood to benefit from the move, since it would enable his businesses to continue to operate without disruption.

The other oligarchs would benefit as well. While reformers in and out of government were applauding the decision of the Naftohaz board to fire Prokopiv, it set off alarm bells for less reform-minded Ukrainians, who feared the precedent of an independent supervisory board firing a corrupt Ukrainian. If the decision stood, it would put a lot of corrupt Ukrainians and their schemes at risk. Which was precisely the point.

Whatever the motivations, the UTH move would have violated key reforms that Ukraine had agreed to in exchange for assistance from the international community. We at the embassy knew this had to stop before this brazen display of corruption imperiled Ukraine's badly needed international financing — and before it undermined U.S. faith in Ukraine's commitment to reform its gas sector and fight corruption.

I FIRST HEARD about the UTH crisis from one of the other donors at a conference on a Saturday afternoon. This issue was arcane, and I had no idea what he was talking about. I consulted with Washington, and late on Sunday night, barely a month into my new ambassadorship, I called Prime Minister Groysman, a man I had met just once. I told Groysman that the decision to move UTH to the Ministry of Economy was ill-advised; if it was not reversed, I explained, the U.S. could not go forward with the billion-dollar loan guarantee that would enable Ukraine to raise bonds on the international markets and finance government spending. I added that I couldn't speak for other donors, but they would likely also withhold their financing. With a child audibly crying in the background, the prime minister told me he didn't understand why the UTH decision violated Ukrainian commitments regarding corporate governance and unbundling, but he said he'd look into it and get back to me.

Two days later I joined other international donors at a meeting that Prime Minister Groysman convened to discuss the matter with select cabinet members and Naftohaz's reform team. It was tense. Billions were on the line, and the international donors were looking to me to lead the charge — the one who had just arrived and who knew the least about the subject, I thought to myself. But I represented the U.S., and the U.S. leads. I plunged in, explained the problem, and as diplomatically as possible noted that billions in international support would not be forthcoming unless Ukraine kept its word and followed through on its promise to reform and to unbundle Naftohaz — real unbundling, not pretend unbundling. Then everyone else had a swing.

Groysman responded by throwing Minister Kubiv under the bus. He alleged that he had been misled into thinking that the transfer of UTH to the ministry constituted unbundling and would meet with international donor approval. That, of course, raised the questions of why it had been done so quickly, in the middle of the night, without consultation, and why the Ukrainians were protecting Prokopiv. Pleasant to the end, Groysman said that he agreed with the international community and declared that the Economy Ministry's takeover of UTH was "suspended."

At least, that's how his interpreter translated Groysman's Ukrainian into English. But when I heard the word "suspended," I knew that wouldn't work. I thought it might be an interpretation error, but I knew I couldn't let it go. A suspension wouldn't solve the problem, and we'd all be back fighting this same fight once the billions had been transferred and the Ukrainians thought the suspension had outlasted the international community's attention. I asked Groysman point-blank whether he meant "suspended" or "canceled." You could have heard a pin drop as Groysman and his interpreter communicated in Ukrainian. The answer came back "canceled" — to a collective sigh of relief.

That precise answer notwithstanding, the decision didn't get undone immediately. It took a meeting several days later between Vice President Biden and President Poroshenko, both of whom were in New York for the annual meeting of the United Nations General Assembly. When Vice President Biden raised the backtracking on Naftohaz, Poroshenko claimed he knew nothing about it and blamed Groysman (just as Groysman had blamed Minister Kubiv). That response infuriated Biden, and he let Poroshenko know he wasn't buying it. Nothing of this magnitude happened in Ukraine without Poroshenko knowing about it, and Biden told Poroshenko he was through with him unless he fixed the UTH mess. Poroshenko called back to Kyiv, and the cabinet finally reversed its earlier decision.

That was a good day. But the entire incident served as both a reminder and a foreshadowing: the old Ukraine still had enormous power, and it wasn't willing to let go without a fight.

I wasn't pleased when the details about my meetings, including my role in laying down the law with Groysman, found their way into the Ukrainian media. No matter how hard the fist inside the velvet glove, I prefer U.S. diplomacy to stay behind closed doors, with everyone saving face and coming out a winner. But Washington wasn't worried. The assistant secretary to whom I reported laughed when I told her and replied, "The legend grows."

I was less sanguine. I hadn't been in Ukraine long enough to present myself to the Ukrainian public, and I wasn't sure who benefited from this kind of leaking. But I knew it wasn't me.

FIRTASH WASN'T the only oligarch trying to influence Ukraine's political system and undermine the government's commitment to reform. The same dynamic that I had seen in the energy sector played out in the banking sector.

It seemed that every oligarch — along with their less wealthy cousins, whom we called the minigarchs — owned a bank. They operated them like their own personal piggy banks, taking deposits from unsuspecting citizens and making loans to themselves at rock-bottom rates. They extended the loans indefinitely, meaning that the owners never needed to pay them back. As a result, many of the banks had turned into so-called zombie banks, institutions with net assets below zero that stayed in business only because their owners found new, unsuspecting depositors to sustain the pyramid scheme. Banks with unfunded obligations to their depositors presented a huge vulnerability; at any moment people could lose confidence, rush to withdraw their savings, and start a run on the banks that would destabilize the nation's economy. The banks escaped being shut down by the government only because there was no effective central bank oversight.

To avoid bank failures and their catastrophic consequences, many countries have central banks that promote the stability of the country's financial system and ensure the integrity of the banking system. The National Bank of Ukraine (NBU) had not been performing that function before 2014, but after the Revolution of Dignity, the fearless reformer Valeriya Hontareva took the NBU helm and along with it the thankless job of launching the wholesale cleanup of Ukraine's banking sector. She conducted stress tests to see which of Ukraine's many banks were viable. By the time I arrived, the NBU had closed approximately eighty of the zombie banks, making lots of powerful enemies for Hontereva in the process.

But the biggest zombie bank of all, PryvatBank, was still open, and fixing it was proving to be an enormous and risky challenge. In 2016 PryvatBank provided services to 48 percent of Ukrainians who used banking services, issued 51 percent of Ukrainian debit and credit cards, and held 54 percent of deposits from individuals. It was practically a dictionary definition of too big to fail. Yet that is exactly what was happening: an audit showed that PryvatBank had at least a $5.55 billion shortfall. More than 95 percent of the bank's corporate loans had gone to businesses connected to the bank's owners, through a myriad of front companies and a blizzard of transactions moving the money through dozens of countries. That money was never going to get repaid. Left to its own devices, in other words, PryvatBank would almost inevitably implode at some point, and an uncontrolled bank crash would likely take the Ukrainian economy down with it.

The only clear path forward was for the government to nationalize PryvatBank — to take over its assets and liabilities and make up the difference from the national budget. It wouldn't be easy or pain-free; a new obligation of $5 billion-plus was difficult to contemplate for a country with a $93 billion GDP. But removing this tremendous risk to Ukraine's economy was so essential to ensure a stable economic future that the IMF made nationalization of PryvatBank a condition for its next loan.

The urgent need to nationalize PryvatBank featured in every call with Vice President Biden in the fall of 2016, but Poroshenko wouldn't move to bring the bank under government control. It's not that Ukraine's leaders didn't understand their enormous vulnerability; they did. They were dragging their feet nonetheless, for one reason, and it wasn't the $5 billion gut punch to the national budget. It was that the most prominent owner of the bank, the powerful oligarch Ihor Kolomoiskyy, wanted to keep his cash cow. Poroshenko, whose relationship with Kolomoiskyy was already strained, was struggling with the difficult decision to seize the bank and possibly make an enemy of someone well equipped to destroy his political future.

Special K, as we called him at the embassy, was one of the richest men in Ukraine. In truth he spent most of his time in Israel, where he also held citizenship, but his absence didn't diminish his influence, in large part because Kolomoiskyy owned 1+1, Ukraine's most popular television station. He didn't hesitate to use the station to sway public opinion against Poroshenko or any other official when they did things that displeased him. His halo of white hair, beard, and twinkling eyes gave Special K the look of a benevolent Kris Kringle, but he terrified many high-level Ukrainians with his take-no-prisoners approach to negotiations. For Hontereva's efforts to nationalize the bank, Kolomoiskyy orchestrated a vicious campaign against her. She received numerous death threats, saw her home spray-painted with epithets, and suffered constant protests at the NBU offices by a rent-a-crowd attacking her work on behalf of the Ukrainian people.

Kolomoiskyy's corrupt reach allegedly extended to our own shores as well. Starting in 2006, he and his partners invested questionably sourced funds in commercial spaces and factories throughout the Midwest and were eventually linked to properties in Ohio, Florida, Michigan, Illinois, Indiana, New York, Kentucky, West Virginia, and Texas. The purchase of these properties in struggling factory towns was often accompanied by hope for urban renewal, but the promised investment never materialized. Instead Kolomoiskyy milked the profits and left in his wake unsafe factories marred by explosions and accidents, empty buildings, unpaid debts, and jobless for-mer factory workers. The FBI eventually raided properties in Cleveland and Miami linked to Kolomoiskyy, and the Justice Department is seeking civil forfeiture of properties allegedly purchased with misappropriated funds. In March 2021 the U.S. sanctioned Kolomoiskyy and members of his family owing to his involvement in "significant corruption" in Ukraine.

The Ukrainian leadership was locked in negotiations with Kolomoiskyy for months, but by 2016 time was running out. If they didn't reach an agree-ment to nationalize PryvatBank soon, there were two likely consequences. First, the IMF would not release the next loan to Ukraine, necessary to keep the government afloat. Second, there would likely be an uncontrolled col-lapse of PryvatBank, which could set off a panic and do serious damage to the Ukrainian economy. Someone clearly was going to have to force the decision with Special K. If Ukraine couldn't get it done alone, the U.S. was ready to provide support.

AT THE EMBASSY we came up with a game plan that aimed to make it clear that the full weight of the United States government was behind the nationalization of PryvatBank. We got word to Kolomoiskyy that the U.S. ambassador would like to meet with him. I was somewhat surprised when he agreed.

Kolomoiskyy flew into Kyiv from Israel on his private plane and came directly to my residence at around nine o'clock on an unseasonably warm night toward the end of 2016. Up close, Kris Kringle was charming and funny. I was less charming and not at all funny. Armed with a short set of talking points that had been cleared by multiple U.S. agencies, I read our position out loud to Special K, so he wouldn't think that I was freelancing.

It was an abbreviated meeting, during which Kolomoiskyy lied to me in the most agreeable and convincing manner. He said the bank was sol-vent and that the Ukrainian government now understood that nationaliz-ing PryvatBank was illegal and had agreed to halt its actions. Then he left for his next negotiating round with the Ukrainian government.

As soon as Kolomoiskyy left, I telephoned Hontereva to give her a heads-up about what he had said. The next day Hontereva called back to report that Special K had told the Ukrainians that the U.S. did not support Pryvat-Bank's nationalization. He was an equal opportunity liar, apparently.

The negotiations with Kolomoiskyy could not go on indefinitely, however. Poroshenko knew from his many calls with Vice President Biden and other international supporters of Ukraine that he had a stark choice to make: he could accept the IMF loan and nationalize PryvatBank, or he could turn it down and live with the risk that any day PryvatBank could go bankrupt and torpedo the Ukrainian economy. Fortunately, even Kolomoiskyy's charm and threats weren't enough to convince the Ukrainian government to forgo the desperately needed IMF loan. Two days after my meeting with Special K, Poroshenko managed to get Kolomoiskyy to agree that the Ukrainian government would nationalize PryvatBank.

But would Kolomoiskyy actually go through with the nationalization? It was a nail-biter, because Kolomoiskyy had a well-earned reputation for reneging on agreements and suing his adversaries. The Ukrainian government braced for the worst, but PryvatBank was finally nationalized in the waning days of 2016. Ukrainian and European bankers canceled their holiday plans so they could start the process of nationalization, stabilizing the bank with an injection of over $5 billion of Ukrainian taxpayer money.

The nationalization proceeded so smoothly that there was no loss of public confidence and no depositor run on the bank. Most Ukrainians never even realized that PryvatBank had been a giant Ponzi scheme that had nearly cost them their life savings. It was a victory for the financial stability of Ukraine. But as with the Naftohaz/UTH situation, it hadn't come as readily as it should have.

Once again I found my satisfaction with the outcome tempered by the publicity for my role in it. The Ukrainian press described my meeting with Kolomoiskyy at the residence as "very difficult" and "the point of no return." I wondered who was talking to the media. Who stood to gain from depicting our efforts in this way?

That a tremendous international effort had been required to implement something that the Ukrainian government should have embraced on its own only served to underscore the power of the old Ukraine. Not surprisingly, Special K didn't consider this game over. In the years ahead he would make repeated efforts to reclaim the bank. By that point, however, I would have bigger problems on my hands.

10

The Transition

NOVEMBER 8, 2016, election day in the United States, was also my birthday. That night Mama and some friends joined me for a low-key celebration at a restaurant in central Kyiv. I ate too much khachapuri, the most delicious Georgian cheese bread, and went to bed relatively early. I had to be up at the crack of dawn to make it to the embassy's election day breakfast. The plan was for Ukrainian dignitaries, the diplomatic community, and the press to see democracy in action as we watched the results coming in together. I fell asleep expecting to see Hillary Clinton elected president by morning in Kyiv.

I had liked working for Secretary Clinton at State. I had seen her in action during her visit to Armenia and when I returned to Washington for her final year and a half as secretary. She had an unmatched work ethic, and she was smart, creative, and funny. Moreover, she never shied away from tough talk with our foreign friends when warranted, something that many high-level American officials just won't do. When foreign leaders tried to muzzle the free press, no one was better positioned to respond. Clinton told them she understood: she too was often criticized by the U.S. media, but a free press is the hallmark of a democracy. There wasn't much anyone could say to argue with that, since everyone knew how viciously she was often pilloried.

The notion of a Trump presidency, though, unsettled me. Trump didn't seem to share many of the bedrock American principles that formed the basis for our partnerships around the world and which had motivated me to join the Foreign Service. He didn't seem to appreciate how alliances with our democratic friends had kept the peace, defeated communism, and enabled us to become prosperous and secure. From my perch, "Make America Great Again" was a dog whistle to our lesser angels. Trump wanted to close our borders, halt inclusion, and shut us off from global engagement — in short, to undermine much that in my view made our highly imperfect nation great, not just to ourselves but to the world. It was because of America's greatness, indeed, that the international community in Ukraine looked to the American embassy, where we represented a country of unmatched principle and power.

Trump seemed troublingly — and triumphantly — ignorant of reality both in the U.S. and abroad. Most relevant to my work, during the campaign he had appeared to support Russia's occupation of Crimea despite international consensus that this constituted an unlawful infringement of Ukraine's territorial sovereignty. I worried about how someone who seemed completely estranged from the facts could lead the country. His slogan of "America First" somehow implied that my colleagues and I did not put America first, which offended me. On a personal level, I found Trump's bullying behavior, his xenophobia, misogyny, and racism not just offensive and immoral but dangerous. I worried about the divisions he was encouraging in our homeland.

I was a government employee, so I did not share my views about candidate Trump. But the hallmark of our free society is that I was (and am) entitled to my own private beliefs. And my belief was that Hillary Clinton would make a better president than Donald Trump.

THE ALARM WOKE me up at 5:30 on the morning of November 9. It was still election night in the United States — Ukraine is seven hours ahead of Eastern Standard Time — and the race had yet to be called. I was planning to get to our election event by 6:45 a.m., and as I was getting ready, I turned on the TV to check the results. Then I sat on my bed, cross-legged in my pajamas, staring at the screen as the returns came in. Absolutely astounded.

By 6 a.m. Ukraine time CNN was reporting a Trump victory in Ohio and Florida. As talking heads took turns explaining the significance of the returns, I felt I was watching a slow-motion car crash. Trump was going to be the next president of the United States. I couldn't wrap my mind about what that would mean for the U.S. — and for Ukraine.

At 7 a.m. my staff called to find out where I was. With no time for a shower, I washed my face and threw on some clothes. At the last minute I pinned on my American flag brooch, which always makes me feel patriotic and protected. I decided I was as ready as I'd ever be. I got to the party at

7:30 with a big smile anchoring what I hoped was a stiff upper lip. I didn't want anyone to see my inner turmoil.

Hundreds of people — embassy staffers, foreign diplomats, Ukrainian officials, expat Americans, and media representatives — were at America House, the U.S. cultural center in downtown Kyiv where we held many public events. I made a quick circuit of the crowd and walked to the stage to give short formal remarks.

Ambassadors don't give partisan speeches. The election hadn't been called yet, and it didn't matter who won; it would have been the same speech. I focused on celebrating American democracy, on the importance of elections — every voice being heard, every vote being counted. I also sought to reassure the Ukrainians that whoever won, America's strong bipartisan support for Ukraine would continue as it had for the twenty-five years since the fall of the USSR. My personal doubts about Trump aside, this is what I truly believed. I repeated that same message to members of the press and Ukrainian politicians who were present and nervous about candidate Trump's seeming coziness with Russia, his willingness to repeat Russia's claims about Crimea, and his opposition to foreign assistance.

After the breakfast wound down, I went to the embassy. By the time I arrived, Clinton had already called Trump to concede. Trump was the president-elect.

Walking into the embassy and down the long hall to my office, I could see a lot of worried faces. Our American staff was committed to Embassy Kyiv's mission to help a democratic Ukraine reform and resist Russia's continued aggression. Like the Ukrainians, they had heard Trump's views, and many of them were anxious about what his election would bring. A couple of midlevel officers came into my office and said I needed to address the American staff. Within ten minutes people were piling into my outer office, my inner office, the DCM's office, and the hallway. I climbed onto a chair in the outer office so that everyone could see and hear me clearly.

I looked at my team, and I saw America. They were from all over the U.S.: Trump supporters, Clinton supporters, and probably some who didn't care. For just a second I wondered what I could say that would keep us united as a team. The words came easily, however, because I was sharing my core beliefs. I reminded the assembled staff about the American experiment, the renewal of democracy through elections. Now that the voters had spoken, it was time for all of us to put aside personal views and help the president-elect succeed. We were professionals, experts. The new president and his team would need us, and we needed to step up. As I had said earlier at the election breakfast, I was sure the bipartisan consensus to support Ukraine would prevail. Privately I believed that the Republican foreign policy establishment would bring Trump into its fold and Trump would eventually embrace the path of his predecessors. I anticipated some rocky moments, but I wanted to project confidence, hoping that confidence would make what I said come true.

Half an hour later I gave the same speech all over again, this time to reassure the embassy's Ukrainian staff members. To my surprise, many of the American staff came to listen again. The only place big enough to accommodate the crowd of several hundred people was the embassy's two-story cafeteria. I spoke from the mezzanine, which made me feel like a second-rate Evita. The distance made it harder for me to communicate, but I did my best to answer the important questions from Ukrainians and Americans alike. They wondered whether the president-elect would support Ukraine. The USAID staff was worried that assistance programming for Ukraine would be cut and local staff fired. Others wondered whether military assistance for Ukraine would continue, given Trump's apparent affinity for Russia. I told them what I believed: that I expected the long-term bipartisan consensus supporting Ukraine to continue, and that while all presidents make adjustments, I did not believe that our foreign policy toward Ukraine would change.

I wish there was an audio recording of these addresses, because I think they were the best speeches I've ever given. They came from my heart and expressed my belief in a nonpartisan Foreign Service, unified as one Team America when we serve abroad. Three years later I read in the press that at least some of the people listening to me that day were disappointed that I didn't criticize President-elect Trump. That was never going to happen. Partisan words would have divided our team, would have been completely at odds with my leadership responsibilities, and would have been contrary to my oath to the Constitution. I can't imagine that any career ambassador addressing his or her employees that day spoke any differently.

BUT IN THE DAYS and weeks that followed, I did privately reflect on what a Trump presidency would mean more broadly and ask myself whether I could in good conscience represent a president with so many views so contrary to my own. I had faithfully executed the policies of presidents for whom I had not voted before, but I wondered whether this time might be different, given all that Trump had said and done. In the end I decided it wasn't different — for three reasons.

First, I had long ago made a commitment to serve whatever administration was in office. My litmus test could never be whether I agreed with everything a president did — that never happens. As I saw it, what mattered was whether I would be asked to implement policies with which I deeply disagreed. Although candidate Trump had come close to that line when he seemed to embrace Russia's claims about Crimea and Ukraine, I expected the Republican foreign policy establishment, which broadly supported Ukraine, to influence the president-elect to do the same. In the near term at least, I didn't anticipate being asked to do anything that would demand a resignation on principle.

Second, I wanted to protect my staff. I had enough years in the Foreign Service that I could retire from government and start collecting a pension before Trump took office, but quitting was a luxury most of my staff couldn't afford. If I left, it would be months before the new president nominated a replacement, and who knew what qualifications that person would have or how long the embassy would have been left adrift? I had been brought up in a culture where leadership brings responsibility.

Third, pride admittedly was at work: I believed that I had the experience and expertise to make a difference in Ukraine, and I owed it to the new administration to share my insights. Plus I loved what I was doing, and I didn't want to leave.

Buttressing my decision, in retrospect, was my naïveté. I thought working in Ukraine, a country that enjoyed a bipartisan policy consensus in the United States, would insulate me from the turmoil that I could sense might overtake Washington. I hoped the Republican establishment would school Trump, and he would temper his views. I knew there would be fights and tumult back home. But in Ukraine, I thought, I would be able to quietly keep working, help the new team understand our equities in Ukraine, and advance our policy.

For two years that was the case.

FOR BETTER OR WORSE, my work in Ukraine was all-consuming, so in the wake of the election I didn't dwell on the unknowns about an administration that wouldn't take office for another two and a half months. I was focused on moving forward with supporting Ukraine in the fight against Russia and on its reform agenda. There was a lot to do, and not just in the realms of energy and finance.

The Ukrainian justice sector also was badly in need of a cleanup, and in late 2016 it was requiring a great deal of my time. Ironically, my efforts in this regard would help to lay the foundation for many of the difficulties ahead. The "telephone justice" so prevalent during former President Kuchma's days — a corrupt system in which politicians and oligarchs simply called investigators, prosecutors, and judges and ordered them to prosecute or protect whomever they wanted — continued largely unabated in post-2014 Ukraine. This was not what the Ukrainian people wanted when they protested on the Maydan. Reformers inside and outside the government continued to insist on change, with the strong backing of the donor community.

The U.S. had been supporting a variety of initiatives, but they were meeting with mixed success, which was a problem. Without comprehensive justice system reform, corrupt officials would feel free to continue their graft, while those fighting for a freer, fairer Ukraine would continue to fear arbitrary arrests — and investors would continue to avoid putting money into businesses that could be confiscated or destroyed because of the uneven playing field. In other words, unless Ukraine tackled corruption and rule of law, our efforts to help Ukrainians transform the country would fail.

There had been consensus that to deal with high-level government corruption, Ukraine needed to try something different. So in 2014 Ukrainian reformers, supported by the donor community, came up with a plan to establish two entirely new and politically independent anti-corruption institutions: the National Anti-Corruption Bureau of Ukraine (NABU) and the Specialized Anti-Corruption Prosecutor's Office (SAPO). NABU would investigate high-level government corruption, while SAPO would prosecute the corrupt actors NABU uncovered. An independent court would also be established to hear these corruption cases. To ensure that Ukraine actually followed through in creating and supporting these new institutions, much of the donor community conditioned their aid packages on the implementation of the plan.

NABU and SAPO opened their doors in December 2015, having built their staff from the ground up. Their investigators and prosecutors were newly hired, freshly vetted, rigorously trained, and well paid. This start-from-scratch approach aimed to ensure that the new agencies wouldn't be infected by long-standing corruption in Ukraine's existing legal structures.

The public had high expectations for NABU and SAPO. Many of Ukraine's politicians, in contrast, greeted the establishment of the anti-corruption agencies with fear, and regret for their earlier support. By the time I arrived just eight months after NABU and SAPO started working, the old Ukraine was throwing as many roadblocks at these organizations as possible. But reformers inside and outside of government were completely aligned, and supported by the international community. Law enforcement reform was worth fighting for.

I was fully in accord. But as it turned out, the price for me personally would be steep.

ONE OF the staunchest opponents to the vital work of the National Anti-Corruption Bureau and the Specialized Anti-Corruption Prosecutor's Office turned out to be the General Prosecutor's Office (GPO), Ukraine's rough equivalent to our Justice Department. It was a typical turf war; NABU's and SAPO's jurisdiction had once belonged to the GPO, and no organization likes to lose power—despite the fact that the GPO's failure to use that power to prosecute corruption was what had triggered calls for these new entities in the first place. GPO's opposition was especially frustrating because it had retained jurisdiction over pretty much every other type of crime in Ukraine, from ordinary street offenses to complex international financial conspiracies. The GPO had even retained what were arguably the most consequential and high-profile corruption cases: tracking down and repatriating the billions of dollars that deposed President Yanukovych and his cronies had taken to Russia and bringing the former president to justice.

It quickly became apparent that the GPO was less interested in pursuing important corruption cases underway than in blocking the work of NABU and SAPO. Before I became ambassador and at the Ukrainian government's request, the FBI had provided experts to support the GPO's forensic work in following the money trail to locate the money Yanukovych and his cronies had stolen. Our agents had worked hard to help GPO investigators but found their effort stymied on the Ukrainian side. After spending half a million American dollars unsuccessfully trying to lead that horse to water, the FBI pulled its experts out of the GPO. The embassy pivoted and instead used the assistance money to fund FBI agents working with the fledgling agency NABU. Some of the funding was also directed to an NGO called the Anti-Corruption Action Center (AntAC).

Institutional rivalry between the GPO and NABU was probably inevitable, but the FBI's defection didn't help. Soon that rivalry took an ugly turn. Shortly before I arrived, GPO agents detained and beat NABU officers who were working undercover on a stakeout at a building connected to the GPO. Ukrainian law enforcement agencies did not have a mechanism for resolving such law-enforcement-against-law-enforcement incidents, and by the time I arrived in Kyiv, the episode was being adjudicated through press statements — never the best way to solve a problem.

So just weeks after my arrival I found myself meeting with other G7 ambassadors, hoping to broker a truce and a path forward between the GPO on the one hand and NABU and SAPO on the other. General Prosecutor (and GPO head) Yuriy Lutsenko, NABU head Artem Sytnyk, and SAPO head Nazar Kholodnytskyy were present to represent their three respective agencies. I hadn't yet met the three Ukrainians, but I arrived at the meeting hoping that Lutsenko would be a constructive counterpart. The U.S. had strongly supported his appointment earlier in the year and hoped that he would do a better job than his predecessor, a Poroshenko ally named Viktor Shokin. The donor community uniformly viewed Shokin as corrupt to the core, someone who would never adopt the reforms or prosecute the cases necessary to make Ukraine a rule-of-law nation. In early 2016 Vice President Biden had made Shokin's removal a condition of another loan guarantee from the U.S. Lutsenko, in contrast, had reform bona fides; he had been an energetic reformer since his days as one of the leaders of the "Ukraine Without Kuchma" movement some sixteen years earlier. Although he wasn't a lawyer, we had hoped that he would turn the GPO around.

But my hope started to fade almost as soon as Lutsenko took the floor. He presented as self-centered, unconstructive, and rude. He seemed to think that force of personality rather than facts would convince us that the GPO was not at fault in the August assault on NABU's investigators. Anyway, that clearly was not what he wanted to talk about, although it was the reason we were gathered that day. He instead lauded the GPO's accomplishments, criticized the ten-month-old NABU, and told us he was asking the Rada, Ukraine's parliament, to pass new legislation to move some of NABU's functions over to his office. When asked to give time to Sytnyk and Kholodnytskyy to respond, Lutsenko stopped talking — momentarily. Then he resumed his filibuster.

It was obvious that the GPO had more than enough work with investigating all other crimes in Ukraine. What's more, reformers and the international community alike had insisted on new anti-corruption entities precisely because the prosecutor's office was still in the business of protecting rather than prosecuting corruption. Yet here was Lutsenko trying to claw back some of that power. He barely addressed the reason for the meeting — his employees' assault on NABU's agents — and over the following months it became clear he wasn't ever going to. It was an inauspicious start for a relationship that would come to define my tenure in Ukraine.

IN OCTOBER, Lutsenko came to my embassy office for our first bilateral meeting. We spent roughly sixty minutes together. Just as he had at the G7 meeting, he held the floor for almost the entire time, speaking from what seemed like the same script. When I could get a word in edgewise, I encouraged him to resolve his conflicts with NABU and to pursue the three goals he had set for himself when he took office: reforming the General Prosecutor's Office, prosecuting the killers of the "Heavenly Hundred" protesters killed near the Maydan, and repatriating the $40 billion that Yanukovych and his crew had stolen.

But Lutsenko seemed more interested in what I could do for him. He wanted two things in particular: U.S. assistance for the GPO, and meetings with top U.S. officials like the attorney general and the FBI director. On the assistance issue, I reminded him why the U.S. had pulled our FBI experts from his predecessor and told him that we could review the assistance request if the U.S. saw progress on his three stated goals. I meant it: although I was already starting to have reservations about his commitment to the reform agenda, his agency was partnering with U.S. law enforcement on a host of transnational criminal cases, from pursuing international drug traffickers to going after networks of computer hackers. Those aspects of the law enforcement relationship were important, and on the whole they had been quite successful. If Lutsenko could show that the GPO was equally serious about pursuing reform, I would have happily advocated for assistance for that effort too.

I was more skeptical about his request to meet with top U.S. officials. Like all ambassadors, I supported direct communication between U.S. leaders and host country counterparts when there was something substantive to be discussed. But American leaders are busy, and they have little time for ego-stroking courtesy calls and even less interest in free-form meetings that might end with surprising and unwelcome requests. We don't advocate for meetings unless we can tell U.S. leaders the purpose and show them how these meetings might benefit the United States and our relationship with that particular country.

I explained all that to Lutsenko but received no insights into the purpose of the meetings he wanted. When I discussed it with colleagues afterward, we concluded that what Lutsenko really wanted was a photo for his trophy wall. He was open about his ambition to become Ukraine's next president and probably calculated that visual evidence of his access to U.S. leaders would boost his political ratings in Ukraine.

Our next meeting, later in the fall, didn't go any better, although it would be several years before I learned just how badly it actually had gone. We covered the same ground as before — me pushing him to fulfill his three commitments and him asking for U.S. assistance and Washington meetings. As before we got nowhere fast.

Lutsenko and I also discussed the importance of the GPO rejecting its long-standing practice of selective — especially political — prosecutions. Decisions based on the facts of a case, not the identity of the person to be charged, were essential for Ukraine's development as a rule-of-law country, one in which all are treated equally. Laying it on a little thick, I reminded Lutsenko that he himself had been convicted during the Yanukovych era on politically motivated charges. We in the U.S. thought he should work to prevent that from happening to other Ukrainians.

I knew that this was a sensitive point for Lutsenko. He saw himself as the white hat, the president-in-waiting, and he wanted us to see him that way. He wanted the accolades, and we were ready to give them to him, but not until he earned them. That would mean trying to reform the GPO, something for which he hadn't yet shown any appetite.

I did not find the meeting remarkable, but as I came to learn two years later, Lutsenko apparently did. My comments opposing selective prosecution seem to have rankled more than I would have expected, since Lutsenko was a self-styled reformer. At the very least, my remarks put him off. Perhaps he had thought that if he couldn't charm me, he'd baffle me with BS — and perhaps, when that didn't work either, he made his decision to go around me and find another way to promote himself with America's leadership. Little did I know then how much better Lutsenko would understand Trump's Washington than I did.

IN THE AFTERMATH of our initial meetings, Lutsenko went about the business of the General Prosecutor's Office in the same old way. He proceeded as if the Ukrainian people's demand for justice system reform could be achieved by giving lofty speeches rather than taking action.

Lutsenko did take the initiative in one area, at least: through public criticism, bureaucratic undercutting, legislative initiatives, and even legal cases against Sytnyk and other National Anti-Corruption Bureau employees, he subverted and distracted NABU from its important job of investigating high-level government corruption. Lutsenko wouldn't reform his own agency, but neither could he accept that other agencies were getting resources and the credit for doing the hard work of building a new Ukraine. In retrospect, his jealousy — and his fear of the force NABU could become — were what made him determined not just to hamper NABU but to bury it.

In November 2017, Lutsenko's feud with NABU turned into a whole-of-government attack on Ukraine's anti-corruption agenda. The vehicle for the expanded war on NABU was a conspiracy that threatened the United States as well as Ukraine.

With the FBI's help, NABU was investigating a wide-ranging plot: government officials from multiple agencies were surreptitiously selling Ukrainian citizenship and Ukrainian biometric passports to unvetted foreigners ineligible to obtain citizenship. A number of agencies connected to immigration or law enforcement — the General Prosecutor's Office, the State Migration Service, and a branch of the SBU, the Security Service of Ukraine — were engaged in the fraud. Investigators suspected that very senior officials were benefiting from the stream of kickbacks.

It was a case tailor-made for NABU, whose mandate was to investigate high-level government corruption. For us the investigation was about far more than helping Ukraine solve its corruption problems. In a post-9/11 world we were seriously concerned about the implications for our own national security. Someone whose true name might appear on a criminal or terrorist watch list, or whose real country of origin would subject him to added scrutiny when traveling, would be able to slip into the United States unnoticed when traveling with an authentic Ukrainian passport issued in his new Ukrainian identity. Once in America, such an interloper could potentially do us untold harm. The corruption of Ukrainian officials now directly threatened the American people.

It all came to a head in late November 2017, when the GPO and SBU disrupted a NABU sting operation, arresting seven NABU detectives, searching NABU property and employees' homes, and confiscating NABU vehicles, equipment, computers, and files. Lutsenko publicly accused NABU investigators of bribing a government employee, and he flagrantly outed undercover NABU agents. As if that weren't enough, when Lutsenko found out that the FBI had been advising on the case, he doubled down and charged that the FBI was acting illegally on Ukrainian soil. Perhaps Lutsenko had a personal motive as well: one of the NABU agents was a witness in a different case, in which Lutsenko was possibly implicated.

His scorched-earth tactics were shocking even for Lutsenko. But while he may have been the loudest voice, he wasn't acting alone. There was no way he could have acted so aggressively without the support of others. Poroshenko and his cronies were as concerned as Lutsenko that NABU was doing its job, couldn't be controlled, and — most dangerously — after a year in operation was starting to show results that might land some of them in jail.

The State Department immediately issued a strong statement highlighting an apparent "effort to undermine independent anti-corruption institutions that the United States and others have helped support" in Ukraine and urging "all branches of Ukraine's government to work together cooperatively to eliminate corruption from public life." That was a good start. What we needed, though, was a high-level U.S. figure to pick up the phone and read Poroshenko the riot act. But Vice President Biden had been gone from office for almost a year, and no one in the new administration had taken on the Ukraine file.

At the embassy we did the best we could. Along with our top FBI representative, known as the legal attaché, I met with the minister of foreign affairs, Poroshenko's foreign policy advisor, the SBU head, and the minister of internal affairs. The legal attaché laid out the facts, and I helped the Ukrainians interpret them by emphasizing that U.S. support for Ukraine would dissolve overnight if a terrorist entered the U.S. on a Ukrainian passport, especially when it became known that this had been facilitated by greedy individuals in multiple agencies in the Ukrainian government. Ukraine couldn't run that risk, I said.

We asked them to do three things: first, shut down the passport scam immediately, no matter who was benefiting; second, allow NABU to continue investigating the scheme so that the perpetrators could be held accountable; third, launch an investigation into the GPO/SBU attack on NABU and develop protocols to avoid future incidents. I emphasized that it was important that Ukraine demonstrate seriousness of purpose, because Ukrainian corruption now threatened not just Ukraine but also the United States.

Privately, the Ukrainians said the right things. They accepted the gravity of the situation and promised to get to the bottom of the issue. I had the impression that the Ukrainian leadership had at least absorbed the magnitude of the misjudgment and that making a few bucks on the side wasn't worth risking a break with the U.S.

The embassy team working this issue unanimously agreed that I should not meet with Lutsenko, who was leading the charge. We didn't see how anything positive would come from such a get-together. Lutsenko had publicly staked his reputation on his unfounded case against NABU and the FBI. He was enjoying the media attention, and we believed he would have spun any meeting with me as the U.S. seeking exoneration for its misguided support for NABU.

In retrospect, it was a mistake not to find a way to constructively engage with Lutsenko directly during this period. No doubt my cold shoulder contributed to his ill will toward me. And the embassy's resolute stand on the matter probably convinced others that we weren't going to back down. That created a problem for those powerful Ukrainians who wanted to continue their self-dealing — and perhaps that made it a matter of time and opportunity before Lutsenko's ruthless tactics were turned against me.

In the moment, though, we thought that Lutsenko's actions left us with no choice but to shun him. He didn't release the NABU detectives in a timely manner, he continued to grandstand, including against the FBI, and he attacked NABU in the press and in parliament. He also championed a change in law that would allow legislators to fire the head of NABU, Artem Sytnyk. That last one especially was a threat to anti-corruption efforts, and President Poroshenko's party was promoting it. The government coalition introduced a bill in the parliament that would permit Sytnyk's dismissal, thereby gutting NABU's independence and rendering it toothless, leaving the field clear for corrupt actors.

I braced myself for a bumpy ride. If the parliament succeeded in neutralizing NABU, the international community would have to respond. We had already seen a lot of backtracking on the commitments of 2014, but this would be an unmistakable break, a clear signal that the Poroshenko government was no longer interested in fighting corruption — if it ever had been.

The vote was scheduled for December 7, and with the ruling coalition supporting the bill, passage appeared certain. But the night before, I received an unexpected request from Minister of Internal Affairs Arsen Avakov, asking me to meet him in the next half-hour at the parliament. He and former prime minister Arseniy Yatsenyuk wanted to discuss the bill with me. It was an intriguing invitation, to say the least: Yatsenyuk and Avakov led the political party that formed the coalition government with Poroshenko's party, and they had supported the bill that was poised to neutralize NABU. Without their votes, there would be no bill. Could they be having a change of heart?

Ukrainian politicians, perhaps like all politicians, are complicated. Erudite and driven, Yatsenyuk was a wunderkind. At forty-three years old, the balding and bespectacled politician had occupied just about every ministerial role in successive governments since 2005. But he didn't have the common touch, so it was a surprise when his party became the second largest in the parliament after Poroshenko's. The two parties formed a coalition government with several smaller parties, and Yatsenyuk became prime minister in 2014. In charge of the economy, he took many tough decisions to reform and strengthen the economy, many of them painful for the average Ukrainian. Inevitably he was blamed for it, including by his coalition partner, Poroshenko. In April 2016, with no top cover from Poroshenko, he resigned. But Yatsenyuk was a survivor, and he kept his party in the coalition, ensuring that even though he was on the outside, he still had influence and ministers in the cabinet. Almost every night, late, late at night, he and other key figures met with Poroshenko to decide the course of the country.

Widely considered to be the second most powerful individual in Ukraine, Avakov too was a complicated guy. A proud member of the Armenian minority, he was a regional power broker in Kharkiv, a northern city on Ukraine's border with Russia. Avakov had been instrumental in taking back the city from Russia-led proxies in the early days of the Donbas war.

Plugged-in, insightful, and candid, he would encourage me to keep diplomatic niceties at the door so we could move through our agenda as quickly and clearly as possible.

The embassy had partnered with Avakov closely to establish the Patrol Police, a signature reform meant to usher out the old era of corrupt cops who used their power to shake down drivers for imaginary infractions and instead begin a new era of honest and helpful police that everyday Ukrainians on the road would appreciate. But we weren't blind to Avakov's troubling sponsorship of right-wing militias, and we regularly called him out on it. I would remind myself that diplomacy is about the art of the possible, which requires working in a world of grays.

I met with Yatsenyuk and Avakov at the Ukrainian parliament building around 10 p.m. In the speaker's parlor that night, I took Avakov's advice and was very blunt. The NABU legislation, I said, was a huge problem. The U.S.—and more broadly anyone who was paying attention—would see successful passage as a big step back from reform, especially since the bill was sponsored by the ruling coalition.

I left at around midnight, when Yatsenyuk and Avakov departed to meet with Poroshenko and his other key advisors. The next day Yatsenyuk and Avakov pulled their support from the bill and the legislation failed. NABU was free to fight corruption for another day.

I greeted the news with an enormous sense of relief, especially as I contemplated what I would have faced if the vote had gone the other way. But as always in Ukraine, it was one step forward and at least half a step back. While reformers had been distracted with NABU concerns, the ruling coalition—both parties—took the opportunity to remove the crusading reformer who headed the parliamentary committee that crafted legislation on corruption, replacing him with a spineless lackey. What's more, the day after the bill's defeat, all the details of my late-night meeting with Yatsenyuk and Avakov were laid out in the press. I assumed one of them had shared the information to demonstrate how they had outmaneuvered Poroshenko by playing the American card. It irritated me that I was again being used in Ukraine's internal intrigues. But otherwise I did not think much of it at the time.

WE WON THAT anti-corruption battle, but the war continued. Even well into the new year we saw no progress on the three requests we had made of the Ukrainian government with respect to the passport investigation: shutting down the passport scheme, allowing the National Anti-Corruption Bureau of Ukraine to continue its investigation into the scheme, and establishing protocols for resolving disputes between NABU and the General Prosecutor's Office. I realized that I had to push to make anything more happen and that the GPO had to be a part of the solution. That meant I would have to meet with Lutsenko.

Because Lutsenko had been the front man for the NABU debacle and the failed legislation, his reputation in Ukraine had taken a hit, and he was clearly trying to dig his way out of the doghouse. He invited me and the embassy team to his private back office, where a gourmet buffet and lots of alcohol awaited. The meeting seemed productive — or at least Lutsenko finally told us that he would work with NABU and SBU to get to the bottom of what happened. But then there was no progress over weeks and months, except more talk, a Lutsenko specialty.

Looking back, I have often wondered whether I could have done anything differently. Diplomacy is after all about human relationships, and clearly I had failed at creating a productive relationship with Lutsenko. But at the end of the day we were at cross-purposes. Just three years after the Revolution of Dignity, which he had supported, Lutsenko, Ukraine's top law enforcement officer, was leading the charge for the forces of corruption and subverting those trying to fulfill the promise of equal justice under the law. No amount of relationship-building could have overcome that.

ALTHOUGH A CRITICAL task of mine was to help push forward Ukraine's reform agenda, it was also important that as the top representative of the United States in Ukraine, I regularly visit the war zone in the Donbas. It may have been a David and Goliath fight, but Ukraine had proven itself a surprisingly redoubtable adversary against Russia. I needed to show the flag and demonstrate American support for Ukraine's efforts to defend itself against the Russian invasion.

International support was strong. Between painful and coordinated sanctions targeting Russian individuals, entities, and sectors, international isolation of Russia, and U.S. and third-country military support, we were showing that America and others stood with Ukraine. Putin claimed that sanctions didn't bite, but the drag on the Russian economy was measurable, and Russia wouldn't have expended the effort on a full-scale lobbying effort to reverse the sanctions unless it mattered. And it was just laughable to think that Putin didn't miss rubbing shoulders with the leaders of the world's most developed economies.

If people wondered why we supported Kyiv, all they had to do was look at the devastation along its eastern border. Beyond the violation of Ukraine's sovereignty, Russia had unleashed a humanitarian disaster in the Donbas. We estimated that the war had displaced over a million and a half people. Approximately 3.5 million needed assistance to survive. Tens of millions of U.S. humanitarian aid dollars went to help these individuals, and I needed to be able to give firsthand reports on the impact of our assistance — another reason for me to spend time in the Donbas.

Perhaps even more importantly, it was impossible to understand Ukraine without seeing the trauma the war inflicted on its people. I needed to talk to people who lived there and to hear directly what they were experiencing and what they needed to rebuild their communities and businesses. It was sobering to witness the destruction that Russia-led forces had left behind, leaving so many homeless and hungry. We needed to report about the suffering, the sacrifice, and the resilience of the people of the Donbas, even if we could access only those on the Ukrainian-controlled side of the line. And our policymakers back in D.C. needed to absorb their stories.

Fighting was intermittent, but casualties were continuous — a hot war in the middle of Europe. Every few days a Ukrainian solder died defending his or her country. The fighting was so unpredictable and so dangerous that whenever we got close to the line of contact, we rode in armored vehicles and wore body armor and helmets. I recall looking out the reinforced windows to see Ukrainians without our elaborate protection going about their daily business and trying to scrape together a living. Many of the women were pushing baby carriages. It seemed we were in two different realities, and I wasn't sure whether to laugh at our precautions or cry at the vulnerability of the population — or both. Even with the damage of the ongoing war all around, even with the sound of incoming artillery rounds, even listening to their testimony, I found it hard to put myself in the shoes of these men and women. I was just a visitor, and I knew that I could go home.

My most memorable trip to the Donbas came on New Year's Eve 2016. Senators John McCain, Lindsey Graham, and Amy Klobuchar were on a multicountry swing through Europe to send a message of congressional opposition to Russian aggression. Senator McCain especially had played a large role in ensuring U.S. support for Ukraine in 2014. When the delegation met Poroshenko in Kyiv on December 30, he invited them to go to the front the following day. Of course they said yes. The embassy scrambled — my staff and I even donated warm clothes and boots to our visitors, who hadn't expected this excursion. It was winter in Ukraine and brutally cold in the east.

For security reasons the Ukrainians didn't give us any information; we didn't even know where we were going. But we did have the forethought to send a message to the Russians through Embassy Moscow that we would have a VIP delegation on the ground. We figured the Russians had no interest in U.S. senators getting killed or injured in this war.

We were told to be at the Kyiv airport in the morning. When we arrived, our Ukrainian handlers said we'd fly out on Poroshenko's plane, pick up helicopters to our unknown destination, and be back in time for dinner and New Year's Eve celebrations. The weather didn't cooperate. The plane took off very late and landed on a barely visible airstrip a couple of hours later. Since it was too foggy for helicopters, we ended up driving to our still unknown destination. Poroshenko was up ahead in what I assume was an armored vehicle. The rest of us boarded an unarmored bus for what turned out to be an approximately six-hour ride. It was a long time on seats that were barely upholstered. Our group, plus assorted Poroshenko aides and Ukrainian journalists, swayed, swerved, and bumped along on pockmarked and barely paved roads on a no-frills, no-food ride. The fog that still hung in the air gave the drive an almost ethereal feel as we passed a snow-covered landscape.

The senators were game. No complaints, even though we still didn't know where we were going. We finally transferred to armored vehicles for the last bit and ended up in the town of Shyrokyne, hard on the line of contact, visiting Ukrainian soldiers stationed there. In a wooden schoolhouse, President Poroshenko gave out awards. Senator McCain said a few words, and the troops applauded, although they looked a little confused about who we were. The real audience was elsewhere. The photo of the senators with the soldiers telling a story of U.S. bipartisan support was beamed around the world — especially, we all hoped, to Russia. A picture, as they say, is worth a thousand words.

We made our way through the icy lane back to the vehicles in the dark. Many of the houses we passed had been abandoned. The ones that were lit told their own tale of destruction and despair. We drove the twelve or so miles from the front to Mariupol, on the Sea of Azov, where we met with a group of Ukrainian Marines. They showed off a new American radar system that they were using to protect the coast — the fruits of American innovation at work for Ukraine. Fortunately, that night we saw no Russian warships menacing the coast, only Ukrainian fishing boats bringing home the catch.

Next was an awards ceremony for the Marines and other Ukrainian troops, held outside to accommodate the hundreds of people present. We stood in the dark and the cold behind Poroshenko, who was giving out an endless series of medals while we were stamping our feet and trying to keep warm. I worried about Senator McCain — no hat, a thin wool coat, and leather shoes. But he was stoic. Senator Graham looked warmer, and I saw he had L.L.Bean boots just like mine. I almost told him that, until I realized they actually *were* mine — I had offered up cold-weather gear to the delegation the night before. I guess Senator Graham shares my shoe size.

President Poroshenko called up a young woman, the mother of a soldier who had been killed several days before. When I explained what was happening to Senator McCain, he was all but propelled toward the mom. Tears slipped down his cheeks, and I couldn't help but sniffle in sympathy as he hugged the woman and spoke some words of comfort. McCain's empathy for a bereft mother was broadcast live all over Ukraine. Not that there was any doubt, but McCain's reputation as Ukraine's best friend was set in stone that night.

By about 8 p.m. the event was over and we got back onto the bus. I dreaded the long ride back on those terrible roads filled with potholes almost big enough to swallow a car, and this time in the dark. Luckily the ride was short: we stopped fifteen minutes later, at a field tent where a table groaned with food and drink. We still didn't have any logistical information, but breakfast had been a long time before, and I applied myself to the food with vigor. I wondered whether we would be celebrating the new year in the tent. But before I could finish my plate, people started filing out to an adjacent windswept runway that I had not noticed in the dark.

We still weren't getting any instructions, and somehow I had lost track of Senators McCain and Graham. I assumed we were still in the Poroshenko pod, so I grabbed Senator Klobuchar and followed President Poroshenko toward a green military helicopter. Out of the corner of my eye I could see the other two senators moving down the airfield in the opposite direction, doubled over against the wind. I ran back to get them and herded them up an icy ladder into Poroshenko's helicopter. We took off less than five minutes later, and I wondered whether Poroshenko would have left us behind if we hadn't hustled onto the helicopter at the last minute.

We were so exhausted that most of us slept until we got to Kharkiv, on the northern border with Russia, where we picked up the presidential plane and flew back to Kyiv. We arrived at around 11 p.m., giving me enough time to get home by midnight for the turn of the year.

It had been a good day. Mama and I toasted the new year. I felt that I had really earned that celebration.

I woke up the next morning to 2017 — and to the realization that I'd be representing a new president in a few weeks' time. I was hopeful that the previous day's bipartisan support for Ukraine would continue into the new year and the new administration. But it wouldn't take long for me to realize just how challenging the next four years were going to be.

11

Diplomacy 101

ONALD TRUMP WAS inaugurated as the forty-fifth U.S. president on January 20, 2017. Mama and I sat in our living room in Kyiv, absolutely stunned as we watched Trump stand behind the podium and paint a dark scene of "American carnage." I couldn't remember ever hearing a speech like that from an American president: poorly written, badly delivered, substantively lacking, and painting a pessimistic vision of an America alone in the world. I hoped the speech wasn't a blueprint for our future.

For better or for worse, I assumed that the new administration would keep me on as ambassador for at least some period of time, as had happened in Armenia through the Bush-Obama transition. New administrations have so much to do in the beginning that replacing ambassadors who come from the nonpolitical career ranks usually isn't high on the agenda. Presidents get to pick their own team, though, and perhaps Trump would want a different ambassador in Ukraine. Until I heard otherwise, there was nothing that I could do about it, so I just kept on doing my job.

Like everyone else, Ukraine's leaders weren't sure what to expect from Trump. They needed the U.S. in their corner and worried that Trump's comments about Crimea, as well as his seemingly pro-Putin leanings, might bring a shift in our policy. Ukrainians and Americans alike in Kyiv also wondered who was going to take over the pivotal role that Joe Biden had played in keeping Ukraine issues on the front burner in Washington and pushing Ukrainians to move reforms forward.

Poroshenko saw it as essential that he meet with President Trump as soon as possible. A meeting between presidents often demonstrates U.S. support for a country, and such a message of continued strong partnership with Kyiv was one that Ukraine — and Russia — needed to hear. Unlike Lutsenko's entreaties, Poroshenko's request was worth advocating for, and not just for the symbolism. The presidents had a full agenda to discuss on the security and reform side. With candidate Trump's pro-Russia comments still hanging in the air, I was concerned about what the *lack* of such a meeting might signal: Putin might see a cold shoulder from Trump as license to take more aggressive action against Ukraine.

I did what I could to promote a Trump-Poroshenko meeting, but I couldn't get any traction for much of the first half of 2017. It isn't uncommon for a new president, as the administration gets its bearings, to take it slow in meeting with foreign leaders. So I initially saw this not as a bad omen but rather as business as usual. In the meantime I recommended an interim meeting between Trump's first secretary of state, former ExxonMobile CEO Rex Tillerson, and his counterpart, Ukraine's foreign minister, Pavlo Klimkin. Tillerson agreed, and I looked forward to joining the meeting, scheduled for early March, when I already had to be in D.C. for other reasons.

The meeting went well for Klimkin but not so much for me. Tillerson had made clear from the moment he took office that he didn't trust the career staff at the State Department. He had fired or sidelined senior officers, implemented a hiring freeze, which left offices severely understaffed, introduced other cost-cutting measures that undermined State's effectiveness, brought in a management consultant team that knew nothing about diplomacy, and generally ignored the experts who were left. Still, I was shocked by his reaction when State's European Bureau scheduled me to join his meeting with Klimkin.

In the past it had been standard practice to include an ambassador in such meetings if they were in Washington. Senate-confirmed ambassadors, because they know both the foreign official and his country's situation, are best positioned to assist the secretary, in a prebrief, at the meeting, and afterward. Including the ambassador helps ensure that our foreign guest doesn't later try to get away with shading the truth or wrongly claiming that a promise was made. Even more, by making it clear that the secretary considers the ambassador a valued member of the team, attendance at such meetings conveys that the ambassador speaks for the administration and must be taken seriously. That makes the ambassador more effective in implementing U.S. foreign policy. It's Diplomacy 101.

It was standard practice, but it wasn't Tillerson's practice. His office came back with not just a no but a *hell* no. Then came an inquiry as to whether I had traveled to Washington at taxpayers' expense just to worm my way into Tillerson's meeting with Klimkin. It was astonishing. As the story spread, it was also humiliating: a colleague later told me that he had been advised "not to do a Yovanovitch" — as though I had done something wrong.

As embarrassing as that was, it wasn't my personal feelings that mattered most; it was the impact on my effectiveness. Ukraine's leaders, unsure of my status as an Obama appointee in the untraditional Trump administration, had already begun to question whether I spoke for the new president. During an early 2017 discussion with Poroshenko's national security advisor on the anti-corruption agenda, the official looked me in the eye and asked me whether my request for action reflected the position of my government. That was a shocker; I had represented the United States through multiple administration changes and had never had my credibility questioned in such a way. More bemused than angry, I told him in no uncertain terms that U.S. policy hadn't changed: I was representing the policy of the Trump administration. And when I spoke those words, I felt certain that I was.

But the Ukrainians were not. Around this time a Washington insider let me know that Poroshenko had called him to complain that I was "still" talking about fighting corruption, when it was clear to him that the Trump administration just didn't care. It was disappointing to hear that Poroshenko was openly expressing his lack of commitment to fighting corruption and that he perceived the new U.S. administration to be similarly indifferent. Yet I was hopeful that once the Trump administration was fully in place, U.S. policy regarding corruption would be clearly articulated at the highest levels. Despite my misgivings about our new president, it still did not occur to me that Poroshenko might have had better insight into Trump's priorities than I did.

BY LATE SPRING 2017, Trump still hadn't agreed to meet with Poroshenko, although a Trump-Putin meeting had been scheduled for July 7. I was worried about the optics of Trump engaging with Putin, whose troops were illegally occupying parts of Ukraine, before showing high-level U.S. support for Ukraine. My concern grew after the Russians published photos of Trump laughing chummily with Russian foreign minister Sergiy Lavrov in the Oval Office on May 10. I wasn't alone.

Vice President Pence stepped up and agreed to meet with Poroshenko in Washington on June 20. Pence reportedly tried to convince Trump to make time that day for his own meeting with Poroshenko, or, as a fallback, at least to drop by the VP's meeting to say hello. That would have given Poroshenko something, although that's not normal treatment for another head of state. If a head of state comes to the White House, he or she rates an actual meeting with our president.

Despite the uncertainty, Poroshenko decided to travel to the U.S. for the meeting with Pence, with the hope of getting in to see Trump. I am sure he saw the prospect of being snubbed by Trump as humiliating, but he no doubt considered it a risk he had to take.

I flew to Washington to participate in Pence's — and, I hoped, Trump's — meeting with Poroshenko. In contrast to Tillerson, the vice president, a former governor and member of Congress, raised no objection to my attendance at the meeting. The sit-down was short on substance but very warm. Poroshenko had studiously prepared, and he knew his audience. The vice president was visibly moved when Poroshenko described not just the courage but also the faith of Ukraine's soldiers (most of whom, like Pence, are Christian). But to my disappointment, there was no tough talk about tackling corruption.

Unbelievably, as the Pence meeting neared its close, we still didn't know whether Poroshenko would get to see Trump. Poroshenko and Pence said their goodbyes, and Poroshenko, his entourage, and I were escorted to a conference room in the West Wing to wait. We weren't sure whether that signaled that there would be a meeting with Trump, just a photo opportunity, or the unthinkable: no presidential interaction at all. Poroshenko sat down, radiating tension as he waited. His delegation gave him a wide berth. Poroshenko is a big man, but he looked like a little boy, alone and ready to explode. I too thought it was wise to keep my distance unless I could say, "The President is ready to see you now."

After about half an hour, a White House aide suddenly appeared and said the magic words. We followed him to the hall outside the Oval Office and watched as briefers streamed out. Even at that moment we didn't know whether Poroshenko would get just a quick stand-up photo op or an actual sit-down meeting — or who would participate in whatever the encounter turned out to be. Usually a meeting between heads of state is tightly choreographed well in advance and down to the last detail. As I had learned in London when I was a junior officer, such planning ensures that logistical issues or cultural miscues don't overshadow the real work of the heads of state. But our group was milling around in the narrow hallway, and it was chaos. I'd never seen anything like it, at least not where a U.S. president is involved.

All of a sudden there was movement, and Trump staffers herded us past the outer office into the Oval Office. One of the president's assistants moved to block my path, but a senior National Security Council staffer came to the rescue and literally pushed me into the Oval Office, so hard that I stumbled as I crossed the threshold.

Vice President Pence, who along with National Security Advisor H. R. McMaster had been in the Oval Office for the president's prebrief, introduced Trump to Poroshenko, Foreign Minister Pavlo Klimkin, Ukraine's ambassador to the U.S. Valeriy Chalyy, and me. President Trump awkwardly reached across a couch to shake our hands. He looked just like he did on TV—big, beefy, and well preserved for his age. But five months into his presidency, he didn't seem to be as confident as I had expected. Pence was the one who seemed to be playing the host as he invited us to sit down.

The two presidents sat in the yellow mama and papa chairs underneath the portrait of George Washington. Pence, McMaster, and I seated ourselves on one of the yellow couches, while Klimkin and Chalyy sat on the opposite couch. Then they let in the press for the all-important photo op.

When the press left, I held my breath. Was that it? Or would there actually be a meeting? Thankfully, the answer to the second question was yes. With the press gone, Trump quickly settled into a conversation with Poroshenko, hitting two points that he would consistently articulate about Ukraine throughout his time in office. The first was that Ukraine was a corrupt country, which he knew because a Ukrainian friend at Mar-a-Lago had told him. Trump's second point was that Crimea was Russian, as the locals spoke Russian. That was surprising enough to hear from one head of state to another, but I got another shock when Trump turned to McMaster and asked him whether American troops were in the Donbas. An affirmative answer to that question would have meant that the United States was in a shooting war with Russia.

I pondered whether it was better to interpret Trump's question as suggesting that the commander in chief thought it possible that U.S. troops were fighting Russia-led forces or instead as an indicator that the president wasn't clear which country was on the other side of the war against Ukraine. Either way, it was disconcerting that he did not seem to know where we had our troops — his troops — deployed. I could only imagine what the Ukrainians were thinking, but everyone kept a poker face on.

In fluent English, Poroshenko ably pushed back against Trump's points. He noted that many people all over Ukraine speak Russian, including himself. Well prepped, he appealed to Trump, the self-described deal maker, and said that Ukraine was ready to purchase coal from the United States, a potentially lucrative deal that would create jobs in the U.S. and that Trump could take credit for. To explain the fighting in the Donbas and the urgent need for U.S. support, Poroshenko pulled out visual aids, which Trump really liked. He then asked Trump to include Javelin antitank missile systems in the planned U.S. security assistance package for Ukraine. The U.S. was already providing massive nonlethal assistance to the Ukrainian military in the form of Humvees, communication gear, counterartillery/mortar systems, medical equipment, and more. But the Ukrainians had long wanted the Javelin shoulder-held missile launchers to help them repel the tanks Russia had deployed in and around Ukraine since 2014. The Ukrainians had seen firsthand just how overmatched they were by Russia's tanks during Putin's full-scale invasion of the Donbas in August of that year. Poroshenko believed that if Russia deployed tanks again, it would take sophisticated weaponry such as Javelins for the Ukrainians to hold their ground.

Although there was broad bipartisan support for the missile transfer in Congress, the Obama administration had declined to approve it out of concern that the Russians might view our sending Javelins to Ukraine as provocative. So Poroshenko concluded his pitch by noting that he had told Congress in 2014 that Ukraine can't win a war with blankets, a dig at Obama that Trump seemed to savor. A deal maker himself, Poroshenko then sweetened the request by suggesting that the U.S. should pay for the first purchase of Javelins but that Ukraine would pay for the next purchase. Trump didn't commit, but he at least seemed open to the idea and later that year agreed to authorize a first Javelin transfer.

Despite the uncertain start, the meeting was congenial, and I hoped it would lay the basis for a relationship between the two leaders. I had the sense that Trump had come into the meeting viewing Ukraine as a "loser" country, smaller and weaker than Russia, and it seemed to me that he was a little surprised by Poroshenko. As physically imposing as Trump, Poroshenko filled the room with his presence. He too was a billionaire businessman who had declined to divest himself of his commercial empire when he assumed elected office. He and Trump had a lot in common, and as the two men shook hands at the end of the meeting, I hoped that Poroshenko had created the kind of favorable impression that would make Trump rethink his views of Ukraine and its importance to our strategic interests.

ALTHOUGH THE TRUMP-POROSHENKO meeting gave us hope that the new administration would support Ukraine's efforts to defend its territorial integrity, Trump's obsequiousness toward Putin was a frequent and continuing cause for concern. As expected, Trump and Putin met in early July, with Secretary of State Tillerson and Foreign Minister Lavrov in attendance. The only other people in the room were translators, and details from the meeting were hard to come by. The Ukrainians were not reassured by Lavrov's assertion that the leaders had discussed working together on Ukraine.

Tillerson traveled to Ukraine right after the Putin meeting for a previously planned half-day visit. He wanted to signal U.S. support and reassurance to a nervous Ukrainian leadership and public. All signs from Tillerson pointed to continued strong support for Ukraine — which was a relief, given Trump's ambiguity.

Secretary Tillerson brought with him Ambassador Kurt Volker, the department's newly appointed special representative for Ukraine negotiations, tasked with leading U.S. efforts to mediate an end to Russia's war against Ukraine in the Donbas. The position wasn't new, but the title and the spotlight were. A former ambassador to NATO and career diplomat, Kurt was bright, experienced, and a Russia hawk — in short, a great pick for this tricky role. We had worked the visa line together in London at the beginning of our Foreign Service careers, and I thought he'd be a great addition to the team.

The short visit's highlight was a sit-down with Poroshenko, a meeting that I was invited to attend, to my relief. But my gratification was short-lived. Tillerson introduced Kurt to Poroshenko as his man to help broker peace with Russia. It was clear that Kurt enjoyed Tillerson's trust and respect. In meetings with foreign counterparts, it is usual for secretaries of state to say something positive about the ambassador in the country, but I wasn't entirely surprised when Tillerson didn't do that, given his obvious distrust of the career officials at the State Department.

Immediately after that first meeting, Kurt started fast and wowed the

Ukrainians. They saw his appointment as a heartening sign of the Trump administration's support. Kurt worked his enormous Rolodex, kept the Europeans close, and courted the press. He tried to test the proposition that the Russians were serious about negotiating an end to the war, which despite repeated ceasefires was bringing additional fatalities every week. But after six months and four meetings, the Russians were done. They clearly did not share our desire for resolving the conflict and seemed disinclined to deal with Kurt, whose explicit criticism of Russia had evidently gotten under the Russian leaders' thin skin. But while Kurt was unable to make progress in bringing the sides together, his vocal support for Ukraine nevertheless mattered deeply to Kyiv and helped to provide a stable counterpoint to the mixed signals that were coming out of the White House.

IN EARLY MARCH 2018, another Russia hawk visited Ukraine: CIA director Mike Pompeo. In keeping with his role, Pompeo didn't make any public appearances, but he had excellent meetings with Ukraine's leaders. He conveyed that he saw the Russian threat clearly and favored strong support for Ukraine. I was pleased with the visit, and so were the Ukrainians. The visit seemed especially significant when, a week later, Trump fired Tillerson by tweet and announced that he'd be nominating Pompeo as secretary of state.

After Tillerson's near-disastrous tenure, I would have welcomed pretty much anyone as his replacement, and Pompeo — West Point grad, former member of Congress, and incumbent CIA director — certainly seemed to have a background that better suited him for the job. His promise to return "swagger" to the department did give me pause, as diplomacy is all about quiet persuasion, not aggressive bluster. Nevertheless, I wanted him to succeed and had high hopes that he would, because as spring crept over Ukraine, it was clear that the country's challenges were only growing.

Among the many U.S. interests threatened by Russia's illegal 2014 occupation of Crimea was the principle of maritime access to the Black Sea and the Sea of Azov. The Crimean Peninsula juts out from the Ukrainian mainland toward the center of the Black Sea. Its easternmost edge lies less than thirteen miles from the Russian coast, across the narrow Kerch Strait. To the north of the strait is the Sea of Azov, a body of water bordered by only Ukraine and Russia and used by commercial vessels from all over the world to take goods to Ukrainian and Russian ports. South of the Kerch Strait lies the vast Black Sea, surrounded by six nations, including three NATO allies — which we have a treaty obligation to defend — and, of course, Russia.

When Russia occupied Crimea in 2014, it seized the bulk of Ukraine's warships berthed in the Black Sea port of Sevastopol. With Ukraine's navy largely out of the way, Russia then set about creating additional facts on the ground and over the sea to consolidate control of both Crimea and the Kerch Strait, and, as a result, the Sea of Azov. In May 2018, Russia completed construction of a road bridge across the Kerch Strait to connect Crimea to the Russian mainland. The West barely took note, but Russia's inspections of foreign-flagged commercial vessels traversing the strait to Ukrainian ports skyrocketed after the bridge was completed. That complicated and therefore disincentivized trade with Ukraine. In principle Ukraine still enjoyed freedom of navigation, but anyone paying attention knew that the next violation of Ukrainian sovereignty was only a question of time.

For the U.S., the consequences for our strategic interests went well beyond Ukraine. Russia's calculated, step-by-step strategy was designed to ultimately dominate the Black Sea and its access to the Mediterranean Sea, the Balkans, and beyond. Control of Crimea gave Russia greater reach across the Black Sea, and with it a commanding position from which to inspect commercial ships from all over the world — or to threaten U.S. and other sovereign vessels, if it was so inclined.

A month after Russia finished the road bridge linking Crimea to Russia, the U.S. Navy used our annual multinational maritime exercise cohosted with Ukraine to remind Russia that we support our friends. Twenty-nine ships from eighteen nations gathered in the Black Sea to participate in the Sea Breeze 2018 exercise. President Poroshenko and the Ukrainian brass made sure to attend. It was quite a show, and as I watched the display of U.S. sea power and leadership — signaling the clear message that we stood by our friends — I was proud to be an American.

The event could not have been better timed. On that very day, July 16, President Trump was holding what turned out to be a disastrous meeting with President Putin in Helsinki. The summit wrapped up with a joint press conference between the two leaders, a spectacle that left observers pondering the depths to which Trump had sunk in his pandering to Putin. The Sea Breeze 2018 exercise at least showed that Trump's administration strongly supported Ukraine, no matter what was going on in Helsinki.

I watched the infamous Trump-Putin press conference at my Odesa hotel that evening while pecking at room-service french fries. I quickly lost my appetite as I saw our president toady up to Putin and take the Russian's word over that of our own intelligence agencies, which assessed that Russia had interfered in the 2016 U.S. presidential election. And that's what was said publicly. God only knows what Trump said in the two-hour one-on-one meeting with Putin, a meeting unusual not only for its length but because Trump did not brief U.S. officials on the discussion later. That raised all sorts of questions.

When the Ukrainian media called, we referred them to the White House for comment on the summit, but we also took the opportunity to reinforce the point that U.S. policy was to help Ukraine defend itself against Russian aggression. Sea Breeze 2018 had just demonstrated that we were backing up our words with action. Unfortunately, it would prove an insufficient deterrent to further Russian hostilities.

BY SEPTEMBER 2018 the situation in the Black Sea had reached a slow simmer. Faced with steadily escalating Russian aggression, the Ukrainians decided to test their ability to navigate freely through the Kerch Strait and the shared internal waters of the Azov Sea. They sent two of their few remaining naval vessels from Odesa to Mariupol, Ukrainian ports on the Black and Azov Seas, respectively. The warships sailed through the Kerch Strait without a problem, and there was a lot of Ukrainian high-fiving, duly noted by Russia. We were sympathetic, very sympathetic, but we warned the Ukrainians that Russia was now on notice. If Ukraine tried it again, the voyage would probably not proceed so smoothly. They needed to plan for success. I was reassured that the Ukrainians seemed to take that advice to heart.

In mid-November I went home for Thanksgiving. The day I was set to return to Kyiv, Sunday, November 25, I was enjoying a farewell brunch with family when I received an urgent text from my extraordinary deputy in Kyiv, Pam Tremont. The Russian coast guard had blocked three Ukrainian navy vessels that were still in international waters and approaching the Kerch Strait. Unless one of the sides backed down, the situation could escalate, with unpredictable and potentially far-reaching consequences.

Over the several hours I had before boarding the plane, I received constant updates from Pam in Kyiv, as well as from State Department and White House Ukraine experts. I also fielded phone calls from anxious Ukrainian officials who wanted the U.S. to weigh in. Senior policymakers at the department recommended that the U.S. issue a statement condemning the Russian action. We needed to give public notice that the U.S. was paying attention, which we hoped would make Russia think hard before taking any additional aggressive actions. It was troubling enough that Russia was broadening its military campaign against Ukraine into the naval domain; we also had to worry that Putin would read U.S. silence as a green light for further unlawful action in international waters.

A statement of this sort is usually standard stuff, even on a Sunday afternoon. In other administrations the State Department would likely have recommended more than just a statement — a high-level call from the secretary of state or the secretary of defense, perhaps even the vice president or the president, to their Russian and Ukrainian counterparts to underscore the need to deescalate the situation. But we knew that the best we could hope for from the Trump administration was a State Department statement.

It turned out that even that was too much to expect; the White House wouldn't let the State Department issue a statement calling for a lowering of tensions. It was mind-boggling. Only later did I learn that the source of the delay was the president himself. National Security Advisor John Bolton had checked with Trump, who thought that the Ukrainians might have provoked the incident and wasn't interested in doing anything quickly. Bolton apparently decided that he had to block the statement.

Outgunned in the Black Sea and with no U.S. diplomatic intervention in the offing, the Ukrainians realized that they had no choice but to retreat. Astoundingly, the Russians wouldn't let them. Rather than accepting victory, the Russians pursued the Ukrainian vessels — in international waters — and rammed one of them twice. The Russians then forcibly boarded and seized the Ukrainian ships, taking twenty-four Ukrainian sailors prisoner, including a number who were wounded.

It was a shocking move and made us wonder whether the Russians had decided to escalate their aggression against Ukraine and whether more attacks would come, including in the Donbas. I had a long overnight flight to contemplate whether an immediate U.S. statement would have put Russia on notice and given it pause in pursuing and capturing the Ukrainian ships and seamen.

The rest of the international community saw the situation for what it was.

The UN Security Council met in an emergency session the next day, Monday, November 26. There was still no U.S. statement, which meant that our UN ambassador, Nikki Haley, was the first high-level U.S. official to speak about this incident on the record. She delivered the modest White House–approved talking points and then added her own fire-breathing thoughts, lambasting "reckless Russian escalation" and Russia's "outlaw action."

Haley's comments gave Secretary Pompeo plenty of cover to belatedly do the right thing, and he issued a statement that condemned Russia's action, called for the release of the vessels and crew members, and urged respect for Ukraine's sovereignty and territorial integrity. Unfortunately, the statement was released late on November 26 and after close of business in Europe. Most Ukrainians — and Russians — didn't see it until November 27. Haley's intervention and Pompeo's statement were at least twenty-four hours too late to make a difference. Ukrainian sailors and ships were in Russian custody. The Russian high command was no doubt toasting in Moscow while Ukraine was licking its wounds. At least Ukraine had world opinion in its corner, I thought to myself.

But I got a surprise when I landed in Kyiv in the afternoon of Monday, November 26. Pam informed me that events were moving rapidly, and not all in the right direction.

THE INTERNATIONAL COMMUNITY was unified in its outrage against Russia's aggression in the Black Sea and fully on Kyiv's side in the standoff with Moscow. But most of Ukraine's international allies were not on board with one of the political measures that Poroshenko was taking in response: imposing martial law within Ukraine for sixty days. Poroshenko justified this draconian measure by claiming to be concerned that Russia could escalate the land war in the Donbas. That was certainly a risk, but it was hard to see how it justified Poroshenko's reaction. And frankly, we couldn't be sure of his motives.

As the end of 2018 approached, Poroshenko was about to embark on what was destined to be a tough campaign for reelection, with elections slated for early 2019. He was lagging badly in public opinion polling and had to know that he faced the possibility of a loss. In fact, much to my consternation, he regularly asked high-ranking American visitors whether President Trump could endorse his reelection. Many Ukrainians wondered whether declaring martial law was a gambit to postpone the upcoming presidential election.

Parliamentarians, who would need to approve the declaration of martial law, worked with Poroshenko on a compromise bill. The final legislation authorized a more limited thirty days of martial law and only in the ten regions closest to Russia. But even that more limited imposition of martial law concerned us.

Later that week I used my previously scheduled remarks at an international conference in Kyiv to put U.S. views on the record. I strongly condemned Russia's actions, made clear our support for Ukraine's freedom of navigation, and discussed the concrete steps that we were taking to beef up U.S. support for the Ukrainian navy. I noted, however, that limiting the freedoms of Ukrainian citizens through martial law was a "grave" decision, and I warned that Ukraine needed to restrict the use of these new authorities only to what was necessary to counter clear Russian threats.

This was a defining moment for Ukraine's democracy, and I thought that it was important for the U.S. to lay down a marker. Whether my remarks had any effect, I can't be sure, but to his credit Poroshenko did not extend martial law past the thirty days, leaving the way clear for the presidential election in early 2019.

Still, I felt a bit like the little boy plugging his finger in the hole of the dike. American influence surely would have been greater in this moment if we had presented a united front guided by clear and coherent objectives. But our commander in chief seemed incapable of that kind of consistency. Instead of a rational Russia policy, the White House seemed only to create confusion. Occasionally this resulted in actions that were appropriate, if surprisingly so. For instance, Trump, who hadn't been willing to issue a U.S. statement condemning Russia's aggression immediately after the naval confrontation, unexpectedly canceled an upcoming meeting with Putin and said he wouldn't reschedule unless Russia released the Ukrainian ships and sailors. We had barely absorbed that welcome, strong signal when the president abruptly nixed a measure to show American support for Ukraine by canceling a U.S. ship visit to Ukraine in December. Compounding the damage, he made the decision after the ship visit had already been announced.

At the embassy it was hard for us to follow the logic. I couldn't even imagine what our Ukrainian counterparts were thinking. Or the Russians, for that matter. Privately I hoped that the chaos of the Trump administration's decision-making would not engulf and irretrievably harm our interests in Ukraine. It didn't occur to me to worry that the chaos might also engulf me.

To be sure, I knew that I was on thin ice. But I thought that it was the Ukrainian president who was getting fed up with me, not our own head of state. By raising questions about the martial law declaration, I had given Poroshenko one more reason to believe that I was insufficiently supportive of him personally — something that he surely found especially galling, given that he was the commander in chief of a country at war.

I assumed that Poroshenko and those around him understood that I was implementing U.S. policy, tumultuous though it was. The U.S. expected Poroshenko to lead not only as a wartime president but also as a democratic president, and so I assumed that nobody doubted that my actions had the backing of the Trump administration. After all, if Trump didn't think I was properly representing him, he could have declared a loss of confidence and recalled me, at any time, for any reason.

Only much later did I realize that I was the one incorrectly reading the tea leaves. Events that I didn't think much of in 2018 were, in retrospect, a clear signal that corrupt forces in Ukraine weren't going to accept my actions without fighting back. And just because Trump hadn't recalled me yet did not mean that he had not begun to consider it — albeit for reasons that, if I had known about them, would have made no sense to me at the time.

12

Warning Signs

Throughout 2018 there had been signs that I was attracting the wrong kind of attention from powerful people, both in Ukraine and in the United States. The first warning that I can recall came from within the U.S. embassy in Kyiv. A staff member, whom I'll call Benjamin Rivers, was friends with Johnny McEntee, who had been a close personal assistant of Trump's before moving over to the president's reelection campaign in March 2018. Beginning in the early spring of 2018, Benjamin periodically informed me that McEntee was asking about me and inquiring whether I was doing a good job.

Those conversations stuck with me because they were so odd. The White House had shown very little interest in Ukraine, and my position wasn't one that usually attracted attention from those close to the president — any president. I told my supervisors back at the State Department about McEntee's questions, and they found them just as strange as I did. No one had heard concerns expressed about my performance or talk of replacing me. So I let it go, if only because I didn't know what else to do.

By early that summer, however, McEntee's inquiries started to seem less isolated. George Kent, at the time my deputy in Ukraine, told me about a call he received from Catherine Croft, a staffer on Trump's National Security Council who was working on Ukraine. Croft reported that Washington lobbyist Robert Livingston, a former Republican congressman, had contacted her at least twice to urge that I be replaced. He was concerned that I was an "Obama holdover" and falsely alleged that I was associated with conservative bête noire George Soros. Croft had no idea who Livingston represented, or even whether he was working for an American or a Ukrainian. I had never met Livingston, and the criticism contained no specifics. His recommendation, fortunately, went nowhere. But when added to the McEntee inquiries, it gave me an uncomfortable feeling.

Those events weren't my only cause of concern. The Ukrainian government, and President Poroshenko in particular, were clearly unhappy with my continued focus on reform. Poroshenko systematically forum-shopped, looking for more sympathetic Americans, ones willing to take at face value his claim that reforms were proceeding apace — or at least not to see it as a problem when they weren't. It worried me, but I couldn't control the behavior of others. So I tried to be professional. I was doing my job and implementing U.S. policy. I didn't need Poroshenko or General Prosecutor Yuriy Lutsenko to like me — they just needed to understand that I spoke for the U.S. government, which I had every reason to assume I did.

Still, it was concerning when even more concrete clues of Ukrainian dissatisfaction with me began to surface near the end of 2018. An embassy staffer who met regularly with Arsen Avakov, the Ukrainian internal affairs minister who had torpedoed the anti-NABU legislation, told me that Avakov wanted me to know that Lutsenko was working against me "personally." I knew from our testy meetings that Lutsenko resented my insistence that he uphold his reform commitments and stop undermining NABU. Still, it seemed far-fetched to think that Ukraine's top law enforcement official would be actively working to undermine the official representative of his country's most important international supporter. After all, in my previous experience serving in countries with dishonest leaders, their machinations did not extend to involving a U.S. ambassador personally.

I didn't know what to make of it. So with the exception of reporting it to George Kent, who had left Kyiv late that summer to be the State Department policy lead on Ukraine and five other countries, I kept to my "ignore it" approach. That had worked so far, and anyway, rumors were common in Ukraine. I had known going into the job that I wasn't going to make friends by pressing for reform. I figured that even if Lutsenko was working against me, it wouldn't amount to anything, especially back in the U.S., where it mattered most. Washington understood the way this part of the world worked and would judge me on the job I was doing for the United States, not the views of a disgruntled and corrupt Ukrainian. Of that I felt sure.

In addition, even in Ukraine it appeared that the consensus was that I was doing a good job. Earlier in 2018 I had landed near the top of a prominent local newspaper's list of the hundred most influential people in Ukraine —a sure sign that the embassy and I had been effective in our advocacy for reform. Perhaps even more gratifying, in the run-up to Ukraine's 2019 presidential elections, three cabinet ministers separately urged my boss, the assistant secretary for Europe, Wess Mitchell, to keep me on past my expected summer 2019 departure date. They foresaw a tumultuous period for Ukraine during and after the country's spring elections, and they thought that the country would benefit from having an experienced Ukraine hand at the embassy. Surely such endorsements would count for more than Lutsenko's conniving.

I TRIED TO keep my head down and move forward with my work, but by early 2019 I could no longer deny that the headwinds blowing against me were real. Not only that, but they were also having an effect.

In the beginning of January, former general prosecutor Viktor Shokin, the corrupt prosecutor whom the international donor community had pushed Poroshenko to get rid of, and whose firing had resulted in Lutsenko's appointment, applied for a visa to visit his children in the U.S. Although Shokin was by then a private citizen, the head of our visa section knew his reputation for corruption and that his application would be politically sensitive in Ukraine. In the spirit of no surprises, she let me know that Shokin had applied.

By law, I wasn't the decision-maker. I advised the visa section to follow whatever process and laws it normally follows when a known corrupt person applies for a visa. That's exactly what happened, and Shokin did not receive a visa. I let George Kent know, in case there was any blowback from Poroshenko, with whom Shokin was reportedly still close.

There was blowback—big blowback. But it came from a surprising place. Not from Poroshenko, but from Trump's White House. And it was bigger than anything I could have anticipated.

Although Shokin had told the embassy that he wanted to go to the U.S. to visit family, a different story emerged in Washington. Former New York City mayor Rudy Giuliani, now Trump's personal lawyer, had complained to the White House Chief of Staff's Office that the visa denial was keeping Shokin from a scheduled meeting with him. I was told that Giuliani had said that Shokin wanted to share information about alleged corruption in the U.S. embassy in Kyiv, corruption claims that—incredibly—involved me. Giuliani asserted that I had wrongly blocked Shokin's visa to prevent him from sharing this information with Washington. This triggered a call from the White House to the State Department, where the top political appointees in two bureaus — Consular Affairs and European Affairs — were forced to respond.

Wess Mitchell, the political appointee who headed the European Affairs Bureau, swung into action, but not in the way Giuliani had wanted. He immediately understood the situation and moved to protect the White House from making a potentially damaging and embarrassing mistake. Working with George, he explained the law to the White House, pointing out how the visa decision wasn't even a close call in Shokin's case. Abetting entry into the United States for a corrupt foreigner would open up the White House to all sorts of questions. Receiving the updates on Giuliani's efforts, I was appalled by his meddling in internal government decisions and gratified that we had strong leadership in the European Bureau, committed to doing the right thing.

The message got through. The decision was not overturned, and Shokin did not receive a visa enabling him to travel to the U.S. It felt like the good guys had won a round. But that feeling would be short-lived.

JUST A FEW weeks later, while I was in Washington for a conference, I met Benjamin Rivers, McEntee's friend and my now former staffer, who was by then back in Washington working at Foggy Bottom. Benjamin again shared what he had heard from McEntee, and what he told me was unsettling. Apparently Giuliani had complained directly to the president about me and wanted me fired. According to Benjamin, Giuliani was angry, and he was claiming that I personally had prevented Shokin from obtaining a visa to meet with him in New York.

This was so strange on so many levels that once again I didn't really know what to do. Shokin was a corrupt operator who was not a friend of the United States. Giuliani had no insight into our embassy's internal decision-making process. He had no basis on which to claim that I was the decision-maker or — most crucially — that the embassy had made a mistake. And he did not work for the U.S. government. If Shokin truly had evidence of corruption at the embassy, why wouldn't he take the direct route and share it with the State Department? Regardless, why was the president's personal lawyer, someone with no foreign-policy or consular decision-making role or experience, involved in any of this?

It made no sense. But if Benjamin's report was accurate, this could very well mean that my job was in jeopardy. In each of the five previous administrations I had served, I would have felt confident that Giuliani's pique would go nowhere. But two years into the Trump presidency, the only thing I knew for certain was that Trump was unpredictable, and he didn't seem overly concerned about the truth or the law.

I could do little about these strange goings-on, but I did recount the story to George, who was as taken aback as I was. He said that he would report it up the chain. The next day I got on a flight back to Kyiv as scheduled, hoping that the Shokin visa was just another bump along the road.

It wasn't long before I found out otherwise. In late February 2019, I attended an unrelated meeting with Internal Affairs Minister Avakov. After we concluded our scheduled business, Avakov asked for a private conversation with me and kicked everyone else out of his office. I appreciated his frankness, but I nevertheless was stunned by what came out of his mouth next. Avakov told me that Giuliani was working with Lutsenko and that the two men had met in Warsaw earlier that month. Later I would learn that Lutsenko, using a previously issued visa, had also traveled to New York in January to meet with Giuliani.

According to Avakov, Lutsenko was partnering with Giuliani to spin a story that Vice President Joe Biden had acted corruptly while serving as President Obama's lead person for Ukraine. Moreover, Lutsenko and Giuliani were trying to sell the idea that Ukrainian reformers, the U.S. embassy, and the Democratic Party had conspired during the 2016 U.S. presidential election in an unsuccessful attempt to help Hillary Clinton win.

Behind these conspiracy theories, Avakov indicated, were two goals. First, Lutsenko knew that Giuliani wanted to undermine Biden's expected candidacy in the 2020 U.S. presidential elections, so he had concocted a tale of lies and half-truths to oblige Giuliani. Lutsenko reshaped actions that Biden had taken to hold corrupt Ukrainians to account and twisted them into the opposite. He said that Biden had been corruptly protecting the interests of his son, Hunter, when the VP had insisted that Poroshenko fire former general prosecutor Shokin. According to Lutsenko, Biden wanted to stop Shokin from investigating a company called Burisma, on whose board

Biden's son served. In fact, of course, the opposite had been true; Shokin was not actively investigating corruption at Burisma, or anyplace else for that matter, which was why the entire donor community had come to believe that Shokin was corrupt and needed to go. This Orwellian construct was just one of the many ludicrous elements of the Giuliani-Lutsenko conspiracy theory.

Second, and most personally troubling, Avakov said that Giuliani and Lutsenko wanted President Trump to remove me as ambassador. They claimed that I too was corrupt, and they were trying to give me a supporting role in the fake narrative whereby I had directed bad actors in Ukraine to interfere in the 2016 U.S. presidential elections to undermine Donald Trump and benefit Hillary Clinton. I hadn't even arrived in Ukraine at the time the alleged events had occurred, but as usual with this crowd, facts didn't matter. Suffice it to say that both men evidently had a personal grudge against me, for reasons that were clear to me in Lutsenko's case and clear enough in Giuliani's — or so I thought at the time. Only later did I realize that Giuliani, in addition to having it in for me because of the Shokin visa issue, wanted me gone for a different reason: he wished to deflect from the consensus that Russia had tried to help Trump in 2016 by creating a fictitious narrative that it was Ukraine that had tried to help Clinton. If he could frame me as part of a fictional cabal of anti-Trump operatives in Ukraine, it might help to obfuscate or at least confuse the very real story that pro-Trump meddling had been coming from Russia.

Avakov told me that I needed to protect myself: *You need to watch your back.* He also told me that the Lutsenko-Giuliani machinations were being openly discussed during meetings of Poroshenko's inner circle. Avakov said that both he and former prime minister Yatsenyuk had warned Poroshenko that it was dangerous for Ukraine to insert itself into American politics. What Poroshenko himself thought about the matter, Avakov didn't say. But apparently he wasn't warning Lutsenko off. And given his omnipresent role in Ukrainian politics, it was hard for me to believe that he hadn't blessed the campaign against me. I was in the capital of a foreign country, and normally I would have felt secure in my position, even with such knowledge. But with people in my own country's capital apparently gunning for me, and Avakov's evident urgency, my anxiety immediately went up several notches.

Avakov added that Giuliani was also working with two Soviet émigrés, now American citizens: Lev Parnas and Igor Fruman. The two had recently traveled to Kyiv to discuss an energy company they hoped to establish in Ukraine. At a meeting that Avakov had attended, the pair had informed Ukrainian officials that I would soon be removed. They were *trouble*, Avakov told me, and he would not meet with them again. Avakov also said that he had declined Giuliani's repeated requests to meet, as it was *too dangerous* — by which I assumed he meant that Ukraine risked losing bipartisan U.S. support if Ukrainians started meddling in American politics.

I believed Avakov. He had been a good partner on certain anti-corruption reforms in the past, and I couldn't see what he stood to gain by making up such a crazy story. I certainly knew that I had made enemies out of Giuliani and Lutsenko. So that part of his story checked out. But I didn't know what to make of Avakov's information about Parnas and Fruman. I had never heard of them, which in itself was odd. American businessmen entering the Ukrainian market usually make their first stop the embassy's commercial section, which provides advice on doing business in Ukraine. They often ask to meet with me as well. If it is legitimate business, of course.

What's more, while I'd seen plenty of whisper campaigns and smear efforts in my many years of working in the former Soviet Union, Americans had never been among the key players driving them. Perhaps that's because anyone considering such an effort would never have gotten close enough to the seat of American power to have an impact. But as I was rapidly learning, where Trump's administration was concerned, all bets were off.

ALTHOUGH IT BECAME more and more difficult to write off the rumors as idle noise, I did my best to compartmentalize. Ukraine's presidential election was approaching, and Poroshenko was increasingly unpopular. With his reelection in doubt, his government seemed determined to roll back some of the reforms that had been achieved, probably in an effort to protect his allies — and himself — while he still could. We and other international representatives held private conversations with key Ukrainians to raise our concerns, but to no avail. So at Embassy Kyiv we looked for an opportunity to make U.S. consternation more public before more damage was done to Ukraine's hard-won reforms. It was time to make clear that the United States had taken note of the backsliding and would call it out for what it was.

On March 5, 2019, I found that opportunity in a speech to honor the fifth anniversary of the Ukraine Crisis Media Center, an NGO devoted to supporting journalism and freedom of information. I acknowledged the center's achievements and, more broadly, Ukraine's significant progress. But I also stated what we all knew: Ukraine was struggling to live up to the aspirations of the Revolution of Dignity. I raised concerns about a recent decision by the top court—a decision that senior government officials likely welcomed and perhaps influenced to gut a provision in the criminal code barring government officials from "illegally enriching" themselves at the public's expense, as well as about court decisions to reverse banking reforms. I also highlighted recent allegations of corruption in the defense sector and in the selection process for judges, and the resulting corrosive effect on the military and the judiciary. But there was one line that seemed to catch everyone's attention: I called for the replacement of Special Anti-corruption Prosecutor (SAP) Nazar Kholodnytskyy.

Kholodnytskyy's prosecutorial unit, the Specialized Anti-Corruption Prosecutor's Office, had been created at the same time as the National Anti-Corruption Bureau of Ukraine and was supposed to prosecute the high-level corruption cases that NABU investigated and developed. Like NABU, it was designed to be independent of Ukraine's leaders. Like NABU, it was an object of great hope and expectation for the Ukrainian people. And like NABU, its creation was a condition of international assistance for Ukraine. Unlike NABU, however, SAPO reported to the general prosecutor, an arrangement that the donor community had reluctantly agreed to. That meant that Kholodnytskyy wasn't really independent—and that in turn created serious issues.

The issues had come to a head when Kholodnytskyy, the man supposedly in charge of prosecuting high-level government corruption in Ukraine, had himself been caught on tape about a year earlier coaching suspects on how to testify in corruption cases that he was prosecuting. The G7 ambassadors and I had spent the intervening year working quietly with Lutsenko to encourage him to find a way to remove the discredited Kholodnytskyy from his position. We had watched Lutsenko go through the motions of trying to dismiss Kholodnytskyy, only to come up short. I wish I could say this was a surprise.

Airing our concerns in a speech hadn't been my first choice, but Kholodnytskyy was doing significant damage—damage compounded by the clear signal sent by Lutsenko and the rest of the establishment that they would protect him. It was time for me to convey a more pointed message in return.

I went right from the speech to the airport to pick up Under Secretary for Political Affairs David Hale, the number-three official at the State Department and the department's highest-ranking career Foreign Service officer. So serious that he looked like he had been born in a business suit, Hale and his presence in Kyiv signaled continuing U.S. support for Ukraine, and I was grateful for the visit.

At a press conference at the conclusion of his three-day visit, Hale was asked about my March 5 remarks. They had caused a furor, with Kholodnytskyy telling everyone that I was not speaking for the U.S. government. Hale responded that "Ambassador Yovanovitch represents the president of the United States here in Ukraine, and America stands behind her statements." He provided the unstinting support that ambassadors need to do their jobs, and I was grateful once again. But my relief would be short-lived.

I HAD ORIGINALLY planned to leave Ukraine in July 2019, three years after I arrived. But during his visit, Hale asked me to stay longer. With no one even in the pipeline to replace me, he was concerned that my departure would leave the post vacant for many months at a pivotal time. A bit embarrassed, I told him about Avakov's report that Giuliani was working with Lutsenko to remove me. It wasn't a long conversation, because I didn't know very much. Still, I thought that Hale should know. He simply responded that he was aware and considered the problem *manageable*. I figured that meant that Giuliani was freelancing — annoying, but irrelevant. Some days later — and somewhat reluctantly — I agreed to extend my tour. Shortly thereafter the State Department personnel system started taking the necessary steps to implement the decision.

But the rumors didn't go away. In mid-March, Avakov, who continued to get updates from Lutsenko and could see that I was going about my duties as if nothing was wrong, enlisted Deputy Foreign Minister Lana Zerkal to convey an urgent message to me. Lana came to my residence and said that Avakov had asked her to warn me that Lutsenko wanted to *hurt me in the U.S.* Sitting in my living room, nursing a cup of tea, I was both alarmed and perplexed. *But what could he do?* I asked. Lana said she didn't know.

From Avakov's prior warnings I knew that Lutsenko was going to try to make life uncomfortable for me in Ukraine. I understood that he had joined forces with Giuliani and that they both wanted me fired. But I still couldn't imagine that they were going to be successful. The notion that an unscrupulous, disgruntled foreign official or even a president's personal dirt-dig-ger could actually manipulate the U.S. government to act against a sitting U.S. ambassador was inconceivable to me. After all, the State Department had just asked me to extend my tenure in Ukraine.

Nevertheless, I dutifully reported this latest bit of unsettling information to George Kent in Washington. He was as much in the dark as I was, but he said that he would share the information up the chain, and I let it rest at that. Even if true, it was beyond my control.

WHAT I WOULD NOT understand for nearly a month was that my ambas-sadorship was already on life support. The scheming against me had spread beyond Lutsenko and Giuliani to incorporate a wider array of purposes and players, apparently reaching all the way to Trump himself.

A reputable American businessman named Dale Perry later revealed that his close associate, then the number two at Naftohaz, had been ap-proached in March by a trio of private American citizens about participat-ing in a plan to remove Andriy Kobolyev, the head of the Ukrainian gas conglomerate. Andriy was a rare Ukrainian in power who never stopped fighting corrupt efforts to benefit the well-connected at the expense of the Ukrainian people. I had worked closely with his team in 2016 to keep the Ukrainian government from moving Naftohaz subsidiary UTH beyond the reach of Naftohaz's reform management—a move we then suspected was made to benefit the U.S.-indicted oligarch Dmytro Firtash.

In April 2019, Perry sent a number of people at the State Department and elsewhere an email, which he characterized as an "open letter." Perry explained that Firtash was back at it (if he'd ever stopped), trying to collect on claims that Naftohaz owed him hundreds of millions of dollars. Perry reported that Giuliani's partners Parnas and Fruman also seemed to be rep-resenting Firtash, and that the two men had joined up with Harry Sargeant III, a billionaire from Florida, who wanted lucrative sole-source contracts to supply gas to Naftohaz. Perry claimed that Sargeant, Parnas, and Fruman wanted to replace Andriy with someone more amenable, someone who would not insist on open competition and would facilitate the sweetheart deal that Sargeant wanted. For good measure, Perry wrote, they wanted to replace me as well. They knew that I would object to the removal without cause of Andriy, a stalwart reformer. They were right about that, since promoting transparent governance of Ukraine's state-owned companies was a key tenet of U.S. policy.

Most astounding of all in Perry's recounting was how high the claimed connections of the three went. Harry Sargeant, Perry wrote, said that he "regularly meets with the President at Mar-a-Lago" and that he had told Trump about their plans — and that Trump had agreed to them. It seemed incredible to Perry. As he wrote, "Is it possible for such a person from Florida to 'appoint' a US Ambassador, with an aim to getting his special deal in Ukraine, at the expense of the fight against corruption in Ukraine and at the expense of the Ukrainian gas consumers?"

If you had asked me the same question as these events were unfolding, I would have had only one answer: absolutely not. But that's only because I then lacked the imagination to see that the corruption that was afflicting Ukraine was also infecting the United States.

For his part, Sargeant later issued a statement through his lawyers that he was not involved in any Ukrainian business nor had he discussed participation in a future Ukrainian venture with the individuals Perry cited — or with Trump at Mar-a-Lago.

IN A WAY it was good that I was unaware of most of these events as the spring of 2019 neared. With just a couple of weeks to go before the first round of Ukraine's presidential elections on March 31, I needed to be firing on all cylinders. I was meeting with the top candidates in the crowded field of thirty-nine, seeking to understand their thoughts on Ukraine, their platforms, prospects, and predictions. We also had an important message to convey: free and fair elections were critical to Ukraine's democracy. To Ihor Hryniv, Poroshenko's campaign manager, we made two additional points: *don't* use the state's resources to affect the outcome, and *do* accept the election results, whatever they may be. We weren't sure whether Poroshenko would try to hold on to power if he lost. We wanted to ensure that he understood that the U.S. would not support extra-constitutional measures. For the Russia-leaning candidates, I noted that we expected Russia and its proxies not to meddle in the elections.

We had a critical message, but I was beginning to wonder whether the attacks on the messenger — that is, me — were undermining that message. Kyiv is a small town, and information and rumors passed efficiently among the elite. Increasingly Ukrainians would ask whether I was leaving, to which I always replied that they shouldn't trust the rumors; I was on the job and staying in Ukraine.

When I gave presidential candidate and former defense minister Anatoliy Hrytsenko this standard response, he looked at me compassionately and said, *You're a professional, you'll work until the day you leave.* I still couldn't believe that Giuliani would prevail, but that comment made me wonder whether Hrytsenko knew more than I did.

The gossip and rumors made a difficult job more difficult, but I still didn't really believe anything more would come of it. State was backing me, and despite the stress and the questions, I thought I could still be effective in Ukraine.

And then I fell down the rabbit hole.

13

Cut Loose

O N WEDNESDAY, MARCH 20, 2019, John Solomon, a conservative opinion writer whom I had never heard of, posted several Ukraine-related
articles on the website of *The Hill*, a moderate to right-leaning publication focused on national politics. Masquerading as news reports and rely-
ing heavily on an interview with Lutsenko, Solomon's postings advanced a
number of conspiracy theories, all of which seemed aimed at showing that
certain unscrupulous people in Ukraine had worked against Trump in 2016
and were continuing to do so in 2019. An entire set of Lutsenko's charges focused on me. Months later *The Hill* would sever its relationship with Solomon; ultimately it would append to his Ukraine columns a lengthy editor's
note calling Lutsenko's credibility into question and offering critical background about Lutsenko and his allegations that Solomon had ignored. But
by that point the damage had long been done.

Solomon's pieces flipped reality on its head and portrayed Lutsenko as
an anti-corruption crusader who had been stymied by a rogue U.S. ambassador. Among the most consequential charges: Lutsenko's claim that I gave
him a "do not prosecute" list. This made-up document allegedly recorded
the names of corrupt individuals whom I wanted to protect from Ukrainian justice. The very idea was ridiculous, but that did not prevent it from
playing an outsized role in the drama that followed. Nor did it prevent Lutsenko from bravely declaring that nobody would stop him from prosecuting crime in Ukraine.

Solomon buttressed his comic-book portrait of me with a fictional story
from Lutsenko claiming that the embassy was wrongly withholding $4 mil-
lion in U.S. assistance monies allocated to his office because I didn't like
that he was investigating people close to the U.S. embassy. According to

Lutsenko, there was "a case for the embezzlement of the U.S. government technical assistance worth 4 million U.S. dollars."

Almost everything Lutsenko said in the article was a lie; in fact, it was typical Russian-style gaslighting. He turned our standard U.S. policy that prosecutors should stick to the rule of law and avoid selective prosecution into a fantasy in which I protected rivals and political opponents from his dogged pursuit. And he completely mischaracterized an official U.S. government decision to transfer its anti-corruption assistance from the ineffective and discredited GPO to two Ukrainian organizations actually fighting graft, NABU and the Anti-Corruption Action Center. He alleged that the embassy had moved the money to undermine his pro-reform work. Never mind that the assistance reprogramming had occurred long before my August 2016 arrival and even before Lutsenko had started at the GPO. Why let facts get in the way of a tale of self-serving heroism?

But there was more. Claiming that concerns about me were widespread, Solomon posted a letter that Texas congressman Pete Sessions had sent to Secretary Pompeo on May 9, 2018, nearly a year earlier. In the letter Sessions called for my immediate "expulsion," claiming that he had proof — unspecified, of course — that I had spoken with "disdain" about the Trump administration.

The congressman's letter looked authentic, but it was the first I had heard of it or the allegations that it contained. They were of course untrue, but even more, they were perplexing. I couldn't remember ever having met Sessions and just couldn't figure out why he'd write a letter about me or Ukraine. He wasn't on the House Foreign Affairs Committee, and as far as I knew he didn't follow Ukraine. What had made him write such a letter to the secretary of state? Who were his unnamed sources? Perhaps strangest of all, why had I never heard of this year-old letter before? When a member of Congress writes to the secretary, the letter usually goes to the relevant State Department office to draft a response. A letter from a congressman charging ambassadorial misconduct would normally trigger a discussion with the ambassador, at a minimum. How had Solomon obtained it when even *I* hadn't seen it before? I wondered how Pompeo's office had handled the response, since there had been no input from the professionals in the European Bureau.

It was disconcerting, to say the least, that what I had thought to be a reputable publication was so readily publishing damaging — and disprovable — lies about me. But naively I thought that if this was the big Giuliani-Lutsenko conspiracy that Avakov had warned me about, it was pretty thin gruel. Every allegation was easily rebutted; a State Department spokesperson made that much clear to Solomon, calling the do-not-prosecute list claim "an outright fabrication" and rejecting Lutsenko's claim of embezzlement by explaining that State had decided not to provide aid to the GPO. Anyone who read the articles with a critical eye would see right through them, or so I thought. Despite my worry, I still had faith that the truth would triumph.

WITH THE U.S.-UKRAINE time difference, I didn't see Solomon's articles until sometime on Thursday morning. I read them, but as usual I had a jam-packed day and didn't have the time to sort it all out. I had to prepare for an early-afternoon meeting with a primarily Republican group of U.S. senators and representatives. They had arrived the night before to familiarize themselves with the situation in Ukraine, and I saw their trip as an important opportunity to build support for Ukraine's defense against Russia and its internal fight against graft. As the delegation and I headed to a meeting with Foreign Minister Klimkin, I told the group, led by Idaho senator Mike Crapo, about the Lutsenko interview and articles. They had already seen the article about me and wanted to know what I thought was behind Lutsenko's claims.

I told them what I thought at the time: that it was retaliation for my March 5 speech criticizing the reform rollbacks and calling for the removal of Special Anti-corruption Prosecutor Kholodnytskyy. Although the warning signs were out there, I somehow still wasn't willing to entertain the thought that this was connected to the Giuliani-Lutsenko partnership Avakov had warned me about. It was just too crazy. The congressional members seemed to accept my explanation, but I wouldn't have predicted what happened next.

Crapo opened the meeting with the foreign minister by forcefully warning that Ukrainian officials attacking the U.S. ambassador made it harder for the U.S. to support Ukraine. Each member took a turn. Louisiana senator John Kennedy told Klimkin that Lutsenko needed to apologize and that Klimkin needed to convey that message from the congressional delegation directly to Poroshenko as well. I hoped no one was looking at me, because the support was so unexpected and so overwhelming that I had tears in my eyes. The delegation repeated their defense of me in their next and final meeting in Ukraine, with the finance minister. It was the way it should be: Team America.

Back in the U.S., my Foreign Service colleagues were also pushing back. Phil Reeker, a longtime colleague and career FSO who had recently started as the acting head of the European Bureau, had called in the number-two official at Ukraine's embassy in Washington and read her the riot act. The ambassador was out of town or he would have been the one to receive the message about Lutsenko's campaign against me. Whether because of Phil's actions or the delegations' forceful words, Ukraine's Ministry of Foreign Affairs issued a statement in my defense within hours of our meeting with Klimkin. It was weak — no doubt a bureaucratic effort to please too many masters — but at least it showed that the Ukrainians were scrambling, and I hoped this was the beginning of the end of Lutsenko's efforts. I was grateful for the support of my countrymen and colleagues.

But if I had any illusions that Team America extended all the way to the players that mattered most in Trump's Washington, they were dispelled later that day, when the embassy's press section shared upsetting news with me. The previous night on Sean Hannity's program on Fox News, a married team of Giuliani-connected lawyers named Joe DiGenova and Victoria Toensing — two more people I had never before heard of — had joined Solomon to talk up his Ukraine articles. The discussion focused primarily on Lutsenko's claims about Ukrainian interference to support Clinton in the 2016 elections, but Hannity also referenced Congressman Sessions's claim that I had bad-mouthed Trump.

Hannity was one of Trump's favorite news sources, and he and the president reportedly spoke frequently. Seeing these right-wing talking heads all together and prepared to speak so soon after Solomon's articles went online gave it the look and feel of an organized campaign. That this campaign seemed connected to both the Giuliani-Trump world and the forces of corruption in Ukraine only made it more ominous and alarming.

The next day I allowed myself a bit of optimism when Poroshenko, in response to the controversy, used the opportunity of a prescheduled public event to say some positive words of support for me. But he notably did not fire or even reprimand Lutsenko for acting improperly — the only thing that would have made a difference in Ukraine. I wasn't entirely surprised by this; according to Avakov, Lutsenko had been keeping Poroshenko apprised of his machinations against me. It looked like Poroshenko was continuing to protect Lutsenko, who was nevertheless furious about even tepid words of support for me. That made two of us who were mad.

That evening I called Senator John Barrasso, a member of the congressional delegation that had just visited, to thank the members for their help. He told me to stay in touch, especially if I needed any further assistance. I was grateful for his offer, even if I still couldn't imagine what kind of assistance I might need in the days ahead.

I HAD DONE what I could in Ukraine to neutralize Lutsenko's absurd allegations, and I hoped that the combined weight of the State Department's rebuttal, the senators' strong support in Kyiv, and Poroshenko's remarks would put those allegations to rest. But what I hadn't yet fully appreciated was that the action that mattered most wasn't any longer taking place in Ukraine. While I had been meeting with the senators and trying to get the Ukrainians to correct the record, the Solomon articles had taken on a life of their own back home.

The embassy press shop, responsible for following news and social media, had assembled press packets for my review. When I finally had the time to closely read the growing mountain of clips that Saturday morning, I was devastated — and feared that I was reading about the beginning of the end of my ambassadorship. It turned out that within an hour of Hannity's Wednesday show featuring Solomon, President Trump had tweeted one of the Solomon articles. Not surprisingly, Trump-world influencers and hangers-on then picked up the falsehoods and circulated them endlessly over the ensuing days. It didn't seem to matter that State had denied the stories. The disinformation campaign against me had successfully taken root in the United States, where Lutsenko's claims seemed to serve Trump's desire to divert public attention from the reality of Russia's election interference to sham claims of an anti-Trump conspiracy involving Ukrainians and Americans.

The Solomon articles were well timed to do just that. Solomon posted his pieces just two days before the March 22 release of the Mueller Report regarding Russian interference in U.S. elections. The Mueller Report was big news, unless you were being distracted by the laundering of Lutsenko's claims through channels impervious to correction.

I spent that Saturday afternoon cycling between disbelief and despair as I tried to get the State Department to defend me and our mission in Ukraine more forcefully. A State Department spokesperson had denied the allegations when the articles first came out, but that wasn't cutting it as the slanders spread like wildfire. The news sources and influencers who we all knew mattered most to Trump were excoriating me, and it was hard to see a happy ending unless someone with Trump-world credibility acted soon and decisively. I told State that the department, preferably the secretary himself, had to weigh in — a point that my Foreign Service colleagues in D.C. agreed with — but by late afternoon it felt like I was on my own.

Rather than hearing that a department statement was imminent, I learned through two different channels that David Hale, the under secretary who just weeks earlier had asked me to extend my time in Ukraine, was suggesting that *I* issue a statement, one expressing loyalty to Trump. But unless the State Department publicly went to bat for me, and soon, I didn't think that my own statement would work. Even worse, I thought such a statement was demeaning — and wrong.

Still, I agonized over whether to record the loyalty pledge Hale recommended. My job, my reputation, and the integrity of our mission in Ukraine were at stake. If Lutsenko's and Giuliani's campaign resulted in my removal, it would raise questions about our policies and especially about U.S. commitment to fighting corruption. Plus it would alert and encourage dubious characters around the world and in the U.S. that they could get rid of American ambassadors who were making life uncomfortable for them.

That Saturday night around nine o'clock I drove over to the embassy and met up with the public affairs team. Still following Foreign Service discipline despite my growing shock, I had decided to tape the pledge Hale had suggested before deciding what to do. But when I tried the loyalty pledge on for size, I couldn't make it fit — not if I wanted to keep my integrity intact. I had my press people tweet out a different video statement the next morning. In it I lauded the merits of democracy on the eve of Ukraine's presidential elections and noted that I had taken a pledge, as a nonpartisan diplomat, to serve whoever the American people elected as their president. That, I explained, was the mark of a true democracy.

As I left the embassy, I held my head up and my shoulders back. But I was grateful for the darkness outside and hoped that my colleagues couldn't see my face as I sank into the back seat of the car. My confidence in having done the right thing didn't make me feel any less miserable. It was a lonely car ride home as I wondered how much longer I would be in Ukraine.

I didn't have much hope that the statement would do the trick, and, as if to validate my pessimism, the situation got exponentially worse on Sunday. Around noon Washington time, Donald Trump Jr. tweeted out an article describing growing calls for my ouster, with the comment "We need . . . less of these jokers as ambassadors." I saw the tweet in the early evening, and I quickly sent an email to Under Secretary Hale. It was short and blunt: Pompeo had to issue a strong statement supporting me; otherwise I couldn't survive. To his credit, Hale interrupted his Sunday to call me immediately. He told me that he would raise the issue with Secretary Pompeo on Monday and recommend a statement defending me. He also asked me to send an email describing what I thought was behind the attacks on me — only to him, with no subject line.

I got to the embassy bright and early Monday morning, and after our daily small staff meeting, I asked not to be disturbed. I closed the door and went to my standing desk, where I kicked off my shoes and started writing. In the quiet I drafted my thoughts in a succinct page and a half. I wanted the email in Hale's in-box at the opening of business in Washington.

I lost access to my State Department emails when I retired in early 2020, so I can't reproduce my note to Hale verbatim. But this is what I recall writing: Lutsenko's willingness to slander a U.S. ambassador on the record was the result of a confluence of nefarious interests. On the Ukrainian side, Poroshenko, Lutsenko's patron, desperately wanted Trump to endorse his re-election, and he and Lutsenko were willing to trade made-up dirt on Biden and me if that's what it took. But even absent an endorsement, smearing me would not only silence an advocate for anti-corruption efforts in Ukraine, it would also undermine my unwelcome messages regarding free and fair elections, which cast Poroshenko in an unflattering light as Ukrainian elections approached. Lutsenko's claims about corruption in NABU, if credited, would neutralize a government entity that actually seemed interested in going after corruption. And of course there was the purely personal motivation: Poroshenko made no bones about the fact that I was too critical of his government, and Lutsenko felt disrespected by me; they both wanted me out of the way.

I knew that Hale wouldn't be surprised that certain actors in Ukraine would want to get rid of me, up to and including the Ukrainian president. But would he be able to believe that they had found willing partners on the American side? "G," as I called Giuliani in the email to Hale — trying even then to avoid spelling out the name of someone so close to the president — was trying to help his own patron, Trump, in his reelection campaign. Giuliani wanted dirt on Trump's possible presidential opponent Joe Biden, and he wanted the Ukrainians to launch an investigation into Biden's alleged unprincipled interference in Ukraine. He also wanted to promote a counternarrative to the recently concluded Mueller Report. Giuliani got what he wanted in Lutsenko's false claims about Vice President Biden's actions in Ukraine and in Lutsenko's willingness to share a tall tale about Ukrainians somehow colluding with Democrats during the 2016 campaign.

I also told Hale that Giuliani probably had a grudge against me, that he was likely furious over the visa to Shokin that he claimed I blocked. Giuliani said that Shokin had been planning to travel to the U.S. to share information about alleged corruption at the embassy, including on my part. He had gone straight to the White House to request a visa for Shokin, but cooler heads had prevailed, which probably made Giuliani angrier. The demonstration that he couldn't reverse the visa decision must have embarrassed him in front of Shokin, Lutsenko, and Poroshenko and cast doubt on his ability to deliver on any other promises. Getting me fired would reclaim his credibility as a power broker.

Finally, I recall writing to Hale that Guiliani may well have had his own business reasons for trying to get me removed. It was unclear to me precisely who Giuliani represented and in what capacity, but he associated with — and may even have represented — individuals in Ukraine who would benefit from an embassy that pursued anti-corruption efforts less vigorously, granted visas to questionable characters more liberally, and was less inclined to recommend adding Ukrainians to American sanctions lists.

Hale replied relatively quickly, and although he didn't comment on the substance of my note, he told me that he would pass it on to Pompeo.

Later that day I got a call from the European Bureau informing me that before issuing a statement, Secretary Pompeo wanted to see whether the media who were making the allegations against me had any evidence of wrongdoing. Either Pompeo or Ulrich Brechbuhl, Pompeo's counselor and West Point classmate, planned to call Hannity and ask him to *put up or shut up*. That hardly amounted to the full-throated and immediate public support I was looking for, but at least it was a start. I hoped that it would ultimately lead to a public statement and the full backing of the State Department, even though I knew that the odds were stacked against me — both for the statement and for the kind of fulsome support I would need to stay on in Ukraine.

So, as practical as ever, I steered the conversation toward the elephant in the room. I urged the bureau to start thinking about who would replace me if I was recalled. I dreaded that dismal prospect, but it seemed to be growing more likely by the day, and we needed to be prepared.

AFTER LEARNING that no immediate statement was coming out of State, I started casting around for any other lifelines that I could think of. First I turned for help to Gordon Sondland, our ambassador to the European Union, who had inserted himself into Ukraine issues and recently visited Ukraine. He was a big Trump donor, having given a cool million to the inaugural committee. Tall and bald, he had the air of someone who enjoyed his position of prominence, and he regularly indicated that he and Trump were tight. Sondland was the only individual I knew personally who was in the president's orbit and likely to answer my call. Maybe he could help me, I thought.

I called Sondland the next afternoon, on Tuesday, March 26, and apparently was the first to inform him about Lutsenko's allegations becoming a big political story in the U.S. He made an "Ewwww" noise when I told him about Trump Jr.'s tweet slamming me. I asked him what I should do, secretly hoping that he would offer to call Trump. Instead Sondland advised me to issue my own tweet or statement. He said, *You know the president, and even if you don't know the president personally, you know what he's like and what he likes. Put out a tweet about how much you love the president.* He concluded by saying, *You need to go big or go home.*

I thanked Sondland for his advice, but I couldn't imagine any Foreign Service officer following it. It was another suggestion for a loyalty oath, and an even more partisan version than the one Hale had suggested. I couldn't do it. I knew I couldn't go big, and my hope that I wouldn't be going home was fading by the hour.

But I still wasn't willing to give up. Remembering the invitation to call on them if I needed anything, I reached out to a staffer from the congressional delegation that had visited Kyiv and been so supportive when the *Hill* articles were published. I hoped the delegation could once again work its magic and get an official statement issued, this time from the U.S. government.

I never heard back. I wasn't completely surprised. It's one thing to support a U.S. ambassador to a foreign government, it's quite another to defend a U.S. ambassador to her own president, especially if that president is Trump.

I had played all the cards I could think to play, both within State and outside it, and had come up empty. Pompeo clearly was never going to utter a public word in my defense; I assumed he didn't want the rug pulled out from under him by Trump. I'm not even sure he ever reached out to Hannity, since the Fox anchor later indignantly termed the suggestion that Pompeo called him "fake news."

One person at least never stopped trying to rebuff the false narrative that had engulfed me. Over the next few weeks, George Kent, the lead officer on Ukraine policy at the State Department, my former deputy in Kyiv, and a good friend, ensured that Washington decision-makers had all the facts. Blessed with a phenomenal memory, an outsized intellect, and a prodigious work ethic, George urged strong departmental action to defend me, which would have been standard in past administrations. His right-minded stance didn't win him friends in the administration, and I was often reminded that when he had been in Kyiv, I had called George "our conscience," as he always championed principled policy, even when it was the harder path.

But it was to no avail. The link between the career professionals and the political leadership was completely broken. What, I asked myself, had happened to the State Department? And what had happened to Secretary Pompeo's promise to stand up for his people? He must have known the allegations against me were false. I couldn't imagine his legendary predecessor Secretary Shultz, who had been renowned for taking care of career employees, suddenly abandoning one of his ambassadors without proof of wrongdoing. It was incomprehensible that I was being cut loose like this, and unclear what it meant for other diplomats who ran afoul of unscrupulous interests. One thing I knew for sure: this was not the department I had joined so many years ago.

I HAD WORKED hard to keep the real work of the embassy and the madness of the Giuliani-Lutsenko affair on separate tracks. Before the *Hill* articles, I hadn't discussed the situation with more than a handful of people at the embassy. It was too political, and I wanted to protect my staff. I was grateful that even fewer people knew about my tour's planned extension, which I assumed would be rescinded, so there was nothing to explain there. However, after the publication of the Solomon articles, I knew that I needed to discuss the situation with my senior staff at that week's regular Tuesday meeting.

About twenty of us were packed into our small conference room, which was windowless and secured for classified conversations. At the end of the usual meeting, I asked for another ten minutes to share personal information. It was really awkward to tell nonpartisan professionals that a concerted campaign against me was being led by the president's personal lawyer. Most of them were unaware of the storm around me, and they were visibly shocked. It was a lot to take in. Disbelief, consternation, anger, and sympathy came and went across their faces as I listed the allegations against me. It was hard to explain it all. Fortunately, I was able to hold it together.

I kept to the facts. I didn't have to explain what they meant; everyone understood that this was really bad. When I finished, there was a moment of stunned silence as the staff wrapped their minds around what I was saying. They knew none of the allegations were true: they worked with me. My colleagues expressed their disbelief, their incomprehension, their anger, and, what touched me the most, their desire to help me. I told them that it was incredibly affirming that the people who knew me and my work best were so supportive. But this was political, and no place for embassy staff.

Later in the day my deputy Pam told me that she and the senior staff had discussed options and proposed sending a joint message to Secretary Pompeo defending me. I instructed her to tell everyone to stay out of it. I was touched, but I knew I had to be tough. It would not help me, and it would hurt them, the future leaders of the department and other agencies. I told her to direct everyone to stay focused on the important work we were doing in Ukraine.

NEAR THE END of the week, Phil Reeker, who headed up the European Bureau, drew the short straw and had to tell me that the extension that Hale had proposed just three weeks earlier was off the table. In fact, he added, the department wanted me to leave Ukraine as quickly as possible. Even on a temporary basis, so the scandal could cool.

I couldn't process it. Ukraine was just days away from an important election. The U.S. had serious interests and serious work to do; I didn't think this was the time to pull out an ambassador, especially since it would be nearly impossible to quickly find a replacement who had anything approaching my years of knowledge and connections. The optics were bad. Yanking me immediately would signal that U.S. diplomacy was in disarray. How would the department explain that?

I suggested to Phil that I leave as originally scheduled — after the embassy's big July 4 celebration, a traditional time for ambassadors to transfer. We went back and forth, and it seemed to be settled that I would leave in July as previously planned. A veteran negotiator, Phil has a great sense of humor and a light touch, but as our discussions proceeded, I began to realize that I was being managed as though I were a problem employee. It was an uncomfortable role reversal for someone who had been managing problem employees for the past twenty-plus years. Now, it appeared, I was the problem employee, who didn't know her time was up and needed to be eased out without causing a ruckus. Some part of me felt sorry for Phil, who was getting stuck with this unenviable task.

But I had less sympathy for the people who had given him these orders. The department's position seemed clearly wrong, not least because if State moved me out early, people would wonder what the real story was. Once the real story came out, it would leave State looking weak and unprincipled — unlikely to protect other American diplomats from similar attacks and unwilling and unable to defend American interests against amateurish but malign foreign and domestic intrigues.

I was devastated, and not just for the obvious reasons. I wanted to stay for the launching of Ukraine's next president, which I knew was going to be a consequential time. I felt that I had earned that front-row seat to history. And I just couldn't reconcile myself to being unceremoniously ushered away.

THAT NIGHT I MET Bill Taylor for drinks. A longtime friend who was himself a former U.S. ambassador to Ukraine, Bill's low-key manner, obvious integrity, and soothing baritone immediately instilled confidence. He was in Kyiv to serve as an election observer for one of the monitoring groups, but that's not what he wanted to talk about. He had been closely following the Giuliani-Lutsenko disinformation campaign and he wanted to help, something he felt free to do since he no longer worked for State.

Bill told me that he had joined with the other retired former ambassadors to Ukraine to draft an op-ed defending me. I was bolstered by the show of support, and not just because of the authors' collective gravitas in the foreign policy community. These people were my mentors as well as my friends. Their willingness to stand by me and vouch for my integrity meant everything to me.

Still, I worried that a group of career diplomats weighing in publicly would merely provoke a favorite Trump-world charge: that the so-called deep state — meaning anyone who had devoted his or her life to public service — was flouting the president, in this case by trying to protect one of its own. So I asked them to hold off. They honored my request and instead wrote a letter to Under Secretary Hale, concluding with the point that "allowing these attacks on a U.S. ambassador in the field to stand without strong rebuttal from senior officials in the U.S. Government weakens the structure of our diplomatic engagement abroad." Hale did not respond.

It was a dark time for me, but I was heartened by displays of support such as these, as well as by a Ukrainian poll at the end of March. The pollsters had queried respondents about whether they believed Lutsenko or me. Polling in Ukraine can sometimes be suspect, but I allowed myself to believe this one: nearly 84 percent chose me over the general prosecutor, and another 11 percent didn't care. Barely 5 percent of respondents trusted their chief law enforcement official over me. In his own country.

THAT SUNDAY, MARCH 31, Ukrainians went to the polls to start the process of electing their next president. With thirty-nine candidates vying for the post, it was little surprise that none of them reached the 50 percent threshold necessary for victory in the first round. A second round was scheduled for April 21, when Ukrainians would choose between the two candidates who received the most votes: political neophyte Volodymyr Zelenskyy, who came in at 30 percent, and President Poroshenko, who got barely half as much at 16 percent.

You didn't need a crystal ball to know what was going to happen next. Zelenskyy, a beloved comedian who played an accidental president on a popular Ukrainian television show, was going to win the next round. The Kyiv elite had a hard time accepting it, though. The dynamics struck me as very similar to what had occurred three years before in the U.S., when the American political establishment had dismissed Donald Trump right up until his surprise election-night win.

At the embassy we had reached out to key politicians once again to take their temperature and urge calm. I stressed that the U.S. expected the second round to proceed as smoothly as the first — and expected that Poroshenko and his allies would accept the will of the people.

Ihor Hryniv, Poroshenko's campaign manager, agreed to meet with me. He was spitting venom, and he had a message: Poroshenko had run a "perfect" campaign. His coming defeat was attributable to the U.S., and more specifically to me. Not understanding anything, he continued, the U.S. had championed civil society, reform, and anti-corruption efforts, all of which had undermined Poroshenko. We didn't understand the Pandora's box that we had opened, Hryniv declared, and now we would reap the results with a pro-Russian president.

Shock, anguish, denial, anger — Hryniv seemed to be experiencing a cocktail of emotions. I decided it was best not to remind him that Poroshenko's impending defeat was more about his record than his "perfect" campaign or any actions that the U.S. had taken.

Three weeks later the final round of elections took place. While Zelenskyy's victory on April 21 had not been in doubt, his whopping mandate of 73 percent came as a surprise. Poroshenko graciously conceded by tweet almost as soon as the polls closed. With all the levers of power at his disposal, Poroshenko deserved a lot of credit for accepting the results. His action that night was a step forward for Ukraine's sometimes struggling democracy.

Late that night President Trump called Zelenskyy to congratulate him. It was a short and positive call, according to the readout I received the next day. Both in Washington and in Kyiv, hope was high that the foundation had been laid for a good working relationship. None of us could imagine how very wrong we were.

14

"I Love Ukraine"

THREE DAYS AFTER Volodymyr Zelenskyy's electoral victory, on April 24, I was hosting roughly two hundred people at my residence for an evening event honoring the late Kateryna Handzyuk. A crusading journalist, a committed anti-corruption fighter, and a courageous human rights advocate, Handzyuk had made life uncomfortable for powerful people in her southern Ukrainian hometown of Kherson. In July 2018 two men threw a liter of sulfuric acid at her, causing burns over 40 percent of her body. She lived in excruciating pain for three months before dying of her injuries.

It was now nine months later, and although the authorities had charged some of the perpetrators, there appeared to be no real desire to actually bring those responsible for ordering the attack to justice. Activists accused Lutsenko, among others, of obstructing the investigation, noting that those who ordered the killing had ties to powerful allies in Kyiv. The cry "Who ordered the murder of Katya Handzyuk?" reverberated across the nation, the presumption being that the plot went way higher than the low-level culprits who had been charged. Civil society activists understood that this was not just a personal tragedy for Kateryna and her family. They rightly understood the brutality of the assault as a warning to others challenging the corrupt status quo, daring them to consider whether they really wanted to risk that kind of slow and agonizing death. It was critical to the reform community to show that they had not been cowed, that they would keep the pressure on until all the perpetrators were brought to justice.

Our embassy team was unanimous in wanting to honor Handzyuk with the Ukrainian Woman of Courage Award. As in Armenia and Kyrgyzstan, I created this annual honor with the hope that the profile it gave its recipients — and the message that the United States was watching — would make unprincipled officials think twice before targeting recipients for retribution. I had never before given it to someone who could not personally benefit from its protective power, but I hoped that recognizing Handzyuk's heroism would comfort her family, pressure the Ukrainian authorities to get serious about the investigation, and telegraph that other activists pushing for change in this dangerous environment were not alone: the U.S. supported their efforts and saw their work as vital to building the new Ukraine.

We had invited friends of Handzyuk to the event, along with the human rights community, the law enforcement community, several key people from the Zelenskyy team, and the press. Deciding whom to invite from the law enforcement community had been tricky, since many of the invited guests believed that Lutsenko and others at his level were complicit in stalling the investigation. Ultimately we decided to invite their deputies, knowing that their bosses would hear that the U.S. remained focused on the Handzyuk investigation. It would also be an opportunity for Ukrainians who didn't normally meet each other to mingle and, we hoped, have serious conversations.

Viktor Handzyuk, Katya's father, electrified the room with a passionate speech about his daughter and the need to bring her killers to justice. That was a tough act to follow, but the reformer cop who spoke next discarded his prepared remarks and spoke eloquently about the responsibilities and challenges of policing. Usually at these events the folks at the back of the room are chattering away. Not at this one. Everyone was rapt; some were crying. This was a moment, and everyone knew it. I hoped it would inspire the Zelenskyy team to put pressure on law enforcement to take the investigation seriously. Even Lutsenko's deputy, Yevhen Yenin, seemed moved. He told me that he had something important to talk to me about but that the evening event wasn't the right place for it. We agreed we'd meet later in the week.

While we were honoring Handzyuk, a parallel drama was going on. Right before the event started, Ewan MacDougall, my staff assistant, pulled me aside. In his midthirties, Ewan was just about as impressive as they come. A third-tour officer, he held degrees from both Harvard and Yale and had served in the Marine Corps, with tours in Iraq and the Horn of Africa, before joining the Foreign Service. He became a diplomat because he wanted to continue to make a positive difference for the U.S. and for the world. Ewan performed the same function for me that I had for Ambassadors Price, Seitz, and Catto in my long-ago second tour in London. He made sure I had everything I needed for my meetings, often drafted my speeches, and sometimes accompanied me to events. He was the best of the best. And he always had my back.

Ewan passed me a message from my administrative assistant, Susan Krause: Washington wanted to talk to me immediately, on a secure line. Susan had told the caller that I would not be available for several hours; I was hosting a high-profile public event, and the residence didn't have a secure line. Complying with their request, she explained, would require me to leave my two hundred or so guests and drive twenty minutes to the embassy to access a secure line. Let's do the call after the reception ends, Susan suggested. Apparently that wasn't the right answer, because over the course of the evening she fielded additional and increasingly urgent calls. She passed on the information to Ewan, who whispered the updates to me. I wasn't sure what Washington expected me to do. Jump off the stage and abandon my guests?

After far too much back-and-forth, Washington eventually accepted the idea of a later call but declined to give Susan much in the way of details, other than that the person who wanted to talk to me was Carol Perez, the director general of the Foreign Service and head of personnel. The topic was still a mystery, but Carol's involvement made it clear that it wasn't going to be good news.

I had known Carol for nearly thirty years, since we had worked in adjacent offices in the Operations Center. Although we weren't close, she was someone I had long admired, as she went from one big job to the next. But the head of personnel doesn't insist on a late-night secure call unless there is trouble. Big trouble. I guessed it had something to do with the Giuliani-Lutsenko madness.

As the reception was winding down, I went upstairs to tell Mama that I had to go back to the embassy to talk to Carol and that she shouldn't wait up. Although I had tried hard to shield her from the day-to-day fallout of the attacks on me, Mama knew what was going on and worried about me constantly. She understood immediately that this was serious.

At around 9 p.m., with the last guests still lingering, Ewan and I walked out to the car waiting to take me to the embassy. At the last minute I had asked Ewan to come with me to make sure I didn't set off the front office alarm. But the truth was that I just couldn't face being alone during what I expected to be one of the worst moments of my career.

Twenty minutes later a Marine Guard let us into the embassy, and we took the elevator up to the front office. Ewan unlocked the door and disarmed the security system. I left him in his closet-sized office and went to my adjoining and far more generously proportioned space. I closed the door and waited for Carol's call. It was pretty lonely, and I was grateful that Ewan was there, even if he was in another room.

Carol's assistant put the call through at around 9:45 p.m. Carol began by telling me that she wanted to give me a heads-up that something was going very wrong. There was lots of nervousness on the seventh floor (a term we use to describe both the political leadership in the department and their location in the building) and "up the street" (a term I had never heard before but that Carol said referred to the White House). She conveyed that I was in some kind of trouble, although she didn't use that word and she had no specifics. I asked her whether this had to do with the Giuliani attacks. Surprisingly, she responded that she didn't know what I was referring to.

Conversations in the department are often compartmentalized, but I found it odd that the seventh-floor decision-makers had foisted this call on Carol but apparently hadn't shared the backstory. This conversation and the Giuliani campaign had to be connected. I couldn't think of any other source of trouble that was out there — and what was out there was certainly enough.

I asked Carol what she wanted me to do, and she told me to sit tight. She said she would try to find out more and call me back at midnight my time. I knew that none of this was good, but I also had faith that Carol was doing her best to look out for me. I used the downtime to write up a meeting that I had had earlier in the day. There was always lots of work to do to keep my mind off my problems.

But midnight came and went, and pretty soon my work wasn't enough to keep me from getting anxious. Finally, at about one o'clock Thursday morning Kyiv time — 6 p.m. the prior evening in D.C. — Carol called back with a startling instruction: I needed to come back to Washington. Immediately. In fact, she wanted me on a plane that day. The new, steely urgency in her voice underlined the order. I pointed out that it was impossible to return immediately — it was the middle of the night in Kyiv, the embassy was closed, and I had no way to make arrangements.

Carol still hadn't told me what the problem was. Was I in trouble? Did

I need to hire a lawyer? After all, the accusations of corruption and disloy-alty were clearly at the root of the directive to come home, even if she wasn't connecting the dots. Now the department was taking action based on those lies. That sounded like I was in the kind of trouble that required a lawyer — fast. Carol seemed taken aback and assured me that no lawyer was needed, even as she wouldn't or couldn't tell me what was going on.

I was becoming increasingly angry, although I was doing my best to stay calm and businesslike and carry on as though this were any other agenda item we were discussing rather than the end of my career. I told Carol that it was unfair to pull me out of post with no explanation at all. All she would say was that my immediate departure was for *my protection,* which prompted me to ask whether there was a physical threat. That question seemed to surprise her, and she replied without hesitation that there was *no physical threat.* The conversation went round and round. I just couldn't accept being yanked out of Ukraine without at least some information as to why the de-partment was taking this action.

After a lot more back-and-forth, I realized I had to stop. Carol was just the messenger, and she had conveyed the only message she was authorized to deliver. I told her that we could both see where this was going. My am-bassadorship was over. Thinking practically, I asked whether I would be al-lowed to return to Kyiv and pack out after my trip to Washington. There was no way my ninety-year-old mama could handle closing up three years of our lives and packing our belongings on her own, and I didn't want her to have to travel back alone.

It was a gut punch when Carol responded that she didn't know whether I'd be able to come back. I tried another tack and asked whether in that case I could stay on in Kyiv for another week to pack out, but Carol couldn't agree to that either. She was not the decision-maker, I had to remind myself, and clearly the decision was not going to change. With nothing more to be said, we ended the call about half an hour later.

I sat silent at my desk, absolutely stunned. This was not the way I had ever imagined my career as a diplomat ending: being pulled out of post in the middle of the night, under a dark cloud, to face an uncertain future. After a minute or two I went over to Ewan's cubby. *You're not going to be-lieve this,* I told him. *They want me to go back to Washington.* Understand-ably he looked confused — he later told me that he wondered if there had been a national security emergency. So I spoke more bluntly, although not necessarily more coherently. *They want me on a plane tonight. I can't leave Ukraine yet. My mother is ninety years old.*

It then dawned on him that I had just effectively been fired. I could see Ewan growing upset, so we went into my office and sat down at the coffee table. It was late, and we were both exhausted. I realized that we were probably sitting in that familiar setting together for the last time. As one of the people closest to me, Ewan had been aware of all the attacks over the past few months. But his reaction as I shared some of the details of my call with Carol was completely unexpected and profoundly physical. He bent his six-foot frame so that his head almost rested on his knees, and he wept.

Only the best and the brightest become staff assistants to ambassadors, and Ewan was no exception. Patriotic and hardworking, he was the future of the Foreign Service. He knew that I was being treated unfairly and that this was wrong, not just for me personally but, more importantly, for our institution and for U.S. interests. Ewan was an idealist, someone who had dreamed of making a difference and had believed that the Foreign Service was the place to do it. I watched helplessly as some part of that dream died.

We left the embassy in a shocked but companionable silence. After I dropped Ewan off, I went home to find Mama waiting up. I told her what had happened, and we were both so stunned that we couldn't even cry. The weekend would bring Orthodox Easter, the holiest day of our faith's calendar — a day our family had always cherished. Even though I had never embraced Orthodox rites to the degree my parents had, I had made it a priority to be with Mama at Easter, especially in the years since Papa's death. As she did every year, Mama had already prepared the traditional kulich and paskha for this year's celebration. Now she was going to be celebrating without me.

We were angry at the unfairness, fearful of the unknown, and sad that three years were coming to an end in this abrupt and incomprehensible manner. I should never have come to Ukraine and dragged my mother with me, I thought to myself. At around 3:30 a.m., getting angrier by the minute, I called my brother, André, in Tennessee to let him know what was happening. It was a short, tense conversation as André absorbed the shock and offered me the unstinting support I could always rely on.

I knew I needed to try to get some rest. I thought that I would never be able to fall asleep, but I was out as soon as my head hit the pillow. Mama called it the sleep of the just. It was really just a long nap. Before leaving the embassy that night, Ewan had emailed three key staffers and asked them to meet us at my residence at 8 a.m. My top staff needed to hear from me that I had been ordered back to Washington, and I needed to brief them on the various tasks that they would now be responsible for handling.

The timing couldn't have been worse. Pam, my deputy, had left just two days earlier for another posting, and the new DCM wasn't scheduled to arrive until July. Fortunately I had recruited the very capable Joseph Pennington, with whom I had served in Yerevan, and he would serve as chargé in my absence. Meanwhile, the planning for the Ukrainian presidential transition — a time when I should have been meeting with key players and making sure our reform agenda was on track — was just beginning. Among many other things, there was that meeting that Lutsenko's deputy had just requested. I sensed it was an important one and asked Joseph to take it for me.

Just as Hrytsenko had predicted a month before, I worked until the very end. Since I couldn't get a flight home until early the next morning, I continued with the day's schedule as planned. I briefed a visiting Baltic foreign minister on the situation in Ukraine. I had lunch with Prime Minister Groysman and then a late-afternoon meeting with the minister of defense. The chief of the defense staff (the top military man) wanted to see me in the evening, but I had to decline so I could pack. The American taxpayers were getting their money's worth, and I thought back to a comment that my first DCM in Bishkek had made when we worked together: he was glad American taxpayers weren't paying me by the hour.

AT FOUR O'CLOCK Friday morning I drove out to the airport, unsure whether this was my final goodbye to Kyiv. I later learned that as I was flying back to Washington, Pompeo was unveiling his "ethos statement" with great fanfare at the State Department. Among the statement's precepts was the pledge to act with "uncompromising personal and professional integrity" and to show "unstinting respect in word and deed for my colleagues." Every Foreign Service officer I knew agreed with these points, but coming from Pompeo, the irony was too much to handle. We were all tired of Pompeo's talk. We just wanted him to walk the walk. He didn't need to swagger.

I arrived in Washington late that Good Friday afternoon. I should have been with Mama then and on Easter Sunday, but instead I spent the weekend worrying about her — and my future. Mama went to church without me, in a foreign country five thousand miles away. But I guess all that really mattered to the seventh floor, which had just pledged its staff "unstinting respect," was that it was able to tell the folks "up the street" that I was no longer in Ukraine.

Over the weekend George Kent let me know that I'd be meeting with Pompeo's number two, Deputy Secretary John Sullivan, on Monday afternoon. George also reported that the department was moving forward with a replacement for me. He had already spoken with Bill Taylor, my friend and a previous ambassador to Ukraine, to ask whether he would be interested in serving as chargé until a new ambassador was nominated and confirmed. I thought Bill was an inspired choice: the embassy and our relations with Ukraine would be in good hands, even if they weren't in mine.

BRIGHT AND EARLY on Monday morning I took the metro to the department. As always on visits to Washington, the first thing I did after settling in an empty office was to check back with the post. Joseph reported that he had met with Lutsenko's deputy, Yevhen Yenin, who had started with a shocker: he had just resigned. The Handzyuk reception, he claimed, had been the last straw. Yenin felt that he couldn't look anyone there in the eye because he knew that the charges for Handzyuk's murderers had just been lowered — for a fee, of course. Yenin also had said that not only were decisions to prosecute or not prosecute for sale, but so were prosecutorial positions in his office. Yenin expected that his own job would go for between four and five million U.S. dollars.

Then, changing the subject, he told Joseph the same thing that Avakov and others were saying: Poroshenko was *one hundred percent in the loop,* which I took to mean that Poroshenko had approved Lutsenko's partnership with Giuliani. I asked Joseph to share the information with the Ukraine desk at State, although I had no confidence that further evidence of corruption in the GPO mattered at all to the ultimate decision-makers in Washington.

Later that day came my main event. Respected by Republicans and Democrats alike, Deputy Secretary Sullivan warmly welcomed me to his ornate office filled with antiques and personal memorabilia. In a thick Boston accent, he wasted no time in cutting to the chase: I was out. He told me he was sorry that it was working out this way, that it was unfair, and that I had done nothing wrong to cause my dismissal. Since midsummer 2018, he explained, President Trump had been calling Pompeo and demanding that I be pulled out of Ukraine. Until the preceding week the secretary had managed to convince the president not to recall me because I was doing important work, especially in light of Ukraine's upcoming election and the possible transition of power. But Sullivan said there had been a *strong and concerted campaign against me for almost a year. Every time Trump called, his concern was greater, and the concern never went back down to zero. This time the secretary had been unable to continue to protect me,* so they had removed me from Ukraine to foreclose the possibility that I would be fired by tweet like Secretary of State Tillerson. Sullivan underscored that this was *for my protection.*

Even in the moment I knew that this was a ridiculous — and ridiculously transparent — justification. If Trump were to fire me via social media, I would have been mortified, but Pompeo no doubt feared the unwanted attention a presidential tweet would have generated for him and the department — not to mention the president himself. A presidential tweet firing an ambassador would have been so unusual that it would have prompted a lot of questions from Congress and the press. I already knew that something strange was going on, and if the whole affair were made public by tweet, so would everyone else. This wasn't about protecting me, it was about Pompeo protecting himself and the president from charges of diplomatic malpractice.

I was also surprised by Sullivan's relative frankness. Phil Reeker had previewed some of the information for me earlier that day, and both times I found it especially unnerving to hear that Trump had personally been trying to get rid of me for some time. But Sullivan had no answers to many of my questions. Why did Trump want me gone? What did he think I had done wrong? Was the department concerned about my actions? Remembering the May 2018 Pete Sessions letter to Pompeo about my alleged disloyalty, I asked Sullivan whether the letter was the cause.

Sullivan had no explanations, and he didn't seem to be aware of the ins and outs of the Giuliani-Lutsenko madness — or maybe he thought it was better not to share them. I appreciated his assurance that the department knew I had done nothing wrong, and his further clarification that he had told other ambassadors they were being *recalled for cause* and that *this is not that.* For a brief moment I felt some relief at Sullivan's acknowledgment, even if it was behind closed doors, that none of it was my fault: the call in the dead of night, the requirement to spirit me out of the country like contraband goods, the shock and the shame.

Just as in the conversation with Carol Perez, we were going round and round. I just couldn't accept the situation and so kept pushing for answers that weren't going to come. But then Sullivan cracked the code and stated, "The president has lost confidence in you." Under our Constitution, it's the president who chooses ambassadors, and we act as his personal representatives abroad. Every ambassador knows that you can't hold the position if you don't have the president's confidence. I guess that's what Sullivan had been trying to say all along, but when he put it in those familiar words, I had no choice but to accept the decision.

But I still wasn't done, and I turned the conversation to policy. I was no longer fighting for my future, but a host of issues were still hanging. I asked Sullivan what we were going to tell the embassy and State Department employees, the Ukrainians, the broader public. How were we going to ensure that this didn't set a very public precedent for bad actors in other countries who wanted to get rid of inconvenient ambassadors? Or private U.S. interests that wanted to do the same? Also, what would it mean for U.S. policy in Ukraine? Were we signaling a change by yanking an ambassador so summarily? And what were we telling the new Zelenskyy administration, which seemed to actually want to tackle corruption?

Sullivan had no answers for any of those questions and just told me he'd have to get back to me on how State planned to answer them. It was troubling that State's number-two official didn't have a ready answer for consequential questions that would arise as soon as my unexpected recall became public.

But I did get two pieces of good news in the meeting. The first was Sullivan's assurance that I could go back to Ukraine and pack out and that I would have some say in my final departure date. He made it clear, however, that sooner was much better than later, and that I would be running a risk if I tried to stay on until my original July 5 departure date. I had the impression as well that if I didn't pick an early enough date, the secretary would just order me out of post; it didn't appear to me that Pompeo was willing to risk the questions that would come if the president were to fire me by tweet.

At the end of the difficult conversation, I got the second piece of good news. Sullivan insisted, *We want to treat you respectfully, honorably.* Although that ship had sailed a long time ago, it appeared to me that Sullivan at least meant it, and he asked me to talk to Carol about my next assignment. It obviously wasn't going to be another ambassadorship, but I was relieved that I would have another job and that I wouldn't have to worry about a paycheck.

Of course, this wasn't altruism. The president could strip me of an ambassadorship, but the department couldn't fire me from the Foreign Service without cause, and Sullivan had repeatedly stated there was no cause. But for the administration there was a silver lining to my continued employment in the department: I couldn't talk to the press without permission, and I couldn't talk to Congress without permission. I could be controlled. Better to keep me inside the tent. Once again I realized that I was being managed.

It's embarrassing to admit, but I was crying throughout the conversation. I had spent the past three months compartmentalizing, pretending that the baseless attacks didn't really matter — that everyone would eventually see them for what they were and everything would return to normal. But Sullivan was telling me that principle would not prevail. I was being quietly let go, with no statement of support other than inside that room, leaving the world to believe that the tweets and other slanders raging outside Sullivan's office were true.

The compartments collapsed, leaving only hurt and anger. And tears. Not the elegant tears you see in the movies, either. These were pouring-down-your-cheeks tears, hot and angry tears, with mascara leaving black channels on my face. It was at least twenty Kleenexes worth of tears, plus red-rimmed eyes and a swollen nose. It was ugly and emotional. It was the kind of crying that leaves your face in such ruins that you can't cover it up when you are leaving the office. And every time that Sullivan said something nice to me, I cried harder. I can be tough when attacked, but when people are kind, my defenses start cracking. In this soul-crushing moment, my defenses fell entirely apart.

When I periodically apologized for the stream of tears, Sullivan waved my concerns away. I had the impression that he had delivered a lot of bad news in his short tenure at State and had seen others in the same condition. It was confirmation, as if any were needed by now, that the Pompeo State Department was a deeply unhappy place.

———

TWO DAYS LATER I got up the courage to think about my future and meet with Carol. Before getting down to business, she shared that the call with me the previous week had been the hardest thing she'd had to do since taking the job. She was thinking about quitting. I told her to stay and fight the good fight. Words couldn't express our emotions, and we both cried. I wondered to myself how the department had come to such a state. I found myself wondering too how it would survive the betrayals of the Pompeo years.

To Carol's question *What does your perfect world look like?* I inquired about Georgetown University, where the Institute for the Study of Diplomacy enlists diplomats as "professors of practice." It turned out that a position was available, and Carol ensured a soft landing for me there.

Since Carol was one of the most senior Foreign Service officers in the building, I also raised the policy issues that I had discussed with Sullivan. Even if the higher-ups didn't care about me personally, I just couldn't believe that the department was willing to condone actions so at odds with U.S. interests in Ukraine and so harmfully consequential to its representatives the world over. As the prior U.S. ambassadors to Ukraine had pointed out in their letter to Under Secretary Hale, allowing these attacks to stand unanswered weakened the structure of our diplomacy.

Carol listened to my concerns. But she didn't — perhaps couldn't — comment. And what was there for her to say? We were through the looking glass, in an America that was beginning to resemble Ukraine more than I wanted to admit.

I let Carol and others know that I would return to Kyiv on May 11 to pack out and then come back to the U.S. on May 20. Those dates seemed satisfactory to everyone. In the meantime I tried to fly under the radar. While I waited to go back to Ukraine, I shared my drama with hardly anyone. It was too raw. I couldn't process it myself, so how could I explain it to others? I just wanted to hide. The only place I felt safe was within our small family — Mama, André, and my niece, Zoë. I leaned into their love and strength, and each in his or her own way held me up during this most difficult and lonely time.

On May 6, Embassy Kyiv issued an internal embassy management notice, announcing my departure "as planned." To no avail, I had objected to that language, as well as to the howler that my departure "aligns with the presidential transition in Ukraine." Anybody familiar with diplomacy knows that presidential transitions are precisely when you want continuity at the top of an embassy. Someone leaked the notice within two hours, and almost immediately Giuliani trumpeted by tweet that I had been removed because I had been "part of the efforts against the President." The department had never controlled this narrative, and it never would.

Others were starting to raise questions, just as I had predicted to Sullivan. The day after Embassy Kyiv announced my departure, House Foreign Affairs Committee Chairman Eliot Engel and House Majority Leader Steny Hoyer issued a statement calling the decision to recall me a "political hit job." They also released a letter that they had written to Pompeo a few weeks earlier, on April 12, expressing concern about the attacks on me. It was the first I had heard of the letter, and it made me feel a little better. I wasn't surprised that Pompeo had not responded.

Pompeo's refusal to defend me underscored the bittersweet nature of the one major outside event that I participated in during my time stateside, before I left to pack out of Kyiv. On May 9 the National Defense University inducted me into its Hall of Fame. The event had been planned months in advance, and as the date approached, hard on the heels of the scandal surrounding me, I wondered whether this Department of Defense entity would ask me to pull out. The State Department, my home of thirty-plus years, was kicking me to the curb, but NDU, where I had spent only two years, stood by its plans to recognize my work with the U.S. military despite the controversy. There was some honor left in Washington, if not at Foggy Bottom.

The next morning I was horrified to read in the press that Giuliani was planning to travel to Kyiv that weekend and meet with Zelenskyy to press him to investigate the Bidens. He actually said, "We're not meddling in an election, we're meddling in an investigation, which we have a right to do." There were deep, substantive problems with this, of course, but my worry was more mundane: I was scheduled to return to Ukraine the next day. There weren't very many flights into Kyiv. I really hoped that Giuliani and I wouldn't be on the same plane.

Fortunately Giuliani caused an uproar by saying the quiet part out loud. Congress and the press wanted to know what the president's private attorney was doing messing around in other countries. The outcry forced Giuliani to cancel his travel plans. Characteristically, he blamed the Ukrainians, saying that he had been "set up." The irony was rich, but I couldn't savor the moment. I had a hard trip ahead of me.

I ARRIVED IN Kyiv on Saturday, May 11, and hid at the ambassador's residence. There was plenty of work to do as Mama and I put our past three years into boxes. But the truth is that I just didn't feel up to seeing anyone. I was mortified; I didn't know what to tell people, and I wasn't in any shape to try. I couldn't process the anger and the sadness. I turned down all invitations — I just didn't have the strength to pretend that everything was all right, that I was all right.

But people found me anyway. Even the owner of the company hired to move us back to the States came to the residence to tell me how much my work in Ukraine had meant to her and the people of Ukraine. Big, wet tears rolled down my face as she spoke, and she just kept on going.

I nixed the idea of a large farewell party. I knew that my recall was ultimately due to American corruption, but a portion of Ukraine's political leadership had been complicit, and I couldn't bear the thought of seeing them while my feelings were so raw. Lutsenko and Shokin may have been in the vanguard, but others were involved in or at least aware of the plotting against me. Ukrainians whom I had worked with and tried to help. Ukrainians whom I knew — and who knew me, and knew that the whole thing was a pack of lies. It was such a betrayal, not just of me but of the bilateral relationship. It made me understand why the Ukrainian people had voted this crew out. Ukraine too had been betrayed.

As painful as I knew it would be, I couldn't leave Kyiv without saying goodbye to the embassy staff — to everyone who had worked so hard over the past three years to support me and make our mission a success. I told myself that I had to be strong when I walked into the cafeteria to a sustained standing ovation from hundreds of employees. But it was useless. I teared up immediately. So did many others.

Seeing so many sad faces made it impossible for me to brush over the loss I felt. I immediately skipped over the first two sentences in the remarks I had prepared; I just knew that I would never be able to get the words out without completely breaking down. "I love Ukraine. That's why I came back." A sentiment left unsaid, but which I hoped everyone could read in the emotions on my face.

I wanted to leave the embassy with a sense of purpose and optimism, and I recalled all the good we had done over the past three years and the good that was still in the future. Because no speech in Ukraine is complete without a reference to the great Ukrainian writer Taras Shevchenko, I concluded with perhaps his most famous line: *"Boritesya — poborete."* "Fight on and you will prevail." It was my last instruction to a great team, and I told them it was important for both Ukraine and the U.S. that Ukraine prevail.

It was also a reminder to myself. I knew that the Giuliani-Lutsenko madness wasn't over. I didn't know what I was going back to, but I knew that there was another battle in my future. I had to fight on. I had to prevail.

15

Survival

MAMA, MY FAITHFUL DOG SCOUT, AND I said goodbye to Kyiv for the last time early on the morning of Monday, May 20, 2019. We barely avoided an airport encounter with Secretary of Energy Rick Perry, U.S. Ambassador to the EU Gordon Sondland, and Special Representative for Ukraine Negotiations Kurt Volker, who arrived that same morning to represent the U.S. at President Zelenskyy's inauguration. With my removal, this group now seemed poised to take control of America's Ukraine policy.

Sondland and Volker later testified about the notable Oval Office meeting the "three amigos," as Sondland dubbed them, had a few days after their return to D.C. They briefed President Trump on their favorable impression of Zelenskyy and urged him to invite his counterpart for an Oval Office meeting to signal continued U.S. support for Ukraine and Zelenskyy's reform agenda.

This was the right recommendation and clearly in America's interest, but Trump was less than receptive. He called the Ukrainians bad people and accused them of trying to take him down, presumably referring to the false conspiracy theory swirling around in Trump-world that Ukraine, not Russia, had interfered in the 2016 election. He then cut the meeting short and, according to Volker and Sondland, told the group to talk to Rudy Giuliani. Even from afar it was apparent that the president's personal lawyer — not the three amigos, not Secretary of State Pompeo, and not National Security Advisor Bolton — now served as the president's chief counselor on Ukraine.

When the amigos reached out to Giuliani, they learned that he wasn't interested in setting up the meeting — at least not before Zelenskyy did Trump a favor. Giuliani saw Zelenskyy's interest in meeting with Trump as an opportunity to move forward with his plan to portray Joe Biden as corrupt. If Ukraine's president would announce that his government planned to investigate Biden, Trump and Giuliani could run with the narrative that Biden must be corrupt; why else would Ukraine be investigating? What was becoming clearer too was that Giuliani was focused on the *announcement* of an investigation rather than an *actual* investigation. Apparently he had completely absorbed the lesson of Russian disinformation: the allegation can be just as damaging as the action, and it's easier, quicker, and cheaper to deploy.

And Giuliani diligently spun a theory of wrongdoing that he eagerly trotted out for the cameras. He claimed that then–Vice President Biden had pushed Poroshenko to fire Viktor Shokin from his post as Ukraine's general prosecutor because Biden wanted to stop Shokin from investigating the Ukrainian energy company Burisma, which Biden's son, Hunter, was affiliated with. The truth was that Shokin, widely considered corrupt himself, wasn't even trying to investigate Burisma at the time. The United States, the international community, and international reformers were united in viewing Shokin, the chief law enforcement official in Ukraine, as an obstacle to fighting corruption and establishing the rule of law. The Giuliani story was entirely untrue.

It must have seemed like a brilliant plan, if you didn't consider the harmful impact on U.S. election integrity or U.S. interests in Ukraine. Whatever Giuliani was thinking, this is what he made clear: until the Ukrainians announced a plan to investigate the alleged Biden/Burisma corruption issue, there would be no meeting between Trump and Zelenskyy.

I WAS NOW BACK in the Washington, D.C., area, no longer involved in Ukraine matters, and unaware of any of these Oval Office actions. While my former colleagues were trying to convince Trump and Giuliani to agree to publicly display U.S. support for Ukraine's new president, Mama and I were engaged in more mundane but still urgent tasks: buying cell phones, purchasing a car, arranging to get our stuff out of storage, and finding a place to live.

I owned a home in northern Virginia, but, like many Foreign Service officers, I rented it out when I worked abroad. As a result, we couldn't just move back in when we returned home sooner than expected. Mama and I camped out in a drab and expensive temporary apartment near National Airport while we considered our longer-term options. Even when my tenants' lease ended, my house would not offer a suitable space for Mama; at ninety-one, she wouldn't be able to climb the stairs to the bedrooms. My plan had always been to renovate the house when we came back, but given the uncertainties around my job and my life, I wasn't sure it was wise to sink my savings into home improvements. Mama understood my worry. Fueled by that immigrant fear of losing everything all over again, she wanted to economize. She said she'd manage the stairs, somehow.

Our nervousness stemmed from more than Mama's childhood traumas. In the normal world, if the president removes a government official amid corruption allegations, a criminal investigation almost certainly follows. I — and State Department leadership — knew that I had done nothing wrong, but that hadn't stopped Pompeo from ordering me home and staying silent as my reputation was trashed. What other crazy demands might State accede to? Would the department launch an internal investigation into my actions? Would I be fired? Would my pension be taken away? Could I be prosecuted?

I went back and forth on the house decision but ultimately decided that I couldn't let Giuliani and Lutsenko derail even more of our lives than they already had. Over Mama's protests, I opted to move forward with the renovations and find a temporary rental for us in the meantime. Unfortunately, what I found wasn't available until the end of July, so to save a little money, Mama, Scout, and I moved out of the airport apartment and began living off the kindness of friends. We moved four times over the next couple of months, trying not to overstay our welcome in any one home. Each time we packed the car so tight that it made me think of our first move to the United States. We were the Beverly Hillbillies all over again. There was barely room for Scout.

REPORTERS AND CONGRESSIONAL staffers trying to figure out what was really going on with Ukraine had been reaching out to me ever since the *Hill* articles first appeared in March. As I had predicted, my abrupt departure from Kyiv only served to make the inquiries more frequent and urgent. I deflected all of them. Still a rules-follower to the core, I turned down all press inquiries and referred congressional inquiries to the department.

To be honest, I didn't want to speak out. I didn't think that it would change anything, and I feared that it would bring such a disproportionate response from Trump-world that it would make my situation even worse.

Even privately it still was hard for me to talk about what had happened. I had been beaten down by the attacks, by State's unwillingness to speak up for me, and by the cognitive dissonance of remaining loyal to an institution whose leaders had betrayed me. Angry and sad, I grew emotional even when I confided in a few of my closest friends.

But mostly I kept my own counsel, because I was worried that if I opened up about what was happening, even to friends, I would be dismissed as a crazy lady with an enormous ego: Rudy Giuliani, the hero of 9/11, was trying to dig up dirt in Ukraine about former Vice President Biden and smear me because I was getting in the way of his schemes. Would you have believed me? I barely believed myself at that point.

I spent most of the next couple of months trying to ignore what had happened. The Georgetown University job that Carol had helped me line up didn't start until late July, so I used years of accrued vacation time to try to decompress. It was a good decision. Each move took Mama and me farther away from Washington, both literally and figuratively, especially when we got in some beach time in North Carolina. The physical distance helped me pretend that things were normal again. That felt so good that I considered retiring and leaving the Washington area entirely.

But I still couldn't imagine leaving the Foreign Service. I knew that I was clinging to a vision of the State Department that no longer existed, but it was strangely comforting to remain connected to my professional home of over thirty years. It was also a relief to have the upcoming State Department assignment at Georgetown — and a salary — at a time when I didn't know whether I would ever be employable again. I was glad that I had once again packed my waitress apron for this last move back to the U.S. I hadn't needed it since I'd gone to work for that New York advertising agency all those years ago, and I hoped that I wouldn't be needing it in the future. But I wasn't so certain.

My brother, André, tried to reassure me that the whole thing would blow over. But I had been around Washington long enough to know better; my ordeal wasn't close to being over. Trump-world wasn't about to stop looking for dirt on Biden or stop trashing me until the political reason to do so went away, either with Biden losing in the Democratic primaries or with the November 2020 presidential election passing into the rearview mirror. There was no way that the Democrats who controlled the House of Representatives were going to let the goings-on in Ukraine go unquestioned. My dismissal was so unusual, and Giuliani's actions were so bizarre, that congressional staffers would undoubtedly be back in touch, probably sooner rather than later. I was the canary in the coal mine, the signal that something toxic had permeated this administration — and probably not just with regard to Ukraine.

I was dreading the idea of returning to reality, but at the end of July we had to go back to Washington. Mama worked to settle us into our new life in the rental house. We were both happy that my twenty-three-year-old niece, Zoë, had found a job in the area, and Mama was looking forward to spending time with her only grandchild. They had a special bond and soon started planning an adventure together: Mama wanted to introduce Zoë to the magic of Paris and to some of our far-flung family in France.

AS IF ON cue, mid-August brought the renewed congressional interest that I had feared. On August 14, I received an email from a House Foreign Relations Committee staffer, who asked to meet with me to discuss some "Ukraine-related" questions she labeled "delicate/time-sensitive." I assumed she wanted to find out why I had been dismissed and what I knew about Giuliani's actions in Ukraine. I responded that I was forwarding the request to State's European Bureau and that they would get back to her shortly. That was the usual protocol with congressional requests, and I assumed it would still be followed here. Pretty quickly, though, the request ended up with the department's lawyers, who seemed unwilling or unable to respond.

Knowing that Congress would not take either silence or no for an answer much longer, I began to think that I needed to hire my own lawyer. Although the department lawyers usually tried to watch out for State personnel, their job was to protect State's interests, not mine. I was a team player, but the past six months had shown me that I could no longer trust the coach.

Even after my two months away, I wasn't looking forward to sharing my experience more broadly, but I did think that Congress had a right to know what was going on. Legislative oversight of the executive branch forms a core part of the checks and balances that make our government work, and I believed that oversight was especially necessary in this case, with so much going wrong regarding Ukraine. The executive branch was not going to self-correct, and this was precisely the type of institutional failure the Framers had anticipated. But the idea of Congress getting involved raised the specter of an interbranch dispute, with me caught in the middle. I needed to know my rights and obligations if Congress pushed me to ignore State's protocols and talk directly to them. But even though my instincts told me that it was time to find someone to look out for me, I worried that hiring a lawyer might somehow signal that I believed I had done something wrong. So I procrastinated.

In late August cousins from England visited, and I shared the story of my previous six months. Seeing how upset I was, my cousin John urged me to seek therapy. He said he thought I had post-traumatic stress disorder and warned that if I didn't come to terms with the experience emotionally, it would eat away at me physically. That was a stunner; I associated PTSD with traumatic military experiences, and it hadn't occurred to me that PTSD could be the cause of my intense and continuing distress. But I had surely experienced stress, and I was finding it nearly impossible to get the events of the spring out of my mind. I told John that I would think about it and resolved to make a few calls.

MEANWHILE, ENTERPRISING REPORTERS had spent the summer digging into the Ukraine story, and on August 28 *Politico* reported that Trump was holding up military aid that Congress had approved for Ukraine. That was deeply troubling: Ukraine's military relied on our assistance to keep up the fight against Russia. But far more important than the actual equipment and training was the political signal of support that the assistance sent to Ukraine.

Although it was unclear what was driving this move by the White House, Ukraine had left a clue in its little-noticed government readout of a July 25 phone call between Trump and Zelenskyy. "Donald Trump," Zelenskyy's office reported in stilted English, "is convinced that the new Ukrainian government will be able to quickly improve image of Ukraine, complete investigation of corruption cases, which inhibited the interaction between Ukraine and the USA." This cryptic sentence, and its indication that Trump saw an incomplete "investigation of corruption cases" as the sticking point in U.S.-Ukrainian relations, perhaps offered a hint about the president's motivation for holding up U.S. aid. Giuliani had made it clear back in early May that he planned to push the Ukrainians to investigate the Bidens. From the Ukrainian readout of the July 25 call, it looked like Trump was now personally wading into the fray and trying to get the Ukrainians to go after Joe Biden.

After reviewing all these developments, the House of Representatives, with a Democratic majority, announced on September 9 that three of its committees would join in a wide-ranging investigation into what they called the "Trump-Giuliani Ukraine Scheme." The committees immediately wrote to Pompeo, asking for a range of documents related to the July 25 Trump-Zelenskyy phone call, the suspension of aid to Ukraine, and Giuliani's effort to get Ukrainian help for Trump's reelection bid. My name wasn't mentioned, but I could tell it was just a matter of time.

A lot was going on, and I was happy that I had taken my cousin's advice and found someone to help me sort through it all. Two days after the House announced its investigation, I met with a psychiatrist. I had thrived in a series of pressure-filled environments and spent years under the microscope of foreign governments ready to exploit any misstep, or to make one up for use against me. But here I was, huddled on a couch, barely holding it together as a result of my own government's actions.

I asked the doctor about PTSD. She observed that such a diagnosis would be premature, but she did say that she thought I was appropriately "anxious." (No kidding, I thought to myself. Why else was I there?) In any event, she said, what I was going through couldn't technically be post-traumatic stress, because any trauma I might be experiencing was ongoing. Each time Trump-world attacked me, each time I read about the issue in the paper, I could be reliving the trauma. Paradoxically, that explanation made me feel better. Maybe my reactions were completely appropriate after all.

Perhaps even more helpfully — and in an only-in-D.C. experience — my psychiatrist offered some nonmedical advice. She had been practicing in Washington for a long time, and she could see where things were headed. She urged me to hire a lawyer immediately.

I was still mulling over her advice several days later, on Sunday, September 15, when I got together with the "yoga girls." These were five friends whom I'd known for years: Jenni Parmelee and Shelley Slade had been my roommates at Princeton, and I had socialized with the others over the years; we had become a more tightly knit group — and gotten our nickname — when we went on a yoga vacation to Costa Rica. Whenever I was back in Washington, we would try to get together. I had last seen them in May at the National Defense University event honoring me. But I hadn't had the courage or the energy to share my story with them back then. It was time to let them know what was going on. When I opened up, I was immediately re-inforced: they lavished me with unconditional sympathy and support, and I soaked it up like water.

Late that night Shelley, a lawyer, called. She bluntly stated that many government workers wait too long to hire counsel owing to a naive view that they don't need a lawyer because they haven't done anything wrong. "Don't make that mistake," she warned.

Shelley's call shocked me out of inaction. Belatedly I received the message that so many people had been sending: after months of enduring the "protection" of the State Department, I finally needed to protect myself. I didn't know where to start, so I spent the next morning asking friends what to do. I knew that lawyers with experience handling both the legal and the political aspects of high-profile congressional investigations could be pricy, possibly costing hundreds of thousands of dollars, and I didn't have that kind of money. But I understood now that I would just have to figure it out.

As it turned out, I started my search just in the nick of time. Later that afternoon, September 16, I received an email from the State Department. Congressional investigators had written to Secretary Pompeo three days earlier, asking him to make me and three other State Department officials available for on-the-record interviews. Department staff weren't asking for my opinion on the matter; they just wanted to let me know that the State Department was reviewing how *it* planned to proceed. If I received any direct inquiries from Congress, they instructed, I should refer the request back to them.

I was being managed for the benefit of the department once again. The need for me to hire my own lawyer was becoming ever more apparent.

Two days later the *Washington Post* reported that a whistleblower in the intelligence community had filed a complaint against the president and that it had something to do with communications between Trump and a foreign leader. The complaint was still secret, but the *Washington Post* confirmed the next day that the foreign leader was Zelenskyy. Reporters surmised that the complaint probably arose from the July 25 Trump-Zelenskyy telephone call, although it was not yet clear what the exact problem was.

Within a few days Trump himself acknowledged that he had raised the matter of the Bidens with Zelenskyy on July 25, although he insisted that it was perfectly appropriate for a U.S. president to allege corruption by a domestic political rival on a call with a foreign head of state. Separately, Giuliani had told reporters that he had pushed the Ukrainians to investigate Biden.

It was unbelievable — and embarrassing to me as an American. The president is the highest-ranking public official in the land, the one person above all others who should be acting for the good of our nation rather than corrupting the office for his personal interests. In the authoritarian states in which I had served I had seen leaders who confused the national interest with their own interests, but I had never thought that I would see this at home. It was devastating.

With all of these developments, and Trump now so openly owning his corruption, there was no way that Congress wasn't going to demand to learn more. They'd very soon insist on an end to State Department intransigence. I was going to be dragged into the spotlight before long, whether I wanted that or not.

These same events increased the pressure to convert the House committees' investigation into a formal impeachment inquiry. House Speaker Nancy Pelosi had previously resisted calls to impeach Trump, given the near certainty of acquittal in the Republican-controlled Senate. But the revelations indicating Trump's possible abuse of presidential power led her to announce on September 24 that the committees' investigation into the Trump-Giuliani Ukraine scheme was now officially aimed at considering whether to make Trump only the third president in U.S. history to be impeached.

It was overwhelming. I was struggling to keep up with the pace and the enormity of events. Every morning brought new and important developments. Every minute, it seemed, my in-box was filling up with emails and press alerts regarding the latest twists and turns. And too often for comfort they directly involved me.

16

"The Moment to Decide"

I WAS WARY OF being caught in a public fight between Republicans and Democrats in the run-up to the 2020 presidential campaign, and I was reeling from the realization that I was no doubt going to be asked to play a role in these historic events. But an even bigger shocker was yet to come. On September 25 — the day after the impeachment announcement — President Trump released a summary of what he labeled his "perfect call" on July 25 with President Zelenskyy.

I was teaching a class at Georgetown when a neighbor texted me with the alarming news that the just-released summary revealed that the presidents had discussed me in their July 25 call. I found the call summary online as soon as the class ended. Someone in the room later told me she saw all the color drain from my face as I absorbed what Trump had said.

Zelenskyy had told Trump that Ukraine wanted to buy more Javelin missiles from the U.S. in order to bolster its defenses against Russia. Trump replied not with a yes, no, or maybe but with this: "I would like you to do us a favor, though." Trump then pressed Zelenskyy to launch investigations into two of the baseless allegations circulating since March in Trump-affiliated media: first that Ukrainians had interfered with the 2016 U.S. elections to aid Hillary Clinton, and second that then–Vice President Biden had corruptly blocked a prosecution in Ukraine to help his son.

That was disturbing enough, but here's what really got my attention: in the course of telling Zelenskyy about how some "very bad people" had "shut your very good prosecutor down," Trump took the occasion to slam me. "The former ambassador from the United States," Trump explained to Zelenskyy, "the woman, was bad news and the people she was dealing with in the Ukraine were bad news so I just want to let you know that." I couldn't believe that an American president was praising a corrupt prosecutor and trashing an American ambassador — *me* — to a foreign president.

Remarkably, Zelenskyy piled on. He called me a "bad ambassador" and said he agreed with Trump's assessment of me "100%." Even more ominously, he requested information "for the investigation to make sure that we administer justice in our country with regard to the Ambassador to the United States from Ukraine, as far as I recall her name was Ivanovich." Zelenskyy got my name wrong and my title backward, but it was clear what he meant: I was at risk of prosecution in Ukraine.

Not to be outdone, Trump got the last word in, declaring, "Well, she's going to go through some things."

It was chilling — and infuriating. Not just Trump's willingness to hold our bipartisan foreign policy and Ukraine's security hostage to his personal political ambitions, but also what he was saying about me personally. Months after he and his cronies had baselessly trashed my reputation and booted me out of our embassy in Ukraine to help Trump's reelection efforts, he was, incredibly, still focused on me. I knew that he had a habit of demeaning women, but I saw red when he reduced me to four words: "the woman" and "bad news." Rationally I knew that his behavior reflected more on Trump than on me, but still, his comments enraged me even as they frightened me.

Apparently losing my job and my reputation hadn't been enough. It appeared the most powerful man in the world was planning more for me. My mind was racing as I tried to figure out what kind of trouble lay ahead in Ukraine — but, more consequentially, what kind of trouble awaited me right here at home.

I was still trying to digest this turn of events as I walked back to my Georgetown office. Just then John Herbst, my old boss from my first, long-ago tour in Ukraine, called. *Listen to the end,* John said, *and don't say anything until I finish.* He told me that his childhood friend Larry Robbins was a top Washington lawyer experienced in high-profile congressional investigations. John said he hoped that he wasn't being presumptuous, but if I didn't already have a lawyer, Larry had offered to help — free of charge.

I was stunned. It felt like the gods were swooping in to save me. I did a little due diligence and quickly arranged to meet Larry two days later.

The following morning, September 26, Trump released the whistle-blower complaint, confirming the earlier reports that it focused on Ukraine.

The whistleblower charged that Trump and Giuliani were aligned with corrupt interests in Ukraine and were using the power of the American presidency to persuade Ukrainian leaders to interfere in the 2020 presidential elections and go after a political rival, Joe Biden. Among the issues that the whistleblower raised in detail was the Giuliani-Lutsenko alliance that had resulted in my dismissal.

Hats off to the whistleblower, I thought. Without that individual's courage, the summary of the "perfect" call would not have been released. As a result, it is doubtful that the first impeachment proceedings against Trump would have been launched, and the public might never have learned the truth about Trump's self-dealing on national security matters. But at that moment I didn't know any of that, and I certainly was not as courageous as the whistleblower. I wasn't thinking about my country or the State Department. I was thinking about myself and about what all these developments would mean for me. My concerns would soon prove to be justified, even if events turned out differently from what I expected.

MAMA HAD ENDURED almost a full year of worry. Back when we were still in Ukraine, I had tried to shield her from the rumors, but that became impossible as they spread and became more public. When David Hale asked me in early March to extend my tour in Ukraine, she didn't want me to accept because of the accusations levied against me — and that was *before* the public attacks in the U.S. had started.

Then Giuliani and company had taken to the American airwaves with the wild accusations that led to my recall from Kyiv. It pained Mama to hear these absurd claims, and it pained her that I wouldn't let her defend me. I was concerned that she would say publicly what she said to me privately: "I have seen this before." She was thinking of the Germany of her youth, when an elected leader had solidified his control over the country by appealing to nationalism, scapegoating minorities, undermining institutions, co-opting the establishment, targeting the opposition, and using egregious falsehoods to manipulate the population and rewrite history. There was power to her analogy, but I couldn't imagine the uproar or the consequences if the mother of a sitting American ambassador compared the United States to Nazi Germany.

Things didn't improve much once we got home. Foreign Service discipline had taught me how to compartmentalize information and to avoid expressing partisan views. That didn't come naturally to Mama, and I continued to caution her to keep her thoughts to herself. Nothing good could come of it, I told her. Her alarm only increased after she read Republican strategist Rick Wilson's book, *Everything That Trump Touches Dies*. The title pretty much said it all. She couldn't protect me, and it weighed on her.

Very early on the morning of Friday, September 27, two days after she learned that the president of the United States had predicted that her daughter would "go through some things," one day after she read the whistleblower complaint that featured my removal from Kyiv, and hours before I was to meet with my new attorney, Mama was gasping for air. In obvious distress, she told me that she felt like she couldn't breathe. I rushed her to the emergency room, so fast that I left the car unlocked and blocking the ER entrance. A nurse walking out after her overnight shift took one look at Mama and turned around to help while I was checking her in. She tucked Mama into a wheelchair, gave her supplemental oxygen, and took her blood pressure and other vitals before I had even gotten through the paperwork. Within minutes Mama had disappeared into the bowels of the ER.

I had to run out to the car to find a real parking place. When I walked back into the hospital, Mama was lying in a curtained-off cubicle, hooked up to all sorts of machines. Even though we didn't know what was wrong, Mama and I both felt a little better knowing that help was at hand. The ER doctor came by and said that they wanted to admit her for observation but that it would take a while for a room to become available.

Mama hadn't been able to sleep well for the past several weeks, and she dozed for most of the morning while I stood guard. It gave me some time to think about what my cousin John had said: if I didn't work out the issues before us emotionally, they would come back to bite physically. He had been talking about me, but it was Mama, in her tenth decade of life, who seemed to be proving his prediction right.

While I was with Mama, I received an email from the State Department telling me that if I received a subpoena, a request for testimony, or any other communication from Congress, I should forward it to the department. The message was clear: State expected House investigators to reach out to me directly, but it wanted to control all communications with Congress. I thought the subtext was clear too: State was planning to do its part to help slow-roll the investigation into the president's actions.

I didn't want to leave Mama, but I felt I had no choice. The email from

State had an ominous feel and left me with no doubt that I was exactly where I had feared I would be: in between the executive branch, led by a Republican president, and the House of Representatives, controlled by Democrats, in advance of the upcoming presidential election.

I took the metro into D.C. and arrived at my new lawyers' K Street office at 3 p.m. sharp. I was ushered into a modern, glass-walled conference room and met my legal team: Larry Robbins plus Laurie Rubenstein and Rachel Li Wai Suen. Larry was a feisty lawyer from New York City, a former federal prosecutor and Justice Department official who had argued a number of cases before the Supreme Court. Even more important for me than his considerable court work was his experience in representing individuals before Congress. Laurie was a Capitol Hill veteran who had spent more than a decade working on investigations from the Senate side, including staffing a senator on the 1999 impeachment trial of President Clinton. Rounding out the team was Rachel, a seasoned litigator with extensive experience in preparing clients facing internal investigations or government enforcement actions. The three had expertise in all the areas where I needed help.

I proceeded to tell my story, tearing up a couple of times. It was the first time I had shared many of the details of my experience beyond my inner circle, and I wondered whether these three strangers would believe me. Would Larry call John Herbst and tell him that they couldn't take on his crazy friend? But to my immense relief, the attorneys didn't seem put off in the slightest by my story or my emotion.

I told them I had two simple goals. I wanted to protect myself, and if I could, I wanted to bring honor to the Department of State, which had been dragged through the mud right along with me. I knew that it sounded strange to want to support the State Department, given the way it was treating me. But to me the real State Department was still made up of the men and women of the Foreign Service and civil service — people dedicating their lives to protecting the interests of the American people. Despite being vilified, these men and women were continuing to serve honorably in Washington and all over the world, often in dangerous places, and I wanted to make them proud and show the American people how worthy we were of their support.

It was an exhausting and emotional meeting. It took so long for me to get my story out that we ended up ordering takeout Chinese food for dinner. We didn't break for the night until after 8 p.m.

I headed straight for the hospital to visit Mama. On my way I saw an email from a House staffer, one that made the earlier email from State make more sense. The House staffer wrote that the committees wanted me to appear for a deposition on October 2. That was just five days away, with little time to prepare for intense questioning in real time and under oath. The message closed with alarming language: "Please note that failure to comply shall constitute evidence of obstruction of the House's impeachment inquiry." This was clearly the communication to which State did not want me to respond.

I was worried, but also relieved that I was no longer dealing with such matters on my own. I immediately forwarded the email to my new lawyers, who quickly reassured me. They told me that this was an opening gambit, that I could ignore the obstruction talk and the specificity of the October 2 date. All I needed to do was send a placeholder email and introduce my lawyers, and they would take it from there. The lawyers would inform Congress that I wouldn't be ready to testify on October 2. Then we'd discuss what to do, and they'd make sure I understood all the options and consequences before I decided my next step.

I had a game plan and three great new coaches. It was confidence-inspiring: they understood the law, but they also understood *me* and the strain I was under. They had been strangers in the afternoon, but as hokey as it sounds, by that Friday night they felt like my knights in shining armor.

WHEN I FINALLY got back to the hospital that evening, I was spent. Mama was, of course, even more tired. She had been moved out of the ER sometime in the afternoon and was in her room. She looked small and wan in her hospital bed, but she was, as always, stoic. She said that she was doing fine. The doctor was long gone, so I talked to the nurses, who assured me that she was indeed okay, although some of her vitals were off. But they couldn't give me a diagnosis — that was the doctor's domain. I sat with Mama until about 11 p.m., and then I went home to get some rest myself.

By Saturday morning Mama seemed a little better. She was her old self, full of life and joy, but I wondered how much of it was an act to reassure us. Her physical frailty worried me. I was hoping to talk to the doctor to get concrete information and advice about next steps. The wait was frustrating, but Zoë had arrived and was working her magic on Mama's mood. They shared knitting problems, and both of them posed in kooky sunglasses and posted the photos on social media.

I had been trying to keep Mama in an information blackout zone to try to protect her from what I saw as unrelenting bad news, but she was as intellectually sharp and inquisitive as ever. She spotted her chance when she received a Saturday afternoon visit from George and Velida Kent, who had become good friends when George served as DCM in Kyiv. Telling the Kents that she didn't need to be coddled, she peppered them with questions about the impeachment inquiry and international developments and proudly showed off her new iPad.

It filled my heart to know that Mama's spirit was as resilient as ever, but it was a tough couple of days nevertheless as I bounced back and forth between Mama's room and the hospital corridor, which I used as my makeshift office. Larry, Laurie, and Rachel worked all weekend, reaching out to congressional investigators and State Department contacts while continuing to familiarize themselves with the ugly details of what had happened in Ukraine. Under normal circumstances I would have been completely on edge as they readied to ask the House lawyers to push back my proposed deposition. But it was hard to focus on their calls and emails while Mama's health was so precarious.

A few days later we had a diagnosis, and it was serious: Mama had congestive heart failure. How can three little words be so terrifying? Her heart wasn't pumping properly, which is why she'd had trouble breathing. Liquid was filling her lungs; I could even hear the gurgle. Given the risks of surgery and Mama's age, the doctor recommended a treatment plan of diet and meds, which they thought would enable us to manage the disease at home. But before getting to that point, Mama's vital signs needed to improve, which the doctors thought would happen by the end of the week. She would spend the following week in rehab, and then she would come home. Or at least that's what we hoped would happen.

Later that week the cavalry arrived, in the form of André and his pup, Fenway. It was a game-changer. They moved in, and André set up mission control at my kitchen island. He worked his day job remotely and took care of all the many issues for Mama's care on the side. He scouted out rehab facilities and eventually moved Mama into one when the hospital approved her discharge. Mama wasn't happy about not coming straight home, but neither André nor I could give her the care she needed. It was wonderful to have André's strong presence during such a volatile time, but I couldn't help but feel guilty about not being more present myself.

BETWEEN MAMA and the impeachment proceedings, I was struggling. As a result, I nearly misjudged the motives of a colleague I had known and admired for decades.

While I was with Mama at the hospital, Mike McKinley, a four-time ambassador then serving as a senior advisor to Pompeo, called to find out how I was doing after the double shock of the Trump-Zelenskyy call summary and the whistleblower complaint. At first I was wary; I was feeling so set-upon that I wasn't sure whether he was being sincere about his concern or was just fishing for information. But then Mike told me that he was pushing Pompeo to issue a statement defending me and the State Department as an institution. He clearly was shocked when I told him that he was the first person to reach out to me from the seventh floor. I hung up the phone, relieved that he was still the same man I had always known.

I knew that I had allies in the State Department, but it felt like a lot of people were afraid to reach out. To her credit, a few days after I talked to Mike, Carol Perez, the head of personnel who had been tasked with recalling me from Ukraine that terrible night, called to check up on me — on her private cell phone. I really appreciated that call, not least because it reassured me that I wasn't the only one looking over my shoulder.

WHILE I TRIED to focus on Mama during her first weekend in the hospital, my lawyers were navigating me through the gulf separating the demands of the State Department and the House investigators. By Sunday they reported that House investigators were willing to push the date of my deposition off a bit but that "no" or "not unless State agrees" did not look to be acceptable answers to their deposition request.

State, for its part, was objecting vociferously to the House demand to talk to me or anyone else from the department. Pompeo said he was trying to protect us from congressional bullying and harassment. That was rich — and remarkable Orwellian doublespeak. I *had* been bullied and treated improperly, but not by Congress. From March on I had been subjected to a campaign of lies and harassment coming straight from Trump allies and sometimes from the president himself. During that period Pompeo hadn't lifted a finger — even though, from what his deputy had said, he had been fully aware that I had done nothing wrong and that I did not deserve such treatment.

State also objected to House rules excluding State Department lawyers from attending the closed-door depositions. Having seen the Trump administration stonewall oversight efforts for close to three years already, Democratic investigators weren't willing to yield on the rule. They expected that State's lawyers, if allowed to participate, would disrupt the depositions and make overly broad assertions of executive branch confidentiality.

To be sure, State had a kernel of legitimate concern that if its lawyers weren't present, a witness might improperly reveal classified material or information covered by executive privilege. But it seemed to me that the department's real interest was in making sure that its employees didn't talk about things that Pompeo didn't want discussed. The House planned to conduct the depositions in a SCIF — a sensitive compartmented information facility, set up to protect classified information — meaning that in the exceedingly unlikely event that anything classified came up, it would be properly protected. Plus everyone in the room would have a security clearance. Since I'd had virtually no interaction with the president and no insight into his decision-making, it was hard to see how my testimony would touch on privileged information.

Even so, it was not my fight. If I was going to testify, I'd be fine with State Department lawyers in attendance or not. I just didn't want to be forced to choose sides.

To that end, my lawyers urged both House investigators and State Department lawyers to try to work out something that would allow Congress to get the information it wanted from me while protecting any legitimate interest that State might assert. Perhaps, they offered, State's lawyers should talk to me separately and directly to determine whether I knew anything that legitimately should be off-limits to Congress. My legal team asked State's lawyers to send over specific objections or language to read if the deposition proceeded without them there. But State never took steps to protect these legitimate concerns; it seemed that the only real goal was to keep me out of the deposition room.

On Tuesday, October 1, Pompeo wrote to the House committees, declaring that the requested State Department officials — myself, Kurt Volker, Gordon Sondland, George Kent, and Pompeo's counselor Ulrich Brechbuhl

—"may not attend any interview or deposition without counsel from the Executive Branch present." It wasn't a direct order to me, but we could all read between the lines. It was only a question of time before I'd receive an instruction not to attend.

Working with the lawyers was starting to make me feel more protected again, but getting caught between two sides of an impeachment investigation wasn't a great place to find myself. I needed to understand the risks before I could decide whether to testify in the face of a likely State Department order not to do so. Would State have the right to discipline me or even fire me for disobeying an instruction? Could they strip me of my pension? Somehow charge me with revealing sensitive or classified information, even though I'd be speaking to Congress in a SCIF? The past six months had shown me that this crew played hardball, and I hadn't forgotten about Trump's promise that I would "go through some things." To the extent possible, I wanted to avoid providing any pretext for bringing these "things" down upon myself.

My lawyers dived into these questions. The stakes were high for me, so I was reassured to learn that a host of expert partners outside the State Department stood ready to help in this task. Three public-interest entities in particular jumped in to assist, most importantly AFSA, the American Foreign Service Association, a union that represents the interests of Foreign Service officers. AFSA had been my first stop when I was recalled in the spring, and it had stood by me ever since. Along with the Government Accountability Project and Co-Equal, two other nonprofit organizations with expertise on the rights of federal employees testifying before Congress, AFSA told us that the administration would have a hard time disciplining or firing me if I testified. Most importantly, they assured me that my pension would be safe.

It was comforting to learn that the administration couldn't put me in jail or the poorhouse for testifying, but I still wasn't confident that I'd be believed—or that I could withstand a repeat of the spring's coordinated attacks. Despite growing increasingly frustrated with State's stonewalling, I was finding it surprisingly hard to break with the institution that had been my home for thirty-three years. I was still a committed rules-follower, and it wasn't in my nature to ignore the practice of a lifetime: that State set the rules and I followed them.

I wanted time to think, but House investigators were pushing me to commit quickly. They had agreed not to insist on the original October 2 date but wanted me to come in by the following Friday, October 11. They told my lawyers that speed would work in my favor. With the House out of session that week, very few representatives would be in Washington. If I came in before they returned, I'd face mostly staffers, who would be far less likely to use my appearance to grandstand and try to score political points. Plus facing staff counsel would undoubtedly be less intimidating than being interrogated by members of Congress. They also pointed out that the sooner I came in, the sooner I'd be done with it. It was highly unlikely, they assured me, that I'd have to testify again or in public.

I was grateful that I had a team of experts helping me work through the decision. But I was surprised when my lawyers asked me what I wanted to do: testify or not? I had thought they would weigh which option protected me most and tell me what to do. No dice, they told me: you're the client, you tell us what you want to do, and we will help you achieve your objectives and make sure you are protected.

Although part of me still just wanted to run and hide, I felt increasingly compelled to testify with each passing day. I didn't think that I had anything to add to the issue at the heart of the impeachment inquiry: whether the president had held America's foreign policy and Ukraine's security hostage to his personal political interests by refusing to release aid to Ukraine or meet with Zelenskyy unless the Ukrainian president agreed to go after his expected 2020 rival. That all happened well after I had left Ukraine.

But it didn't really matter what I thought. Congress was considering whether to impeach the president of the United States, and the committees thought that I had pertinent information. As an American by choice, I cherished the constitutional system of checks and balances that gave them the right to request that I come forward. Under the circumstances, I couldn't imagine refusing. Anyway, I wasn't being asked to opine on whether the president's actions constituted impeachable offenses; I was being called as a fact witness to share what I knew. I was continuing to be what I always had been: a nonpartisan professional.

Secretary Pompeo, of all people, should have understood. As is customary, I had regularly talked to Congress over my years as a Foreign Service officer and ambassador. I was appalled at the notion that State would try to stop me from doing so now, not just because of the disrespect it demonstrated toward Congress and the Constitution but also because that disrespect came right from the top, from Secretary of State Pompeo, who in his former position as a representative had embraced a very different view about the role of Congress. This was the same man who had zealously participated in the congressional investigation of the tragic death of four Americans at the U.S. consulate in Benghazi, Libya, demanding that the secretary of state herself talk to Congress. His hypocrisy was galling.

As melodramatic as it sounds, I found myself coming back to the lyrics of a hymn that we used to sing in chapel at Kent School: "Once to every man and nation comes the moment to decide, / In the strife of Truth with Falsehood, for the good or evil side." I thought to myself that if this was my moment, then I needed to do what was right. I needed to stand up for the truth. It's what Papa would have done.

I decided to testify.

17

Three-Dimensional Chess

I WAS ALREADY an unhappy visitor to Mama's new world of doctors, illness, and pain. The decision to testify would send me deep into yet another strange realm, this one of high-stakes political investigations, legal strategies, and media attention. The time that I would spend in these two worlds was without question the worst period of my life.

Trump's promise that I was going to "go through some things" echoed in my mind. It made me wonder what else was in store for me. During the rare moments that I wasn't desperately worried about Mama, I was worried about myself. The one bright spot was that I had good guides to help me navigate all this unfamiliar terrain, but sometimes it was hard for me to accept their advice.

My lawyers cautioned me not to talk to anyone about the events being investigated — not to colleagues, not to friends, and especially not to anyone who worked on Ukraine matters. They wanted to make sure that I didn't inadvertently drag someone new into the investigation by giving reporters or investigators additional people to query about what I was saying. Even more importantly, they explained, we didn't want anyone to accuse me of trying to coordinate testimony with other potential witnesses or attempting to influence what others said.

I understood the attorneys' reasoning, but I bristled at it. I had finally begun to regain my sense of self and longed for the comfort and counsel of my wider circle of friends, but most of them were in the foreign policy community, even if they weren't working on Ukraine, and at this point Ukraine was all that anyone in the foreign policy world was talking about. It was frustrating to have to avoid friends and to censor my speech, and it added to my resentment of Trump, Giuliani, and Pompeo. They had taken so much from me already, and now they were depriving me of my support system too.

I wasn't the only one being thrust into this Kafkaesque world. It seemed like every colleague who had ever touched Ukraine policy in 2019 — all formerly obscure government employees like myself — was pulled into the investigation over the next months. On a dime they had to navigate a new universe of congressional investigations, private legal representation, potentially enormous lawyers' bills, and intense media scrutiny. It's hard to convey how disorienting it was. It's one thing to be in front of the cameras to talk policy, something we had all done before. It is completely different to have that attention focused on you personally — on your actions and your thoughts — and to face questions from people who you know have an agenda that doesn't include what's best for you. To make it harder, while diplomats usually work together, each of us had to face this new challenge on our own. I was in a bubble and felt very much alone.

THE TWO WEEKS between when I first met my lawyers and when I appeared for my deposition, now scheduled for October 11, were overwhelmingly intense. Not only was I making sure that Larry, Laurie, and Rachel knew everything possible about what I had experienced, contemplating the decision whether to testify if State ordered me not to, and — of course — fretting over Mama and supervising her care, I was also trying to keep up on what seemed like daily developments in the investigation.

Among the most disturbing of these was the urgent request from the State Department's inspector general, Steve Linick, for a closed-door briefing with congressional staffers. He went to the Hill on October 2 and dramatically delivered a packet of documents that found its way to the press by evening. The core of its contents was almost laughable: presented in a Trump Hotel folder, it included a haphazard set of poorly photocopied news articles from dubious sources trying to smear the Bidens and me. The packet was not just unprofessional, it looked like the sort of thing a slightly unhinged relative would throw together and harass the rest of the family with. How could anyone take this seriously? I thought to myself.

Giuliani had reportedly delivered the packet to the White House in late March, right after Lutsenko's allegations were published in The Hill. The White House had then forwarded the collection of materials to Pompeo's office, and it had eventually made its way to the inspector general's office and over to the FBI. It appeared that nobody in the long chain of recipients had deemed the slanders worth taking seriously. This made me grateful that our government still retained at least some checks to prevent Giuliani's absurd allegations from leading to an investigation, criminal charges, or worse. But I was still disappointed that nobody had been willing to stand up publicly and take Giuliani to task or defend our government from his corrupting influence. It was appalling that his stunts could nevertheless have such serious repercussions.

By the time Linick forwarded the packet to Congress, he had added to it a series of emails from State Department officials criticizing the contents of the packet as, among other things, a "fake narrative." But those emails seemed like a fig leaf for a naked attempt to change the story from Trump's malfeasance back to Biden and me by reviving these discredited materials in the face of the impeachment inquiry. Coming from the department's inspector general, it also was a sad illustration of what Giuliani and Trump had done to our government.

The parallels with Ukraine, where patronage and politics often outweighed principle and patriotism, were uncomfortably close for comfort. So although the packet was almost laughable, I wasn't laughing. I was alarmed by the revelation that the FBI had received Giuliani's materials. Now that the stakes were so much higher, with a possible impeachment on the horizon, I wondered whether presidential pressure could influence the FBI to investigate me. My lawyers reassured me that I had nothing to worry about on that front, but I couldn't fully put my fears to rest.

Nonetheless, I was heartened by almost daily revelations that made it harder and harder to believe the Giuliani-Lutsenko narrative about Ukraine, at least from the standpoint of any rational person. The day after Linick delivered his "urgent" briefing to Congress, Kurt Volker, who had resigned his position as special representative for Ukraine negotiations the previous week, went to the Hill for the first deposition of the impeachment inquiry. His October 3 testimony was closed to the public, but the House panel released an astonishing set of text messages that he had provided. The texts showed Volker and Sondland working to implement Giuliani's demand that Ukraine announce an investigation into Burisma as the price for Zelenskyy's requested Oval Office meeting. One text suggested that the plot may have gone even further: Bill Taylor, then serving as chargé at Embassy Kyiv, incredulously asked whether congressionally approved military aid to Ukraine was being held up in the push for investigations.

I had known Kurt for a long time, and I couldn't understand how he could have expected that any good could come from working with Giuliani. I imagine he probably thought he could get Giuliani to do the right thing for the bilateral relationship and for Ukraine. Instead it appeared that Giuliani got Kurt and Sondland to do his bidding in the effort to convince the Ukrainian government to announce a corruption investigation into Biden. When I read through the texts that Kurt provided to the committee, I was shocked, angered — and saddened.

And, oddly, I experienced some hope. The disclosures in the text messages were so sensational, I thought, that surely Americans — even some Republicans in Congress — would now see that the president of the United States had tried to trade his office for personal favors from foreign governments.

On the one hand, it was dangerous for our adversaries to know that our president was motivated by causes other than the good of our country. But it was also true that foreign countries already knew exactly who Donald Trump was and how to manipulate him. On the other hand, the more the truth came out, the less likely it was that Americans would tolerate this sort of behavior and therefore the less likely it was that our country would slide further into the kind of self-dealing that I had seen firsthand in so many other countries. I had to believe this to be true.

KURT'S DEPOSITION drove home the reality of my impending participation in the proceedings, and I paid close attention to the theater surrounding it. The press had swarmed Kurt as he arrived at and departed from the Capitol, and his Hill appearance became front-page, top-of-the-broadcast, trending news. I also took note that Republican representatives had periodically left his deposition to brief the press, spinning their versions of what was taking place behind closed doors. This would be my world in just a week's time — a gut-turning vision for an introvert.

Closed-door questioning of this sort was something I had never before experienced, so my lawyers spent some time walking me through what to expect. I'd face questions from both Republican and Democratic staff from each of the three House committees that were pursuing the investigation. Unlike in a courtroom, the deposition would feature neither jury for the questioners to play nice for nor judge to make sure that the questions had some relevance to the matter at hand — in this case, whether Trump should be impeached. Instead, each questioner would come at me with an agenda.

For the Republicans, we expected, uncovering the truth would not be the priority item. No matter how many damning revelations emerged about what Trump and Giuliani had done, House Republican support for Trump never seemed to waver. We were pretty sure that Trump's defenders would try to show that Lutsenko and Giuliani were right about me and attempt to portray me as a corrupt and disloyal ambassador.

We thought that the Democrats, by contrast, were actually interested in finding out the truth, which they had good reason to believe would benefit their cause. They would want my testimony to connect Giuliani and Trump to misdeeds regarding Ukraine, to the extent that I could provide such evidence. Since many of the Lutsenko/Giuliani allegations took place either before or after my time in Ukraine, the Democrats would probably also ask me probing questions about how I had been treated by the Trump administration. Reliving painful memories before a roomful of strangers who were likely to broadcast them even further was not an appealing prospect, and I knew that it would be difficult to maintain my composure.

I spent a lot of time reviewing my detractors' allegations as well as my own actions in Ukraine. But my lawyers warned me to expect questions about events I barely remembered, questions premised on twisting things I had said beyond all recognizable meaning, and questions that would seem just completely crazy. I no longer had access to most of my State Department materials to review, which made it hard to prepare for such a wide array of contingencies. It was going to be a challenging day.

I also had to decide whether I wanted to do more than just respond to the agenda my questioners set. Did I merely want to survive the day? Or did I want to do more? I had a complex tale to tell, one that required context about both Ukraine and my work to be fully understood. I resolved that my first goal was to ensure that the committees — and ultimately the American people — had the full story regarding the false accusations against me. So many allegations had been flung around that there was a lot of Trumpworld spaghetti to scrape off the wall.

My second goal was more complicated. I knew that for most of my fellow Americans, Ukraine was an unknown and its importance to our national security unclear. The events were so complicated that it probably wasn't obvious either how dangerous Trump's and Giuliani's actions had been for our nation. Closest to my heart, I doubted that very many observers had processed the broader impact these events had had on the critical ability of America's diplomats to function the world over. I wanted to give Congress and the American people the context and help them understand that their representatives abroad needed their support as we worked to defend U.S. interests.

From my previous and far less dramatic experiences testifying before Congress, I knew that I could not count on either Republicans or Democrats to ask questions that would allow me to get out my story, let alone these broader points, in a coherent and comprehensible way. If I wanted that done, I would have to do it myself, by delivering a statement up front. With years of Capitol Hill experience, Laurie confirmed that unless I did so, I risked losing control of the narrative, especially with the different sides of the House committees focused on the conflicting goals of proving Trump guilty or innocent.

Opening with my own account, however, would be a stark departure from my previous silence, most especially because no honest statement could be complimentary to the current administration. But I was starting to feel braver, and I believed strongly that this wasn't just about me. Of course I wanted to defend myself, but I also wanted to defend my colleagues and the Foreign Service in general. So I drafted some remarks and then set them aside. I would decide later whether to use them.

MEANWHILE THE STATE DEPARTMENT escalated its effort to prevent its personnel from cooperating with the investigation. When Volker had testified, he had already resigned from his special envoy position, so State had no control over his actions. That wasn't the case with witnesses like me, still employed by the department.

Just after midnight on Tuesday, October 8, State's leadership played its hand. They directed Gordon Sondland, still our ambassador to the European Union, not to appear for the voluntary testimony he had scheduled for later that morning. Sondland felt that he had no choice but to comply with the demand. The instruction arrived so late — no doubt intentionally so — that House investigators weren't able to subpoena Sondland in time to compel his appearance for that day's testimony. The investigators regrouped and subpoenaed Sondland for an appearance the following week — after my

October 11 deposition date. That meant that I'd be the first witness to appear who still worked for the U.S. government.

My lawyers had warned me to expect State to direct its personnel not to testify, but now it was no longer theoretical. If Pompeo's lackeys had given Sondland this order, they would no doubt give me the same one. I had made the decision to testify, but it was still hard to reconcile myself to the idea of doing so against the express instructions of the department that I had served for almost my entire professional life. Hard, but also important: as the first government witness up, my decision to appear despite a directive to the contrary would set a precedent for those called after me.

As if on cue, White House counsel Pat Cipollone followed up that night with a letter to Speaker Pelosi and the three chairmen conducting the impeachment inquiry. Cipollone labeled the entire impeachment inquiry invalid and declared that "President Trump cannot permit his Administration to participate in this partisan inquiry." He wasn't writing directly to me, but no doubt someone from State soon would.

With that instruction likely imminent, my lawyers explained that I should expect a subpoena from House investigators to follow — and that I should see this as a good thing. All the same, the thought of being subpoenaed upset me. In my work with law enforcement over the years, subpoenas went to the bad guys who had done something wrong or who had refused to cooperate with law enforcement. That wasn't me. I hadn't done anything wrong. I had made a decision to cooperate and to respect Congress and the Constitution, and it bothered me to think that anyone might think I had something to hide.

My lawyers set me straight. The House staff knew that I was willing to cooperate and that the State Department was not. They told me House investigators often deploy subpoenas to protect witnesses from outside retribution, making clear that they have no choice except to comply. A subpoena did not imply that I was a reluctant witness.

CLEARLY WE WEREN'T the only ones discussing the implications of Cipollone's letter. Almost immediately House investigators called my lawyers about a plan to subpoena me. As predicted, the House staff had no interest in portraying me as a reluctant witness. In fact, now that I was up first, my testimony might be seen as an inflection point. If I was willing to testify despite State's efforts, other government employees probably would as well, and the investigators would have a chance of getting to the bottom of what happened. On the flip side, the House investigation could be stalled if State somehow succeeded in stopping me from appearing.

The investigators clearly were worried about that possibility, concerned that once they subpoenaed me, State might counter by sending me a directive not to testify even in the face of a subpoena or by trying to go to court to get an injunction. In light of the department's twelfth-hour directive to Sondland, they wanted to wait until the morning of my deposition to subpoena me. This would give State little time to stop the deposition.

I felt like a pawn in a game of three-dimensional chess. The most recent moves also gave me a new worry. Would the State Department actually take me to court to prevent my deposition testimony? If the House thought that was a possibility, what else might State try to do? Would they try to go after me or my pension, even if they, like we, knew they'd likely lose? It was profoundly alienating as we were talking about the possible hostile actions of my longtime employer. But I felt that I was doing the right thing, which gave me the determination to move forward.

THE PRESSURE INCREASED by the day. On October 9, barely forty-eight hours before my scheduled appearance, House staff told my lawyers that Adam Schiff, chairman of the House Intelligence Committee and the congressman leading the impeachment inquiry, planned to attend my deposition. This was not welcome news. Investigators had told us that staff would be handling most of the questioning, with minimal member involvement. But if Schiff came, it wasn't going to be a low-key event. I wondered who else would be there. But I couldn't dwell on that, because I had to focus on the task at hand: making sure I was ready for my deposition.

The next day I was back in my attorneys' glass-encased conference room on K Street, nervous about what the following morning — deposition day — would bring. A fancy flat-screen television hung recessed in one of the side walls, turned on but muted. My lawyers and I sat around a big conference table with a long list of items to get through. Shortly before 10 a.m., Steve Castor, the lead counsel for the Republicans in the impeachment inquiry, called. Larry had previously reached out to introduce himself to Castor and ask whether he had any issues he wanted to discuss. Now Castor wanted to know if I had reached a decision about testifying the next day. He reported that I would probably receive an order from State not to testify and that the

Republican committee members thought that State Department witnesses, beginning with me, should decline to appear if the committee excluded the department's lawyers from the room.

Castor was cordial, and he noted that Trump administration officials in past investigations had ignored House subpoenas under such circumstances and suffered no repercussions. It wasn't subtle. This congressional investigator — or at least his bosses — thought that I should flout the congressional investigation. Larry told Castor that if I received a subpoena, I was unlikely to ignore it.

I wasn't quite sure what Castor's message meant for how the Republicans planned to treat me once I showed up to testify. But we had to prepare for the worst and assume that their goal would be to destroy my credibility, just like the president's men (and a couple of women) had been trying to do for months.

Then, at 10:23 a.m., everything changed. We looked up at the muted television and noticed the headline of a breaking story. CNN was reporting on the arrest of two of the key players in the campaign against me, Giuliani associates Lev Parnas and Igor Fruman. At Dulles Airport. With one-way tickets to Vienna, Austria. The home, I recalled, of the indicted and corrupt Ukrainian oligarch Dmytro Firtash.

We scrambled to find the remote and turned on the sound to get the details. Federal prosecutors in the Southern District of New York had indicted Parnas and Fruman on charges of illegally funneling foreign money into U.S. campaigns. The indictment accused them of using their resulting influence to try to remove me on behalf of one or more unnamed Ukrainian officials. The prosecutors had kept the indictment under wraps while continuing to investigate but presumably felt they had to act quickly when it appeared that Parnas and Fruman might be fleeing the country.

It had been more than six months since the *Hill* articles had broken the smear campaign against me into public view, and I still didn't have a full understanding of where all the accusations against me had originated. I knew that Parnas and Fruman had been the middlemen connecting Giuliani and Lutsenko. I had seen the Dale Perry email back in April that indicated that Parnas and Fruman were working with other individuals who wanted me removed as ambassador. But the indictment revealed more: they and "one or more Ukrainian government officials" — which I assumed referred to Lutsenko at a minimum — had also been behind the strange letter that Congressman Pete Sessions had written in May 2018 to Secretary Pompeo, pushing falsehoods about me and seeking to have me removed as ambassador. Some of the pieces, at least, were coming together.

If this had happened in a movie, I wouldn't have believed such a plot twist. But this was real life — my life. Trump's own Justice Department was charging two of my chief accusers with illegally trying to corrupt American campaigns and promote foreign interests — the day before I was to testify. I wondered what else Justice knew about them and whether the prosecutors knew the source of the money that Parnas and Fruman had donated. Most of all, I wondered how the House Republicans would adjust their line of questioning the next day, since presumably they could not rely on the disinformation supplied by these two plus their allies Lutsenko and Giuliani regarding what had happened in Ukraine. I sent a silent little prayer of thanks to the Southern District of New York for the timely and unexpected arrests.

I knew it wasn't game over, even though the conduits of much of the disinformation about me had just been indicted on charges specifically related to me. I was quite sure that the Republicans, with the task of defending the president in an impeachment inquiry, would still be intent on undercutting my testimony. Even though the stated purpose of the investigation was to examine Trump's actions, it was beginning to feel to me like I was the one on trial. I knew I had to be ready for anything.

While my lawyers tried to chase down the details of the indictment and make sure we had a response ready to go if State tried to stop my appearance, I sat at the conference room table quietly preparing. I had decided to give an opening statement after all, and I spent considerable time trying to get it right. I also reread a lengthy timeline we had prepared and wrote out a one-page list of key names, dates, and actions to have with me in case I needed reminders the next day. At the top I wrote in big block letters: "THE TRUTH IS ON MY SIDE."

In the afternoon the attorneys and I did some role-playing to get me used to what it would be like in the hearing room. In depositions like this, they told me, it wasn't uncommon for questioners to load their questions with incorrect facts or suppositions. I needed to listen carefully to every question and answer only what was asked.

That last part was harder than it sounded, and Rachel and Laurie pulled me aside to explain that this was a common issue for women. Like so many of us, I was socialized to be helpful, which could translate to helping ineffective questioners by answering the question I thought they were driving at rather than the question they had actually asked. That would be a sure recipe for saying things that could be used out of context to hurt me. It could allow my detractors to twist an answer I gave to what I *thought* they were asking into some type of admission to the incoherent query they had *actually* posed.

Our role-playing also gave me a chance to confront questions that would throw me for an emotional loop. At one point Larry asked me whether I thought the president had acted properly. He was trying to think of ways the Republicans could try to probe the baseless Pete Sessions claim that I had repeatedly expressed disdain for the president. I hadn't done that, but Larry didn't ask what I had done; he asked what I had thought.

I was surprised to find I couldn't respond. I was just paralyzed. To have answered honestly would have required me to state that the president of the United States had used his office for his own personal and political gain. It was wrong and made our country vulnerable. It would have put America in the same league as struggling transition countries — Ukraine, Kyrgyzstan, Armenia, Somalia, and, Russia — where I had spent so much of my career trying to help reformers establish the rule of law to protect against avaricious oligarchs and kleptocrats.

The purpose of my entire career had been to strengthen the United States, to defend our country, and not to divulge any insights that could be used against us. By this point I knew that foreign powers had been much quicker than me to assess Trump, but even after the events of the past year, it was hard to contemplate stating out loud that the president of the United States had acted dishonorably.

I choked up, my eyes filling with tears. I told myself I had to get it together — that those were the last tears I could allow myself. Surprisingly, Larry said, *If you tear up tomorrow, maybe it will make them realize what they've done.*

That took some of the pressure off. But I knew that no matter what Larry said, I couldn't cry the next day. I would be the weeping woman. Forever. I could already imagine the tweet.

AS THURSDAY AFTERNOON turned to evening, we still had heard nothing from the State Department. I found the waiting and the uncertainty unsettling. Finally, around 7:30 p.m., Under Secretary of State Brian Bulatao sent the letter we had been bracing for, with instructions that I should not appear for the next day's deposition. Within minutes the department lawyers were on the phone with Larry, wanting to know what I planned to do. Larry explained that the situation was fluid and my decision would depend on whether and when the House issued a subpoena.

State's lawyers asked for a heads-up if we received a subpoena, to which Larry asked whether the department was considering going to court to stop my testimony if a subpoena was issued. State's lawyers declined to answer, so Larry ended the conversation without committing to any advance notice of our decision. The department wanted me to be transparent, but they weren't willing to be transparent in return.

An hour later House investigators called Larry, who had shared State's letter with both Republican and Democratic staff. Burned by the administration's last-minute maneuvering before Sondland's scheduled deposition, the Democratic staff weren't about to be outplayed again. They proposed waiting to serve me the subpoena until after I arrived at the Capitol for the deposition.

Larry said no to that. I was under instructions from my employer not to testify voluntarily, and he would not give State any reason to claim that I was disobeying that order by going to the Capitol before a subpoena was served. After a bit of discussion, Larry and the House investigators reached an agreement on the way forward. I would be at the lawyers' office before nine o'clock the next morning. If the House investigators served a subpoena at that time, we would accept it, consider it a legal order to testify, and then head to the Hill for my 10 a.m. deposition.

I was still sitting at the lawyers' big conference table while all this was going on, keeping an ear open to all the back-and-forth among my lawyers, the department, and the Hill. Watching them in action, I thought of all the people who had asked me why I needed a lawyer. In the beginning I hadn't known the answer. I just knew in my bones that I needed counsel. But on that night, if on no other, I could tell that if I hadn't had Larry, Laurie, and Rachel in my corner, I would have been pulverized between the gears of the Hill and the State Department. Once again I felt profoundly grateful that these three were on my team.

I HAD WANTED to go home early, to see Mama at the rehab facility and reassure her. I had also really hoped I'd be able to relax a little before a good night's sleep. But I didn't leave the law firm until around 8:30 p.m., so I called Mama on the ride home and told her I was feeling confident and that there was nothing to worry about. I might have had my fingers crossed when I said it. Mama said what she always said: she would pray for me.

André was waiting for me at the house. We talked about the next day and wondered what it would bring. My personal concerns aside, I told him, I would never forgive myself if I didn't testify. This was the moment to share what I knew.

I hadn't asked anyone other than André and my lawyers for input on my opening statement, but even at this late hour, lots of people were sending me lots of advice on what to say and do. Most didn't seem to understand what was at stake for me. They thought it was "cool" that I was testifying and hoped that I would "give Trump hell." I wish I could say that I saw it that way too. But honestly, my life was flashing in front of my eyes. I had come a long way over the preceding two weeks, but I couldn't fully shake my anxiety about the possible consequences of the next day's event.

What's more, as committed as I was to testifying, I had no plans to burn down the house. I *was* angry: at corrupt forces in Ukraine for how they had treated me over the past year, at Trump's inner circle for their eagerness to trade our national security for the president's political advantage, at Trump-world overall for its seeming lack of concern about telling the truth, and most of all at the State Department, an institution to which I had devoted my working life, for not standing up for me. But I knew that I couldn't allow myself to express my anger and hurt or to be strident in my testimony.

My reasoning was as simple as it was depressing: what had happened was so complicated, so insane, that if I allowed myself to sound even remotely angry about it, I would be dismissed and labeled as partisan. This risk was all the greater because I am a woman. If I used anything other than a measured, factual, and professional tone, I knew, I'd be called hysterical, and my testimony would be discounted.

I stayed up past midnight rehearsing my statement. I wanted to make a good first impression. Then I followed Mama's advice from when I was a little girl. Whenever I was about to take a test, she'd say, *Put your book under your pillow and get a good night's sleep. The information will travel right into your brain.* So I put my statement and my notes under my pillow, and I slept like a baby.

18

No More Tears

B Y 6 A.M. on Friday, October 11, I was emailing with the legal team and making last-minute edits to my statement. Too nervous to eat, I quickly showered and dressed.

I had given some serious thought ahead of time to what I should wear. For better or worse, men only need to pick out the right tie, but women know that we are judged by our appearance. What I wore would matter. I wanted to be comfortable, because it would be a long day, and the investigators had warned us that the chairs were hard and the room cold. But I also needed to look like a professional, someone to be treated with respect. I selected my favorite power suit, professional but feminine — and decades removed from the boxy suits I had worn at the beginning of my career. Grayish black with white flecks, the skirt's kick pleat made it easier to move, and the jacket's rounded collar softened the look. I added a jeweled American flag pin to my lapel. I wanted to send a patriotic message.

André drove me into Washington to meet the lawyers, listening as I rehearsed my opening statement for the final time. I wished he could have accompanied me to the deposition for moral support. After an emotional goodbye, he promised he'd go sit with Mama at the rehab facility and try to take her mind off the deposition. An impossible task, I thought to myself.

AS PROMISED, the House emailed the subpoena just before nine o'clock on Friday morning, commanding my appearance at the deposition one hour later. A phone call with State revealed, to my enormous relief, that the department did not plan to intervene.

We called a Lyft and ran down to K Street, but in the "nothing is ever easy" category, we had trouble finding our escort at the designated meeting point at the Capitol. We finally met up and walked across the large plaza to the Capitol Building, where the press was waiting. Rachel and Laurie walked close on either side of me, forming a physical barrier between me and the media. I tried to keep my face expressionless and my breathing even as reporters shouted questions and TV cameras and still photographers trailed us. I tried hard not to think about the events of the past year or ponder how I, an ordinary public servant, had ended up being called to testify in a historic impeachment inquiry.

Once inside, we went through airport-style security, walked by a second press gauntlet, and navigated a maze of narrow corridors and stairwells as we descended to the House Intelligence Committee's suite of subterranean offices. The outer door closed, muting the shouted questions from yet a third press scrum. Security guards made us check all our electronics, severing our connection with the outside world, and we entered the sensitive compartmented information facility, or SCIF, where I would deliver my testimony.

The hearing room inside the SCIF was surprisingly small, and between the very large rectangular table and the extra chairs packed tightly against the walls, there was almost no room to move. My legal team and I sat at the head of the table, Democrats to our right and Republicans to our left. Two stenographers sat near us, positioned to catch every word. The room was very cold.

The first thing I noticed was that virtually every seat was occupied. The second was how many members of Congress were attending. I didn't count them in that moment, but before the day was out more than a dozen legislators would make an appearance. The promise of a relatively informal, low-key, staff-led interview had convinced us to agree to a quick appearance on Capitol Hill. It looked like this was going to be anything but low-key.

ADAM SCHIFF, the Intelligence Committee chairman, opened the deposition by praising my record of service, excoriating the "shameful attacks" against me, and assuring me that Congress would protect me from any possible retaliation. Then Congressman Jim Jordan, who was taking the lead for the Republicans, spoke — but not about me. He and a couple of Republican colleagues who followed argued that the entire impeachment inquiry was unfair and that Schiff's committee didn't have proper authority to conduct it.

Jordan's comments foreshadowed the entire day. The Republicans at the deposition didn't seem remotely concerned about the events that had brought us together. Trump's own Justice Department had charged just a day earlier that foreign money had illegally funded a scheme to get me, our nation's ambassador, removed from office, at the behest of a "Ukrainian government official" whose "political interests" the indictment accused Parnas and Fruman of serving. But despite the gravity of these accusations, the focus of my GOP questioners was and would remain on poking holes in the inquiry, defending President Trump, and trying to find a way to justify the treatment I had endured. If I had been angry before about how blithely the president and his enablers seemed to trample on the truth, I was growing more so by the hour as I watched them in action and up close.

Schiff let the procedural points play out for a bit and then he cut the Republicans off and asked the Democrats' lead counsel, Dan Goldman, to swear me in. After so many months of standing by as others spun tales about me, after so many months of following the department's rules, declining to speak publicly, even to defend myself, it was finally my turn to speak.

As I had been preparing my remarks in the days leading up to this moment, I had tried to keep my twin goals in mind. I wanted the members not only to hear my personal story but also to understand how allowing unscrupulous forces abroad and at home to orchestrate my dismissal had been deeply harmful to our national security. Now, as I began to recite my opening statement, I tried to keep my voice steady as I pressed this second point in particular. I explained to the assembled members of Congress and House investigators how the anti-corruption work I had done in Ukraine on behalf of our government had threatened the business model of unprincipled Ukrainians, and how those Ukrainians had conspired with dubious Americans to get me out of the way. I addressed the key allegations against me and pointed out that Lutsenko, the source of most of them, had already recanted significant parts of his claims. I made clear that I had never broken faith with my duty to advance the official policy of the presidents under whom I had served, including President Trump.

Most urgently, I argued that my story was about much more than just me. It was about foreign and private interests successfully manipulating the presidency to advance their own agenda. It was about the hollowing out of the State Department, whose professionals were the frontline defenders of our national security interests. It was about the need to ensure that bad actors, both foreign and domestic, would not be emboldened to further weaken our country. "Anti-corruption efforts serve Ukraine's interests," I explained. But then I continued:

> They serve ours as well. Corrupt leaders are inherently less trustworthy, while an honest and accountable Ukrainian leadership makes a U.S.-Ukraine partnership more reliable and more valuable to the U.S. A level playing field in this strategically located country — one with a European landmass exceeded only by Russia and with one of the largest populations in Europe — creates an environment in which U.S. business can more easily trade, invest, and profit. Corruption is a security issue as well, because corrupt officials are vulnerable to Moscow. In short, it is in our national security interest to help Ukraine transform into a country where the rule of law governs and corruption is held in check.

As far as I was concerned, the need to hold accountable an American president who, with his enablers, had undermined this mission in pursuit of his own self-interest was not a partisan issue. It was a question of our security — and it was a national emergency. I had never thought that I would be alarmed about the resilience of American institutions or the integrity of our leaders. But that's where we were.

I SPOKE FOR about twenty minutes. Then we were off, as the proceedings switched to a series of alternating rounds of questions from Democrats and Republicans. Staff counsel took the lead for both sides, but members frequently stepped in. The Democrats led me through the details of my tenure in Ukraine, from my first meetings with Lutsenko, through the accusations that had exploded against me, through what State had told me when I was recalled. The Republicans, for their part, seemed less interested in what had happened to me and more in casting doubt on my actions in Ukraine, presumably hoping to undermine my credibility.

There were a few dustups during the day, and Larry didn't hesitate to jump in if he thought a question was badly put or inappropriate. My bulldog lawyer was making me feel very protected, but I still found the experience difficult. And emotional, as much as I was trying to keep my feelings in check.

At one point Dan Goldman, the Democrats' top lawyer, asked me to describe the meeting in which Deputy Secretary Sullivan had told me that my ambassadorship was over. Reliving the worst moment of my professional career for the committee members — not all of them sympathetic — was painful, and Goldman could see the tears shimmering in my eyes. He sympathetically asked if I wanted to step out for a minute. I did, furious with myself as my lawyers and I escaped to a holding room. Larry gave me a minute to compose myself and then he said, *Let's go back. It doesn't matter if you cry.* But I knew it did matter — that my detractors were looking for any opening and could use my tears to paint me as an emotional woman, someone not to be taken seriously. So I steeled myself and went back for more questioning.

The deposition seemed to go on forever, and the afternoon session frequently felt disjointed. The Democrats pursued one line of questioning, and the Republicans hared off in a different direction when it was their turn, including down a few avenues that they seemed to think might show me in a bad light. They didn't have a lot to work with. If they had been planning to rely on what Parnas and Fruman had said, those two were at that moment sitting in a federal prison about twenty miles away. The Republicans had to know that Lutsenko had already publicly acknowledged that I had never actually given him a "do not prosecute" list of corrupt Ukrainians whom I wanted to help avoid justice — one of the key allegations that he had made about me in his interview with *The Hill.* Still, the GOP side beat that dead horse until it was bloody, asking garbled question after garbled question, trying to get me to say that I had told Lutsenko not to prosecute corrupt actors. It seemed they were pushing for that *Perry Mason* moment when I would jump up and say, "Yes, I gave Lutsenko a list of names of corrupt people not to prosecute!" It wasn't true, so it wasn't going to happen. I found it incomprehensible — and offensive — that any American official was pretending to take the word of someone like Lutsenko over my own. Lutsenko: the man who had since recanted and who appeared to be connected to actions the Justice Department had just the day before labeled criminal.

Oddly, the Republicans also spent a lot of time trying to make a Democratic Foreign Relations Committee staffer's August outreach to me look suspicious. To me, there was nothing odd about State's oversight committee wanting to know why State had so suddenly recalled an ambassador. As everyone sitting in that room knew, committee staff routinely reach out directly to government workers who may have evidence of mismanagement or wrongdoing. No doubt Republican staff members sitting in the room had done the same during their own investigations. Yet the Republicans insisted on asking questions seemingly aimed at casting standard practice in a nefarious light.

Another Republican effort focused on a theory being pushed in some Trump media circles that I was illegally "monitoring" right-wing figures. In the wake of Lutsenko's March interview with *The Hill,* my press staff had tried to ensure that we were aware of what was being said about me in the media, especially since the stories were being circulated in Kyiv. Everything the press shop compiled, whether blogs, tweets, articles, or talk-show appearances, was public, put out there by people who presumably wanted others to read or watch what they said. Yet somehow my Republican questioners seemed intent on twisting our effort to follow the public statements of my detractors into an act of illegal surveillance. It was ironic, I thought, as this standard embassy practice of following media and influencers was one I was sure that every member of Congress routinely asked his or her staff to perform. New Jersey Democratic congressman Tom Malinowski later joked that he'd be honored if those present would follow him on Twitter, and he wouldn't accuse anyone of "monitoring" him if they did.

By late afternoon, just as I was getting really tired, the Republicans asked to return to my earlier testimony about a brief conversation between me and George Kent regarding the Trump-Zelenskyy July 25 phone call. All ears had perked up when I had mentioned that George had told me about the call before the White House had made its summary public. George, who himself wasn't on the call, had not mentioned that I featured in it, but I did remember him sharing that Trump had asked for help with the Burisma/ Biden investigations. I also, perhaps incorrectly, recalled understanding that Zelenskyy had demurred.

I figured that, after answering the Republicans' first, second, third, and fourth set of questions about the conversation, we were done with the matter, especially since my vague recollection of a short recounting of the call clearly did not shed any light on what the committees were investigating. But near the end of the day, Castor came back to it again, asking me to go over the event "from beginning to end." Since this was by now well-plowed ground, I said I had nothing to add, but that didn't satisfy him.

It is impossible to answer the same broad questions exactly the same way every single time. I was telling the truth, but it felt like the Republicans were picking at me, trying to get me to vary my words or say something that would give them even a tiny opening to say that I was inconsistent in my testimony. My lawyers pushed back, and after a spirited exchange among them, Schiff, and a number of Republican members, a compromise was reached. Jim Jordan refined the question, I answered, and we moved on.

The deposition finally ended at 7:31 p.m. It had been an exhausting day, but I felt relieved that the Republicans hadn't drawn blood. My lawyers thought that the Republican members had treated me relatively gently, but as the one in the hot seat, I had a different point of view. I was indignant and angered by their hypocrisy. This was an investigation led by the House Intelligence Committee, after all, and the members surely knew the intelligence-world adage "Consider the source." They had to know by then that there was no basis to doubt my credibility, whereas there were a whole lot of reasons to doubt Lutsenko's. Yet I had been forced to play defense all day long. I felt disrespected. It was infuriating.

WE HAD SPENT nearly nine hours isolated in the SCIF. Except during a brief lunch break, we had had no communication with the outside world. We had little idea of how my testimony was being reported, and we were especially curious about the reaction to my opening statement, which we had released to select reporters before entering the SCIF that morning.

I had thought long and hard about putting my statement out there — it was probably the first time in my career I had ever released a statement without prior authorization — but I was speaking for myself this time. It was the only way to make sure that my views were accurately conveyed. While we were stuck in the SCIF all day, I knew that committee members would be cycling in and out to put their own spin on my deposition, and that anonymous administration officials would probably add their views. I thought it was important to make sure that my story, in my own words, was out there from the start.

We left the Capitol building around 8 p.m. The Capitol Police had hailed two cabs for us, but we had to walk back across the plaza once again, and through an enormous media gauntlet to reach them. It wasn't easy. It was a dark night, and the wall of camera flashes made it impossible for our eyes to adjust. Rachel grabbed my arm after I tripped while trying to avoid bumping into the reporters and photographers who were pushing in close to yell a question or get their shot. We finally made it to the waiting taxis. Larry took one to Union Station, while Rachel, Laurie, and I jumped into the other.

The three of us sat in silence. We had met only two weeks earlier, but our time together had been intense, nonstop, and I felt like we had forged an unbreakable bond. I knew Laurie and Rachel were committed at this point, but I had to ask: That Friday afternoon when we had first met, had they believed me? Laurie and Rachel just looked at me. So I asked again, and this time they understood it was a serious question. "Of course," they replied in unison. "Of course we believed you from the very beginning." Much later Laurie told me that the question had floored her. Only at that moment did she understand how much the gaslighting had made me question everything, including myself.

AFTER DROPPING OFF Rachel and Laurie, I called Mama from the cab. She was relieved the day had gone reasonably well, but she was tired and wanted to sleep. I told her I'd come over the next morning. I spent the rest of the ride looking at my phone, which was exploding with good wishes. When I got home, I found a very relieved André and Zoë waiting with flowers, champagne, dinner, and lots of hugs. We hadn't known what this day would bring, but I was done — and I felt free.

André and Zoë filled me in on everything I had missed while in the SCIF. I was the same person, but somehow it felt like the world — or at least the world's reaction to me — had changed. We had CNN on, and my face was all over the news. Even our Slavic last name was being pronounced correctly, at least for the most part. MSNBC's Rachel Maddow read my opening statement on her show practically verbatim. How was it possible that Rachel Maddow knew my name, let alone was singing my praise?

Most startling was a comment Trump made while I was still testifying: "I just don't know her. She may be a wonderful woman." I couldn't even begin to wrap my head around his change of tone. But I allowed myself to hope that it meant I wasn't going to "go through" any more "things."

For me, October 11, 2019, was a through-the-looking-glass experience. I had walked into the Capitol that morning as a relative unknown but somehow walked out a hero to many of my fellow Americans. That public acclaim, though, didn't match the way I viewed myself, and I found it all a bit disconcerting. The media was lauding my walk across the Capitol grounds on the way to the hearing as a defiant thumbing of my nose at the president and Pompeo, my choice of dark sunglasses a testament to my "badass" nature. The *Washington Post* even referred to my "swagger," a word I had become allergic to after Pompeo appropriated it. The truth was that I had been apprehensive about the deposition and had wanted to drive into the underground garage to avoid the press waiting at the Capitol entrance, but the committee staff had said that that wasn't possible. As for my sunglasses, they were just regular prescription lenses that darken automatically in sunlight.

I didn't even know exactly what the word "badass" meant. My millennial interpreter, Zoë, had to explain it to me, and when she did, I had to question how anyone could think it applied to me, although I've always aspired to be the person that word describes. The way I saw it (and still do), my new status derived in large part from an accident of timing. After State's last-minute directive postponed Sondland's testimony, I was the first government employee to comply with a subpoena and testify. Whoever went first would have been hailed as a hero, at least by some. Every civil servant and Foreign Service officer called before the committees after me made the same decision that I did; we could have defied Congress, as some of Trump's political appointees had done, but that's not what nonpartisan public servants do. Each one of us knew that our oath to the Constitution comes first.

I appreciated the applause, don't get me wrong. But in some ways it seemed like a sad testament to the serious challenge of our times that a public servant speaking the truth could be seen as heroic.

I HAD A GOOD WEEKEND, the first time in a long time that I felt really relaxed. I capped it off with a Sunday afternoon visit with Mama at the rehab facility. She was looking good and feeling good, and we were both happy to make plans for the following week, when she would be back home. We would both be free. I was done with the impeachment inquiry, or so I thought, and she would soon be done with the rehab facility.

At some point Mama excused herself for a minute. After she had been gone for an unusually long time, an aide checked on her. She found her, still breathing but not with us. We moved her to her bed, and it was obvious even to me that she had suffered a stroke. Very quickly the paramedics arrived. I followed the ambulance back to the same hospital Mama had left less than a week earlier. On the way I called André to tell him to meet us there.

In the emergency room the doctors asked us to consent to an injection of tPA, a miracle drug that can bust clots in ischemic strokes if administered within the first several hours. We weren't sure what to do. Mama had always been very clear that she did not want extraordinary measures used if they left her without quality of life. The doctors told us there was reason for hope, because Mama had been active prior to the stroke, and tPA, if successful, would give her a chance to regain substantial function after rehab. There were no guarantees, they cautioned, and even the best-case scenario would require a lot of hard work on Mama's part. But they were optimistic that it could bring her back.

André and I gave our consent and spent the next few hours pacing. When the specialist finally emerged from the operating room, he told us that the clot had been destroyed. That was great news, although we knew there was still a long and uncertain road ahead. After Mama was settled into the intensive care unit around 2 a.m., we were able to see her quickly, but she had been through a lot and wasn't able to respond.

We drove home to get some sleep, but a short five hours later we were both up. André went back to the hospital to check on Mama, but I had to wait at home. A long-planned delivery of some six thousand pounds of our household belongings was arriving from Kyiv. With Mama in the hospital again, it didn't feel like the right thing to be doing, but I hadn't been able to cancel on a Sunday night. I told myself that it was probably as good a time as any, given how unpredictable life seemed to be at the moment. The movers worked fast, and I was back in the hospital by midafternoon.

I found Mama barely awake and only semiresponsive. She seemed unable to speak at all. It was devastating. Sitting by her bed, I thought how appropriate it was that the Russian word for "stroke" is pronounced almost like the English word "insult." This stroke was a tragedy, but it was also an insult to Mama. She had always been a gifted communicator, fluent in three languages. The stroke had taken all of that away.

Mama seemed to improve a bit later in the day. She was weak, but at least she seemed to recognize us. I thought that was a good sign. When I finally went home that night, I glanced at my calendar and saw an entry noting that Mama and Zoë were scheduled to fly to France that night. It was another blow as I realized that Mama wasn't ever going to get to introduce Zoë to the City of Light or to our family in France.

EVERYTHING ELSE PALED in comparison with the need to focus on Mama, but the impeachment process wasn't slowing down and I had to do certain things in the aftermath of my deposition. I stayed in close contact with my lawyers as we turned down a stream of interview requests and tried to stay on top of the news stories that Trump-world was launching to undermine the credibility of my testimony. I also needed to keep up with what the other witnesses, most of them friends and colleagues, said. I was validated and comforted to hear them confirm what I had experienced in Ukraine. And I was amazed by the new information coming out of their testimony, and further amazed that the Republicans refused to budge from their hear-no-evil, see-no-evil stance, with all the contortions it required.

Amid it all, I tried my best to keep my attention where it belonged: on Mama. André and I divided our time between keeping her company and consulting with the team of physicians and experts who had suddenly become an integral part of our lives. The doctors started Mama on physical and speech therapy almost immediately, and she was trying hard to follow their regimen. When we think about courage, we don't often think of a ninety-plus-year-old in a hospital bed, but that's what I saw. It was excruciating to watch, but Mama was a tiger, fighting to do the therapies with the same grit that she had demonstrated when she had literally run through fire as a young girl.

The neurologists were optimistic. There was no reason, they said, that she couldn't regain her health, although they repeatedly warned us that stroke recovery is never assured or predictable. We had our fingers crossed, and with Mama appearing stable, André drove back to Nashville to take care of some issues that had cropped up during his much-longer-than-expected trip to Washington.

But around day four in the hospital, Mama's progress stalled. She started displaying the same kind of swings I remembered from Papa's final decline. It filled me with fear. Tests revealed an infection, one causing both pain and damage to her organs. It was unbelievable, and so unfair. Her brain was functioning, but now her body was failing. Every day seemed interminable, so much so that I was startled to realize that it had been less than a week since she'd had her stroke. As her condition worsened, we had to face the unthinkable: we were losing her.

On Monday, October 21, I asked my friend Lisa Bon Tempo to begin researching hospice options and family friend Velida Kent to sit with Mama. I wanted to do both those things myself, and I felt terrible that I wasn't doing either one. The impeachment inquiry was intruding again, sending me back to the Capitol to review the deposition transcript with Laurie and Rachel. Investigators planned to make it public, and I needed to make sure the transcript was accurate. I had the uncomfortable sense that I was outsourcing my devotion to my own mother.

To make matters worse, Dan Goldman stopped by our review room to tell me that I would likely be called as a witness at upcoming public hearings that were planned as part of the ongoing inquiry. That was not what I had expected to hear. I felt that I'd done my duty, and I had been counting on the investigators' initial assurance that I'd be done with testifying after the deposition. I told Goldman that I didn't know anything more than what I had already shared, and that anyway the information I had provided wasn't material to the key issues of the impeachment inquiry. The things that Trump was accused of — using his office for personal gain by withholding first a meeting and then hundreds of millions of dollars of security assistance to pressure Zelenskyy into investigating the Bidens — had happened long after I departed from Ukraine. What could I possibly contribute to the congressional investigation?

No final decision had been made yet, but my testimony was important, Goldman told me. I could see where this was headed, and I was not happy to think that I would have to go through the whole ordeal all over again, in public this time — and while Mama was so sick.

After he left, Laurie and Rachel reviewed with me what Goldman had said. The investigators were looking at the impeachment inquiry as a conspiracy case and arguing that my dismissal was the first so-called overt act that proved that the conspiracy was more than just talk. After all, long before Zelenskyy became president of Ukraine, and long before Trump tried to extort him, Trump had blessed Giuliani's alliance with Lutsenko and others so that he could tar Joe Biden and tout fabricated claims that countered the American intelligence community's conclusion that Russia had interfered in the 2016 election. For that to work, Giuliani needed to show his Ukrainian cronies that he wasn't all take and no give; he had to prove that he could wield the levers of American power if the Ukrainians provided him with dirt. Viewed through that widened lens, the lawyers explained, my removal was the deed that showed Giuliani's coconspirators that Trump was all-in on whatever Giuliani was plotting to get Trump reelected. It's what connected Trump to all the dishonest and scandalous things that had happened regarding Ukraine over the past year.

When my attorneys spelled it out for me, I could see why the Democrats wanted me back for public testimony. Not to put too fine a point on it, every crime needs a victim. When Trump used his office for his own benefit rather than the benefit of the American people, Americans were the very real victims, of course, but it would be easier for the Democrats to illustrate that point by highlighting my story, the story of a real person who had been unfairly slandered and mistreated simply for trying to do her job.

Once again I knew that I could not refuse to testify, this time in the public hearings. I had to participate, to do my duty, even if, in this case, my duty put me right where I did not want to be: on a public stage in between Republicans and Democrats in the run-up to a presidential election. Although the historic nature of this impeachment inquiry demanded a somber approach to the task at hand, I was quite sure that the two sides would turn it into a spectacle, with me right in the middle of it. But really, what choice did I have?

THE IDEA OF testifying under the klieg lights of a nationally televised impeachment inquiry hearing filled me with dread. But I had to put it out of my mind so that I could finish the deposition review and head back to the hospital. I had been gone for over seven hours. Seven hours more than I should have been gone.

It was after 7 p.m. when I got to Mama's bedside. Velida told me what I could see with my own eyes: Mama was declining rapidly. Fortunately the doctor was still there. The decision of whether to keep her in the hospital with continued interventions or place her in hospice care was ours, she said, but to me it seemed senseless to prolong Mama's suffering. I called André, and we agreed to move Mama to hospice as soon as possible. André said he'd fly back the next day. Neither of us could believe that we had started a theoretical conversation with Lisa about hospice options just that morning and already it was a reality.

It was heartbreaking. I knew how lucky I was to have had an incredible and loving mother, who was also my best friend. She was old, and she had lived a long and rich life, but I couldn't help but feel that this was not her time to go.

On the late afternoon of Tuesday, October 22 — eleven days after my deposition, and the day on which Mama and Zoë had once been slated to return home from their French adventure — I found myself settling Mama into hospice care. I'm not sure that Mama registered the move. She was slipping away.

André made it to the hospice around 8 p.m., and he, Zoë, and I tried our best to reflect back to Mama all the love she had given us throughout our lives. We thought that she would last a little longer, but it turned out that she must have been waiting for André. Mama died that night, shortly after midnight.

For someone who cries easily, I had no more tears. I was actually glad that my mother had died relatively quickly, because she had been suffering, and now, I hoped, she was at peace. But I was also angry and racked with guilt. It wasn't Mama's time to depart from this life, and there was no doubt in my mind as to why she had left us prematurely. She had watched her eldest child being dragged through the mud, and she couldn't do a thing about it other than worry. At her age, there was only one place for all that worry to lead.

At home that night I wasn't sure what to do with myself. I nervously started eating tortilla chips. Propped up against the kitchen island, I thought about the past four weeks and how I had been spending my time. Whatever else I had been doing, I had not spent enough time with Mama. That was time I was never going to get back.

The last tortilla chip did me in. I could feel my tooth crack, and I winced as I spit part of a molar into the palm of my hand. I went to bed wondering how much more terrible 2019 could get.

ANDRÉ AND I decided to hold Mama's funeral that Saturday in Washington and then to bury Mama next to Papa in Connecticut the following Saturday. André handled the administrative details with the funeral parlor, I worked out the funeral details with our priest, and Beth Jones, the woman who had first put me up for an ambassadorship and who was now a good friend, notified everyone and organized the reception afterward. All the busywork was a blessing, protecting me from the awful realization that Mama was gone. Not just at the hospital gone, but gone gone.

The day after Mama died, I went to see my dentist. She told me that I was suffering from the classic Washington disease of grinding my teeth because of stress. The tortilla chips were not to blame, she said; the tooth had been under strain for a long time. Oh, and I'd need a root canal. Evidently 2019 could still get worse.

19

"The Best America Has to Offer"

IDON'T KNOW THAT I will ever get over how Mama's life ended. But at least André and I were able to give her the sendoff that she would have wanted, and that she deserved.

The local parish that Mama had joined upon our return from Kyiv was small and didn't have adequate space, so we held her funeral at the imposing St. Nicholas Orthodox Cathedral in Washington. She would have loved its soaring ceilings and the walls covered with colorful murals and icons, and even more that the parish's founders had dedicated it to the White Russians who had died fighting for their country and their faith during World War I and the Russian revolution. It seemed to bring her life full circle from Wiesbaden's St. Elizabeth's Church. It was the perfect place from which to send her soul to join Papa.

Even more moving was how many of our friends came to say good-bye. Mama's sparkle had touched many lives all over the world, and here in Washington, where she had only just moved, her reach was palpable. We drew comfort from Father Michael's eulogy remembering her indomitable spirit.

But even in Mama's death, the impeachment inquiry continued to intrude. After I had spent more than three decades in the Foreign Service, many of my colleagues were also my friends and wanted to attend Mama's funeral and the reception afterward. A number of them had been deposed, and by then we knew that some of us would be called up again. I worried that if word got out that we were together, it would be portrayed as an attempt to collude on our testimony. I shared this concern with my lawyers, who responded with choice language and told me that they were eager for anyone to try to put that spin on Mama's funeral. I loved them for that. I hoped they were right.

A week later we flew up to Connecticut for the burial. Now it was my turn to come full circle. We held a simple, beautiful service at the Kent School's chapel, where André and I had spent so much time when we were growing up. Once again I was touched by the outpouring of support. Friends came from all over the country to show their love and respect for Mama. When the service was over, we drove up to the mountain cemetery where Papa and so many of our friends had been laid to rest. I hoped that the tranquility of the site would bring Mama peace, especially given the final tumultuous year of her life.

After the last prayer, each mourner had a chance to say a personal goodbye and throw white flowers into the open grave, an Orthodox tradition. How can such an ordinary gesture be so moving? I wondered.

We drove down the mountain and headed for the reception, which was held at the Kent School headmaster's house. It was an opportunity to remember both my parents but also to catch up with people we had known throughout our lives, including some I had not seen since high school.

And then this introvert had had enough. I needed some time away from the crowd, so Zoë and I sneaked away and walked down Kent's Main Street. I picked up a pair of red and green socks featuring Maya Angelou and the word "courage" on the sides. On the sole of each sock were printed the words "And still I rise." I thought the socks would give me a private boost at the public hearing that was coming up — a boost I was sure I would need.

WITH MAMA GONE and her funeral over, I had to face my own reality. At some point over the next two weeks I would probably be testifying before a nationally televised audience of millions. I wanted to quietly mourn Mama and settle her affairs, but I wouldn't be allowed that option for now. I hoped I would be strong enough to get through the personal trial ahead. Frankly, I didn't have a choice. I *had* to be strong enough.

The outpouring of support from friends, colleagues, and even strangers really helped. I appreciated that Deputy Secretary Sullivan, who had delivered the news that my ambassadorship was over, was straightforward publicly about what had transpired. When he was asked about me during an October 30 Senate hearing, Sullivan corroborated much of what I had said about my recall from Ukraine, including that I had been the subject of a smear campaign by Giuliani. Most gratifyingly, he left no doubt that State's highest levels did not believe Giuliani. I had served "admirably and capably," Sullivan declared.

Secretary Pompeo, in contrast, continued to maintain his shameful public silence about me, although in early November he did manage to send to all State Department employees one of his regular missives, "Miles with Mike." It opened with the following line: "Team, As champions of American diplomacy, we are in the truth-telling business." Given everything else going on, I had missed the email, but an army of colleagues forwarded it to me, underscoring the irony that while his employees had told the truth, the chief champion of American diplomacy had tried to prevent us from doing so.

Meanwhile others in Trump-world continued to try to undermine me, regardless of how slim the pickings. One of the oddest claims came from Lee Zeldin, the congressman who at my deposition had tried to turn a normal email exchange between me and a staffer on the State Department's oversight committee into something nefarious. Like a dog with a bone, he tweeted that a newly discovered email chain showed that "under oath" I did not "accurately answer" his question about the staffer's outreach.

Zeldin's claim showed up that night on Fox News, when Tucker Carlson announced that I had given a "dishonest" answer under oath. Several other prominent Republicans, including Republican whip Steve Scalise, piled on via Twitter. The actual email exchange, which the Democrats quickly made public, showed that I had told the truth, but that didn't seem to matter to those trying to launch a coordinated campaign to distract from the impeachment inquiry.

The case for perjury was ridiculous, and I never heard a word about it from Trump's Justice Department or any other law enforcement entity. Still, for me, being accused of a crime — and by a member of Congress, no less — was troubling. My lawyers told me to ignore it, but I worried nevertheless. I still hadn't completely internalized that the president's enablers lived in an alternate universe of distorted facts and outright fabrications, and that they didn't care whether they shredded logic, or truth, or my reputation, so long as it served their ends. Even after all my time observing disinformation at work in the former Soviet Union, I was continuing to be schooled.

I DIDN'T KNOW what this and other, similar episodes meant in terms of how Republicans would approach my public testimony, which soon was scheduled for November 15. But I expected that they would likely pursue the same approach as before: question the legitimacy of the proceedings, undermine me, and/or ignore me. The Democrats meanwhile would continue to highlight that my dismissal set the stage for all that was to come.

Both sides knew what I was going to say, since they had heard it in the deposition. This was their chance to score points on the record before their slice of America — or perhaps, in the Republicans' case, for an audience of one. A politician could rise or fall depending on how he or she performed. I wasn't expecting surprises in the hearing, but I sure was expecting drama.

Having survived the deposition and seen my testimony confirmed by everyone who came after me, I no longer worried about not being believed — at least by those I respected. And I was starting to feel that some good was coming from our collective appearances. The media were reporting positively about the Foreign Service, characterizing us as a cadre of dedicated professionals, crucial to American security, and as patriotic as the brave members of the military with whom we so frequently served. It was vindicating for us, and I hoped educational for the American public.

Just as important, I think, our testimony provided encouragement for the many Foreign Service officers who felt beaten down after years of Tillerson's hostility and Pompeo's faux swagger. Colleagues from all over the world reached out. Among the hundreds of emails and letters that made me smile was one from a friend and colleague who shared that her sister-in-law had just named her new puppy Masha. The puppy got her name, my friend reported, because she was the "bravest girl puppy" in the litter, who wouldn't "allow the boy dogs to push her around."

I took that message and all the others to heart and tried to store that reserve of goodwill to draw strength from later. I would need it, because I would be largely on my own at the hearing. Although I'd have Larry sitting right next to me, I didn't want anyone to think I couldn't answer on my own, or that I needed to hide behind a man.

On the positive side, the open setting meant that I could bring guests for moral support. I wouldn't be *totally* alone. In fact House investigators encouraged us to fill the row of seats behind the witness table, to serve as a buffer between me and the press tables directly behind us. I knew that I wanted André there, but we reluctantly decided to tell Zoë it was best for her not to come. We wanted to protect her, just in case the hearing turned into an ugly scene.

I thought hard about who I wanted with me in addition to André and my lawyers. I decided that I wanted friends there who not only supported me but whose presence would send a broader message about the importance of the State Department mission to our national security — both to State employees and to the greater American audience. I didn't want to put any current department employees in an awkward position, so I invited several retired friends, each of whom represented a different aspect of my career.

I asked Beth Jones to come, because she was a a wonderful friend and mentor as well as a Foreign Service legend and role model for generations of women FSOs. I invited Grace Kennan Warnecke, a friend and mentor from my early tours in Russia and Ukraine as well as the daughter of celebrated Cold War–era diplomat George Kennan. Her presence symbolized the history, the greatness, and the enduring impact of the legions of diplomats who preceded me. Finally I asked John Naland to attend. An A-100 classmate and friend, John had also served as a past president of AFSA, the Foreign Service union that had been my rock for the past seven months. Sitting behind me, these three friends would literally have my back, and I hoped would send a message to State Department employees that I was not alone, and neither were they.

I was fortunate that this time around I wasn't the first witness to testify. On Wednesday, November 13, that privilege went to two of my friends and colleagues: Bill Taylor, the former ambassador to Ukraine who took over as chargé after my recall; and George Kent, my former deputy in Ukraine who from summer 2018 on had been working as State's lead on Ukraine policy and my lifeline to Washington.

I spent the day at the tiny rental that until recently I had shared with Mama, absolutely glued to the TV. Seated next to each other, Bill and George presented as exactly what they are: salt-of-the-earth public servants. Their testimony was riveting. Simply by recounting what they had witnessed, they offered compelling and detailed evidence that the president had used his office to advance his personal interests. Even more, they showed just how damaging Trump's behavior was to our national security and our interests in Ukraine.

It was a hearing of highs and of lows. While it should not have been surprising by then, it still was shocking for me to see the Republicans on the House Intelligence Committee try to defend Trump's behavior. But the highs outweighed the lows, at least in my estimation. When Schiff gaveled the hearing to an end, I jumped up from the sofa and cheered my friends, so suddenly and so loudly that Scout joined in with some celebratory barks.

It was a great moment, and sorely needed. But I couldn't revel in it for long. Because two days later it would be my turn.

ON FRIDAY, NOVEMBER 15, I woke up early. In the predawn darkness, just like last time, I reviewed what I was going to wear. Warned to expect a glacially cold hearing room, I settled on a black pants suit and a warm red knit top. The American flag pin went back on, and I added a patterned silk scarf. The Maya Angelou socks were hidden by my trousers, but I knew I would draw strength from their message of courage.

Before the deposition Mama had said that she would pray for me. I wished she were here to tell me the same thing now. But I knew both she and Papa were watching over me. To remind myself of their protective presence, I tucked Papa's cross underneath my top and slipped Mama's rings onto my fingers. In the same spirit, André put Mama's watch in his pocket.

When I finally, belatedly, walked out of the house, André had to call me back. He was holding up my suit jacket, which I had forgotten to put on. I had given great thought to what to wear, but I was so distracted that I hadn't finished the job. Good thing he was, as always, looking out for me.

André and I arrived at the lawyers' office thirty minutes late and slightly flustered. As we were about to leave, Rachel pulled me aside. She looked me in the eye and said, "Don't listen to that little voice of doubt in your head. You are going to be fine." It was precisely what I needed to hear at that moment. How did she know? I wondered to myself.

Then my lawyers, my guests, André, and I piled into two large Suburbans for the trip to the Longworth House Office Building, directly across the street from the Capitol. It was one of a handful of buildings dedicated for the use of members of Congress, and I had been there many times, although never for anything as challenging as this. On the ride over I tried to center myself by rereading two poems, Rudyard Kipling's "If" and Angelou's "Still I Rise." The two poets had created their respective works across a vast divide of history, culture, and race, but their wise words regarding the importance of integrity and self-confidence had helped me through the years, and they helped to steady me now.

I was ready when we arrived, but nevertheless I felt disembodied, like a character in a movie, as I climbed out of the SUV to face the waiting press, shouting questions that they knew I wouldn't answer. Thankfully, the Intelligence Committee had provided an escort to guide us through security, past a long line of people waiting to enter the hearing room, and into a private conference room. We nibbled on bagels and tried to make idle chitchat while we waited to be called in to the hearing. I went to the corner of the room to clear my mind and channel my parents. Papa always used to say, Just do the best you can, that's all we can ask. On this, of all days, I took his words to heart.

I FOCUSED MY EYES straight ahead as our escort cleared a path for us to enter the ornate and cavernous hearing room. A wall of flashbulbs greeted us, and I tried not to blink as I made my way to my seat. The witness table stood just a short distance from an elevated two-tier dais, where seats for the twenty-two members of the House Intelligence Committee loomed. Photographers were set up in the space in between my table and the dais, their cameras flashing as Larry and I sat down and organized ourselves. The rest of my legal team and my guests spread out in the designated row behind me, and behind them sat more press and members of the public. As promised, it was very cold. The couple of hundred people in the closely packed room didn't seem to have elevated the mercury one bit.

After the photographers had thoroughly blinded me, the members took their seats. Schiff gave a strong opening statement, followed by a dismissive response from ranking minority member Devon Nunes, who labeled the proceedings a "farce" and didn't acknowledge my presence. I tried to regard this approach as auspicious: if the Republican strategy was to ignore me, maybe I'd emerge from the day unscathed.

Then Schiff turned to me for my opening remarks. Having seen the impact of my deposition statement, I wanted to speak directly to the millions of Americans watching about why they should care about what happened in Ukraine, why Trump's and Giuliani's actions had weakened our national security, and how wrong the White House was when it dismissed loyal public servants testifying truthfully in the investigation as "radical unelected bureaucrats waging war on the Constitution." So in addition to again walking the members through Ukraine's recent history and my experience, I talked about what the life of a diplomat is really like, both the hardships and the rewards. I shared my experiences in Somalia, in Moscow, and in Uzbekistan, where my work had put my life in danger. I tried to explain exactly what we did overseas and why it mattered to every American. "Let me be clear on who we are and how we serve this country," I said. "We are professionals. We are public servants who by vocation and training pursue the policies of the president, regardless of who holds that office or what party they affiliate with. We handle American citizen services, facilitate trade and commerce, work security issues, represent the U.S., and report to and advise Washington, to mention just some of our functions, and we make a difference every day. We are people who repeatedly uproot our lives, who risk and sometimes give our lives for this country." I hoped that the members of Congress in the room and the American people watching at home understood that our diplomats could not continue to be an effective front line for America without the support of the American people and the U.S. government.

I closed by reiterating my dedication both to the mission of the State Department and to my adopted country. "I count myself lucky," I said, "to be a Foreign Service officer, fortunate to serve with the best America has to offer, blessed to serve the American people for the last thirty-three years." The room fell quiet for a moment, and I hoped the statement had served its purpose. Then the questioning began.

At first the hearing proceeded predictably. Dan Goldman led me through the story of my recall from Ukraine, just as he had done during the closed-door deposition. But when we got to the part of the story where I recounted how fear of a Trump tweet was what had likely kept Pompeo from defending me, the chairman interrupted. "It seems like an appropriate time," Schiff said, to let me know that "the president is attacking you on Twitter." Schiff wanted to give me an opportunity to respond.

I tried not to react as I listened to Schiff read the president's words: "Everywhere Marie Yovanovitch went turned bad. She started off in Somalia, how did that go?"

It felt like time was standing still. I am always overprepared, but I wasn't prepared for this: a presidential tweet about me in real time on national TV. My reaction surprised me: I simply marveled that once again the president of the United States was spending any time on me at all. It was ridiculous. Not just that the president was attacking me, but that the line of attack was crazy. I knew Trump must have known better and was probably just trying to change the conversation. There was no way that our nation's commander in chief really believed that while serving as one of the most junior administrative employees at our embassy in Mogadishu, I had somehow precipitated an entire country's collapse, let alone one occurring three years after I had departed. It was such a wild statement that I found it inconceivable that anyone would believe it, or tweet it. Trump had done the inconceivable yet again.

But of course I couldn't say any of that when Schiff asked me to respond. I reminded myself to be cool and not to express anger. It was difficult to come up with a dignified response to such an undignified tweet, so I channeled Papa and did the best I could on the spur of the moment.

"I don't think I have such powers," I said, "not in Mogadishu, Somalia, and not in other places." I went on to say that I thought that I had done some good in my postings, and then I tried to return the focus to where it belonged: my work as ambassador in Ukraine, where I actually had had authority and responsibility and used it to make a positive impact.

I didn't fully appreciate it in the moment, but it would become clear later that Trump's tweet had helped me out. The president's bizarre action — in real time, before an audience of millions — reinforced everything that I had said about how wrongly I had been treated. He pulled the rug out from underneath the Republicans, and after that there was no serious effort to tar me with the original claims of corruption or disloyalty. Maybe the Republican side had already decided not to be confrontational, but the tweet left them with no other option. The optics would have been terrible. As disturbing as it is when the most powerful person in the world attacks you, for once it was working for me. I knew I couldn't relax, but I felt like I could at least exhale.

I had come to the hearing expecting drama but not surprises. I had gotten both. But the rest of my testimony proceeded without much of either. Each side tried to make its points through me. The Democrats highlighted a number of episodes from my final months in Ukraine to emphasize how strange the decision to withdraw me had been, and to rebut the Republican spin that there was nothing unusual about my recall. The Republicans, in contrast, just tried to make my experience seem irrelevant and unconnected to the president. They implied that I hadn't really suffered any harm and repeatedly asked me to acknowledge that I worked at the pleasure of the president, something that I did acknowledge — repeatedly — even though it was beside the point. Given the president's unconditional authority to remove me for any reason or no reason at all, I asked my questioners at one point why it had been necessary to trash my reputation in the process.

Republicans also tried, unsuccessfully, to get me to support the debunked theory that Ukrainians, not Russians, had interfered in the 2016 elections. Their evidence was that some Ukrainian officials had publicly criticized candidate Trump in 2016 for his anti-Ukraine comments. But publicly expressed opposition to a potential president's statements about one's own country bears no resemblance to the surreptitious and illegal election-meddling efforts that our intelligence community had determined Russia had engaged in. I declined the invitation to agree that the public comments constituted anti-Trump interference by the Ukrainian government.

That led to one of the only humorous moments in the day, when Republican counsel Steve Castor alleged that a Ukrainian minister "said some real nasty things" about Trump on social media during the 2016 campaign. With Trump's bizarre tweet still front of mind, I dryly responded, "Well, sometimes that happens on social media," to a ripple of laughter in the room. Even Castor had to chuckle.

Of course, the day also offered some emotional moments for me. Representative Terri Sewell sympathetically asked how the events of the past year had personally affected me and my family. I immediately thought about Mama and then just as immediately put her right out of my mind. If I went down that path, there was no telling where my sadness and my anger would take me. I simply couldn't lose control in the hearing. I responded that I preferred not to share private matters.

Perhaps the most moving moment of the day came from representative Denny Heck of Washington State, who had impressed me at the deposition with his kindness and sincerity. He made an impassioned statement about the importance of public service and connected it to the obviously still-painful memory of his brother's death in Vietnam. It took a lot not to tear up at that.

In the midafternoon, Schiff concluded the hearing with a statement that almost shredded what remained of my composure. "What you did in coming forward and answering a lawful subpoena," he said, "was to give courage to others that also witnessed wrongdoing, that they too could show the same courage that you have, that they could stand up, speak out, answer questions." He then proceeded to state the truth that Pompeo was still refusing to acknowledge publicly:

> And you were viewed as an obstacle that had to go, not just by Giuliani but by the president of the United States. And if people had any doubt about it, they should do what the president asks: read the transcript.
>
> And what they'll see in that transcript is, the president praises the corrupt. He praises the corrupt, Lutsenko. He condemns the just, you. And then he asks for an investigation of the Bidens. There is no camouflaging that corrupt intent.
>
> We are adjourned.

Just like that it was over. I looked at Larry and then at André. I was tired and a bit dazed. We gathered our belongings and walked back through the forest of flash bulbs. I noticed the sound of the still photographers' rapidly moving camera shutters and also heard clapping. I turned to see members of the public standing and cheering. I had never witnessed that before at a congressional hearing. But I was so focused on leaving the room, I didn't realize until later that they were clapping for me.

WE PILED BACK into the two Suburbans, the lawyers in one SUV, my guests and I in the other. My Suburban dropped my party of five back at the rental, where Zoë was waiting with a big spread. We celebrated that the impeachment inquiry was over — at least for me — and we celebrated that the truth was coming out.

The television in the corner was showing wall-to-wall coverage of the hearing. Playing on a seemingly endless loop was the moment when Schiff informed me that Trump was tweeting about me. I was taken aback to realize that my poker face had failed me completely. My inner reactions were visible for all to see: disbelief, resignation, frustration, anger, and, frankly, a little contempt. I was shocked to see that I had actually even rolled my eyes.

I confess that I allowed myself to bask in the generally positive coverage. I was particularly delighted to find among the reams of hard news stories an article by Robin Givhan, a *Washington Post* columnist who often covers the intersection of fashion and culture. It was fun to read someone

I had so long admired analyze my outfit. I did put a lot of thought into it, and she got my intent right in emphasizing patriotism through the flag pin. But she gave me way too much credit when she viewed my Hermès scarf as a "stately declaration of military might, of a willingness to fight for one's honor and the importance of respected traditions." When she wrote "Is that reading too much into a few feet of silk?" I had to answer to myself, Yes, I just liked the way it looked.

The unexpected plaudits extended even further. That Saturday night I got an ovation from friends as I walked into a long-planned party. On Sunday morning I woke up to the news that *Saturday Night Live* had aired an impeachment parody in which I featured. Even my friends who didn't follow politics knew about that. Sunday evening I met friends at Blues Alley in Washington to catch jazz great Arturo Sandoval, and there was another ovation, from strangers. Someone caught that moment on a cell phone and tweeted it out. Over a million people eventually viewed it.

It all was stunning — and humbling. And a little uncomfortable for this introvert. But it sure beat being tweeted about by Trump.

OVER THE NEXT WEEKS I couldn't keep up with my in-box. Female colleagues reported to me that Foreign Service women were asking themselves, "Who will be my Beth Jones?" — an homage to Beth's stalwart support as she sat behind me at the hearing. Old friends and former colleagues reached out across the decades to tell me they were proud of me or how I had helped them along the way. I joked to André that it was like going to my own funeral. Since I was still alive, I was enjoying it.

People I didn't know were reaching out as well. I received hundreds of letters and postcards from people all over the U.S. thanking me for my service, for giving them hope, for standing up for our values. Many suggested that I write a book.

One woman sent me a beautiful afghan that she had knitted during the testimony. She included the yarn information so I would know how to care for it, just like Mama would have done. A U.S. Air Force veteran sent me his leather flight jacket and movingly wrote that he had worn it on missions all over the world as he "sought to support and defend the Constitution." Since I had done the same, he added, he wanted me to have it.

I received postcards with my face printed on them, and I got letters with photos of the writers' families. I also received a custom-printed card with the message "Thanks for being a genuine Badass." I loved that card and ordered several boxes for myself. The coolest honor, however, arrived by email from Georgetown University's Potomac-Chesapeake Dolphin Project. The project director wanted to know whether I would consent to have a dolphin named after me. Can you imagine?

There was more good news. By the time the impeachment inquiry ended, AFSA had come through in yet another big way by raising money for a legal defense fund, a godsend to my colleagues who had been on the hook for their legal bills. So many members of the public had been moved by our collective testimony that AFSA was even able to offer some compensation to my own lawyers, who had steadfastly refused to take a penny from me personally throughout the process.

AS THE IMPEACHMENT inquiry continued, I watched as friends and colleagues testified publicly, and every one of them impressed me with their integrity. Together these fact witnesses made a compelling case that President Trump had abandoned the national interest in favor of his own, that he had commandeered the powers of our government to try to destroy a political rival, and that in doing so he had made clear that he didn't care about the impact his actions would have on our national security. If this didn't qualify as a high crime and misdemeanor, I couldn't imagine what did. The Democratic-controlled House agreed and voted to impeach the president on December 18, 2019.

Nevertheless, with the Constitution requiring a two thirds vote in the Senate to remove a president from office, it was a foregone conclusion that the Republican-controlled upper chamber would not convict him. President Trump would survive. In the end only one Republican senator, Mitt Romney, was willing to hold the president accountable for his actions and vote for impeachment on February 5, 2020.

It was disappointing, to say the very least. But while some wondered whether all the effort that had gone into exposing Trump's wrongdoing had been worth it, I believed that it was important that the truth had come out. I hoped that when the history of our era would be written, it would show that the House had done its duty and that our democracy had been strengthened as a result. I also hoped against hope that the impeachment would chasten the president and force him to govern in accordance with the Constitution and our laws. In this, of course, my optimism would be disappointed.

MY ROLE IN the impeachment inquiry had ended with the hearing on November 15. Although I watched the rest of the process play out with enormous interest, my main focus was on getting my life back to my new normal — a life without Mama and a job at Georgetown that didn't involve traditional Foreign Service work.

Thanksgiving came quickly and was very hard — my first without either parent. I still couldn't shake the thought that Mama had been meant to live longer, but I told myself I had a lot to be grateful for: my family and friends and the support of a community of colleagues that I admired and respected. The Trump-world critics hadn't disappeared, but I was trying not to pay attention to them.

I was also thankful that I had a job. I was the newest staff member at Georgetown University's Institute for the Study of Diplomacy, but by far the most trouble. Ambassador Barbara Bodine, the ISD director, was a champ, standing by me throughout the difficult fall. She kept on standing by me, joining with the ISD board to award me the prestigious Trainor Award for Excellence in the Conduct of Diplomacy. After the previous year, the award held special meaning for me. It confirmed that my colleagues believed that I had acquitted myself well.

The Trainor Award ceremony was still months away, but I would be expected to give remarks. As I started thinking about what I wanted to say, it became increasingly apparent that a truthful speech would include such a stinging rebuke of the current administration that I would need to retire from the State Department before I could deliver it. That was unsettling. I had spent thirty-three years, more than half my life, in the Foreign Service. It was my profession but also an important part of my identity. Who would I be if I wasn't a Foreign Service officer?

It was a hard question to answer — hard, indeed, even to contemplate. But as invitations to speak and write started coming my way, I began to understand that opportunities awaited me outside the State Department, and that I could probably do more good outside government than in. Plus there was still at least another year of the Trump presidency and the Pompeo State Department and the real possibility of a four-year extension for this crowd. I did not see a place for myself in Trump-world: not then, not ever.

In December I made my decision. I could now leave the State Department on my own terms, and I was ready to do so. I submitted my papers and retired on the last day of January 2020.

The past year had been a year of loss, both personal and professional. I hoped that 2020 would be a year of opportunity and renewal. I was starting to look forward to the future, because it turned out that while the optimism that had shaped my life had taken a beating in 2019, it had survived, just as I had. I was luckier than most: surrounded by people who loved and supported me, able to have a rewarding career which allowed me to do some good. My parents had left me a legacy of faith, hope, and love, gifts that would enable me to do whatever I wanted in the next chapter of my life, in the greatest country in the world.

I started believing in myself again. As I was finally unpacking my boxes from Kyiv, I came across the black waitress apron that had traveled the world with me, and I pushed it to the back of my bureau drawer. If I knew one thing, it was this: wherever I was going, I wouldn't be needing it anymore.

Epilogue

Keep Faith

Two weeks after I retired, on February 12, 2020, I accepted the Trainor Award for Excellence in the Conduct of Diplomacy. Before a packed audience at Georgetown's historic Gaston Hall, I finally got to voice my thoughts on the way forward for American foreign policy, expressing ideas and opinions that I had dutifully kept to myself throughout the months and years leading up to this moment.

"We need to be principled, consistent, and trustworthy," I said to the assembled students, professors, foreign policy experts, and journalists. "To be blunt," I continued, "an amoral, keep-'em-guessing foreign policy that substitutes threats, fear, and confusion for trust cannot work for long, especially in our social-media-savvy, interconnected world." Our erratic behavior toward other countries was symptomatic of a deeper problem. I shared my concern that President Trump's assault on facts and truth, his attacks on the press, and his disruption of government institutions weakened our democracy, endangering our people and undermining our values — our most critical strategic advantage.

Finally breaking my silence was a cathartic experience. I felt renewed as I looked out at so many friends and former colleagues who had come to support me, showing their appreciation for how I had handled the past year's trials. It had been almost nine months since I had been recalled from my post in Ukraine, but so much had happened in the interim, and so much more was on the horizon.

When I'd returned to the U.S., I'd been able to see that our country had serious work ahead, both to get our domestic house in order and to right our ship of state. What I hadn't anticipated was how much worse things would get over the ensuing year: an impeachment investigation and trial that further divided our country; a pandemic and then a mismanaged response that resulted in the avoidable deaths of hundreds of thousands of Americans; Trump's denial of and disdain for the social justice movement that erupted after the murder of George Floyd; and a malignant and determined effort to subvert the electoral process and obstruct the peaceful transfer of power.

Like so many Americans, I have spent much of this cataclysmic period in angry disbelief. During the January 6 insurrection and beyond, Trump and his cronies exhibited the same traits and behavior that I had witnessed when I was attacked and then fired as the U.S. ambassador to Ukraine. Just as in the Trump-Giuliani Ukraine conspiracy, we saw a ruthless, single-minded obsession with staying in power; a manifest lack of moral values, shame, and civility; and a stunning disregard of and disrespect for facts, truth, and expertise. Since Trump had not been held accountable during the first impeachment trial, he continued, unchastened, unchecked, and emboldened, precipitating a previously unimaginable assault on our democracy. I had seen such attempts to illegitimately grab power in other countries but had never thought I'd see something like this at home.

By the time he left office, Trump held the dubious distinction of being the only president in U.S. history to have been impeached twice. Through the time of this writing and undoubtedly beyond, he has continued to sow misinformation and outright lies and to threaten the very survival of our centuries-long experiment in representative self-government.

It is a humbling truth that the Ukrainians did far better in transferring power peacefully after their 2019 presidential elections than we did in 2020. On the night in March 2019 when I chose not to issue a loyalty pledge to Trump, I instead recorded a message to the Ukrainian people on what I thought to be an American truism. I said it was the mark of a true democracy that "after an election, whether the incumbent is reelected or a new president comes to office, citizens come together and reaffirm their support for the nation and the will of the voters." Never in my wildest nightmares had I thought that some Americans would disregard this same principle, our founding principle. But as the Trump administration came to a close and a sizable percentage of our population rallied around Trump's "Big Lie" that the election had been stolen from him, that is where we stood.

THE EVENTS FOLLOWING my recall from Ukraine have made me appreciate as never before that democracy is neither inevitable nor permanent, whether in the U.S. or in Ukraine. Rather, democracy will be constantly tested, and thus it must be tended and defended.

The good news to come out of the aftermath of the 2020 elections is that our institutions may have been shaken but they stood firm. Upstanding men and women did the right thing. Election officials all over America performed their jobs showing neither fear nor favor. Republican Department of Justice officials refused to countenance fabricated cases of election fraud brought by the Trump campaign. Honest judges, appointed by both Republicans and Democrats, ruled according to the merits of these cases, not party loyalty. Reporters illuminated the facts so that the public could know the truth. And Congress reconvened just hours after the January 6 insurrection, meeting into the night and fulfilling their constitutional duty of counting the Electoral College vote. With that single courageous step, along with the individual acts of countless conscientious citizens, democracy held fast in America.

But although Trump is out of power, the forces that he rode to office and the conditions that led to his election in the first place have not dissipated. Our country faces serious challenges. We remain on edge and in need of renewal, and it is up to each one of us to do our part. Right now, and in the years to come, we must keep on doing the hard work of making our union more perfect for all our citizens, even as we continue to be challenged by stressors both external and self-made.

While writing this book, I witnessed a great deal of hand-wringing about the degree to which the Trump years exposed that our country is in no position to hold up our system of governance as a model for the world. I disagree. We can pick ourselves up; we can keep striving to ensure that all our citizens enjoy liberty and security and that we remain a government of, by, and for the people. We still have an enormous amount to be proud of and share with others. We need to own our mistakes, and to do better. We need to be humble and to listen more, to each other as well as to those overseas. Underlining this point, two days after the January 6 insurrection my colleague, Ambassador Natalie Brown, wrote:

When we speak out against human rights abuses, we do so not because such abuses do not occur in America. When we speak out for press freedom, we do so not because American journalists are entirely free of harassment. When we call for judicial independence, we do so not because judges in America are free of external influence. On the contrary, we do so because we are mindful of the work still to be done in the American experiment with democracy and because our history has taught us that democracy must be defended if it is to endure. While our work begins at home, we will continue to share the lessons we have learned from our own experience as we look outward toward the world around us.

Just as Natalie advised, our work — the work of every American citizen — does begin at home. We must try harder to live up to our own values and expectations and to tackle the problems we knew we had prior to January 6 and to address the ones that day's horrific events laid bare. We must offer all Americans the dignity of equality and freedom. We must work to make sure that all Americans believe that they have a stake in our communal future, that regardless of our differences we are all part of one united country.

And our work at home is tied to our work abroad. If we fail at home by denying Americans their rights, we will not have the moral authority abroad to create the international environment that makes our country more just, more secure, and more prosperous. We will also be increasingly vulnerable to foreign threats, both at home and abroad.

Dictators around the globe are betting on continued divisions in the U.S. and the opportunities to exploit them. They are hoping that our country becomes more like theirs and uses the tools of democracy — laws, elections, referenda — to produce undemocratic results. Putin calls it "managed democracy." And Putin and his ilk are doing whatever they can to influence our choices and our politics. Getting our house in order is a necessary first step to opposing their interference, whether by cyberattack, a disinformation campaign, or other assaults on American sovereignty.

Our friends are watching too. Although Trump's slogan of "America First" often meant "America Alone," our allies and partners were still hoping for America's continued partnership and engagement during the four years of his administration, just as we have so often cheered them on during their moments of challenge. We have provided moral encouragement or material assistance to most of the countries of the world, and those who believe in us have not forgotten. The world's oldest continuous democracy still serves as a beacon of hope for others. Despite strains over the years, America's leadership is missed when, at the highest levels, we turn inward.

ISOLATION IS NEVER a winning strategy; in order to ensure our own security, we need to engage with the world. Make no mistake: we are not going back to a unipolar world, where America is the sole superpower. The U.S. is neither the world's policeman nor the world's nanny, and no one wants us to be, least of all the American people. But we still have an outsized role to play on the world stage, if we can get our act together. As my old boss Bill Burns has suggested, recognizing that we no longer have an undisputed claim to the sole superpower title is not tantamount to ceding a leadership role in the world: "We can remain the world's pivotal power, best placed among our friends and rivals to navigate a more crowded, complicated, and competitive world. We still have a better hand to play than any of our main competitors, if we play it wisely."

The world today is smaller and more interconnected than ever before. For better or worse, when something happens in another country, Americans often feel the aftershocks, whether we want to or not — and whether we want to admit it or not. The events may be far away, the causality sometimes tenuous, our attention span inadequate, and our domestic issues pressing. It is often easier for most people to look away when the issues and events are not yet front-page news in the U.S.

But ignoring a problem does not keep it away from our shores. Poor governance, civil strife, and collapsing economies can and do lead to pressure on the U.S. A failed state in Central Asia can and did become a safe haven for terrorists, enabling the September 11 attacks on our homeland. An epidemic in a far-off country can and did lead to a global pandemic, resulting in over 750,000 deaths in the U.S. as of this writing. An assassination and an earthquake in the Caribbean can and did catalyze a mass migration, precipitating yet another crisis at our border.

For four years, as great-power competition from China and Russia pressured us at every turn, rising powers clamored for a seat at the table, and transnational challenges continued to multiply in number and severity, the mantle of American leadership gathered dust. We must work hard to refashion that mantle, attempting to transform our global role into that of the "pivotal power" that Burns has encouraged the U.S. to become.

The last hundred years have shown that the world is a safer place when the U.S. is actively engaged in the search for global solutions to global challenges. Working with the international community, we must modernize our institutions to prepare for the trials of the twenty-first century and to mitigate today's developing threats. Our allies are a force multiplier. They amplify our message, share our burden, and help us create the norms and the institutions that make the world a safer, better place, first and foremost for Americans.

We learned that lesson the hard way in the twentieth century, which witnessed two world wars in the span of thirty years. In 1945, after World War II, we worked alongside our allies to establish a rules-based international order that largely kept the peace and raised global living standards. We also took the counterintuitive decision not to enact punitive measures against the Axis powers but rather to help our enemies rebuild into modern and successful democracies, turning them into our best partners in the process.

Our record as a world leader is far from perfect. But for much of the twentieth century we ensured our own security while helping much of the world to thrive. We can do it again, and we must, albeit in new and different ways. If we don't step up, others will. And they most certainly will not have our best interests at heart.

MY DIPLOMATIC CAREER was primarily spent working in the former Soviet Union. My experiences there naturally have shaped my worldview as well as this book. They have given me the insight to fully appreciate that despite arguments from some quarters that Russia has neither the means nor the muscle to assume a preeminent role on the world stage, Putin's Russia has created one of the pressing tests for U.S. power today. Russia's malign actions around the world constitute a call for urgent American engagement with the world. We cannot afford to turn away — not now.

There is no doubt that China is the bigger, richer, more competent rival and Russia the waning power. But despite President Obama's public dismissal of Russia as a "regional power" acting out of "weakness," Russia has shown that it can nonetheless continue to cause great damage on the way down, whether through Moscow's direct actions or proxy action originating in Russia or encouraged by the Russian government. The country's military interventions have imperiled our partners and shaken the international order. Its cyberattacks have damaged infrastructure and businesses both in the U.S. and abroad. Its election meddling and disinformation campaigns have helped accentuate divisions in our society.

Although Russia has been deploying similar tactics in its self-proclaimed sphere of influence for years, the U.S. was caught flat-footed when Putin started targeting us. We found it hard to conceptualize the threat, which in turn made it difficult to come up with an effective response. Because Russia in such cases often denies involvement and its aggressions fall below the threshold of war as traditionally defined, it has been challenging for the U.S. and our allies to counter Russian hostilities.

Russia also has become bolder in its efforts to implement its traditional zero-sum strategy through more conventional means: invading Georgia and Ukraine, sending its military or proxies to the Middle East and Africa, and trying to stake a claim to the Sea of Azov, the Black Sea, and the strategic shipping lanes of the Arctic. Russia deploys its relatively modernized and capable military to neighboring countries with disturbing regularity. And lest we forget, Russia still retains a formidable nuclear arsenal.

Russia doesn't limit itself to corrupting leaders in Ukraine or Kyrgyzstan; it seeks to subvert other, more distant countries as well. Moscow ruthlessly leverages its economic advantage by supplying arms to nations in the Middle East, Central Asia, and beyond. It also sells oil, gas, and nuclear power plants to NATO and EU member countries. Putin's business model too often relies on putting retired politicians and business leaders on corporate boards with lavish remuneration or on paying generous under-the-table payments to foreign leaders. This tactic is so common that it's acquired a chilling term: "elite capture."

Russia gains markets and money from these transactions, but that is not the ultimate goal. Once elite capture is accomplished, country capture is not far behind; that is because owning a nation's elite buys Russia political power there. The strategy inevitably also involves collecting potentially compromising material about its partners (and their political rivals) to keep everyone in line and on Russia's side. Sometimes it also accomplishes more: with the construction of the Nord Stream 2 gas pipeline, for instance, Russia not only managed to divide European countries from each other and from the U.S., but it also established another geopolitical tool with which to hold Europe hostage by controlling the gas supply.

Russian money is laundered in countries with lax laws and regulations, including many in the West. The U.K., for example, is one of the favorite destinations for dirty Russian money. Russian oligarchs and politicians have fostered a whole ecosystem of bankers, lawyers, real estate agents, and others to help them launder their ill-gotten gains. Prominent individuals receive plum posts on Russian company boards. British political parties receive donations from Russia-linked sources. Even the British court system has been abused by oligarchs to settle scores with rivals and intimidate journalists, authors, and their publishers. As a result, London has acquired a number of nicknames, including the poetic-sounding "Moscow on the Thames," as well as the less complimentary "Londongrad" and "the Russian laundromat."

We in the U.S. are no less vulnerable to Russian corruption than our British friends. Russian oligarchs donate to American think tanks and cultural projects, shaping the way we think and enjoy ourselves. As in London, questionable Russian money often gets laundered through American real estate, including through the Trump empire. Russian investors seek to finance American tech startups, a move so worrying that the FBI has warned that the purpose could be to gain access to classified research and sensitive technologies that the money men can then share with the Russian military.

We need to be clear-eyed about what is happening. The Russians don't play by our rules — or any rules, for that matter — but their aim is straightforward: to undermine our institutions and expand Russia's influence. Russia's leaders seem to have made the calculation that since they cannot dominate militarily, financially, or politically by following internationally recognized rules and norms, they will foment chaos by undermining us domestically and probing our resolve abroad.

Anyone looking at U.S. politics today can have no doubt that this strategy has paid off handsomely for Russia. As tempting as it is to focus only on China and write off Russia, with its dwindling population, its economy one tenth the size of our own, and its managed democracy (and the resentment that it breeds domestically), Russia has repeatedly demonstrated that it can wreak havoc. There is no indication that it will stop as long as sowing chaos costs so little and gains Russia so much.

SO, TO BORROW a phrase from the influential Russian philosopher Nikolay Chernyshevskiy, what is to be done?

In the first place, while we must be sober about the threat that Russia poses, we must recognize that historically we have been able to work with its leaders on critical shared interests. Arms control is the best example, where we have lowered the threat posed by our respective conventional and nuclear arsenals. Russia cooperates when it is in Russia's self-interest to do so. So while we need to be hard-nosed, we also must continue to find areas of overlapping interest beyond the disagreements that divide us, because that is in our interests. Success in one area can create the confidence to continue to pursue other mutually beneficial goals.

Second, we must ramp up our cultural diplomacy. It's the low-profile, nonpolitical way of winning hearts and minds, one individual at a time. If a Russian has studied at an American university, participated in a conference hosted by a heartland state on the best technologies to grow sturdier crops, or visited our national parks or Disney World, it will be difficult for him or her to believe all the disinformation coming out of the Kremlin spin machine. Putin recognizes the power of our exchanges and has deliberately made these kinds of programs much more difficult to implement. Our response should be to find more innovative ways to reach out directly to the Russian people and define ourselves, so that Russian state propaganda doesn't do it for us. People around the world love American blue jeans, burgers, and Broadway, and the Russians are no exception.

The "soft power" of attraction remains America's greatest strength. We pull people toward us because they admire some aspect of our culture. Our excellent educational system, our innovative economy, and our foundational values have always drawn the citizens of the world to America's side, and that remains true even today. This is a far more effective way of leading than pushing people to do something against their will; the military should be the tool of last resort. But too often over the past few decades it has been overutilized — and that sometimes may have seemed like the only avenue available, given that diplomacy has been underresourced and disrespected for much of this time.

To be clear, we need both military might and cultural diplomacy. We were willing to spend billions to develop the F-35 fighter jet; why not fully fund our exchanges with mere millions? Just as we can't secure our safety solely with ballots, we can't win hearts and minds with bullets. And just as we are willing to wait years to build a new military platform, we shouldn't expect a foreign student's college studies in the U.S. to pay dividends immediately. We need to think beyond the short-term needs of a U.S. election cycle and utilize all the tools in our government toolkit.

That said, even as we look for ways to expand cooperation and direct dialogue with the Russian people, we need to be realistic about the challenge before us. In the short term, Russia is unlikely to engage in broad-based constructive partnerships with the West. Indeed, stoking grievances against the West is critical to keeping Russian domestic discontent under control and maintaining Putin's grip on power. Today's Russia cannot compete in a rules-based liberal order, so Russia's leaders cling to the kleptocratic model at home, export that alternative economic model abroad, and sow doubt and dissension about the international system.

We must be prepared to ride out a turbulent relationship with Russia until domestic unrest or international pressure begins to put it on a different path. Meanwhile we cannot allow Russia's malign ambitions to continue to go unchecked. The country is not so weak that we can ignore it, but neither is it a ten-foot-tall adversary which we cannot counter. The sooner we come to terms with this, the sooner we will be able to mount an effective response, whatever form that takes.

The U.S. prefers to reach out with an open hand. That is the American way. But we need to remember that Putin's Russia respects a closed fist. All bullies do. In the past decades the Kremlin has had virtually free rein to create trouble. Whether illegally trying to expand its territory or assassinating supposed enemies on foreign soil, weaponizing information against American citizens or corrupting leaders and their societies, Russia has kept on pushing against the rules-based order. We have failed to call out Russia's behavior in a way that Russia finds persuasive or taken steps to stop it that Moscow finds compelling. If we continue to fumble around, we will someday, maybe soon, find ourselves in a serious confrontation in a context not of our choosing and not to our advantage. So while we wait for Russia to moderate its behavior, we need to make clear that we are ready to limit its transgressive actions.

During this difficult transitional period, we need to be up front with Putin — and the American people — on where the U.S. stands. We need to be prepared to increase the costs to Russia as necessary, while being cognizant of the risks of escalation and where they could lead. At the same time we need to harden our defenses and become more adept at mitigating Moscow's destructive actions. Putin exploits the openness of Western democracies and our respect for the rule of law, individual liberties, and free markets. We need to help American citizens be better able to detect and reject

Russian manipulation and disinformation. We need to continue to ramp up our cyber defenses, and we need to overhaul and strengthen our financial laws and regulations and protect our legal systems from being used against us. We need to put more resources into investigating the money trails left by Russia's campaign of corruption against the West, and we need to better combat U.S. corruption and create a climate in which self-dealing and abuse of power are culturally unacceptable. We need to double down on prosecuting and convicting the guilty, whether they're from Russia, America, or any other country.

And we can't allow Russia's desire to control the sovereign nations in its neighborhood to deter us from continuing our post–Cold War policy of supporting countries that want to transition to democracy and free markets. When the U.S. doesn't speak out about human rights abuses overseas, the silencing of foreign independent media voices, or the wrongdoing of another country's leaders, we shrink in the eyes of the world and embolden authoritarians. Commitment to democracy around the globe may waver as a result. That's a problem, because Americans are better off in a more democratic world.

Some critics in the U.S. and elsewhere do not believe we should spend U.S. dollars on helping countries with their democratic development. Throughout my career I have been told that people in certain countries aren't ready for democracy, or that they don't want democracy, or that it would be destabilizing, or that third parties, such as Russia, would feel threatened. All these claims seem condescending to me. Who are we to tell the citizens in an autocratic or semiautocratic regime that they're not ready for democracy, that they don't deserve the same rights and liberties that we enjoy? Why should Russia or any other country get a veto on how countries develop? The age of spheres of influence, when we conceded swaths of the world to other nations, rightly ended with the Cold War.

We also need to understand that supporting the aspirations of people who want a representative government is not the same as nation-building. Our policies don't have to be all or nothing. We need to understand countries on their own terms and meet people where they are — and where they want to be. We can provide assistance and support governments and civil society activists without imposing our own vision or sending U.S. forces, especially since representative governments come in many different forms. My experience tells me that while some people may not think they want the label of democracy, almost everyone wants what democracy brings. They want leaders who govern well so that ordinary people and their children can live well; leaders who are not corrupt but who are held accountable if they are; a system that reliably allows people to pick new leaders and everyone respects the outcome of the vote; and a system where the law treats everyone equally, no matter how high their rank or how low their status. People want the dignity of freedom and equality. And democracy, while never perfect, is the best vehicle to deliver that.

AMERICANS KNOW THAT we need to rebuild our shining city on the hill — to retool our democracy, which animates us as much as it inspires others. But beyond the necessary rejuvenation of the American experiment, how do we shape a foreign policy that meets today's challenges? There is much to be done, and I could never cover most of it, but I would like to emphasize a few key points.

For starters, we need to recognize the essential role that diplomacy plays in ensuring our security. We need to give diplomats the support and resources that befit that critical role but that have been lacking for far too long. The problem has become so acute that successive secretaries of *defense* have asked Congress to provide the necessary funds for the Department of State. Secretary of Defense Jim Mattis, before he took on that role, famously stated that "if you don't fund the State Department fully, then I need to buy more ammunition."

The military understands that diplomats are our global front line. When diplomats are successful at keeping the peace — as they so frequently are — the U.S. doesn't need to deploy our military, and we save both blood and treasure. Diplomats work tirelessly to advance American interests large and small in other ways as well, from helping tourists replace lost passports, to assisting businesses expand their markets, to pressing counterparts to abide by their international obligations.

But diplomacy is hard, often tedious, and sometimes dangerous work. Most diplomatic work takes place behind the scenes, moreover, invisible to most Americans at home and distinctly lacking in glory. This contributes to the undervaluing of the Foreign Service too; when its officers succeed, very few people back home know what crisis was averted or what accomplishment was achieved, which makes it difficult for the public to rally behind diplomats.

Inevitably, much of what diplomats do will never be well known, which is probably as it should be. But the nature of their work should be better understood. That starts with presidential administrations, Democratic and Republican alike, supporting our diplomats. Leaders in the State Department, especially the presidential appointees at the very top, must make communication with the American people a priority. American citizens need to recognize that our diplomats work as hard to protect the American people as our soldiers do, and sometimes make sacrifices that are just as great.

Furthermore, we must ensure that the Department of State is an apolitical organization and that the secretary of state, along with everyone else in the building, honors that norm. In the 1940s, Republican senator Arthur Vandenberg coined the maxim "Politics stops at the water's edge," meaning that American politicians must work together on America's foreign and security affairs and not air their disagreements abroad. The fraught tenure of Secretary Pompeo should remind us that the U.S. is weakened when the State Department becomes just another political tool for partisan gain.

In order to be the foreign policy instrument of all the people, the State Department also needs to recruit, retain, and respect a workforce that is as diverse as the nation. As I told my overseas counterparts, no country can afford to ignore the talents of huge numbers of its potential workforce. That's as true in the U.S. as it is in any other country.

Finally, we need to place truth, facts, and data back at the foundation of our policies once again. Even the best policies may fail, but our best efforts are guaranteed to fail if they are based on ignorance or falsehoods. We need to embrace curiosity, expertise, and critical thinking — encouraging robust policy debates while honoring dissent.

Most importantly, we need to welcome back that most old-fashioned of values: integrity. Only then can we meet the challenges of the future with as much success as we have met the greatest challenges of our past.

HISTORY IS A double-edged sword. The past can illuminate the future, but it can also burden us with traumas that limit our ability to adapt to the demands of that future. Ultimately what we do with history's lessons is up to us. Do we throw up our hands, or do we get to work on fixing the problems?

Writing this book has been a sobering experience, especially when I have reflected on the countries where I served. Our policies in the former Soviet Union over the past thirty years have produced a mixed report card. We got some things wrong — and so did I. But we also got a lot of things right, and I take pride in our record of supporting freedom and the rule of law for the peoples of the former Soviet Union.

When I look back and ask myself whether the U.S. was right to try to help the countries where I served when their governments and civil society leaders asked us to do so, it isn't even a close call. Of course we were right to do so. We didn't impose our assistance; countries requested it. Some countries prospered as a result of our help; others did not. Rather than any assistance on our part, those countries and their people were the single most determinative factor in their own success or failure. And we need to remember that failure in the past doesn't preclude success in the future.

When the Ukrainian people staged a second revolution in 2014, progress was erratic and frustrating for Ukrainians and foreign partners alike. In 2019 they voted in President Zelenskyy to accelerate reform and eradicate corruption. As I write these words, Zelenskyy is trying to take on the oligarchs and their distorting influence on Ukraine's economy and politics. After some ambivalence about NATO, he has decided that membership is the only way to secure Ukraine's future.

Will Zelenskyy succeed in his ambitious plans — plans that would set Ukraine on a better path and turn the country into a better partner for the U.S.? No one can say, but I hope so, and I place my faith in the Ukrainian people, who persist in demanding a new Ukraine. We should continue to help them. In Ukraine as elsewhere, almost everything we do serves our own interests, including democracy promotion. In this case as in so many others, doing the right thing is also the smart thing.

We only have to look a little north and west of Ukraine to see what is possible. During World War II, the Soviet Union took over Estonia, Latvia, and Lithuania, an occupation that the U.S. and a number of other countries never recognized, giving hope for decades to the Baltic peoples. Thirty years after the Soviet Union's demise, all three are democracies, members of the EU and NATO, and the staunchest of U.S. allies. Our determination — and theirs — not to capitulate to Soviet pressure paid dividends, and our support for these three nations has been reimbursed in full. The same thing could happen in the former Soviet Union if we can learn the right lessons from history.

Since the dawn of the twenty-first century, it has proven depressingly easy to look around the globe and wonder whether collectively the human race is on the right track. But there are also people and places that inspire. Over the past twenty years, the Ukrainian people have launched two revolutions and voted in a protest candidate for president, making it crystal-clear that they won't accept the status quo. While critics (including me) point to the glacial pace of change in Ukraine, it would be foolish to bet against the will of the Ukrainian people. They've said what they want. Three times.

I also look at other countries in the region: Armenia, Belarus, and Moldova, where the road to democracy has been even rockier but where the people nevertheless keep on making an affirmative choice for democracy. It may take longer for these countries to become full democracies, prosperous and secure. But I believe they will. Some will call me naive, but I believe that if the people keep on demanding change and the West continues to support them, ultimately these countries will be successful.

At its core, diplomacy is an optimistic profession. The State Department that I joined was all about engagement to advance our country's interests and fix global problems, or at least manage them until the conditions were right for a resolution. Our diplomats helped to deliver many stunning accomplishments. Who would have believed that after the devastation of World War II, Germany and Japan would adopt democracy, develop into economic powerhouses, and become some of our best allies? Who would have believed that the Cold War would end without a major military confrontation between East and West?

More geopolitical successes surely lie ahead, but they won't come of their own accord. The present is determined by the past and the actions that others took. But the future is determined by us and the actions we choose to take now. The outcome is not preordained, so we need to put our shoulders to the wheel and ensure that the chapter of history that we are writing today leaves the world a better place.

To be sure, this moment is full of peril, but I remain hopeful that future generations in the countries of the former Soviet Union, as well as in our own, will be free to determine their own destinies, and that those destinies include the justice, prosperity, and security that come with democracy. There is much work to be done, and our success is never guaranteed. But today, despite our difficulties, we are on the edge of creating a world order better suited to twenty-first-century challenges. Still a diplomat at heart, I am optimistic that if we keep faith with our ideals and commit to doing the hard work necessary to preserve and defend them, we will get it right.

Acknowledgments

As I wrote at the outset, I was surprised to find that writing a book is not the solitary activity that I had imagined. I am deeply grateful to my many communities around the globe — family, friends, mentors, and colleagues — whose wisdom, support, patience, and enthusiasm helped me turn the idea of this book into a reality.

I am indebted to my agents, Keith Urbahn, Matt Latimer, and Robin Sproul, at Javelin (an auspicious name in the Ukrainian context), who helped launch this effort and then guided me through the complex literary and publishing process. Their combined knowledge of the Washington scene, public relations, and the publishing world have made all the difference to this project.

I am most especially grateful to my editor, Alex Littlefield, whose talent in teaching this first-time author how to write a book is nothing short of remarkable. His patience, wisdom, and ability to find the right structure, right phrase, right tone have made this book more insightful and more readable. Alex's tact and skill make me almost sorry that he opted for a career in publishing over diplomacy.

There are many other experienced experts I would like to thank at Mariner Books (and its earlier incarnation, Houghton Mifflin Harcourt) for helping to bring this book to the page and the electrons: Bruce Nichols, Megan Wilson, Maureen Cole, Andrea DeWerd, Peter Hubbard, Chloe Foster, Emily Snyder, David Eber, Heather Tamarkin, Fariza Hawke, and Jessica Vestuto.

There would literally not be a book if it were not for Laurie Rubenstein, who started as one of my lawyers during the impeachment inquiry, became my writing partner, and is now a dear friend. Laurie's probing questions, perceptive observations, and accomplished writing and editing skills have made this into the book it is.

I also want to thank the other members of the legal team at Robbins Russell who provided me with invaluable counsel and a new lease on life: Larry Robbins, Rachel Li Wai Suen, Dick Sauber, Carolyn Forstein, Nadia Turner, and Christina Edwards. I am grateful to three organizations, the American Foreign Service Association, the Government Accountability Project, and Co-Equal, which provided expert advice during this time. At AFSA, which also provided moral and financial support to me and to many others, I especially want to thank Barbara Stephens, Eric Rubin, John Naland, Sharon Papp, and Raeka Safai.

During the difficult 2019–2021 years, I was fortunate to have two places to hang my hat, at least metaphorically, since so much of that time was during the Covid-19 quarantine. Barbara Bodine, director of the Institute for the Study of Diplomacy at Georgetown University, provided me with a landing spot when I returned from Kyiv, kept me on when I retired, and has continued to give me unstinting support. Bill Burns, at that time president of the Carnegie Endowment for International Peace, believed that I could write a book long before I believed it myself and arranged for a fellowship at CEIP so I would have the time and space to do so. Chief Operating Officer Liz Dibble ensured that I was warmly welcomed, and my colleagues at CEIP'S Russia and Eurasia Program, led by Andrew Weiss, have been both patient and supportive. I particularly value the research assistance and excellent advice of the gifted Grace Kier.

At the State Department, I am grateful to the ever-calm and ever-professional Behar Godani, her supervisors, and her team for reviewing and clearing the manuscript: Brandi Garrett, Jeffrey Charlston, Eric Stein, Daniel Sanborn, and Anne Barbaro. It was a pleasure to work with a crew that is so committed to ensuring that diplomats can lift the veil and share their stories with the public.

One of the unexpected joys of writing this book has been the opportunity to revisit so many different parts of my life and to connect — and sometimes reconnect — with extraordinary friends, family, and colleagues, as I sought to clarify and confirm our shared experiences. Some provided memory-joggers and insights through their written works or extended calls. Others offered academic expertise. Many read parts or all of the manuscript, and each one generously gave advice, perspective, and moral support (sometimes even food) to this novice: Vera Theokritoff, Xenia Crockett, Mariumna and Misha Fortounatto, Margaret Crockett and Iain Brown, Alex and John Abraham, Beth Jones and Don Ruschman, William Meinecke, Ewa Wampuszyc, Greg Foster, Srdja Pavlovic, Igor Lukes, Anne Kremidas, Sam Mok, Susan Barnes, Richard Figueroa, Kathy Fitzpatrick, Don Yamamoto, Ilona Kwiecien, Nancy and Vlad Sambaiew, Kathy Kavalec, Nancy Pettit, Anne Hall, Susan Thornton, John Ordway, Dick Hoagland, John Heffern, Lynne Tracy, Joseph Pennington, Alex Russin, Bart Putney, Dan Hastings, Maya Nazarian-Hastings, Chris Smith, Susan Christy, Salpi Ghazarian, Jim Kalustian, Lilit Ohanian, Anahit Mkhitaryan, Don Lu, Eileen Malloy, Robert Burgess, Paul Poletes, Tamara Burkovskaya, Dustin and Cori Bickel, Jenni Parmelee, Shelley Slade, Karla Drewson, Adrian Kuzel, Gabrielle Gallegos, Joan Mower, Norine MacDonald and Mick Nicholson, Natalie Brown, Robin Wright, Kent and Michelle Logsdon, Lisa Bon Tempo and Bill Pierce, Maria Longi, Jennifer Watkins and Amanda Simpson, Carlos Pascual, John Herbst, Steve Pifer, Nick Burns, Mike McFaul, John Tefft, Mike McKinley, Melanne Verveer, Mark and Alice Sandy, Amos Hochstein, Iryna Vozianova, Catherine Belton, Matthew Murray, Alex Vindman, Dominic Bustillos, George and Velida Kent, Chris Anderson, Matthew Werner, David Holmes, Stephanie Holmes, Yaryna Ferencevych, Susan Fritz, Chip Laitinen, Ellie Seats, Anya Brunson, Anne Benjaminson, Jeff Anisman, Ewan MacDougall, Pam Tremont, Kristin Hawkins, Kristina Kvien, Walter Braunholer, Luke Meinzen, Vadim Kovalyuk, Lesia Trachuk, Vitaliy Makarenko, Sofiya Willis, Danila Galperovich, Catherine May, Grace Kennan Warnecke, Tom Pickering, Dan Yergin and Angela Stent, Ruth Pojman, Sharon and Dick Miles, Fiona Hill, Ellen McHugh, Nancy McEldowney, Phil Gordon, Jim Seevers, Elizabeth Richard, Kathleen Doherty, Jen Davis, Brent Hartley, Julieta Noyes, Amanda Sloat, Hoyt Yee, Yuri Kim, Conrad Tribble, Dereck Hogan, Jacqueline Ramos, Carolyn Cornish, Melinda Haring and Barbara Zigli.

Gene Fishel, Sheila Gwaltney, Rachel Li Wai Suen, and Bill and Deb Taylor deserve special acknowledgment for their generous and repeated readings of the manuscript — and for improving it every time.

I was beyond fortunate to have had loving parents who protected and inspired me, teachers and mentors who encouraged me, friends and colleagues in the Foreign Service and beyond who supported me, and work that fulfilled me. And I am blessed to always be able to count on André and Zoë, who had my back during the worst of times and celebrated with me during the best of times.

I also want to say a word of thanks to the many who sent me letters after the impeachment inquiry. Their words lifted me up and led me to write this book in response.

To all of you, including those who cannot or would prefer not to be named — especially the whistleblower who risked all to force scrutiny of the former president's actions and whose courage and resolve inspired a nation — my gratitude and my thanks.

Photo Credits

Every effort has been made to trace the copyright holders of the photographs used in this book. We apologize for any inadvertent omissions and would be grateful to be notified of any corrections, which will be incorporated in future printings.

Papa in uniform: Author's personal collection.

Theokritoff family photo: Author's personal collection.

Yovanovitch family photo: Author's personal collection/Vera Theokritoff.

With Mama and André at the State Department: Author's personal collection.

Standing in a park: Author's personal collection/Nadia Yovanovitch.

With Somali locally employed staff: Author's personal collection/U.S. State Department.

In a ball gown: Author's personal collection/Margaret Crockett.

The Russian White House burning: Peter Turnley, Getty Images.

With lion statue: Author's personal collection/Barbara Zigli.

2002 election monitoring: Day Newspaper.

Swearing-in photo #1: Author's personal collection/U.S. State Department.

Swearing-in photo #2: Author's personal collection/U.S. State Department.

Swearing-in photo #3: Author's personal collection/U.S. State Department.

Oath of Office: Author's personal collection/Marie Yovanovitch.

With Colonel Reese and President Bakiyev: Author's personal collection/Vyacheslav Oseledko, Getty Images.

With General Oruzbayev: Author's personal collection/U.S. Defense Department.

With Stanley Jordan and Armen Blbulyan: Author's personal collection/U.S. State Department.

President Obama and President Sargsyan: Author's personal collection/U.S. government.

Talking to the press about U.S. elections: Author's personal collection/Lesia Trachuk, U.S. State Department.

President Trump and President Poroshenko: Author's personal collection/Mykola Lazarenko/Presidential Press Service.

Lutsenko: NurPhoto, Getty Images.

Kolomoiskyy: Vladyslav Musienko, Getty Images.

Firtash: Bloomberg, Getty Images.

Sytnyck and Kholodnytskyy: Barcroft Media, Getty Images.

Parnas: Bloomberg, Getty Images.

Fruman: Bloomberg, Getty Images.

Giuliani: Alex Wong, Getty Images.

With Klobuchar, McCain, Poroshenko, Graham, and Ukrainian soldiers: Author's personal collection/Mikhail Palinchak, Getty Images.

With Admiral Voronchenko: Author's personal collection/Lesia Trachuk, U.S. State Department.

At wall honoring military personnel killed in Donbas: Author's personal collection/Vitaliy Makarenko, U.S. State Department.

With former Ukrainian detainees: Author's personal collection/Lesia Trachuk, U.S. State Department.

Giving a toast with George Kent: Author's personal collection/Lesia Trachuk, U.S. State Department.

Giving award to Viktor Handzyuk: Lesia Trachuk, U.S. State Department.

Women's mentoring event: Author's personal collection/Lesia Trachuk, U.S. State Department.

With Senators Barrasso, Crapo, and Kennedy: Author's personal collection/Lesia Trachuk, U.S. State Department.

With Ambassador Smith and NDU President Roegge: Author's personal collection/U.S. Defense Department.

With lead counsel Larry Robbins before the hearing: Author's personal collection/Chip Somodevilla, Getty Images.

With Zoë and André: André Yovanovitch.

Index